Taking a Stand

A GUIDE TO THE RESEARCHED PAPER WITH READINGS

SECOND EDITION

CONTRIBUTORS

ANGELA M. HAAS

DENISE K. KARSHNER

ANN M. WESTRICK

PROJECT LEADER

JOHN M. CLARK

ADAPTED AND REVISED FROM THE BOOK BY IRENE L. CLARK

A CUSTOM EDITION FOR THE GENERAL STUDIES WRITING PROGRAM, BOWLING GREEN STATE UNIVERSITY

Pearson
Custom
Publishing

Addison
Wesley
Longman

PEARSON CUSTOM PUBLISHING
75 Arlington Street, Suite 300, Boston, MA 02116
A Pearson Education Company

CONTENTS

1   Academic Writing as Argument: An Overview

Many first-year college writers find that the essays they are expected to write in their college courses differ substantially from the essays they were accustomed to writing in their high-school classes. Let's consider Malcolm, a college student who works hard in his classes and usually earns good grades. Malcolm attends classes faithfully, studies hard, hands his work in on time, and performs well on exams. However, in one of his courses, Malcolm was given an assignment which required him to choose an issue that particularly interested him, find at least six credible sources, and write a researched essay that was at least six to eight pages long, suitably documented. "No problem," Malcolm thought, after reading the assignment. So Malcolm went to the library and found several sources describing an old Native American burial custom, a topic he thought was interesting. He then read the source information, incorporated it into a paper that included many facts and quotations, and submitted a 10-page essay, suitably documented.

When Malcolm received his essay back from his instructor, however, he was disappointed to discover that he had not received as high a grade as he had hoped. His instructor explained that apparently Malcolm had not understood the requirements of the assignment, although he obviously had worked hard on his paper. "You have a lot of really interesting information, Malcolm," his instructor said, "and the paper is organized and clearly written. But you didn't focus your information in support of a main point or a clear purpose." In other words, Malcolm had not developed his essay around a **position.**

Malcolm's misunderstanding of what is expected in a research paper is one that is shared by many college students. Although it might be acceptable on certain, non-typical assignments for a research paper to consist simply of a lot of well-organized and documented information, most college-level research papers are really arguments. That is, they use outside information purposefully in support of a thesis, claim, or position. Ideally, Malcolm's essay should have argued his position on a controversial issue relating to Native American burial customs instead of merely informing his readers about this practice.

Many first-year college writers think, like Malcolm, that writing a research paper means simply collecting an assortment of interesting information, blending it together with clever transitions, and documenting references carefully. And yet, when they receive their papers back, they discover that their instructors had expected them to have established a clear purpose for their research and to have developed a strong argument. College-level researched essays usually argue a position, evaluate options, propose solutions, or make some other sort of strong argumentative point that is supported using appropriate evidence and reasoning.

The ideas that informative and argumentative writing are synonymous and that all researched essays are alike are common misconceptions some students may have. The following Calvin and Hobbes cartoon humorously illustrates another possible student misconception—the idea that a clear plastic binder will ensure a good grade.

This book was assembled to help college writers avoid misunderstandings such as Malcolm's and learn strong skills for writing **argumentative academic**

Calvin and Hobbes   by Bill Watterson

Students often have misconceptions about research papers. (Calvin and Hobbes. Copyright 1989 Universal Press Syndicate. Reprinted with permission. All rights reserved.)

Figure 1

essays, purposeful position papers that develop a strong argument and that utilize, not simply display, ideas and words from sources. Different kinds of academic arguments—what may be called different "genres" of persuasive academic writing—and different elements of academic writing and reading are targeted in each chapter. One very common type of academic writing, the **critique,** is introduced in Chapter 2. Critiques, analytical evaluations of an individual piece of writing, differ from research papers in that only one "source"—the original text under scrutiny—may be referred to. Learning to write an effective critique gives you valuable experience examining the validity of source information for future researched essays. Another common academic essay assignment, the **multiple-source essay,** calls for students to use a particular group of sources—or to use several sources of their choice from an instructor-specified group—as support for an essay on an assigned topic. Although the multiple-source essay is a source-based essay, the sources are generally supplied by the instructor. Conversely, in **researched essays** students must identify all the sources they need and also determine how to find these sources before they can begin drafting their papers. In each of these three types of academic essay assignments—in critiques reacting to a single text, in essays utilizing multiple, assigned sources, and in researched essays using student-discovered sources—academic writers are expected to make, sustain, and support an argument. Certainly, some academic writing is intended only to inform or to share information gleaned from reading, and some "pure information" of various kinds can be very helpful, even crucial, *within* an academic essay. But when most college teachers assign source-based writing, they expect the paper to have a strong thesis (position or claim) and an argumentative focus.

Unlike Malcolm's (and many other students') misconception of a research paper, a documented argumentative essay has the following characteristics:

1. It argues a **thesis, position,** or **claim** on a controversial issue.
2. It **integrates outside sources** as a means of developing and supporting its thesis.

Furthermore, when you write a critique, multiple-source essay, or researched paper, you will be engaging in a number of activities that are part of the writing process for each essay. These activities, along with other supporting materials such as definitions, explanations, and examples, are divided into manageable components and incorporated into the nine sections of this book. Specifically, the chapters in this book are organized as follows:

1. **Chapter 1,** "Academic Writing as Argument," provides an overview of the process of writing an argument.
2. **Chapter 2**, "Reading, Summarizing, and Evaluating," discusses critical reading strategies—including annotating, analyzing, summarizing, and evaluating texts—and provides several textual samples for critical reading practice. Chapter 2 concludes with discussion of the academic critique as an essay genre, including techniques for evaluating (and selecting) published works, critique assignments, and model critiques.
3. **Chapter 3**, "Selecting Issues," describes techniques for identifying, finding, and exploring issues in preparation for academic essay assignments.
4. **Chapter 4**, "Finding Information," shows both techniques and resources for academic writing and research.
5. **Chapter 5**, "Argumentation and Synthesis," presents various models of argumentation and explains the concept of **synthesis** as used in academic writing.
6. **Chapter 6**, "Planning the Researched Argumentative Essay," gives detailed suggestions for approaching, planning, and drafting multiple-source or researched essays. Included in Chapter 6 are strategies for analyzing assignments; foundational techniques for building synthesis; essay organization patterns; and both assignments and models for exploratory drafts, essay proposals, assigned-source essays, and researched essays.
7. **Chapter 7**, "Working with Information," offers tips for maintaining academic honesty (and meeting conventional expectations) in your writing, integrating source-materials into your own arguments, and improving "flow" and coherence in your argumentative writing using transitions and metadiscourse.
8. **Chapter 8**, "Revising Academic Argument Essays," explains revision strategies for academic critique, multiple-source, and researched essays.
9. Finally, an appendix, "Working Together," presents effective strategies for working in writing groups.

WRITING THE RESEARCHED ESSAY: WORKING THROUGH THE PROCESS

To help you understand what is meant by **developing a position** in a researched essay, we will consider portions of the writing process of Elisa, a student in a college composition course. Often, when you read about how someone completes a task, you get the impression that the task was completed neatly and easily. As you read in various chapters of this book about Elisa's experience with her assignment, you might think that Elisa's work is too good to be true, since it appears as if she wrote her paper without taking many wrong turns. In actuality, though, the task of writing an argumentative essay is not one that most students can successfully complete without spending a great deal of time rethinking and revising. In fact, the following two related points are crucial for all kinds of writing, whether or not outside research is included:

1. **Writing takes time.** As you watch Elisa work through her assignment, it may seem as though she somehow managed to leave enough time to write several drafts, get help from others, rethink her position, and polish her sentences. And you might say to yourself that this organized approach is something you could never manage. Most of us have difficulty leaving enough time for writing, even though, ideally, it is very helpful to leave time for thinking, locating information, writing multiple drafts, obtaining feedback from others, and editing. As you practice academic writing and learn from your experiences, estimating the time needed for each step in the writing process will become easier.

2. **Writing is a recursive, messy process.** The process of writing rarely occurs in the neat linear sequence that some textbooks and teachers recommend. You may have been taught that the process occurs by first thinking of an idea, then writing an outline, then writing your paper, and finally, editing for correctness and style. However, for most people, the writing process does not happen this way. When you write, you may have an idea, start to write, then change your idea, discover that you need different or additional sources, begin to write again, change your idea once again, and even rethink your position after several drafts. Even experienced and professional writers spend a lot of time rewriting, rethinking, rearranging, adding to, and deleting from their texts. Writing does not usually occur in a neat or orderly fashion. Over time, as you learn which process or processes work best for you, you will grow more and more comfortable with writing as a process, and your writing likewise will improve. What's important, especially in the early stages of your college writing, is that you avoid over-rigid process thinking which can restrict the potential of your writing. Don't be afraid to tinker with your writing in process; tinkering is good!

With the above ideas in mind, let's begin considering Elisa's writing process. Elisa was assigned to write an argumentative essay based on the following situation:

> In a prominent American town of moderate size, many parents are concerned that the local high school library contains books that they feel are unsuitable for their children to read. In particular, they point to many modern novels that, they say, contain explicit sex and gratuitous violence. These parents feel that exposure to such books will contribute to what they perceive as an already violent and promiscuous society. To prevent the library from acquiring additional books of this nature, these parents have requested that a committee of concerned parents be formed to screen new book acquisitions.

The details and specific instructions for Elisa's essay assignment were as follows:

> Develop a position on whether you feel the above committee should be formed. If you decide a screening committee should be formed, how should it be formed, and how would it operate? Be sure that you present strong evidence in support of your position, show an interaction of multiple sources in most (if not all) of the body sections of your essay, and include in your response a discussion of whether such a committee would be consistent with the values stated in the United States Constitution, particularly the First Amendment. To help you formulate your position and to serve as additional support, please read the following:
>
> > Loudon Wainwright, "A Little Banning Is a Dangerous Thing"
> > Frank Trippett, "The Growing Battle of the Books"
> > Ruth McGaffey, "Porn Doesn't Cause Violence, But a Fear of New Ideas Does"
> > Susan Brownmiller, "Pornography Hurts Women"
> > Stanley Kauffman, "Pornography and Censorship"
> > Garry Wills, "In Praise of Censure"
>
> [Note: These readings can be found on pages 17–34 in Chapter 2.]

Elisa's assignment resembles argumentative essay assignments in many college composition classes—or in other classes such as Political Science or Sociology, for that matter. You will find that the multiple-source and researched essay assignments included in this book typically, like the assignment above, emphasize not just source-use but *synthesized* source-use. Synthesis is explained in great detail and frequently referred to in Chapters 5, 6, 7, and 8.

Elisa's assignment asks the writer to address a question that is controversial and significant. Note, too, that the assignment requires Elisa to develop a position or argument about her topic. In order to express an informed opinion, she will have to consider several sides of the situation or issue; however, Elisa's paper will be primarily concerned with arguing **a point of view,** not simply showing how much information she has found. Finally, Elisa's assignment is based on the idea that one does not form a position in a vacuum. In fact, the ideas of others are important in helping us develop a perspective, and skill at incorporating and acknowledging other's positions is essential to researched writing. Elisa, then, will write an essay in which she **develops a position.** Throughout the remainder of this book and in your academic writing, you also will be asked to write essays developing positions. Like Elisa, one of the first resources you may want to consider in approaching an academic writing assignment is the published writing of others, especially the writing of so-called authoritative sources. Chapter 2 gives you many tips for approaching such sources, for becoming a critical reader, and for both informally and formally evaluating what you have read. Although your writing process need not always begin with reading, in the recursive, interlocking processes of academic reading and writing, it's as good a place to begin as any.

2 Reading, Summarizing, and Evaluating

READING

Effective academic writing requires careful reading, and sometimes a great deal of it! Understanding what you read at both the "global" and "local" levels—seeing both the forest and the trees—is best accomplished through a series of careful processes, including reading, annotating, summarizing, analyzing, and note-taking. These processes often culminate in a formal or informal evaluation of the texts you have read as you consider not just the content of the texts you read but also the author's methods of presentation, attitude toward readers, values, and assumptions.

In this chapter, you will learn more about reading critically, analyzing and evaluating what you read, and writing a type of academic paper known as a "critique," a formal analysis and evaluation of a text of some kind. As you read this chapter and work with its materials, pay close attention to what you are reading and be an active reader, one who writes questions, reactions, or other comments in the margins and underlines or highlights noteworthy ideas. Becoming an active, responsive reader is among the most important steps—and possibly the *first* step—one needs to take toward becoming a knowledgeable and respected college-level writer.

APPROACHING YOUR SOURCE

Before you begin reading a source, ask yourself the following questions:

1. *What information is this source likely to provide?* Is this a source that will provide you with background information? Will it help you understand what happened during a particular time period? Will it familiarize you with key terms and concepts concerning your topic? Will this source provide you with a particular point of view? What can you expect from this source?
2. *What opinions do you already have on the issue?* Can your opinion be changed? Is this source likely to change it?
3. *How can thinking about your own position on this issue help you set your source into a framework?*

Perhaps you already have a very strong position, which is unlikely to be changed by anything you read. This is worth knowing if you are thinking about developing an argument and acknowledging alternate points of view. If you can sense in advance what impact the source will have on your own opinion, you can then determine how it might help you to formulate ideas or serve as a support.

Clues about Your Source

There is a great deal that you can determine about a source before you actually read it. To get a sense of it, you should check all of its standard features as if they were clues. Here are some clues to examine:

1. *Title:* Think about the title. What does the title suggest about the author's attitude toward the subject or purpose for writing? Does the title mean anything to you? Can you guess what the article or book is about simply from the title?
2. *Author and Topic:* Is the author addressing a controversial issue or critical question? Are you familiar with different positions on this issue or answers to this question? Can you determine the author's attitude about the issue? Is the author well known in the field? Can you determine the credentials of the author by reading the introduction or, with books, the information on the back cover? Can you use the resources of your department or library to assess the credentials of the author?
3. *Publishing Information:* For books, check the copyright date and the publisher to determine whether the work is current or if you recognize the publisher's name. Is the book a second or third edition? If you are reading an article, you should similarly note the publication date and the journal, magazine, or newspaper in which it appeared. If published in a journal, note that some journals are known for a particular political orientation; thus, it is possible to predict the position of articles on the basis of your knowledge of the journal.
4. *Overviews:* If you are reading a book, look through the table of contents and note the chapter headings. Think about what the chapter headings suggest about the structure of the text. See if there is a chapter summary at the beginning or end of each chapter or group of chapters. Also, you may want to look over the index to see how much information the source contains about your particular topic. When reading an article, check to see whether it includes an abstract, or short overview of the article, that you can read quickly to get a sense of what it is about. Finally, keep in mind that skimming over section headings or words that appear in bold type might provide you with additional insight into the main ideas of the text.

➤ **Exercise in Approaching a Source:** In small groups, look through your reader to find an article with an abstract provided. First, note the title, then skim over the background provided on the author, abstract, and publishing information; next, answer the following questions based upon the information provided:

1. What does the title suggest about the article?
2. What information can you glean about the author? Is there enough information to form an initial opinion on the credibility of the author?
3. Does the publishing information help you to determine how relevant the information might be to your topic?
4. Does the information provided in the abstract give you an ample overview of the article?
5. Does the information provided in the abstract relate to the message the title conveys? Why or why not?

Utilizing Available Resources

If you are enrolled at a college or a university, you probably have many resources available to you that you can use to help assess the value of a particular source. Your instructor or professor may know something about the author of a source you have found or may even be familiar with the source itself. Your librarian may also be able to suggest other resources that will help you make this assessment.

Many students, though, are reluctant to avail themselves of these resources because they are concerned about appearing foolish or ignorant. Thus, they refrain from asking questions that could save a lot of work. If you can overcome these very natural fears, though, we suggest you consult the authorities and resources available to you for additional assistance with finding and understanding source material. Most of the time, you will find that instructors and librarians are quite happy to assist you.

BECOMING A CRITICAL READER

Interacting with the Text

Once you have gained a "sense" of the text, you are then ready to begin reading. However, reading a text for a potential essay does not mean that you simply open to the first page and read steadily until you come to the end. Rather, it means that you read critically, maintaining a questioning attitude toward your material and interacting with it as much as possible. A useful way of thinking about the difference between passive reading and critical reading is to consider the metaphor of a sponge and a filter. If you read like a sponge, you simply absorb everything you read passively, without questioning whether or not it is true. But if you read like a filter, you read actively, "filtering" or straining out impurities—that is, you accept some pieces of information or points of view, but reject others as biased or inaccurate. Becoming a critical reader means that you interact with the information you are reading.

Understanding Context and Meaning

Reading a text critically means being able to question what it says and place it in the context of other texts concerned with the topic. Very few authors sit down and write an article or book on a controversial issue unless they have a strong reason for doing so, and understanding the situation or context of a piece of writing is the first step in becoming a critical reader. Think, then, about why the author may have written this particular text. Was he or she responding to a particular event or news item? Was it perhaps a response to another piece of writing? Then consider the audience, the particular sort of reader, for whom this piece of writing may have been written. Finally, try to really understand the text's meaning, purpose (in particular its main point), presumed value system, means of support, and method of organization.

Finding the Author's Position on the Controversy

Understanding the main point of a text means that you understand the issue or controversy it addresses. It also means that you understand the position that the author wishes the reader to accept. Sometimes the author tells you straight out which controversy is being addressed and what his or her position is in reference to it. Often, the main point is found either at the beginning or at the end of the text. Wherever you find it, try to determine the author's position in reference to a controversy before you begin reading carefully, so that you will be in a better position to ask critical questions and evaluate what you read.

> ➤ **Exercise in Finding an Author's Main Point or Position:** Closely read the article "Teenagers Need Drug Testing," by Brian Noel Mittman, and then comment on the following:
>
> 1. What controversy does the author address?
> 2. What is the author's position on the controversy? Highlight or underline in the text what you believe to be the author's main point, or thesis.

Finding the Author's Values and the Conflicts in Values

Understanding the main point of a text frequently involves understanding the author's values, those ideas the author considers fundamentally important. Authors often support their position by appealing to values, since questions of "right" and "wrong" usually depend on what one considers to be important. Freedom of speech, equality, and individualism are examples of values that are considered important in our culture, and an author may support a position because it promotes one of these values.

Sometimes, though, disagreements on controversial issues occur because a particular value may conflict with another one, and sometimes issues are difficult to decide because of divided values. For example, many of us are in favor of individual freedom. We do not wish the government to tell us what to do, we value being able to come and go as we please, and we worry about the implications of a government that is too controlling. Yet, we are also in favor of living in a safe environment, where we need not worry about being robbed or assaulted, and we feel that it is the role of the government to ensure that our society is safe. But if a crime wave developed in our neighborhood and the police began to enforce a curfew to ensure public safety, many of us would object strenuously. Even though we value individual safety, we also value individual freedom. In this situation, our values would be in conflict, and we probably would develop a compromised position, to some extent sacrificing one value to another.

Similarly, a person may value certain traditions, particularly those of the home and family. Yet she may also value individual self-fulfillment and the opportunity to pursue happiness. Therefore, she might experience a conflict in values if she learned that a friend had left her husband and family for another man. (Although, because she also values friendship, she may support her friend's decision.) Understanding an author's values and how those values might conflict with other values can help you understand and evaluate what you read.

Evaluating Reasons and Quality of the Supporting Evidence

Reading a text critically also means understanding how the author supports his or her position. Such support may take the form of reasons that are backed by facts, claims of fact, information from authorities, or examples (in the form of statistics, case studies, and anecdotes). The quality of support is crucial to whether or not we accept the author's position; therefore, we must examine carefully any facts or claims of facts, which may not actually have been proven.

If we examine the Mittman article at the end of this chapter, for example, we will see that it gains its support primarily by Mittman's own claim of "inside" information about drug use in high school. Mittman begins his article by stating that he has seen many high school students "stoned," and he uses his own observations to claim that there is a "massive drug problem" in the schools. He also points out that, according to his experience, most adults are unaware of the problem, and those who are aware of it feel incapable of dealing with it. Mittman's tone is one of concern; he presents himself as a responsible young adult who is interested only in solving a serious problem. Yet even if we feel that Mittman is completely trustworthy, and credit him with only the most noble of motives, we do not have to accept his suggestion for mandatory drug testing. Our acceptance of his main point depends on the quality of his reasons or support.

If we examine Mittman's reasons carefully, we will see that most depend simply on his claim that a problem exists. Moreover, we can also note that some of Mittman's support is not clearly presented. For example, early in the essay, Mittman makes the following claim: "In interviews conducted by *USA Today*, teenagers themselves were the strongest advocates of hard-line legislation to handle drug abuse." On the surface, this statement appears to be straightforward. Yet if we read closely, we will note that Mittman does not mention which issue of *USA Today* he is referring to, nor does he include some important information, such as which and how many teenagers were interviewed, what sort of questions they were asked, or what he means exactly by "the strongest advocates." The omission of this information casts serious doubt on whether most teenagers are in favor of mandatory testing. Moreover, even if most teenagers are in favor of the testing, it does not necessarily mean that testing is the best means of solving the problem. Finally, one might question whether *USA Today* is the most credible source for information of this type.

Another problem one might find with this essay is that Mittman gives only a passing mention to a possible opposing position, the idea that the policy of mandatory drug testing might be considered a violation of students' right to privacy. With a quick statement that drug abuse, by definition, disqualifies students from the right to privacy, Mittman goes on immediately to discuss how such a policy could be implemented, without considering possible implications and consequences. A careful reader might say, "Wait a minute. If a person breaks the law in one way, does that mean all rights are forfeited?"

In evaluating the use of support in a source, then, be sure to ask the following questions:

1. What is the main basis of support?
2. Are there any unsupported statements?
3. Is adequate information provided to support the author's position and for you to understand the issue?
4. Are sources adequately backing up the author's claims and documented?
5. Are the sources reliable?

Finding the Organizational Pattern

A helpful method of understanding a text is to create a brief outline of the text to see if you perceive the author's method of organization. After finding the main point, try to locate the first reason in support of that point. Note the evidence that develops that reason. Then go on to the next point or reason, noting whatever evidence the author provides and seeing if you understand how such evidence is lending credibility to the text.

Looking for Cues

While it is true that patterns create structure in writing, structure is also created by **cues,** which are signals in the text that indicate a change of some sort is about to occur. Cues are commonly used to **introduce new content** while reminding the reader of previous content appearing earlier in the text and thus **function as a transition.** Often, in longer texts, readers cannot retain information that has been introduced at an earlier point. Therefore, the reader must be reminded of this information before new content can be introduced.

Examine the following excerpt adapted from an essay about suburbs, by Fred Powledge:

Although the suburbs may be considered cultural wastelands and wasp nests of racism, they have created a great American social institution—the giant shopping center, our most fitting possible memorial to greed and bad taste. Suburbia's young people may be seen loitering day and night at these Eastgates and Westgates and asphalt encrusted Green Acres, their glassy eyes reflecting the vacuity of the suburban landscape, their brains forever soft-boiled by the Muzak that issues from endless chains of K-Marts and Woolcos. Some young people manage to escape into the real world, but many do not. The only salvation for many of them is rock music and killer weed.

(Powledge)

Note that in the first sentence, the writer reminds his reader of his two previous points—the cultural lack and racist characteristic of the suburbs—before introducing his next point, the problems with shopping centers.

> ➤ **Exercise in Finding Organizational Patterns:** Skim again through Mittman's article—all the while looking for cues—and generate a scratch outline based upon what you perceive to be the basic organizational structure. Bring your outline to the next class meeting to discuss.

Annotating Texts as We Read

Annotation is a process in which readers write down their internal dialogue with the texts they read. While many different techniques for annotating exist, each technique—or combination of techniques—is effective in its own way. The most important issue with regard to annotation is that you try to actively respond to a text as you read and develop a set of techniques that work for you. Below, you will find some tips for annotation. Perhaps these tips or methods will give you some ideas you will want to adopt. In some specific instances, more than one method is recommended for the same function.

1. Underline or highlight the thesis of the text you are reading, or jot down the dominant impression of the piece in the margin.
2. Do the same for paragraphs, underlining the topic sentence if there is one, or jotting down the main idea of each in the margin.
3. Carry on a dialogue with the author as you read; write questions and/or comments in the margins.
4. Use abbreviated symbols for particular cases. One example might be a question mark next to or a wavy line beneath a sentence that seems confusing or contains questionable ideas. Another example might be underlining an idea you find particularly strong or placing an exclamation point in the margin next to it. You also might wish to adopt specific symbols to indicate ideas or information with which you agree or disagree. "Emoticons," facial representations often used in email, work well for these purposes. ☹ works well for disagreeable ideas, and ☺ effectively identifies agreeable ideas.
5. Circle words that seem significant, but you are unsure of their meaning.
6. Summarize, briefly, your overall reactions to the text at the end of the piece.
7. Make particular notes of lingering questions or other concerns, as well as how the author's views might differ from or substantiate the views of others on the issue.

In order to see how annotations may look in practice, look at the annotated Hentoff article later in this section.

> ➤ **Assignment on Annotating:** Read Nat Hentoff's "Presumption of Guilt" on pp. 51–57, paying close attention to the annotations in the margins. Next, critically read and annotate—based upon the above annotation suggestions—two articles that you might use for a critique assignment. Bring your annotated articles to the next class meeting to share in small groups.

MAKING SENSE OF INFORMATION

Summarizing

Summarizing means **condensing** a piece of writing into a shorter form; therefore, a summary is always shorter than the original source. In writing a summary, you are attempting to **grasp the main points** of your source from the perspective of its author; that is, you focus on the author's main point and include what you feel are the most important ideas. When you write a summary, you are also gaining an understanding of the relative importance of and relationships between the component ideas of the text. Learning to summarize will help your performance in any class you take, even those that do not involve writing, since the act of summarizing forces you to understand the material and its main points and can help you to remember material long after you have read it. The following suggestions for writing summaries can help you summarize both articles and chapters in books.

Thinking about the Author's Purpose

Before you write a summary, you should consider what the author of the article or book is trying to accomplish. Is the author arguing for a particular position? Is the author reacting against someone else's position? From the title, can you determine where the author's ideas fit among other points of view on the topic? Before you begin to summarize a piece of writing, think about why the author may have written it. Figuring out the author's purpose will help you decide what points to include in your summary.

The Role of Audience in Writing a Summary

Summaries can be written just for yourself or for other readers, such as your teacher or other students. Usually, when you are assigned to summarize a source, you assume that your reader has not read it. Therefore, you should make sure that even a reader who knows nothing about the topic or the source will be able to understand its main points, and you should mention the author and/or the article's title. Even when you summarize a source for yourself, you should assume that once a period of time has elapsed, you may not remember it clearly yourself. Therefore, in writing a summary, you must be sure to include sufficient details so that any reader will be able to understand it without confusion.

Writing the Summary

Writing a summary involves making many decisions about which details to include. Those decisions are based on a number of factors: your own research purpose and the relationship of the article or book to that purpose, your previous knowledge of the topic, your assessment of the author's purpose in writing, and your intended use for the text you are summarizing. Thinking about these issues before you begin to write your summary may be useful. The following suggestions, derived from research in reading comprehension, may also help you:

1. **Scan your source before reading it carefully. Do not attempt to write the summary before you understand the source's main point.** Because a summary represents an overview of what a work is about, it is a good idea to scan the piece before writing anything down, even though this method may seem to take more time. See if you can locate the main point that the author is trying to prove or explore. Then look for subpoints that might be related to that main point. Are there terms central to the topic that seem to jump out at you from the page? Can you quickly determine how the article is structured?

   Some students think that they can whip off a summary as they discover the meaning of a source; they copy down bits of the text as they read. But when students attempt this sort of shortcut, their summaries are not usually well written, nor do they serve as useful a function. A summary written this way may include elements that are not really central to the main point of the text. Also, students may be so busy writing that they are unable to think about and remember what they are reading.

   To scan an article, look at the first paragraph or two. Often this is where the main argument or thesis may be found. Glance at the conclusion. This might give you an overview of the results or the emphasis of the text. Then look quickly over the subdivisions of the text. Perhaps it uses headings; if not, look at the opening sentences of each paragraph. See if you can trace the general line of the argument.

   After you have scanned your potential source, keeping the above ideas in mind, you should have a sense of whether or not the text contains valuable information that will help provide support for your argument. If you decide to examine the source further based on your initial evaluation of its thesis, major ideas, supporting points, and overall structure, you should read and annotate it more carefully during your second reading of the text. However, save more detailed information gleaned from the source to use in supporting points made in your argumentative essay. Remember, summaries only address major, overriding ideas contained within a text.

2. **Ask yourself if you understand the purpose and intended audience of the text.** Look at the title of the excerpt or article you plan to summarize. Does the title give you insight into what the text is about? As you read the article more closely, think about the main **purpose** of the text. Is the purpose of the text to present information? Or does its tone suggest that the main purpose is to express an opinion or argue a position? Does the

author sound seriously concerned about the issue? Or do you feel that the tone is impersonal, which suggests that the author is not terribly involved? Often, if you get a sense of the tone, you can also determine the author's purpose.

Thinking about the purpose of the text will also lead you to think about the **audience** for whom the text was intended. Was this text written for a particular group? Does this group have a particular opinion? Was it designed to change the audience's mind about a particular topic? Did the author assume that the audience knew a lot or a little about the topic?

3. **Examine the "plan" of the text.** Understanding the "plan" of a text can be very helpful in writing a summary. Like any plan, the plan of a text may be defined as a set of directions about how the overall purpose is to be achieved. In other words, if you understand the purpose of a text, focusing on the plan will help you see how that purpose is achieved. Thus, as you examine the plan, you are gaining insight into how the source has been "put together," or—more specifically—how the chosen content, and organization of that content, helps the text to fulfill its purpose.

➤ **Assignment on Understanding Purpose and Audience:** In small groups, choose an article you all are interested in critiquing. Independently scan the article—according to the suggestions outlined above—and try to fill in the following statements:

The intended audience for this text is _____.
The purpose of this text is to _____.
The plan of this text reflects the author's purpose by _____.

Next, share your answers with your group and come to an agreement on the intended audience, purpose, and plan of the article.

Understanding the "Plan" and Writing the Summary

The plan of a text is essentially the structure, or organization, of the information provided within that text. For argumentative articles, then, the plan is the structure of the argument throughout the text. Knowing the plan of a text helps you to decide its main point and determine how other parts of the text relate to that main point. Understanding the interrelationship between the parts will help you know how to condense the ideas presented. Below are some tips that may help you in recognizing the plan of the text and then writing a summary of that source:

1. *Look for Topic Sentences:* Often authors use sentences that encapsulate a main idea in the text. Sometimes such a sentence is the topic sentence of a paragraph. Paraphrasing these sentences—rewriting an individual source's ideas in your own words—can help you write your summary.

2. *Collapse Paragraphs:* Some paragraphs expand the ideas in other para-graphs. Some paragraphs may have a transitional function, moving the reader from one idea to another. Other paragraphs may serve to remind readers of previously discussed information. In writing a summary, de-cide which paragraphs contain the crucial ideas of the text and rephrase the topic sentences of these paragraphs. Eliminate any paragraphs you find unnecessary; also, leave out supporting details within each para-graph as you summarize. Not all information in a text is equally impor-tant. The author may have included numerous examples or repeated some information in several places. In writing a summary, do not include repet-itive or nonessential information.

3. *Use Synonyms and Restructure Sentences:* You should be writing in your own words and style. You should not copy whole phrases or sentences from the text, particularly if you plan to use the summary in a piece of writing. Rephrasing also helps you understand what you read.

4. *Collapse Lists:* If you see a list of items, try to think of a word or phrase name for the entire list so that you can condense the information within the list. For example, if you see a list such as cake, pie, candy, and cook-ies, you might refer to them simply as "sweets." If you see a list that in-cludes books, rulers, pencils, and pens, you might condense the list by calling them "school supplies."

Please note that there is one final step you should carry out before consider-ing your summary complete: *Rewrite your summary so that it reads easily and gracefully.* This is particularly important if you plan to include your summary in a piece of writing. To illustrate, an example of a summary is provided below. This summary paragraph of the article "Teaching *All* Children: Four Develop-mentally Appropriate Curricular and Instructional Strategies in Primary-Grade Classrooms," by David Burchfield, was written for an English 112 course at Bowling Green State University. (Burchfield's entire article can be found at the end of this chapter). In this summary, student-writer Amy Burton effectively condenses and collapses paragraphs, rephrases main ideas, and reworks word choices so that her summary flows smoothly:

In his article, Burchfield first states that as schoolrooms continually become more diverse, new teaching methods are necessary. He then offers four new methods to solve the problem; they include knowing multiple intelligences and teaching according to them, using the Project Approach, utilizing the writer's workshop, and developing a balance of reading strategies and cue-ing systems. According to Burchfield, multiple intelligences means children become gifted in different areas. Examples of the different intelligences in-clude musical intelligence, spatial intelligence, and social intelligence; he concludes that children have difficulty in school when they are not taught in their area. The Project Approach, then, tries to make subjects in school re-late to everyday life, and the writer's workshop encourages students to write about the world they live in. Lastly, reading strategies help children form words, and therefore make it easier for them to learn to read. He be-lieves these methods will encourage, help, and motivate all children.

> ➣ **Assignment on Writing a Summary:** Using the suggestions offered in this chapter on writing summaries, compose a summary paragraph or two of an article you might critique or use in a researched essay.

READINGS ON CENSORSHIP

A Little Banning Is a Dangerous Thing

Loudon Wainwright

My own introduction to sex in reading took place about 1935, I think, just when the fertile soil of my young mind was ripe for planting. The exact place it happened (so I've discovered from checking the source in my local library) was the middle of page 249, in a chapter titled "Apples to Ashes," soon after the beginning of Book III of a mildly picaresque novel called *Anthony Adverse*. The boy Anthony, 16, and a well-constructed character named Faith Paleologus ("Her shoulders if one looked carefully were too wide. But so superb was the bosom that rose up to support them . . .") made it right there in her apartment where he'd gone to take a quick bath, thinking (ho-ho) that she was out.

Faith was Anthony's sitter, sort of, and if author Hervey Allen was just a touch obscure about the details of their moon-drenched meeting, I filled in the gaps. "He was just in time," Allen wrote, "to see the folds of her dress rustle down from her knees into coils at her feet . . . He stood still, rooted. The faint aroma of her body floated to him. A sudden tide of passion dragged at his legs. He was half blind, and speechless now. All his senses had merged into one feeling . . . To be supported and yet possessed by an ocean of unknown blue depths below you and to cease to think! Yes, it was something like swimming on a transcendent summer night."

Wow! Praying that my parents wouldn't come home and catch me reading this terrific stuff, I splashed ahead, line after vaguely lubricious line, exhilarated out of my mind at Anthony's good fortune. "After a while he was just drifting in a continuous current of ecstasy that penetrated him as if he were part of the current in which he lay." "I still don't understand *that* line, but I sure feel the old surge of depravity. And reading it again, I thank God there was no righteous book banner around at the time to snatch it from me. *Anthony Adverse* doesn't rank as literature, or even required reading, but I'm convinced it served a useful, even educational, purpose for me at the time.

Loudon Wainwright, "A Little Banning Is a Dangerous Thing," *Life*, 1982. Copyright 1982 Time Warner Inc. Reprinted with permission.

Alert vigilantes of the printed word worked hard to suppress the novel then. The wretched little war to keep the minds of children clean is always going on. In fact, it has heated up considerably since President Reagan came to power, with libraries around the country reporting a threefold increase in demands that various volumes even less ruinous then *Anthony Adverse* be withdrawn. School boards, too, are feeling the cleansing fire of assorted crusaders against dirty words and irreverent expressions of one sort or another. Protesters range from outraged individual parents to teachers to local ministers to such well-organized watchdog outfits as the Gabler family of Texas, Washington's Heritage Foundation and, of course, the Moral Majority.

The victims are fighting back. Writers are leading public "read'-ins" of their banned works. One school board case, which actually dates to 1976, has gone all the way to the U.S. Supreme Court. Before the end of the current term, the court is expected to rule on whether or not the First Amendment rights (to free expression) of five students in Island Trees, N.Y., were denied when the board took nine books out of circulation. A far more personal thrust against censorship was made recently by author Studs Terkel. At the news that his book *Working* was in danger of being banned in Girard, Pa., Terkel went there and standing before the whole school in assembly made his own eloquent case for the book, for the so-called bad language in it and for reading in general. Six weeks later the school board voted unanimously to keep *Working* in the reading program where it had initially been challenged. Presumably they were persuaded, in part at least, that Terkel was *not*, as Kurt Vonnegut wrote in a furious and funny defense of his own *Slaughterhouse-Five*, one of those "sort of ratlike people who enjoy making money from poisoning the minds of young people.

What gets me is the weird presumption that the book banners actually know something about the minds of young people. Vonnegut, among others, suspects that a lot of censors never even get around to reading books they suppress. And just the briefest scanning of the list of titles currently banned or under threat in various communities calls the banners' credentials to rude question. *The Scarlet Letter, The Great Gatsby, A Farewell to Arms, Huckleberry Finn, The Grapes of Wrath* are a few of the variously seminal works challenged as somehow being dangerous to the stability of impressionable young minds. *Mary Poppins and The American Heritage Dictionary* have been under attack, too, the former after protests that its black characters were stereotypes, the latter presumably as a storehouse of words that shouldn't be viewed by innocent eyes, much less defined.

More critically, the censors forget, if they ever knew, many of the needs of childhood. One, obviously, is the need for privacy, for a place to get away from the real world, a place where one is safe from—among other things—difficult or boring adult demands. The world that a reader makes is a perfect secret world. But if its topography is shaped by adults pushing their own hardened views of life, the secret world is spoiled.

Yet the world of the young human mind is by no means a comfy habitat, as much as a lot of interfering adults would like to shape it that way. In *The Uses of Enchantment,* Bruno Bettelheim's book about the great importance of folk and fairy tales to child development, the author writes: "There is a widespread refusal to let children know that the source of much that goes wrong in life is due to our very own natures—the propensity of all men for acting aggressively, asocially, selfishly, out of anger and anxiety. Instead, we want our children to believe that, inherently, all men are good. But children know that *they* are not always good; and often, even when they are, they would prefer not to be." In the fantasies commonly churned out in the mind of a normal child, whatever that is, bloody acts of revenge and conquest, daredevil assaults and outlandish wooings are common currency. To achieve the bleak, cramped, sanitized, fear-ridden state of many adults takes years of pruning and repression.

Books, as everyone by the censors knows, stimulate growth better than anything—better than sit-coms, better than *Raiders of the Lost Ark,* better than video games. Many books, to be sure, are dreadful heaps of trash. But most of these die quickly in the marketplace or become best-sellers incapable of harming the adults who buy them.

It's often the best books that draw the beadiest attention of the censors. These are the books that really have the most to offer, the news that life is rich and complicated and difficult. Where else, for example, could a young male reader see the isolation of his painful adolescence reflected the way it is in *The Catcher in the Rye,* one of the *most* banned books in American letters. In the guise of fiction, books offer opportunities, choices and plausible models. They light up the whole range of human character and emotion. Each, in its own way, tells the truth and prepares its eager readers for the unknown and unpredictable events of their own lives.

Anthony Adverse, my first banned book, was just a huge potboiler of the period. Still, it tickled my fantasy. And it sharpened my appetite for better stuff, like *Lady Chatterley's Lover.* Actually I didn't read that tender and wonderful book until I was almost 50. I wish I'd read it much sooner while we were both still hot.

The Growing Battle of the Books

Frank Trippett

Written words running loose have always presented a challenge to people bent on ruling others. In times past, religious zealots burned heretical ideas and heretics with impartiality. Modern tyrannies promote the contentment and obedience of their subjects by ruthlessly keeping troubling ideas out of their books and minds. Censorship can place people in bondage more efficiently than chains.

Thanks to the First Amendment, the U.S. has been remarkably, if not entirely, free of such official monitoring. Still, the nation has always had more than it needs of voluntary censors, vigilantes eager to protect everybody from

Frank Trippett, "The Growing Battle of the Books," *Time,* January 19, 1981. Copyright Time Warner Inc. Reprinted by permission.

hazards like ugly words, sedition, blasphemy, unwelcome ideas and, perhaps worst of all, reality. Lately, however, it has been easy to assume that when the everything-goes New Permissiveness gusted forth in the 1960s, it blew the old book-banning spirit out of action for good.

Quite the contrary. In fact, censorship has been on the rise in the U.S. for the past ten years. Every region of the country and almost every state has felt the flaring of the censorial spirit. Efforts to ban or squelch books in public libraries and schools doubled in number, to 116 a year, in the first five years of the 1970s over the last five of the 1960s—as Author L.B. Woods documents in *A Decade of Censorship in America—The Threat to Classrooms and Libraries, 1966–1975.* The upsurge in book banning has not since let up, one reason being that some 200 local, state, and national organizations now take part in skirmishes over the contents of books circulating under public auspices. The American Library Association, which has been reporting an almost yearly increase in censorial pressures on public libraries, has just totted up the score for 1980. It found, without surprise, yet another upsurge: from three to five episodes a week to just as many in a day. Says Judith Krug, director of the A.L.A.'s Office for Intellectual Freedom: "This sort of thing has a chilling effect."

That, of course, is precisely the effect that censorship always intends. And the chill, whether intellectual, political, moral or artistic, is invariably hazardous to the open traffic in ideas that not only nourishes a free society but defines its essence. The resurgence of a populist censorial spirit has, in a sense, sneaked up on the nation. National attention has focused on a few notorious censorship cases, such as the book-banning crusade that exploded into life-threatening violence in Kanawha County, W. Va., in 1974. But most kindred episodes that have been cropping up all over have remained localized and obscure. The Idaho Falls Idaho, school book review committee did not make a big splash when it voted, 21 to 1, to ban *One Flew over the Cuckoo's Nest*—in response to one parent's objection to some of the language. It was not much bigger news when Anaheim, Calif., school officials authorized a list of *approved* books that effectively banned many previously studied books, including Richard Wright's *Black Boy.* And who recalls the Kanawha, Iowa, school board's banning of *The Grapes of Wrath* because some scenes involved prostitutes?

Such cases, numbering in the hundreds, have now been thoroughly tracked down and sorted out by English Education Professor Edward B. Jenkinson of Indiana University in a study, *Censors in the Classroom—The Mind Benders.* He began digging into the subject after he became chairman of the Committee Against Censorship of the National Council of Teachers of English. His 184-page report reviews hundreds of cases (notorious and obscure), suggests the scope of censorship activity (it is ubiquitous), discusses the main censorial tactics (usually pure power politics) and points to some of the subtler ill effects. Popular censorship, for one thing, induces fearful teachers and librarians to practice what Jenkinson calls "closet censorship." The targets of the book banners? Jenkinson answers the question tersely: "Nothing is safe."

Case histories make that easy to believe. The books that are most often attacked would make a nice library for anybody with broad-gauged taste. Among them: *Catcher in the Rye, Brave New World, Grapes of Wrath, Of Mice and Men, Catch-22, Soul on Ice,* and *To Kill a Mockingbird.* Little Black Sambo and *Merchant of Venice* run into recurring protests basd on suspicions that the former is anti-black, the latter anti-Semitic. One school board banned *Making It with Mademoiselle,* but reversed the decision after finding out it was a how-to pattern book for youngsters hoping to learn dress-making. Authorities in several school districts have banned the *American Heritage Dictionary* not only because it contains unacceptable words but because some organizations, the Texas Daughters of the American Revolution among them, have objected to the sexual intimations of the definition of the word bed as a transitive verb.

Censorship can, and often does, lead into absurdity, though not often slap-stick absurdity like the New Jersey legislature achieved in the 1960s when it enacted a subsequently vetoed antiobscenity bill so explicit that it was deemed too dirty to be read in the legislative chambers without clearing out the public first. The mother in Whiteville, N.C., who demanded that the Columbus County library keep adult books out of the hands of children later discovered that her own daughter had thereby been made ineligible to check out the Bible. One group, a Florida organization called Save Our Children, has simplified its censorship goals by proposing to purge from libraries all books by such reputed homosexuals as Emily Dickinson, Willa Cather, Virginia Woolf, Tennessee Williams, Walt Whitman and John Milton.

Most often, censors wind up at the ridiculous only by going a very dangerous route. The board of the Island Trees Union Free School District on Long Island, N.Y., in a case still being contested by former students in court, banned eleven books as "anti-American, anti-Christian, anti-Semitic and just plain filthy." Later they discovered that the banished included two Pulitzer prizewinners: Bernard Malamund's *The Fixer* and Olivia La Farge's *Laughing Boy.* For censors to ban books they have never read is commonplace. For them to deny that they are cen-soring is even more so. Said Attorney George W. Lipp Jr., announcing plans to continue the legal fight for the Island Trees board: "This is not book burning or book banning but a rational effort to transmit community values."

Few censors, if any, tend to see that censorship itself runs counter to cer-tain basic American values. But why have so many people with such an out-look begun lurching forth so aggressively in recent years? They quite likely have always suffered the censorial impulse. But they have been recently em-boldened by the same resurgent moralistic mood that has enspirited evangeli-cal fundamentalists and given form to the increasingly outspoken constituency of the Moral Majority. At another level, they probably hunger for some power over something, just as everybody supposedly does these days. Thus they are moved, as American Library Association President Peggy Sullivan says, "by a desperation to feel some control over what is close to their lives."

Americans are in no danger of being pushed back to the prudery of the 19th century. The typical U.S. newsstand, with its sappy pornutopian reek, is proof enough of that, without even considering prime-time TV. But the latter day inflamed censor is no laughing matter. One unsettling feature of the cur-rent censorial vigilantism is its signs of ugly inflammation. There is, for in-stance, the cheerily incendiary attitude expressed by the Rev. George A. Zarris, chairman of the Moral Majority in Illinois. Says Zarris, "I would think moral-minded people might object to books that are philosophically alien to what they believe. If they have the books and feel like burning them, fine." The notion of book burning is unthinkable to many and appalling to others, if only because it brings to mind the rise of Adolf Hitler's Germany—an event marked by widespread bonfires fed by the works of scores of writers including Marcel Proust, Thomas Mann, H.G. Wells and Jack London.

Unthinkable? In fact, the current wave of censorship has precipitated two of the most outrageous episodes of book burning in the U.S. since 1927, when Chicago Mayor William ("Big Bill") Thompson, an anglophobe miffed by a view sympathetic to the British, had a flunky put the torch on the city hall steps to one of Historian Arthur Schlesinger Sr.'s books. In Drake, N. Dak., the five-member school board in 1973 ordered the confiscation and burning of three books that, according to Professor Jenkinson, none of the members had read: Kurt Vonnegut's *Slaughterhouse-Five,* James Dickey's *Deliverence* and an anthology of short stories by writers like Joseph Conrad, John Steinbeck and William Faulkner. Said the school superintendent later: "I don't regret it one bit, and we'd do it again. I'm just sorry about all the publicity that we got." In Warsaw, Ind., a gaggle of citizens in 1977 publicly burned 40 copies of *Values Clarifications,* a textbook, as a show of support for a school board that decided to ban both written matter and independent-minded teachers from its system. Said William I. Chapel, a member of that board: "The bottom line is: Who will control the minds of the students?"

An interesting question. It baldly reveals the ultimate purpose of all censorship—mind control—just as surely as the burning of books dramatizes a yearning latent in every consecrated censor. The time could not be better for recalling something Henry Seidel Canby wrote after Big Bill Thompson put Arthur Schlesinger to the flame. Said Canby: "There will always be a mob with a torch ready when someone cries, 'Burn those books!'" The real bottom line is: How many more times is he going to be proved right?

Porn Doesn't Cause Violence, But a Fear of New Ideas Does

Ruth McGaffey

I must respond to the Meese Commission's Report on Pornography as well as several comments that have appeared in these pages regarding pornography and censorship. My purpose is not to defend pornography, but if my commitment to the First Amendment makes that necessary, I am willing to do so.

I find much pornography disgusting as well as demeaning to women. The same is true of much commercial advertising, including the ring-around-the-collar commercial. Both depict a woman I do not like.

Ruth McGaffey, "Porn Doesn't Cause Violence, But a Fear of New Ideas Does," *The Milwaukee Journal,* September 28, 1986. Reprinted by permission of the author.

I also find racist stereotypes offensive. I think uniformed people, ignorant students and religious bigots are offensive. When I taught at Northwestern University last semester and had to live in Chicago, I found Chicago Bear fans repulsive. Neither the First Amendment nor any other part of the Constitution, however, guarantees me a right to live without being offended. Those who would ban sexually explicit material are no different from those who would censor *Huckleberry Finn* because of racist stereotypes, those who criticize other books because of sexist stereotypes and still others who object to curriculum materials because of offensive ideas on religion or values.

Americans are scared stiff of ideas and people with whom they disagree. We have persecuted all sorts of religious and political groups. We are afraid that these strange groups will influence us and, worst of all, will influence our children.

Those who fear sexually explicit material rejoice in the Meese Commission's report because it agrees with their intuitive fear of pornography. They believe that it has established a link between pornography and violent crimes against women. Yet no respectable social scientist would agree.

Fear of pornography or any other sort of message is based on the theory that messages can magically make people do things they wouldn't otherwise do. That theory is not true. People don't change their behavior very easily. After 30 years of research, scholars have not been able to prove that even subliminal persuasion works. Nor has research on brainwashing shown that to be effective. Modern communication research indicates that the response of any audience to a message depends more upon the predisposition of the audience than upon the power of the speaker, writer, or film-maker. People generally search out information that supports what they already believe. The danger is much more acute when people are not exposed to all kinds of ideas. Then, without experience in questioning ideas, without a "critical mind," they may be more easily persuaded. Researchers believe, for example, that the apparent success of some totalitarian propaganda results not from some magic techniques but from a monopoly control over information.

What kinds of ideas do rapists and child abusers and wife beaters already have? What we might find by looking at their testimony is that this society really believes that men have the right to make decisions for women. Analysis of the background of wife beaters does not reveal pornography, but rather parents who considered women's role to be appropriately subordinate to men. I have met very well-educated women who don't work or go to school because "My husband won't let me." Grown women who think they have to have permission to do something for themselves are sick, and the men who assert that dominance are sicker. It is not much of a jump from that attitude to believing that men have a right to control women sexually. An amazing number of men admit that they would rape if they could get away with it. Date and marital rape are common. It is highly simplistic to say that pornography either caused this widespread cultural attitude or that it causes acts of violence.

Furthermore, that claim is counterproductive. It allows men to excuse their actions. We laugh when we hear "the devil made me do it," but saying that "pornography made me do it," is exactly the same thing.

Instead of worrying about all the dangerous ideas and pictures and films in the world, we should be worrying about developing minds that are comfortable with uncertainty and complexity, not obedient minds. We must teach our children to question what they are told even when it comes from us. In this society we have rejected the elitist notion that some should make choices for others. That at least is the theory of the First Amendment.

Our founding Fathers did not envision a nation of cowards. Freedom of expression was put in a primary position in the Bill of Rights because a self-governing people must be able to discuss all ideas regardless of how repulsive they might be. Anti-Jewish, anti-black, or anti-Catholic statements offend most decent Americans. Swastikas as well as the white sheets of the KKK and the pornography of *Hustler* are not only offensive but also frightening to the majority of our people. These ideas we hate, however, must be protected if the marketplace of ideas is to survive for those ideas we love.

Pornography Hurts Women

Susan Brownmiller

Pornography has been so thickly glossed over with the patina of chic these days in the name of verbal freedom and sophistication that important distinctions between freedom of political expression (a democratic necessity), honest sex education for children (a societal good) and ugly smut (the deliberate devaluation of the role of women through obscene, distorted depictions) have been hopelessly confused. Part of the problem is that those who traditionally have been the most vigorous opponents of porn are often those same people who shudder at the explicit mention of any sexual subject. Under their watchful vigilante eyes, frank and free dissemination of educational materials relating to abortion, contraception, the act of birth, and female biology in general is also dangerous, subversive and dirty. (I am not unmindful that frank and free discussion of rape, "the unspeakable crime," might well give these righteous vigilantes further cause to shudder.) Because the battle lines were falsely drawn a long time ago, before there was a vocal women's movement, the antipornography forces appear to be, for the most part, religious, Southern, conservative and right-wing, while the pro-porn forces are identified as Eastern, atheistic and liberal.

But a woman's perspective demands a totally new alignment, or at least a fresh appraisal. The majority report of the President's Commission on Obscenity and Pornography (1970), a report that argued strongly for the removal of all legal restrictions on pornography, soft and hard, made plain that 90 percent of all pornographic material is geared to the male heterosexual market (the other 10 percent is geared to the male homosexual taste), that buyers of porn are "predominantly white, middle-class, middle-aged married males" and that the graphic depictions, the meat and potatoes of porn, are the naked female body and of the multiplicity of acts done to that body.

Discussing the content of stag films, "a familiar and firmly established part of the American scene," the commission report dutifully, if foggily, explained, "Because pornography historically has been thought to be primarily a masculine interest, the emphasis in stag films seems to represent the preferences of the middle-class American male. Thus male homosexuality and bestiality are relatively rare, while lesbianism is rather common."

The commissioners in this instance had merely verified what purveyors of porn have always known: hard-core pornography is not a celebration of sexual freedom; it is a cynical exploitation of female sexual activity through the device of making all such activity, and consequently all females, "dirty." Heterosexual male consumers of pornography are frankly turned on by watching lesbians in action (although never in the final scenes, but always as a curtain raiser); they are turned off with the sudden swiftness of a water faucet by watching naked men act upon each other. One study quoted in the commission report came to the unastounding conclusion that "seeing a stag film in the presence of male peers bolsters masculine esteem." Indeed. The men in groups who watch the films, it is important to note, are *not* naked.

When male response to pornography is compared to female response, a pronounced difference in attitude emerges. According to the commission, "Males report being more highly aroused by depictions of nude females, and show more interest in depictions of nude females than [do] females." Quoting the figures of Alfred Kinsey, the commission noted that a majority of males (77 percent) were "aroused" by visual depictions of explicit sex while a majority of females (68 percent) were not aroused. Further, "females more often than males reported 'disgust' and 'offense.'"

From whence comes this female disgust and offense? Are females sexually backward or more conservative by nature? The gut distaste that a majority of women feel when we look at pornography, a distaste that, incredibly, it is no longer fashionable to admit, comes, I think, from the gut knowledge that we and our bodies are being stripped, exposed and contorted for the purpose of ridicule to bolster that "masculine esteem" which gets its kick and sense of power from viewing females as anonymous, panting playthings, adult toys, dehumanized objects to be used, abused, broken and discarded.

This, of course, is also the philosophy of rape. It is no accident (for what else could be its purpose?) that females in the pornographic genre are depicted in two cleanly delineated roles: as virgins who are caught and "banged" or as nymphomaniacs who are never sated. The most popular and prevalent pornographic fantasy combines the two: an innocent untutored female is raped and "subjected to unnatural practices" that turn her into a raving, slobbering nymphomaniac, a dependent sexual slave who can never get enough of the big, male cock.

There can be no "equality" in porn, no female equivalent, no turning of the tables in the name of bawdy fun. Pornography, like rape, is a male invention, designed to dehumanize women, to reduce the female to an object of sexual access, not to free sensuality from moralistic or parental inhibition. The staple of porn will always be the naked female body, breasts and genitals exposed, because as man devised it, her naked body is the female's "shame," her private parts the private property of man, while his are the ancient, holy, universal, patriarchal instrument of his power, his rule by force over *her.*

Pornography is the undiluted essence of anti-female propaganda. Yet the very liberals who were so quick to understand the method and purpose behind the mighty propaganda machine of Hitler's Third Reich, the consciously spewed-out anti-Semitic caricatures and obscenities that have an ideological base to the Holocaust and the Final Solution, the very same liberals who, enlightened by blacks, searched their own conscience and came to understand that their tolerance of "nigger" jokes and portrayals of shuffling, rolling-eyed servants in movies perpetuated the degrading myths of black inferiority and gave an ideological base to the continuation of black oppression—these very same liberals now fervidly maintain that the hatred and contempt for women that find expression in four-letter words used as expletives and in what are quaintly called "adult" or "erotic" books and movies are a valid extension of freedom of speech that must be preserved as a Constitutional right.

To defend the right of a lone, crazed American Nazi to grind out propaganda calling for the extermination of all Jews, as the ACLU has done in the name of free speech, is, after all, a self-righteous and not particularly courageous stand, for American Jewry is not currently threatened by storm troopers, concentration camps and imminent extermination, but I wonder if the ACLU's position might change if, come tomorrow morning, the bookstores and movie theaters lining Forty-second Street in New York City were devoted not to the humiliation of women by rape and torture, as they currently are, but to a systemized, commercially successful propaganda machine depicting the sadistic pleasures of gassing Jews or lynching blacks?

Is this analogy extreme? Not if you are a woman who is conscious of the ever-present threat of rape and the proliferation of a cultural ideology that makes it sound like "liberated" fun. The majority report of the President's Commission of Obscenity and Pornography tried to pooh-pooh the opinion of law enforcement agencies around the country that claimed their own concrete experience with offenders who were caught with the stuff led them to conclude that pornographic material is a causative factor in crimes of sexual violence. The commission maintained that is was not possible at this time to scientifically prove or disprove such a connection.

But does one need scientific methodology in order to conclude that the antifemale propaganda that permeates our nation's cultural output promotes a climate in which acts of sexual hostility directed against women are not only tolerated but ideologically encouraged? A similar debate has raged for many years over whether or not the extensive glorification of violence (the gangster as hero; the loving treatment accorded bloody shoot-'em-ups in movies, books and on TV) has a causal effect, a direct relationship to the rising rate of crime, particularly among youth. Interestingly enough, in this area—nonsexual and not specifically related to abuses against women—public opinion seems to be swinging to the position that explicit violence in the entertainment media does have a deleterious effect; it makes violence commonplace, numbingly routine and no longer morally shocking.

More to the point, those who call for a curtailment of scenes of violence in movies and on television in the name of sensitivity, good taste and what's best for our children are not accused of being pro-censorship or against freedom of speech. Similarly, minority group organizations, black, Hispanic, Japanese, Italian, Jewish, or American Indian, that campaign against ethnic slurs and demeaning portrayals in movies, on television shows and in commercials are perceived as waging a just political fight, for if a minority group claims to be offended by a specific portrayal, be it Little Black Sambo or the Frito Bandido, and relates it to a history of ridicule and oppression, few liberals would dare to trot out a Constitutional argument in theoretical opposition, not if they wish to maintain their liberal credentials. Yet when it comes to the treatment of women, the liberal consciousness remains fiercely obdurate, refusing to be budged, for the sin of appearing square of prissy in the age of the so-called sexual revolution has become the worst offense of all.

Pornography and Censorship

Stanley Kauffmann

One pleasant aspect of pornography discussions is that they never end, even within oneself. No set of arguments can be air-tight, and one can always think of points to be added or changed in one's own arguments. But here are some of my present views:

I dislike pornography; and I dislike censorship laws.

I dislike pornography; because after the excitements there comes tedium; and with the tedium comes a sense of imperfection. After sex itself comes no such tedium (languor is something else) and no such basic sense of inppropri-ateness. Porno excites me because all my neural systems seem to be adequately hooked up, but after the shock of crossing the threshold into that "world" wears off, which doesn't take so long, I begin to think that porno represents an ideal—essentially male—of sexual freedom and power, unrelated to reality as is, or as is desirable. I am an anti-idealist; ideals seem morally and functionally corruptive. I am against this ideal as well.

I dislike censorship laws because they intrude on personal rights. Most laws operate between at least two people: they protect me from you and vice-versa. Laws against pornography, like laws against drinking and drug-taking and suicide, come between me and myself. I object to the state's arrogance.

People want pornography.

Stanley Kauffmann, "Pornography and Censorship." Reprinted with permission of the author from: *The Public Interest,* No. 22 (Winter 1971), pp. 28–32. © 1971 by National Affairs, Inc.

This has been true of many cultures, especially for men, in many areas. Porno producers are not philanthropists or missionaries; they're in business because people want what they produce. What right have some of us to tell others that they may not have what they want? (I know some intelligent, cultivated men—and a few such women—who delight in porno.) I disbelieve in the legislation of taste.

DEFENSE AGAINST REPRESSION

The question of theatrical productions like *Oh! Calcutta!* is self-solving. If you want to go, go; if not, don't. The concept of "the dram of eale" is a puritan delusion. Gresham's Law doesn't operate in art. If bad art drove out good, there would not be any good art at all because for centuries there has been more bad art than good.

Most films are now clearly labeled by the ratings system of the Motion Picture Association of America. That system has manifest defects, but I have argued for it—and would still—as the best defense against repression. The X rating is, as is often said, a license for opportunists, but numbers of people want what the opportunists offer and I don't recognize anyone's right to deny it to them. More important, the X rating is a license for the serious film maker who wants to deal with sexual subjects. I'm glad that *Midnight Cowboy* (whatever its faults) was made and widely distributed, something that was difficult anyway and would have been nearly impossible without the protection of the X rating.

DANISH SURVEY

The concept of the state's interest in pornography, possibly related to the Roman concept of the republic of virtue, is gradually being eroded by scientific research. The researchers in the Lockhart report, incomplete though they are, support the belief that there is no connection between porno and sexual crime. A Danish study (*New York Times,* Nov. 9, 1970) finds that sex crimes have sharply declined in Denmark—coincidentally?—in the three years since censorship laws have been eased there. The data and conclusions of the British Arts Council report on obscenity laws (full text in the *New Statesman,* August 8, 1969) support a recommendation for repeal of the Obscene Publications Acts. The state surely has a legitimate interest in the moral welfare of the community, but every ground for including porno in that interest is weakening.

The only real legal question is the protection of children. And it is a *question.* I can't define what a child is—six, yes, but sixteen?—and I can't define what "protection" is. I'm simply not convinced that a young person without sexual experience and some maturity of judgment can see pornography as pornography: that is—aside from understanding the acts themselves and understanding the unconventionality (even impossibility) of some of them—can see the relation of porno to experience, as commentary and stimulant and revenge. "Depravity and corruption" are supposed to be considerations, too, though no one seems to know much about them. I have no wish to be blithe about parents' concern for a child (particularly since I have no children), but my guess is that a parent's attitude toward his child's exposure to porno is as much secret embarrassment at revelation of his own fantasies as it is protection of the young.

PROTECTION FOR MINORS

Censorship legislation for minors, however, only moves the semantic and moral problem to a different locus. Two sociologists on the Lockhart commission recommended the abolition of *all* statutory legislation, for young persons as well as adults, on the ground that obscenity and pornography have long proved undefinable. They would rather rely on "informal social controls" and "improvements in sex education and better understanding of human sexual behavior" than on "ambiguous and arbitrarily administered laws."

Nevertheless I confess that, even without scientific data to prove harm, I'm uneasy at the thought of children being exposed to pornography before those "improvements" are realized.

Porno is of two distinct kinds.

I don't mean the difference between porno and erotic art nor the argument that sections of recognized classics—Rabelais, Joyce, etc.—are pornographic. (An argument I cannot accept. A sexual portion of a genuine artwork cannot—in my understanding—be pornographic. The latter means, for me, material devised *only* for sexual stimulation.)

The real difference is between imagined porno—written or drawn or painted—and performed porno, done in actuality or on film or in still photographs. The latter entails the degradation of human beings. It doesn't seem to me to matter that these performing men and women always seem cheerful and busily engaged, or that (reportedly) some of the occupants enjoy it or that some of them perform public sex acts as part of lives that are otherwise quite conventional. Obviously conditionings and rationales can vary widely, but I cannot believe that the use of human beings for these purposes is socially beneficial or morally liberating. On the contrary, I think it socially stultifying and morally warped.

I'm not talking about nudity and simulated intercourse in such plays as *Che!*, which are frequently done quite self-righteously as an attempt to *épater le bourgeois*. I mean (currently available in person and on film in New York and other cities) the public performance of coition, fellatio, cunnilingus, and mutual masturbation—with the coition usually interrupted so that the male ejaculation can be seen.

ACTS OF VINDICTIVENESS

I've been as excited by watching some of those films as a human being ought presumably to be. But essentially those films seem to me acts of vindictiveness by men against women in return for the sexual restrictions and taboos of our society and for the cruelties of women towards men that those restrictions have produced. The vindictiveness is essentially mean-spirited and exploitative. I would hope that the socio-sexual improvements on which the Lockhart sociologists relay may affect performed porno first.

In any event, I think that the lumping-together of all porno—imagined and performed—is a conceptual error. The one-to-one relation of writer and reader is a different matter, in psychic and social senses, from the employment of people to enact fantasies.

Conclusions, *pro tem.*

I am not a swinger. I don't believe in pornography as a healthful reminder of the full genital life amidst a pallid and poky society, or as an extender or consciousness in any beneficial way. These views seem to me phony emancipation—in fact, a negation of the very fullness of life that is ostensibly being affirmed. Much better to concentrate on our silliness about the romanticized restrictions of love and the shortcomings of marriage, on the humiliations of both men and women in our rituals of courtship and bedding and wedding, that make pornography such a popular form of vengeance.

But the legal suppression of pornography seems to me anticivil and anticivilized (because it misses the anticivilizing reasons for porno), and also shows a failure in sense of humor. (If the idea of sex is funny, as it often is, the idea of porno is funniness multiplied.) I'm against censorship laws just as I'm against laws against certain kinds of sexual practice, or against any sexual practice between unmarried people, that still exist in many parts of this country. I want to be able to have porno if I want it. The purely personal opinion that I don't happen to want it very often should not be made the law of the land.

To put it entirely subjectively, I think that one way to cure my uneasiness on the subject of porno is to repeal all the laws restricting it, except possibly the ones forbidding the advertising and sale to minors. The more mature the individual, the more he resents the idea of being forbidden something that affects him alone; and the more mature individuals there are, the better the polity.

In Praise of Censure

Garry Wills

Rarely have the denouncers of censorship been so eager to start practicing it. When a sense of moral disorientation overcomes a society, people from the least expected quarters begin to ask, "Is nothing sacred?" Feminists join reactionaries to denounce pornography as demeaning to women. Rock musician Frank Zappa declares that when Tipper Gore, the wife of Senator Albert Gore from Tennessee, asked music companies to label sexually explicit material, she launched an illegal "conspiracy to extort." A *Penthouse* editorialist says that housewife Terry Rakolta, who asked sponsors to withdraw support from the sit-

Garry Wills, "In Praise of Censure," *Time,* July 31, 1989 The Time Inc. Magazine Company. Reprinted by permission.

com called *Married . . . With Children,* is "yelling fire in a crowded theater," a formula that says her speech is not protected by the First Amendment.

But the most interesting movement to limit speech is directed at defamatory utterances against blacks, homosexuals, Jews, women or other stigmatizable groups. It took no Terry Rakolta of the left to bring about the instant firing of Jimmy the Greek and Al Campanis from sports jobs when they made racially denigrating comments. Social pressure worked far more quickly on them than on *Married . . . With Children,* which is still on the air.

The rules being considered on college campuses to punish students for making racist and other defamatory remarks go beyond social and commercial pressure to actual legal muzzling. The right-wing *Dartmouth Review* and its imitators have understandably infuriated liberals, who are beginning to take action against them and the racist expressions they have encouraged. The American Civil Liberties Union considered this movement important enough to make it the principal topic at its biennial meeting last month in Madison, Wis. Ironically, the regents of the University of Wisconsin had passed their own rules against defamation just before the ACLU members convened on the university's campus. Nadine Strossen, of New York University School of Law, who was defending the ACLU's traditional position on free speech, said of Wisconsin's new rules: "You can tell how bad they are by the fact that the regents had to make an amendment at the last minute exempting classroom discussion! What is surprising is that Donna Shalala [chancellor of the university] went along with it." So did constitutional lawyers on the faculty.

If a similar code were drawn up with right-wing imperatives in mind—one banning unpatriotic, irreligious or sexually explicit expressions on campus— the people framing Wisconsin-type rules would revert to their libertarian pasts. In this competition to suppress, is regard for freedom of expression just a matter of whose ox is getting gored at the moment? Does the left just get nervous about the Christian cross when Klansmen burn it, while the right will react only when Madonna flirts crucifixes between her thighs?

The cries of "un-American" are as genuine and as frequent on either side. Everyone is protecting the country. Zappa accuses Gore of undermining the moral fiber of America with the "sexual neuroses of these vigilant ladies." He argues that she threatens our freedoms with "connubial insider trading" because her husband is a Senator. Apparently her marital status should deprive her of speaking privileges in public—an argument Westbrook Pegler used to make against Eleanor Roosevelt. *Penthouse* says Rakolta is taking us down the path towards fascism. It attacks her for living in a rich suburb—the old "radical chic" argument that rich people cannot support moral causes.

There is a basic distinction that cuts through this free-for-all over freedom. It is the distinction, too often neglected, between censorship and censure (the free expression of moral disapproval). What the campuses are trying to do (at least those with state money) is use the force of government to contain freedom of speech. What Donald Wildmon, the freelance moralist from Tupelo, Miss., does when he gets Pepsi to cancel its Madonna ad is censure the ad by calling for a boycott. Advocating boycotts is a form of speech protected by the

First Amendment. As Nat Hentoff, journalistic custodian of the First Amendment, says, "I would hate to see boycotts outlawed. Think of what that would do to Cesar Chavez." Or, for the matter, to Ralph Nader. If one disapproves of a social practice, whether it is racist speech or unjust hiring in lettuce fields, one is free to denounce that and to call on others to express their disapproval. Otherwise there would be no form of persuasive speech except passing a law. This would make the law coterminous with morality.

Equating morality with legality is in effect what people do when they claim that anything tolerated by law must, in the name of freedom, be approved by citizens in all their dealings with one another. As Zappa says, "Masturbation is not illegal. If is it not illegal to do it, why should it be illegal to sing about it?" He thinks this proves that Gore, who is not trying to make raunch in rock illegal, cannot even ask distributors to label it. Anything goes, as long as it's legal. The odd consequence of this argument would be a drastic narrowing of the freedom of speech. One could not call into question anything that was not against the law—including, for instance, racist speech.

A false ideal of tolerance has not only outlawed censorship but discouraged censoriousness (another word for censure). Most civilizations have expressed their moral values by mobilization of social opprobrium. That, rather than specific legislation, is what changed the treatment of minorities in films and TV over recent years. One can now draw opprobrious attention by gay bashing, as the Beastie Boys rock group found when their distributor told them to cut out remarks about "fags" for business reasons. Or by anti-Semitism, as the just disbanded rap group Public Enemy has discovered.

It is said that only the narrow-minded are intolerant or opprobrious. Most of those who limited the distribution of Martin Scorsese's movie *The Last Temptation of Christ* had not even seen the movie. So do we guarantee freedom of speech only for the broad-minded or the better educated? Can one speak only after studying whatever one has reason, from one's beliefs, to denounce? Then most of us would be doing a great deal less speaking than we do. If one has never seen any snuff movies, is that a bar to criticizing them?

Others argue that asking people not to buy lettuce is different from asking them not to buy a rocker's artistic expression. Ideas (carefully disguised) lurk somewhere in the lyrics. All the more reason to keep criticism of them free. If ideas are too important to suppress, they are also too important to ignore. The whole point of free speech is not to make ideas exempt from criticism but to expose them to it.

One of the great mistakes of liberals in recent decades has been the ceding of moral concern to rightwingers. Just because one opposes censorship, one need not be seen as agreeing with pornographers. Why should liberals, of all people, oppose Gore when she asks that labels be put on products meant for the young, to inform those entrusted by law with the care of the young? Liberals were the first to promote "healthy" television shows like *Sesame Street* and *The Electric Company.* In the 1950s and 1960s they were the leading critics of television, of its mindless violence, of the way it ravaged the attention span needed for reading. Who was keeping kids away from TV sets then? How did promoters of Big Bird let themselves be cast as champions of the Beastie Boys—not just of their right to perform but of their performance itself? Why should it be left to Gore to express moral disapproval of a group calling itself Dead Kennedys (sample lyric: "I kill children, I love to see them die")?

For that matter, who has been more insistent that parents should "interfere" in what their children are doing, Tipper Gore or Jesse Jackson? All through the 1970s, Jackson was traveling the high schools, telling parents to turn off TVs, make the kids finish their homework, check with teachers on their performance, get to know what the children are doing. This kind of "interference" used to be called education.

Belief in the First Amendment does not pre-empt other beliefs, making one a eunuch to the interplay of opinions. It is a distortion to turn "You can express any views" into the proposition "I don't care what views you express." If liberals keep equating equality with approval, they will be repeatedly forced into weak positions,

What is at issue here is not government suppression but government subsidy. Mapplethorpe's work is not banned, but showing it might have endangered federal grants to needy artists. The idea that what the government does not support it represses is nonsensical, as one can see by reversing the statement to read: "No one is allowed to create anything without the government's subvention." What pussycats our supposedly radical artists are. They not only want the government's permission to create their artifacts, they want federal authorities to supply the materials as well. Otherwise they feel "gagged." If they are not given government approval (and money), they want to remain an avant-garde while being bankrolled by the Old Guard.

A case in point is the Corcoran Gallery's sudden cancellation of an exhibit of Robert Mapplethorpe's photographs. The whole matter was needlessly confused when the director, Christina Owr-Chall, claimed she was canceling the show to *protect* it from censorship. She meant that there might be pressure to remove certain pictures—the sadomasochistic ones or those verging on kiddie porn—if the show had gone on. But she had in mind, as well, the hope of future grants from the National Endowment for the Arts, which is under criticism for the Mapplethorpe show and for another show that contained Andres Serrano's *Piss Christ,* the photograph of a crucifix in what the title says is urine. Owr-Chall is said to be yielding to censorship, when she is clearly yielding to political and financial pressure, as Pepsi yielded to commercial pressure over the Madonna ad.

What is easily forgotten in this argument is the right of citizen taxpayers. They send representatives to Washington who are answerable for the expenditure of funds exacted from them. In general these voters want to favor their own values if government is going to get into the culture-subsidizing area at all (a proposition many find objectionable in itself). Politicians, insofar as they support the arts, will tend to favor a conventional art (certainly not masochistic art). Anybody who doubts that has no understanding of a politician's legitimate concern for his or her constituents' approval. Besides, it is quaint for those familiar with the politics of the art world to discover, with a shock, that there is politics in politics.

Luckily, cancellation of the Mapplethorpe show forced some artists back to the flair and cheekiness of unsubsidized art. Other results of pressure do not turn out as well. Unfortunately, people in certain regions were deprived of the chance to see the *Last Temptation of Christ* in the theater. Some, no doubt, considered it a loss that they could not buy lettuce or grapes during a Chavez boycott. Perhaps there was even a buyer perverse enough to miss driving the unsafe cars Nader helped pressure out of the market. On the other hand, we do not get sports analysis made by racists. These mobilizations of social opprobrium are not examples of repression but of freedom of expression by committed people who censured without censoring, who expressed the kinds of belief the First Amendment guarantees. I do not, as a result, get whatever I approve of subsidized, either by Pepsi or the government. But neither does the law come in to silence Tipper Gore or Frank Zappa or even that filthy rag, the *Dartmouth Review*.

EVALUATING INFORMATION

> *"Now I'll give you something to believe."[said the White Queen]. "I'm*
> *just one hundred and one, five months and a day."*
> *"I can't believe that!" said Alice.*
> *"Can't you?" the Queen said in a pitying tone. "Try again: draw a long*
> *breath and shut your eyes."*
> *Alice laughed. "There's no use trying," she said: "one can't believe im-*
> *possible things."*
> *"I daresay you haven't had much practice," said the Queen. "When I was*
> *your age, I always did it for half-an-hour a day. Why sometimes I've*
> *believed as many as six impossible things before breakfast."*

In *Through the Looking Glass* by Lewis Carroll, the White Queen claims that believing information is simply a matter of effort and practice, and, of course, we all know that this is nonsense. Actually, what is not usually recognized is that it is sometimes easier to believe what we read and hear than it is *not* to believe because the act of questioning information often involves effort and practice or at least awareness. This section of Chapter 2 is concerned with helping you consider when to believe and when to doubt—that is, how to decide whether a piece of information from an outside source is true or worth considering.

ASSESSING YOUR ATTITUDE TOWARD PRINTED MATERIAL

In order to develop skill at working with outside sources, it's a good idea to consider how you generally react when you read information in articles or books. Do you usually believe what you read? Or do you tend to be skeptical? Think about this the next time you read a text you consider to be nonfiction. To help you focus your thinking, consider whether the following statements should be answered "true" or "false."

1. Information from a published work is always true.
2. When a work is published, all statements made by the writer are carefully checked by the editor to see whether they are true.
3. Articles that cite statistics are more likely to be true than those that do not.
4. An article written by an expert in a field is more likely to be accurate than one written by a non-expert.
5. Recent publications are more useful than those written long ago.

Here is a general response to all of these statements concerning reading: When you first read a source, begin with an attitude of acceptance so that you can glean the main ideas from the text. Then, when you read the article again more closely, or more critically, question what you read by asking critical questions.

The following responses to the statements above should help you to see why critical reading is important. You should know, though, while the following responses are generally considered correct, the answers to each are relative and may vary according to specific situations:

1. **Information from a published work is always true.**
   False: Even published works are subject to error, both intentional and unintentional. Be wary of believing everything you read.
2. **When a work is published, all statements made by the writer are carefully checked by the editor to see whether they are true.**
   False: Reputable publishers do have a staff of people who check information. But even then, errors can occur. Plus, many publishers do not check sources or facts very carefully at all.
3. **Articles that cite statistics are more likely to be true than those that do not.**
   False: Although most writers do not actually make up or lie about their figures, they can use them to create an impression that may actually be a distortion of the truth. For example, look at the following paragraph:

   > Increasingly, college men are inclining toward a return to the traditional family structure of the past. A questionnaire given to entering freshmen at State University revealed that 253 wished their future wives to stay at home and care for their children. This is an increase of 50 students over the responses given to the same questionnaire in 1980.

   In the above paragraph, the statistics have been distorted to suit the author's purpose because we do not know what percentage of the entering freshmen the number 253 represents. If the enrollment of male freshmen had increased considerably since 1980, then the figure of 253 might actually represent a decrease. Moreover, we do not have access to the questionnaire, which may have contained questions designed to elicit certain responses.
4. **An article written by an expert in a field is more likely to be accurate than one written by a non-expert.**

True: Established experts are more likely to know what they are talking about than non-experts. Yet even experts may use information to suit their own purposes.

5. **Recent publications are more useful than those written longer ago.**
   Sometimes, but not always: In developing fields, such as the sciences or social sciences, recently written articles contain more current information than those written longer ago, and, in these fields, new information may mean that the writer has greater insight into the issue. In fact, sometimes new studies directly contradict older ones. At other times, though, you may be dealing with a subject that generated controversy some years ago, and for that subject, articles and books written longer ago may be more useful to you. For historical topics especially, older source materials may be more valuable.

SHOPPING FOR SOURCES

Two Metaphoric Scenarios

Scenario 1: Anwar enters a big and tall men's clothing store. He comes upon a rack of jeans and selects a pair without checking the price, size, or fit. Next, he sees a display of sweatshirts and selects a green one, again without doing any further checking. His eye then lights upon a display of slacks, tennis shoes, and jackets; he quickly selects one of each in the same way. Anwar pays for everything and leaves the store, satisfied that he has done a good day's shopping and that he will be able to use everything he has purchased.

Scenario 2: Before going shopping, Carol carefully surveys her wardrobe, noting exactly what she needs. She makes a careful list, which includes the name of the item, the quantity, the color and size, and the expected price. She then goes to the store, finds everything on her list, and goes home, well satisfied with her shopping excursion.

Think about these scenarios. You are probably thinking that both scenarios are neither realistic nor desirable. In Scenario 1, Anwar obviously knows very little about shopping and is unlikely to have purchased suitable articles. He did not enter the store with a specific purpose in mind, he did not plan his choices, nor did he examine and evaluate his purchases in terms of how appropriate they were for his particular needs. His behavior suggests that he believes any item he finds will be useful, regardless of the size, color, fit, or price, and most of us would be critical of anyone who shopped in this way.

On the other hand, Carol's narrow list did not allow for much flexibility, nor did it enable her to do much looking around. Most stores are unlikely to have carried every specific item on Carol's list, and since she was focused so narrowly on finding only those particular items, she did not get any ideas from simply browsing. Her behavior suggests that she had thought of everything beforehand and that she was uninterested in anything new or surprising.

These two scenarios represent two extreme metaphors of how students look for sources. Some students, like Anwar, scout around the library and, as soon as they discover a source remotely concerned with their topic, they open it and begin reading passively, from beginning to end, satisfied that they have found something useful. They then go on to the next source, and when they have found the required number, they feel they have fulfilled their assignment. Other students, like Carol, plan very carefully what they think they need from a library and look only for these items. If the library doesn't have exactly what they are looking for, they feel extremely frustrated, and even if it does, they miss out on valuable opportunities for browsing and getting new ideas.

Actually, an initial search for sources is probably best when it is a compromise somewhere between randomly selecting sources and searching for specific sources to fit a specific need. It is a good idea to plan for what you might need, but it's also desirable to remain flexible, open to new possibilities and ideas. After working initially on a topic, you might expect to skim through anywhere from 12 to 20 sources in order to find 6 worthy of your close attention.

Choose Sources Purposefully

You would not select clothing at random; you would be unlikely to wear just anything, simply because you happened to come upon it. Neither should you randomly select your sources for inclusion in your researched paper. People who engage in academic research approach their sources with a questioning attitude, and before they read a source, they check several features of it to see whether it will be useful. Then they consider whether the source is likely to fulfill their particular needs or purposes before reading it through. Furthermore, as they read, they ask questions—in their minds, in their notes, and sometimes in the margins. Because the act of critically examining a source is so complex and involved, the following sections provide you with guidelines to help you assess the validity and usefulness of each source you might use in a research project.

Discovering Logical Fallacies or Errors in Logic

Not every argument you may read is developed logically. Many rely on errors in reasoning that do nothing to provide support. Being aware of some of these common "logical fallacies" can help you evaluate the strength of your sources' evidence when researching a topic and the strength of your own evidence when writing essays.

Post Hoc (Presuming Cause and Effect): The post hoc fallacy is one in which one event is said to have caused another simply because they occurred in sequence. This type of thinking presumes a causal relationship between events without recognizing other factors that may have contributed. Post hoc reasoning is a very common way of thinking, but it does not incorporate logic. Here are some examples:

"Don't take Susan on a picnic. Every time I go somewhere with her, it rains!" [Obviously, Susan could not have had anything to do with the rain, despite the coincidence.] "We have discovered that all of the criminals in the county ate white bread as children. Therefore, white bread leads to criminal behavior." [The white bread obviously did not cause the criminal behavior.]

Hasty Generalization (Generalizations from Insufficient Evidence): Related to the fallacy of presuming causality is the hasty generalization, which bases claims on insufficient evidence. An example of a hasty generalization follows:

"We shouldn't allow girls from that part of town into our club. I once knew a girl from there, and she was a thief."

Loose Generalization: A loose generalization is an overly broad, unqualified statement that does not allow for exceptions or complexity. For example:

"Girls are not good in math."

False Analogy: This form of argument presumes that if two things or people are alike in one or two ways, they will be alike in other ways also. Here is an example:

"People should be allowed to smoke in restaurants. If they are allowed to drink in restaurants, they should be allowed to smoke as well." [This analogy ignores the fact that smoking in restaurants is harmful to others, while drinking, at least in moderation and not while driving, is not.]

Ad Hominem (Attacking the Person Rather than the Issue): An ad hominem argument attacks a person, rather than an issue or position. To illustrate:

"Don't listen to Fred's ideas for a new computer system. He watches professional wrestling."

Appeals to False Authority and the Bandwagon: Television ads frequently use well-known stars to advertise products for which they really have no expertise. If a famous movie star endorses a particular product, this does not mean that the produce is worth buying. Similarly, if a famous person endorses a particular social or ethical position, this endorsement does not mean that the position is right and just.

The bandwagon effect is a logical fallacy maintaining that if everyone (or a great deal of people) believe or do something, then it must be right. Here is an example of bandwagon thinking:

"Millions of people are in favor of the death penalty. Therefore, it must be right."

Circular Reasoning: Circular reasoning is another common form of illogical thinking. It occurs when you state your position and then restate it in different words as your reason for believing in the position. An obvious example of circular reasoning follows:

> "Excess drinking is detrimental to health because it causes harm to the body."

A more complicated form of circular reasoning is illustrated in the following:

> "Corporations, too, would benefit from the decrease in taxes because businesses need the advantages a decrease would bring."

Black and White (Either/Or) Thinking: This is a form of reasoning that presumes only two possibilities when, in fact, there may be many. Black and white reasoning is exemplified in the following statement:

> "Either we must institute a strict dress code or employees will dress inappropriately." [This statement overlooks the possibility that general specifications about dress might be sufficient or that employees might dress appropriately even without a dress code.]

Non Sequitor (Does Not Follow): This is a fallacy in which a piece of evidence does not relate directly to the idea that it supposedly supports. For instance:

> "Aquabright toothpaste is the best brand because the company has a wonderful marketing department."

Slippery Slope: This type of fallacy inaccurately presumes a chain of events likely to occur as a result of one original event. An example of a slippery slope argument is as follows:

> "I can't allow my son to join that mountain climbing club. If he does, he will be climbing mountains at least once a week, then twice a week. Before you know it, he will be spending all his time climbing mountains and won't be able to keep up with his studies."

Ad Populum: The translation of this Latin phrase is "to the people," and in argumentation, it means appealing to the prejudices of the audience without providing necessary support. This sort of appeal can be seen in the following bread advertisement:

> "Homestead bread is a superior brand because it brings your whole family to the table at dinner time; so, if you care about strong family values, you'll pick up a loaf for your family today!" [This advertisement plays on the common concern parents have today about family values but does not demonstrate that the bread is superior in any other way.]

> ➤ **Exercise in Identifying Logical Fallacies:** For the following list of claims, try to determine which kind of fallacy each exhibits (refer to the descriptions above, if necessary). Be prepared to explain your answers to your classmates.
>
> 1. If birth control devices become available at our school, all students are going to think it is acceptable to have sex before marriage.
> 2. Since Michael Jordan promotes Nike, they must make the best basketball shoes.
> 3. I wouldn't hire Hosam as your interior decorator. He is a man, and you should know that men don't have any taste when it comes to decorating.
> 4. Camilla is the best writer; she is from England after all.
> 5. If you want a good grade in Physics, don't take Dr. Woo. My friend Sarah took her class, and Dr. Woo flunked her!

Checking for Ambiguity and Distortion

We are all familiar with ambiguity in the language of advertising. We would be suspicious of an ad for a face cream that claims it will "bring out all of your natural beauty" because we really don't know what "bring out" or "natural beauty" means. A toothpaste ad that claims that the product "fights cavities in six ways" would mean little if we were not told anything about those six ways. Writers concerned with social or political issues often use abstract words that have different meanings for different people, words such as "freedom," "obscenity," or "privacy," for instance. In reading a source, check to see whether the term is adequately defined and whether the examples support that definition. In the Mittman article, for example, there is a claim that "teenagers themselves were the strongest advocates of hard-line legislation to handle drug abuse," yet the term "strongest advocates" is not clearly defined or supported.

Note also whether the author uses inflammatory language, exaggerated comparisons or examples, or inflated statistics to support the main position. Often extreme situations and hysterical language are so compelling that they distract us from questioning their appropriateness. Think about whether such examples are truly representative and whether the author has omitted other equally representative examples.

GETTING IN THE HABIT OF EXAMINING YOUR SOURCES

As we have discussed, it is imperative that you examine your sources with a critical eye to ensure that the information provided is valid, and, if an argument is asserted, that the reasoning is sound. On the next page is a form that can assist you in reading and evaluating your sources critically:

Source Evaluation Worksheet

Author:

Title:

Publisher:

Copyright date:

What information is this source likely to provide?

My opinion on the topic:

Significance of the title:

Author's relationship to, or likely position on, the issue:

Main point:

What is the controversy?

Reasons for the controversy:

Method of organization:

Ambiguous terms?

Inflammatory examples?

Omissions or unstated assumptions?

Representative quotations:

➤ **Exercise in Using the Source Evaluation Worksheet:** If you haven't already done so, read the essay "Presumption of Guilt," by Nat Hentoff, on pp. 51–57. Next, generate a source evaluation sheet for the essay, using the model above, and fill out your source evaluation sheet as completely as possible. Finally, compare your worksheet to the one provided on pp. 42–43. Jot down any discrepancies between your worksheet and the one provided here in the text.

Two Methods of Interacting with a Source

Two students in a composition class read the essay "Presumption of Guilt," by Nat Hentoff. As a means of generating critical thinking about this source, one filled in the Source Evaluation Worksheet. The other interacted with the text by annotating it—underlining key points and writing questions and comments in the margins. Both methods are useful for better understanding and for evaluating your sources.

Source Evaluation Worksheet

Author: Nat Hentoff

Title: "Presumption of Guilt"

Publisher: *The Progressive*

Copyright date: May 1986

What information is this source likely to provide? This article is likely to provide reasons against mandatory drug testing.

My opinion on the topic: I am concerned about possible drug abuses in certain industries in which public safety is at stake. I think I am probably in favor of drug testing, at least for certain industries.

Significance of the title: The title refers to the general idea that, in our culture, someone is thought innocent until proven guilty. This seems a reversal of that idea.

Author's relationship to or likely position on the issue: This article was published in a journal called *The Progressive*. The title of this publication suggests that the author might be in favor of maintaining freedom from government interference. He is probably somewhat "left-wing" and worries about abuses.

Main point: Mandatory drug testing is a violation of a person's right to privacy under the Fourth Amendment. It can lead to all sorts of abuses.

What is the controversy? Some say that there should be mandatory drug testing because there are too many instances in which drug users cannot do their job adequately. Others say that mandatory drug testing will lead to a "Big Brother" society in which the government will know all sorts of things about everyone, which they will be able to use against them.

Reasons for the controversy:

1. Mandatory urine tests are an invasion of privacy.
2. They aren't accurate.
3. They violate the Fourth Amendment because they allow searches without probable cause.
4. New tests will soon provide employers with all sorts of private information about employees' body chemicals or their likelihood of catching a disease, information that employers could then use against employees.

Method of organization: Shows how prevalent mandatory drug testing has become, both in government and in the private sector. Then presents reasons against it. Then states how more sophisticated tests could lead to further abuses.

Ambiguous terms? Although the author says that drug use might be considered simply a "disability," and although it is forbidden by law to fire someone because of a disability unless it affects job performance, there are no examples of how drug abuse won't affect job performance.

Inflammatory examples? Compares drug testing to eavesdropping or hidden microphones I'm not sure this is the same thing. Brings up Orwell's "Big Brother." "Massive and official attack on workers' privacy." This seems a little exaggerated. "Having one's bodily fluids forcibly and randomly inspected."

Omissions or unstated assumptions? The author doesn't address industries where it is really necessary for safety to have employees drug-free. Cites only extreme cases of potential abuse.

Representative quotations: "As for coming attractions that verify the prescience of George Orwell, the *Washington Post* reported in mid-1984, 'Researchers in academia and industry say it is now possible to envision a product that could instantaneously assess whether employees are concentrating on their jobs by analyzing their brain waves as they work.'"

The worksheet enabled the first student to perceive that the author had a strong bias on the question of drug testing and that a balanced argument would have to include at least one other point of view on the subject. Gaining this overall perspective enabled the student to understand the reasoning and viewpoint of the text more thoroughly than if he had simply begun to read it unquestioningly.

> ➤ **Exercise in Comparing the Two Methods for Interacting with a Source:**

Turn to the Hentoff reading at the end of this chapter (pp. 51–57) and note how the second student interacted with the text through annotation, that is, writing his questions and comments in the margins. Consider the following:

1. How are the two methods similar?
2. How do the two methods differ?
3. Which method do you think was most effective? Explain your choice.
4. Which method do you feel most comfortable using? Explain your answer.

Next, in small groups, compare your answers. Remember that each of you is entitled to your own opinion—and that everyone learns in different ways. Be prepared to present a summary of your group's discussion to the class.

WRITING THE CRITIQUE

Establishing and Applying Criteria

When we formulate an opinion on whether or not we consider something to be positive, negative, or somewhere in between these extremes, we usually base our position on several concrete, specific areas of evaluation. These areas of evaluation, or criteria, are the objective standards we use to determine the worth or merit of whatever it is that we're evaluating. By applying our criteria to the object we are evaluating, we can more readily ascertain its value.

Using Criteria to Make Qualitative Decisions

Judging the merit, or worth, of a particular thing based on a set of objective standards is an activity we engage in quite often in our everyday lives. For example, if you were getting ready to move and searching for the perfect apartment, you might first come up with a list of various criteria to apply to your potential choices. By first determining which criteria to apply to each apartment, you could more easily establish whether or not each candidate measures up to these qualities you've determined are necessary for an ideal apartment. So, you might generate a list of criteria for your dream apartment that includes new appliances, large bedrooms, and central air conditioning. Then, when you visit each apartment, you can judge the merit of each one by seeing how it compares to your established criteria. If the first apartment has deteriorating or non-existent appliances, very small, cramped bedrooms, and no air-conditioning, you can justify your negative opinion of it based on how it fails to meet your criteria. On the other hand, if you look at another apartment that has brand-new appliances, gigantic bedrooms, and efficient central air, you would feel comfortable with your positive evaluation of the apartment (and your decision to write a check for the first month's rent). The second apartment, then, warrants a positive evaluation, for it clearly measures up to your predetermined standards of evaluation, or criteria.

THE CRITIQUE ESSAY: APPLYING CRITERIA TO EVALUATE WRITING

Just as you might do in assessing the merits of different apartments, in judging the merits of a piece of writing you should base your judgments on an established list of qualities which, in your opinion, are crucial to an effective essay, article, poem, book, or any other type of composition. One type of essay commonly assigned in both first-year college writing classes and in upper-division, subject-specific courses is the critique, an essay which requires you to write an argumentative essay based on a critical, directed reading of a particular text. Writing a critique essay is a worthwhile endeavor, for it allows you to develop competence with skills you will use often in future college writing assignments. Some of these important skills include:

1. reading, understanding, and analyzing a written piece critically;
2. determining the relevance, usefulness, or worth of a reading based on an objective set of standards which you feel are imperative to the type of writing you are assessing (criteria);
3. writing a position paper which successfully argues your assessment of the strengths or weaknesses inherent to a text and its argument.

Deciding on Specific Criteria

In order to establish whether or not a written text has merit, you must first decide on the objective standards, or criteria, you consider vital to an article's effectiveness. For instance, does the article present facts gleaned from reputable sources in support of the author's thesis? Is the language used in the article engaging and easily understood by its intended audience? Does the author organize his or her supporting arguments well to validate a rational thesis? The choice of which criteria to use in support of your critique is up to you, but you will probably find it very helpful to look at the following section for a multitude of suggestions for getting started.

Establishing Criteria for Evaluating Sources

Skill at comprehending and evaluating textual materials of varying length and complexity is crucial for most college courses, especially those courses that require researched writing. The ability to understand and evaluate sources will be showcased when you write critiques of specific sources. Critique assignments are common in many disciplines, since critiques show college instructors which students are able to comprehend and critically analyze research in their field. Remember that you are not expected to passively read what is assigned to you by your instructors. Instead, you are expected to interact with what you read, creating a dialogue between yourself and the source and analyzing what is written therein. To determine an article or book's merits and/or faults, you must first read it to understand what was written. Next, once you grasp the content, you must re-read the source, all the while questioning what you read.

Below is a list of questions that you should ask yourself about every source that you read—especially those that you consider using in your research:

1. Who wrote the article/book? Is the author credible on the subject? You should carefully examine the author's credentials, training, expertise, and experience and decide whether his or her qualifications are relevant for the subject of the text.

2. When was it written? Is it a timely piece of writing? Is it up-to-date? You should determine whether or not the author is writing about a current and relevant subject. The author should also be using up-to-date, relevant evidence (e.g., current studies, statistics, etc.) to support claims.

3. Why was this piece written (author's purpose)? What is the author intending to do in this text? What function does this text serve for its readers? Does it fulfill the purpose it intends? For example, if the author's purpose is to entertain readers, then the author should be using humor effectively; if the author's purpose is to gain support for a proposed solution, he or she should provide readers detailed ideas for implementation.

4. What kind of reading is it (genre)? What would you normally expect from a text of this genre? You should determine whether or not the piece of writing meets typical expectations college-educated readers have of this genre.

5. What is the author's thesis? Do the main points/ideas support the thesis throughout? Is the thesis clear? Remember that the author of an effective piece of writing makes the thesis clear for readers.

6. How does the author support the thesis/main points/arguments throughout? Are the thesis/main points/arguments supported with solid evidence and reasoning? Generalizations? Biases? Contradictions? Repetitive points? Does the author ignore any important arguments, counterarguments, or information that should have been addressed? Remember that an effective argument has ample evidence and solid reasoning to support its claims.

7. Are the main points or arguments logical/valid? Persuasive writing that contains logical fallacies and invalid conclusions is not effective. For more on fallacies, refer to the previous section on logical fallacies within this chapter.

8. How is the author's tone/attitude conveyed? Does the author's tone support or detract from the article's purpose or meaning? Is it appropriate for the audience and purpose? It should be.

9. Who are the intended readers of the text? Is the appropriate audience addressed? Is the subject, stance, word choice, and so forth suitable for the intended audience? With any published work, the author(s) should anticipate readers' background knowledge on the subject and specific issue.

10. Is the text comprehensive enough for its subject matter? Is there enough information? Too much information?

11. Are the details, facts, and statistics accurate and verifiable? Are there reliable sources backing the author's claims? Are the sources adequately documented? Remember that a credible author provides adequate information for readers to assess the accuracy, reliability, and verifiability of the details used.

➤ **Exercise in Establishing Criteria:** Using the heuristic offered above, begin assessing the merit, or worth, of Brian Noal Mittman's article, "Teenagers Need Drug Testing," found on pp. 57–59 later in this chapter. Jot down your answers to each of the questions. Be prepared to share your tentative assessment of the article with your classmates and instructor during the next class.

➤ **Assignment on Establishing Criteria:** Using the heuristic offered above, begin assessing the merit, or worth, of an article you are considering critiquing or using in a researched essay. Jot down your answers to each of the questions. Be prepared to share your tentative assessment of your chosen article with your classmates and instructor during the next class.

Using Your Criteria to Formulate Your Position

As previously explained, when writing a critique you should base your evaluation of a text's merit upon an established list of criteria that, in your opinion, are crucial to its effectiveness. Thus, once you have critically examined a text using the heuristic above, you will need to determine which criteria you find to be most important to the text's success or failure—and those you would most likely be able to address clearly, fully, and comfortably in a written critique. As a general rule, in order to convince readers of a text's merits and/or faults, you will need to develop at least three or four criteria to support your **position**, or **thesis**—your overall assessment of the text. Therefore, we recommend that you first choose the criteria that you find to be most important to the text's ultimate success or failure; then, you should base your overall assessment on your judgment of how well the text meets those criteria.

For example, if the text successfully meets all the criteria you believe to be crucial to a text's effectiveness, your position within your critique should convey an overall **positive review** to readers so that they know that you are recommending the text without reservation. However, if the text only meets some of the criteria you decided upon, your thesis should present a **mixed review**. But how do you recommend a text with a mixed review? To answer this, we suggest that if the text meets those criteria you find to be more important than the criteria it does not meet, you should still recommend it to your readers as worthwhile. Conversely, you might choose to persuade your readers that although the text has redeeming qualities, it would be worth their time to find another, more valuable text on the same subject. Finally, when the text you are evaluating does not meet any of the criteria you have established, your position should convey a **negative review** in which you let readers know that the text's faults are too numerous to warrant a positive recommendation.

> ➤ **Exercise in Using Your Criteria to Formulate Your Position:** Using the answers you generated in response to the "Establishing Criteria" heuristic when assessing the merit, or worth, of Brian Noal Mittman's article, "Teenagers Need Drug Testing," determine which 3–4 criteria you find to be most crucial to its ultimate success or failure. Next, with those criteria in mind, would you give Mittman's article an overall positive, negative, or mixed review? Jot down your position and explain why you decided upon that position. Be prepared to share your position with your classmates and instructor for the next class.

> ➤ **Assignment on Using Your Criteria to Formulate Your Position:** Using the answers you generated in response to the "Establishing Criteria" heuristic when assessing the merit, or worth, of an article you are considering critiquing or using in a researched essay, determine which 3–4 criteria you find to be most crucial to its ultimate success or failure. Next, with those criteria in mind, would you give the article an overall positive, negative, or mixed review? Jot down your position and explain why you decided upon that position. Be prepared to share your position with your classmates and instructor for the next class.

Considering Your Audience

An important consideration when writing a critique (or any other essay) is your potential audience and your purpose for writing. It might help to envision an academic audience willing to be persuaded to accept or dismiss the text you critiqued, based on your review. As you compose your essay, you'll want to make a conscious effort to be as clear and concise as possible since your readers may not be familiar with the article you are critiquing. Keep your audience in mind as you write and give them honest feedback about the quality of the article.

Critiquing Versus Debating

Another very important consideration to keep in mind as you write a critique essay is that this writing assignment requires you to assess the strengths or weaknesses of an article, *not* the issue being debated. For instance, suppose you are evaluating an article in which the author advocates treating juvenile offenders as adults. If you disagree vehemently with this position, you might be tempted to condemn the article as narrow-minded and inaccurate. However, because the critique essay compels you to evaluate the article (and the position it promotes) impartially, based on objective criteria, you must still look at whether or not it presents the author's stance effectively. Notice the important distinction here—instead of taking issue with the author's point of view, you need to assess how the author relays that point of view (effectively or ineffectively). Although you might ultimately decide to write a negative critique of the article, it should be based on specific, criteria-based issues such as the author's insufficient evidence, fanatical tone, or incoherent organization, rather than his or her position on the issue.

BASIC FEATURES OF A CRITIQUE

A critique is a systematic evaluation of a reading written in order to provide your reader (and yourself) with a deeper understanding of that reading, its intended meaning, and its merits and faults. Most critique essays contain the following elements:

1. **introduction**—interests readers in the text being critiqued;
2. **summary**—provides background information;
3. **analysis and evaluation**—assesses the text's effectiveness based upon an established set of criteria;
4. **conclusion**—reminds readers of your overall judgment of the text.

These essential features of the critique essay are discussed in detail below to help you plan and write your critique essay:

Introduction

In the introduction to your critique essay, your main purpose will be to introduce the text you've decided to critique, its subject, its purpose, and your assessment (briefly, at this point) of its merits and/or faults. Early in the critique essay, it is also helpful to provide the name of the author, title of the work, and the date of publication for your readers. Additionally, you'll want to identify author's central argument (or thesis), since your critique will be based on how well the author argued his or her position. Again, remember to avoid taking a stance on the issue itself, especially as you begin your evaluation of the article. Your goal is to critique the quality of the argument, not the position itself.

When introducing your evaluation of the text's overall effectiveness based on its merits and/or faults (your thesis), be sure to provide your readers with a clear understanding of your assessment and your arguments that support that assessment. Remember to base your supporting arguments upon relevant criteria. Your criteria, again, are the three or four strengths or weaknesses you intend to point out which, in your estimation, either add to or detract from a written text's usefulness or validity.

Summary

A summary of the text must be included to give the reader enough background information to be able to follow your critique of it. This summary should be concise, comprising no more than one-fourth of your entire essay. You should strive, in your summary of the text you are critiquing, to include only the essential, main points of the essay—try not to overwhelm your readers with too many details. Your summary should be provided in one of the following locations:

- early in the essay—after the introduction—to facilitate your reader's understanding of your subsequent critique of the text (as student-writer Amy Burton does in her critique at the end of this chapter), or
- interspersed throughout the analysis portion of the critique, provided that you include enough of a brief, yet comprehensive, overview of the text within the introductory portion of your critique so that readers can get a sense of the text's purpose and main point before you begin critiquing it (as student-writer Sara Carrasquillo does in her critique at the end of this chapter).

For more specific tips on writing the summary, refer to the "Writing the Summary" section earlier in this chapter.

Analysis/Evaluation

Your analysis of the effectiveness or ineffectiveness of the written text will provide the bulk of your essay—all of your supporting paragraphs (besides the summary) will be developed using the criteria you've chosen to judge the strength or weakness of the text. You might choose, for example, to focus on the quality of the author's research, the consistency of the author's focus, or the accessibility of the author's language, to name just a few possibilities.

In this critical section of your essay, you'll evaluate the validity of the text and the argument it upholds, stating whether or not your find it to be strong or flawed overall and providing your readers with three or four examples of strong or weak areas as support for your stance. Each example should be based upon a clear criterion and backed by two-to-four pieces of evidence. Remember that the more evidence (quotes and paraphrases from the text) you include to support your argument, the more credible and persuasive you will be to your readers. While your summary should report the ideas presented in the text and your interpretation of the author's purpose, your analysis should report your interpretations of what the writing was trying to accomplish and how effective it was at doing so. You might also consider, as part of your analysis, including what the author failed to discuss or might have discussed in more detail.

Conclusion

To wrap your essay up, remind your readers of your overall judgment. The conclusion should include a logically reasoned claim about the overall validity of the article based on the criteria used to evaluate it. You may remind the reader of the three-to-four strengths or weakness of the argument that you developed in your essay and comment on whether or not the author's argument was ultimately successful.

> ➤ **Exercise in Analyzing an Article's Strengths and Weaknesses:** If you haven't already done so, please read the following two articles, "Presumption of Guilt," by Nat Hentoff, and "Teenagers Need Drug Testing," by Brian Noal Mittman (found later in this chapter). Next, consider the following questions:
>
> 1. Which article did you find most effective?
> 2. What were its strengths and weaknesses (based upon 3–4 criteria)?
> 3. Which article did you find least effective?
> 4. What were its strengths and weaknesses (based upon 3–4 criteria)?

Presumption of Guilt

Nat Hentoff

> *"I don't take drugs and I don't believe I have*
> *to piss in a bottle to prove I don't."*
> —*Bob Stanley, pitcher, Boston Red Sox*

> *"If you hang all the people, you'll get all the guilty."*
> —*Tom T. Hall, country singer*

In March, Ira Glasser, executive director of the American Civil Liberties Union, sent a letter to twenty of the

Nat Hentoff, "Presumption of Guilt," *The Progressive,* May 1986. Reprinted by permission from *The Progressive,* 409 East Main Street, Madison, WI 53703.

nation's largest labor unions inviting them to take part in a series of seminars this fall to work out a strategy, for the unions and the ACLU to protect the privacy of Americans where they work.

"Government employees and employees of private industry, railway workers and baseball players," Glasser wrote, "are being required in ever greater numbers to prove their innocence by submitting to intrusive and humiliating urine and blood tests." The seminars, he said, would deal not only with "random drug testing of people not suspected of using drugs," but also with "other violations of the right to privacy of the workplace."

As many workers can testify, privacy rights in the workplace have been eroding for a long time by means that range from management eavesdropping on employee telephone calls to placement of hidden microphones in employee washrooms in order to pick up intelligence concerning "troublemakers." What prompted Glasser's rallying cry, however, was the proclamation of an unprecedented massive and official attack on workers' privacy.

Main thesis: privacy rights are being eroded

On March 2, the President's Commission on Organized Crime strongly recommended—in the name of "national security"—that all Federal employees be tested for drug use. Not particular individuals about whom some reasonable suspicion of drug abuse exists, but *all* employees. Furthermore, the Commission urged all private employers who have Federal contracts to begin dragnet testing of their workers. If the contractors refuse, they should be denied any further Government business.

The Commission went on to recommend that all private employers, not just those with Federal contracts, start collecting urine samples and otherwise screen their workers from drug use. Peter Rodino, chairman of the House Judiciary Committee and a member of the President's Commission on Organized Crime, objected strenuously, noting that such wholesale testing "raises civil-liberties concerns." Nonsense, said Attorney General Edwin Meese, a mail-order scholar of the Framers' intentions on these matters. No unlawful search and seizure is involved, Meese explained, because, "by definition, it's not an unreasonable seizure because it's something the employee consents to as a condition of employment."

In other words, when the boss tells you to pee in a bottle if you want to keep your job, you consent to the condition if you don't want to lose your job.

A pretty brash example

At the press conference with the Attorney General was the chairman of the President's Commission, Judge Irving Kaufman of the Second Circuit Court of Appeals. Kaufman was the judge who sent Ethel and Julius Rosenburg to the electric chair after praying earnestly for guidance, thus making God an accomplice in the execution. As the years went on, Kaufman, extremely sensitive to charges that he was the prosecutor's judge in the Rosenburg case, has developed an exceptional reputation as a defender of First Amendment rights of defendants, especially the press, against the Government. But now, in the twilight of his career, Kaufman has again become the prosecutor's judge by supporting dragnet drug testing of millions of Americans.

Discusses Kaufman's role in the Rosenberg case to show that he might be overly zealous now

The testing he and the majority of the Commission advocate, says Kaufman, is no more an invasion of privacy than requiring any American to walk through metal detectors at an airport. However, as Tom Wicker noted in *The New York Times,* "Having one's bodily fluids forcibly and randomly inspected is substantially different from putting one's luggage through an electronic device."

Urine testing is invasive

What's more, the drug tests aren't even accurate. "The most commonly used urine test is notoriously unreliable," Ira Glasser noted in an ACLU statement. "It cannot identify specific drugs and it cannot distinguish between common cold medicine and illegal substances like marijuana and cocaine. The test cannot determine when someone used a particular drug, or to what extent. And it cannot measure impairment of the ability to function on the job."

Drug tests are not always accurate

There are also blood tests for drugs, and they reveal much more than the Government or a private employer claims to be testing for. Charles Seabrook, an unusually probing science writer, pointed out in the *Atlanta Journal & Constitution* last year that "from a single ounce of a person's blood, sophisticated computerized tests can determine, or at least strongly suggest, whether a person is predisposed to heart attacks, whether he smokes, drinks to excess, has had a venereal disease, or is epileptic, schizophrenic, or subject to depression. . . . 'Given enough blood and enough lab technicians, I could find out hundreds of things about you—what you eat, what drugs you take, even the kind of booze you drink,' says Dr. James Woodford, a forensic chemist in Atlanta, who is frequently consulted in drug-related cases."

Drug tests can reveal too much

Ambiguous. How many is 'enough'?

Judge Kaufman and the Attorney General may have unwittingly rendered a considerable service to the nation because their proposal has begun to focus attention on routine invasions of privacy in the workplace. A growing number of large corporations have been doing just what the President's Commission on Organized Crime is pushing.

As an index of the dragnet testing that is already in place, everyone who applies for work at United Airlines, IBM, Exxon, Du Pont, Federal Express, Lockheed, Shearson Lehman, TWA, and a good many other companies has to undergo urinalysis. Indeed, at least a quarter of the *Fortune 500* companies test all applicants for drugs. Even without prodding from the President's Commission, many other firms, large and small, would have joined the list. Any time management has a chance to control its work force more firmly, it seizes on that chance. Now, the notion that every worker is guilty until proven innocent also has the imprimatur of a blue-ribbon Government commission that insists on regarding urinalysis and other forms of testing workers—before and after they're hired—as essential for national security.

Drug testing is pervasive

Is this really true? It seems inflammatory.

At the ACLU seminars with labor unions to be held in the months ahead, the first distinction to be drawn will be between the Government and private employers. Although Kaufman and Meese claim there are no constitutional problems with regard to testing public employees, case law indicates otherwise. When the State is the employer, the Fourth Amendment prohibition against unreasonable search and seizure comes into play. The Fourth Amendment requires that there be probable cause—or, in some instances, the lower standard of reasonable suspicion—that *particular* individuals may be doing or holding something illegal.

Unions have been agitating for rights for private workers.

In 1984, for example, the Eighth Circuit Court of Appeals affirmed a decision granting prison guards an injunction against random urinalysis even though they certainly perform crucial security functions. The court ruled that for the bodily fluids of public employees to be seized there has to be an *individualized,* reasonable basis for the search.

Shows that public institutions have not been allowed to conduct invasive searches.

In East Rutherford, New Jersey, last year, the school board ordered all students to undergo urine and blood testing for drugs and alcohol as part of an annual physical examination. Any student who tested positive would be suspended or expelled from school. The ACLU of New Jersey, representing five of the students, took the case to court and the rule was struck down because, said the judge, it violated each student's "legitimate expectation of privacy and personal security" under the Fourth Amendment.

Also in 1985, the school board of the Patchogue-Medford School District on Long Island decided that to be given tenure, a teacher would have to submit to a urine test to determine the presence of absence of illegal drugs. In Suffolk County Supreme Court, Justice Thomas Stark could not have been more clear in his decision declaring that the school board had acted unconstitutionally:

"The Fourth Amendment of the United States Constitution, applicable to state action through the Fourteenth . . . protects individuals from unreasonable searches of the person. <u>The compulsory extraction of bodily fluids</u> is a search and seizure within the meaning of the Fourth Amendment." Such a search is permissible, he added, only when there is particularized, reasonable suspicion "based on objective supportable facts."

Inflammatory phrase

Workers in private employment, however, do not have Fourth Amendment protections because the order to give up bodily fluids does not come from the State. Alternative sources of protection are available, however. Union contracts can include, through collective bargaining, provisions extending to workers the equivalent of First Amendment, Fourth Amendment, and other constitutional rights. Some United Auto Workers locals, for example, have won contracts with clauses that make it difficult to fire an employee for anything he says or puts on a bulletin board or wears on a T-shirt.

Union agitation for private workers

Drug testing should require a search warrant.

Until now, most workers and their unions have been slow to recognize the importance of battling for such contract clauses. It may well be that the Meese-Kaufman assault on workers' privacy may spur more collective-bargaining strategy to get language that will give workers the same rights on the job as they have on the streets and at home. As bus driver Randy Kemp of Seattle put it in *Time,* "You've got to have a search warrant to search my house. Well, my body is a lot more sacred than my home."

Another route to protecting privacy is through state constitutions and local statutes. Some state constitutions have stronger privacy provisions than the U.S. Constitution, and if the language covers private employees, dragnet and random searches can be banned. Richard Emergy, a Fourth Amendment specialist with the New

York Civil Liberties Union, also points out that under some local human-rights statues, it is illegal to fire anyone who has a disability if that disability does not affect his job performance. Drug use can be a disability, but not necessarily one that interferes with worker competence. Accordingly, if a local statute includes drug dependence as a disability, and if the worker is doing his job efficiently, he can't be fired if he fails a drug test.

Compares drug abuse to a disability. One shouldn't be fired for a disability. But is this a good comparison?

More directly specific is a San Francisco ordinance—the first in the country—that prohibits employers from administering random, dragnet blood and urine tests. And state legislatures in California, Maine, Oregon, and Maryland are considering bills that would limit or regulate testing of employees.

Clearly, there is potential for a natural alliance between workers and civil libertarians to educate local and state legislators and to lobby for protective statutes. Invasion-of-privacy horror stories and realistic remedies ought to be covered in union newspapers, general publications, and—never to be underestimated—letters to the editors of all kinds of papers and magazines.

For many workers, civil liberties have long seemed to be a class issue. If you look at the composition of most ACLU affiliates and chapters, the overwhelming majority of members are lawyers, academics, enlightened businessmen, and a very few union officials. Blue-collar workers are seldom represented. The rights that have appealed most to workers are economic rights, and they don't see the ACLU and other civil liberties organizations as being particularly concerned with take-home pay and benefits. But when a worker can lose his job if he won't piss into a bottle, the Fourth Amendment, at least, becomes much less abstract, and that's why a coalition between the usual civil-liberties activists and workers is not only plausible but potentially effective.

Drug testing should require a search warrant.

The possibility of protests within certain shops also exists. Job actions not for more pay but to be a free citizen at work could put some heat on certain company officials.

Take the *Los Angeles Times.* Its editorial page has been among the most forceful and lucid in the nation in fighting to keep the Bill of Rights in working order. Yet, according to Daniel Jussim, writing in the ACLU's *Civil Liberties* newsletters, "The *Los Angeles Times,* though its director of employee relations says there's no particular drug problem at his newspaper, recently adopted a mandatory urinalysis program 'to stay current with what other employers are doing.'"

Imagine the impact in Los Angeles if Anthony Day, the civil libertarian who is editor of the *Los Angeles Times's* editorial page, were to lead a picket line outside the paper with such signs as:

JAMES OTIS, FATHER OF THE FOURTH AMENDMENT, FOUGHT BRITISH GENERAL SEARCH WARRANTS ON BEHALF OF WORKING PEOPLE—NOT JUST PUBLISHERS.

The need for alliances to preserve what's left of privacy grows greater by the day. Charles Seabrook writes of new tests that can "detect the presence of the abnormal levels of chemicals found in patients with severe depression, schizophrenia, and manic-depression that can detect chemical 'markers' that may mean a person is at high risk of developing diabetes, arthritis, or cancer . . . that can screen for more than 150 genetic diseases, including sickle cell anemia . . . and cystic fibrosis."

A call to arms!

It soon will be possible to detect all sorts of other things through testing.

Would an employer hire someone who is at risk of developing cancer? Should an employer have access to such private information?

Use of extreme examples

On a modest level, a new test developed by Werner Baumgartner, a Los Angeles chemist, bypasses such old-time procedures as requiring the random suspect to urinate into a cup or bottle. The new test uses radiation on hair and discloses not only what drugs have been taken but when they were taken, something urinalyses can't do.

As for coming attractions that verify the prescience of George Orwell, the *Washington Post* reported in mid-1984, "Researchers in academia and industry say it is now possible to envision a product that could instantaneously assess whether employees are concentrating on their jobs by analyzing their brain waves as they work."

Drug testing compared to Orwell's 1984 "Big Brother" concept.

This seems extreme

There isn't much time left to create, in law, the best possible defenses against Government and employer intrusions into privacy, including intrusions that now seem inconceivable.

Teenagers Need Drug Testing

Brian Noal Mittman

As a recent high school graduate I've seen rampant drug use—in schools, where students take a few "hits" before entering class; at parties, from which many kids drive home completely stoned; and even at a high school prom,

Brian Noal Mittman, "Teenagers Need Drug Texting," Manchester, NH *Union Leader,* October 26, 1986. Reprinted by permission of the author.

where cocaine usage was high. Today's younger generation is often too accepting of drugs as a part of its life, and adults are too unwilling to implement necessary anti-drug laws. With the massive drug problem that exists in our schools today, new legislation is necessary to discourage substance abuse. Cities in Texas, New York, California and Tennessee have already implemented mandatory drug testing in some of their public schools. Such a program is needed on a national scale.

Many adults who oppose mandatory drug testing in schools are completely oblivious to the severity of the problem. Students see signs of drug usage in school, with friends, and on the street far more often than their parents. In interviews conducted by *USA Today,* teenagers themselves were the strongest advocates of hardline legislation to handle drug abuse. Many parents fail to realize how rampant drug addiction is. It is no longer monopolized by problem-plagued students and inner-city schools—good students and promising athletes are often victims as well. I attended an academically-oriented, highly-competitive, affluent, suburban high school. The number of students dealing and using drugs was shocking. Parents of friends on drugs feel incapable of dealing with the problem, while others choose to ignore a child's addiction. Mandatory testing in schools would raise teenage consciousness about drug danger and could reduce students' abuse of toxic substances without depending upon their parent's guidance.

Most opponents of mandatory drug testing in schools argue that such legislation is an invasion of students' privacy—the mere fact that so many teenagers do abuse drugs is sufficient evidence that they are not mature enough to handle such problems independently.

Mandatory school drug testing should be administered to students beginning at the junior high level where many drug problems start. The test should be given by an outside organization, unassociated with our public schools. Without prior warning, testing should take place for all students at a given school on Mondays, when drugs ingested from weekend partying can still be detected. Repeated testing should be administered before reporting results to parents in order to reduce uncertainties inherent in the drug test itself. This would reduce unfounded parental suspicions of frequent use if a child simply "tried" a drug for the first time before the test date, had recently kicked a drug habit, or if the test result itself was inaccurate. Finally, all information should be kept confidential between parent, child and the administering agency. Results should be kept by the administering agency—not by the school—to lessen "leaks" of confidential information.

Such drug testing could reduce teen substance abuse in six ways. (1) Younger, more immature students might be deterred from future drug abuse through junior high testing and heightened awareness. (2) Individuals might refrain from drugs due to embarrassment before drug testing personnel. (3) Students would fear that surprise drug testing could result in parent notification of abuse. (4) Parents notified of their children's drug problems would seek help for them. (5) Students already addicted, fearing they might be detected, might seek help on their own. (6) School administration could take action if heavy drug use over a long period of time is detected.

State laws (required inoculations against various diseases and periodic medical checkups) have already affected health mandates for students. Today, drug abuse has become a terrible health menace in our public schools. Any attempt to reduce this growing disease should be implemented. It's time to institute drug testing for teens.

ANALYZING STUDENT CRITIQUE ESSAYS

"Education for All," by Sara Carrasquillo, and "Critiquing 'Teaching *All* Children,'" by Amy Burton, were both written for a first-year writing course at Bowling Green State University in response to David Burchfield's article, "Teaching *All* Children: Four Developmentally Appropriate Curricular and Instruction Strategies in Primary-Grade Classrooms."

After reading the following student critique essays closely, you should be quite familiar with the basic features of this type of essay and feel comfortable embarking on your own criteria-based evaluation of an article.

Both of these student responses to David Burchfield's essay were written using the strategies discussed in the "Writing the Critique" section earlier in the chapter. Each critique essay reflects the students' critical reading of the text, thorough contemplation of its effectiveness, and thoughtful analysis of how it meets (or fails to meet) specific criteria. Yet, each writer presents a very different judgment as to the overall effectiveness of Burchfield's article.

Burchfield's article and the students' critiques of it are reprinted below:

"Teaching *All* Children: Four Developmentally Appropriate Curricular And Instructional Strategies In Primary-Grade Classrooms" (David W. Burchfield. *Young Children*, November 1996: 4-10. Reprinted by permission from the National Association for the Education of Young, Washington, D.C.)

The classrooms of our nation's public schools are becoming increasingly diverse places. Old models and traditional structures for teaching and learning are not working well for all children entering our school doors, nor are these approaches challenging children to reach their full potential so that they may succeed in school, the workplace, and in life.

Teachers and support staff in schools and school systems, major professional organizations, and many parents attest to this claim (MASBE 1988: Bredekamp & Rosegrant 1992; Davis 1992; NCREL 1992). Educators and communities are actively searching for ways to meet the varied educational needs of their children. The future of public education and of our society rests in part on the ability of educators and concerned community members to develop and implement ways to support and teach *all* children well.

As even our graded classrooms begin demographically to take on the characteristics of one-room schoolhouses, practitioners must continue sharing with each other *what is working* in the context of teaching and learning that encourages children to learn and reach their potential. Educators of primary-school children are embracing more and more the idea of moving away from grade-leveled thinking toward more *child-focused* (Burchfield 1994) or *child-sensitive* (Katz 1992) attitudes and approaches.

Teachers must be given opportunities to develop, implement, and evaluate developmentally appropriate curricular and instructional strategies that go beyond the traditional "high-middle-low group" way of looking at, organizing, and teaching the children in their classroom communities (Burchfield & Burchfield 1992).

Whether we work with and advocate for children in communities that are exploring new models, such as nongraded and multi-age structures (Goodlad & Anderson 1987; Katz, Evangelou, & Hartman 1990) or are involved in conversations in graded-school communities that acknowledge the challenge of heterogeneity, we must continually examine our philosophies and belief systems about children and teaching and learning to ensure that they are developmentally appropriate and child focused. It will be a consequence that we develop new models of curriculum and innovative instructional strategies for the sake of our children and their learning.

For the past decade I have been fortunate in having opportunities (as a preschool and primary-grade teacher, early childhood grant administrator, consultant, and now a principal) to learn about and implement strategies that have worked with children, from whom I have learned so much. What I learned and now practice is the consequence of my own interaction with and observation of children; many professional development opportunities; much reading, research, and reflection; and a result of collaboration with other educators and members of school communities.

For much of this century, leading early childhood educators have been advocating that we view children in more diverse ways than those represented by narrow and traditional IQ measures, that we engage primary-school children in authentic project work, that we involve children in meaningful writing for a variety of reasons, and that we challenge young readers to develop a repertoire of decoding strategies while learning to read. The theorists and researchers cited in *this* article, however, represent current best practice in the field and have particularly served as useful to this author.

The four curricular and instructional strategies outlined and described below have improved my understanding of children and increased the quality of my teaching and their learning so that all have had the opportunity to succeed in the primary years and beyond.

1. Multiple Intelligences and Different Ways of Knowing

A number of years ago, in my graduate studies, I became familiar with Howard Gardner's theory concerning multiple intelligences (Gardner 1983) and what is now often referred to as "different ways of knowing."

Gardner's theory holds that children and all people are much more complex than once viewed by traditional theories of intelligence, learning, and development. The premise of Gardner is that people naturally have specific areas of both strength and weakness and that ability and intelligence exist in not only the traditional curricular focus areas of language and numero-mathmatics (which are also the aim of most instruction, assessment, and reporting), but also in five other areas of development or ways of knowing: bodily-kinesthetic, spatial, musical, interpersonal, and intrapersonal.

Gardner's theory is related to the seemingly all-too-simple and yet quite profound premise that *children are different* and they are much more capable than previously was conceptualized. A theory of difference asserts that people learn on a continuum from novice to expert in any given domain of learning and development (Hatano & Inagaki 1983; Walsh 1991).

If we truly adopt the belief that children are different and unique; if we expand our view to include a broader concept of intelligence and then accept the idea that there may be as many as seven "ways of knowing" and understanding what we learn, dramatic implications consequently result for the whole scope of teaching and learning.

No longer can we conduct themes or units of study with our students by simply sequencing for a period of a week or two teacher-directed activities that seem to go in no specific direction. Nor can we narrowly focus our unit study solely on reading, writing, and math or demand that most or all children do the same thing at the same time. When we gather together young people (who vary on a continuum from novice to expert) to be involved in and to think about a topic, question, or skill for an extended period of time, we must build in a progression for learning, such as the one advocated by DeVries and Kohlberg (1987), which outlines four major steps in the learning cycle: awareness, exploration, inquiry, and utilization.

Children first are made aware of the idea and can discover what they already know and have experienced about the topic. Students will ask lots of questions, design ways of figuring out some answers, and become involved in making decisions about the ways they inquire and share what they learn and understand.

A unit of study designed by practitioners who hold Gardner's theory to be true would allow children to experience a concept or skill in a variety of ways and demonstrate their learning and understandings by using their strong suits *and* by being challenged to develop their ability in areas identified (by parents, teachers, and even the children) for more emphasis and improvement.

During a unit of study about parks, for example, children could demonstrate their understandings in the following ways:

1. sing a song or compose an original piece of music about their study,
2. build a model of their park,
3. share a drawing or a piece of writing about a field trip to their park,
4. listen to read-alouds of picture books about animals that live in their park,
5. represent in dramatic play the way a worm moves through earth,
6. interview a groundskeeper about her responsibilities and report the findings,
7. share their feelings about the homeless people who live in the park, or
8. estimate the number of trees in the whole park based upon study of a small area

The possibilities are endless.

Gardner's theory is being considered and put into practice in many schools across the country. Gardner and organizations such as the Galef Institute (1994) have created comprehensive ways of organizing curriculum, instruction, and assessment and reporting of children's progress based on the seven ways of knowing. Gardner's theory, along with an acceptance of the belief that children are different, has far-reaching implications for teaching and learning in classrooms and schools where difference is not only valued but viewed as an asset for the community of learners.

2. The Project Approach

The most mature, balanced, and practical model that complements Gardner's theory is the Project Approach proposed by Katz and Chard (1989), which builds on a long history of process-oriented project work and a focus on integrated teaching and learning in early childhood education.

The Project Approach encourages meaningful and relevant engagement in units of study chosen cooperatively by teachers and children, depending upon the needs of the school and school system. The units of study can be extensively interdisciplinary in nature or be adapted to explore one angle of the curriculum if the local school district demands a separate focus on other skills and domains of learning (such as math and language arts—reading, writing, and spelling/word study).

The greatest strength of the Project Approach, perhaps, is this: It is a flexible and adaptable model and process that can fit with local curricular demands. Katz and Chard (1989) acknowledge that it may not be possible or even desirable to integrate all skills and areas of learning into every unit of study in which we become engaged. The Project Approach is a real-world, user-friendly guide to organizing purposeful, social, active, and engaging units of study that allow children to be involved in making decisions about the direction, implementation, and evaluation of their learning.

Once I had read the Project Approach, my own classroom practice began a transformation. I finally had a process and scaffolding for unit studies substantial enough to hold onto, a model that gave me an actual process to work through with children (and for a teacher who desperately wanted to move beyond the superficial).

Similar to the learning cycle outlined by DeVries and Kohlberg (1987) and the Transformational Curriculum advocated by Rosegrant and Bredekamp (1992), Katz and Chard's approach encourages teachers and children, in the context of the classroom community, to be involved as scientists in significant studies.

Initial awareness of an idea or skill is built through active discussion, brainstorming, webbing, and shared experience. Children and teachers then wonder and ask questions that form the basis for further investigation.

Something sets the Project Approach apart form other related approaches and processes: Children are encouraged to be involved in the discussion and planning of ways to inquire about the chosen topic and in devising methods to investigate the questions generated or those that arise. "Projects" for individuals, small groups, or the whole class are designed and negotiated that allow children to inquire and then demonstrate and utilize their learning and understandings.

There may be some non-negotiable activities, experiences, and projects that are built in by the teacher over the course of the unit of study. The powerful motivators for the children, however, are that they are involved in decisions about the course of the study, the topic and hand is relevant, and the children are actively and socially involved in making sense out of the concepts and skills.

3. The Writer's Workshop

Although the use of the "writing process" and children writing for authentic reasons have been advocated for decades, a way of thinking about the teaching of writing, using the "writer's workshop," (Calkins 1983; Graves 1983) has spread like wildfire and now affects thousands of classrooms and millions of children.

Teachers have been trained in "writing projects" at universities and colleges and have read influential authors who have thoroughly researched the movement and been involved in teacher-training themselves (Newkirk & Atwell 1988; Calkins 1991, 1994; Graves 1991; Routman 1991; Harwayne 1992).

What began as a fledgling movement to encourage authorship in children by allowing them to use the writing process has now developed in many locations into classrooms and schools deeply involved in authentic and meaning-based writer's (and reader's) workshops. The writer's workshop is often the favorite, cherished time of the day by both children and teachers who regularly practice the model in classroom communities.

Carved out of an often-dissected day, the workshop is a place dedicated to the individual making sense out of significant moment and ideas, using the written word. In my own classroom the writer's workshop was so revered and powerful that, if a field trip or assembly displaced its position in the day, the children would often demand to miss recess in favor of making up the workshop and having the opportunity for written expression.

Topics and reasons for writing emerge from many sources along a continuum from child to teacher. With young children in the primary grades, the most motivating sources come from their own experiences and ideas. Topical or thematic units of study, author studies, and even genre studies of tales, picture books, songs, rhymes, and poems (and many others) also provide the impetus for inspiration.

Ironically, perhaps the least-effective way to encourage meaningful, relevant, and child-sensitive writing is the typical "Story starter" on the blackboard (which many of us experienced in school ourselves during an occasional creative writing lesson). Such a teacher-driven written command narrows both the choice of topic and the reason to write at all and often leads to boring product accomplished only to "get your seat work done," to please the teacher, or to receive external rewards, such a stickers, smiley faces, or grades.

It is difficult to develop new knowledge and skills in an area of teaching (such as writing) with which we ourselves most likely had little significant experience or success as students in our early years of schooling. Yet Lucy Calkins (1994) challenges us to allow writing not to be deskwork, but "lifework," to create an intimate atmosphere in our workshops where "significance is grown" and we as teachers and children hold onto a time, place, and process to "make sense of our lives."

The workshop can vary in length from 45 minutes to two hours, depending upon the age of the children, the time of the year, and other demands on the classroom schedule. The time often begins with brief (five to eight minutes) mini-lesson (or group time) in which the class may focus on examples of children's work or ideas, revisit and reflect upon a quality piece of children's literature, or focus upon a skill that will lead the class forward in their technical ability in writing.

During the heart of the workshop is a lengthy time for writing, reading, and conferring. Children draw and write about topics mostly of their own choice and yet may draw on classroom-based or teacher-guided ideas and suggestions. The teacher confers with children during this time about the content, process, design, or evaluation of their writing. The greatest challenge while conferring with a child is to truly listen first and then to respond in a child-focused way that challenges the child, if necessary, to explore a new idea, book, or skill that might assist with the development of their idea or piece of writing.

The workshop concludes with an "author's chair" or "author's circle," as children talk about their drawings and ideas. Young authors also share pieces of writing that are in progress or may be nearing completion and possible publication.

The writer's workshop taps a powerful desire on the part of the child to express relevant and significant ideas. In fact, it is my experience that children, when allowed to write from their earliest years in school, choose to write more than read, quite possibly as a result of the basic human need for expression and the yearning we have in life to truly be heard. The writer's workshop is a age-appropriate place for the individual to flourish while both learning to write by writing and making sense of significant ideas.

4. Develop a Balance of Reading Strategies/Cueing Systems

Teachers nationwide are being asked to make reading instruction more whole and relevant, whether the source of text is the traditional basal textbook, emergent literacy reading material, or trade books. Staff development in this process is often aimed at learning how to access a student's instructional level in reading ability, then matching child and text so that the reader is operating on the margin of development. Focus is placed on what children read and how to determine a reader's instructional ability level, and often not as much on how the child attacks new words in the text.

In my own development as a teacher of young readers, I became aware of the work of Marie Clay, a New Zealander and creator of the Reading Recovery Program (Clay 1979), which advocates that teachers build on what children can do and know in their learning to read.

Clay's idea is that although children typically develop two major cueing systems, or decoding strategies (semantic and graphophonemic), at least two major approaches (syntax and visual clues) exist. She encourages teachers of young readers to develop all of these strategies with children, which will encourage readers to be increasingly independent in comprehending and decoding text of a given instructional level.

In addition to Clay, Strickland (1994) and Goodman (1993) also advocate a balanced approach to helping children develop strategies for unlocking new words while reading.

As a teacher it became clear to me that the question is not: Is it phonics *or* meaning *or* whole word? Rather, we must ask, "How can I understand what my students already know and can do, and then help them develop a repertoire of strategies upon which to draw to maximize their reading development and ability?"

As a consequence of this new understanding, I developed a schema (based on Clay's model) for organizing my thinking and for my children's reference as we were involved in reading. I challenged myself and the children to draw upon these strategies while unlocking new words. The strategies (Figure 1) are listed in order of priority and in the language we used in the classroom.

Figure 1: Strategies to Unlock New Words

1. **What makes sense** (context, meaning, semantics) using pictures to make sense of our new words reread: go back to the beginning of the sentence and start again
2. **What the letters tell us** (graphophonemics) beginning letters: "get your mouth ready to say the word" vowel patterns
3. **Words we use often** (see Figure 2) high-frequency sight words 36 words make up 50% of all the words we read
4. **How words are built** (structure) length of the word compound words (block out one part of the word) prefixes and suffixes
5. **How our language works** repeat the sentence back to the child as it is read can we say it that way?

In the context of reading instruction, these strategies (posted on charts) became reference points for children's learning. Eventually and with much practice, the strategies become more habitual and automatic with young readers.

The first strategy, "What makes sense," draws upon meaning and context clues. Children are encouraged to figure out unknown words by looking at the pictures or by going back to the beginning of the sentence and rereading the text and coming up to the unknown word with increased fluency, expression, and understanding.

The second strategy, "What the letters tell us," primarily asks very young readers to "get your mouth ready to say the word." Instead of isolating a sound and beginning to break the word apart by sounding it out at the beginning of the word, which often does not really represent the sound the letter makes as a part of the whole word, the reader is asked to learn how to form the mouth properly to begin to pronounce the word.

For example, the word *monkey* can be started by putting lips together, but without making an *m* sound. The child learns to form the mouth to get ready to say letters and blends. Young readers in the classroom, for some reason, learned the *th* formation particularly quickly. I told them that the only time they were allowed to stick their tongue out at the teacher was when they were beginning a word that began with *th*!

In the debate between advocates of phonics and advocates of meaning, another important strategy, widely used for 40 years or more, had been lost: high-frequency sight words or, as we referred to them, "words we use often." Practitioner colleagues and I recognized that it was these short, rather meaningless words that often gave children the most trouble, even while engaged in reading meaningful text (including words such as *it, was, saw, but, of, who*, etc.).

As we decided to focus more on these words, the idea of creating "Club 22" and "Club 60" was born. These clubs, membership in which depends upon the child calling these high-frequency words in isolation from word cards and listing on a chart in the classroom (see Figure 2), were motivators for children to learn these basic sight words. Children were not highlighted

---

Figure 2: Words We Use Often

"Club 22"

I   a   and   am   at   on   me   my   we   no   said

You   the   they   it   is   in   of   for   from   was   saw

"Club 60"

(In addition to the above words . . .)

off   come   she   he   your   see   not   be   get   are   if   can

do   all   an   what   why   where   when   who   that   there

then   these   those   their   want   went   now   one   ask

would   could   should   before   after   knew   know

---

as "in" or "out" of the club, although it was celebrated when every child reached a new plateau (even intermittent) in word knowledge.

As the young readers in the classroom community developed from emergent to beginning-reading levels, children began to work on the other two strategies: "How words are built," which emphasizes such ideas as compound words and knowledge of prefixes and suffixes, and "How our language works," which asks children to listen to how they read a sentence and to reflect as to whether or not it sounded right (grammar and usage rules).

The result of shifting from believing that only one or two ways exist to teach young readers (and that these ways are necessarily antithetical) to understanding that children bring different strengths and weakness to the act of reading was powerful in practice. This understanding was more consistent with my emerging knowledge base and beliefs about children, teaching, and learning and with my goal of helping each child reach his or her potential as an individual.

Summary
As practitioners search for ways to challenge individual children to learn and reach their potential in meaningful and age-appropriate ways, we must share with each other what is working in order to promote best practice.

The existing challenges of diversity and heterogeneity are most likely here to stay. As grade-leveled thinking is broken down, we must develop, implement, and evaluate more child-focused and child-sensitive curricular and instructional methods and strategies that encourage teachers and children to achieve their best for the sake of learning.

Howard Gardner offers a useful and real-world way to look at children, their intelligence and ability and consequently a framework in which to organize curriculum. The Project Approach complements well this view of children and offers the teacher a user-friendly way to engage children in relevant and meaningful units of study.

By implementing the writer's workshop and offering young readers a repertoire of strategies in the primary years, we can better respond to the individual learners who inhabit our communities and create more literate classrooms and children as well.

As educators, we must rise to the challenge of the diversity and the heterogeneity in our schools and classrooms. Inherent in the philosophy of developmental appropriateness is the ultimate and most important call: *To maintain our focus on children.* Then practices, like those above that encourage success for *all* will follow.

SAMPLE STUDENT CRITIQUE ESSAYS

The following essays were written in response to the article above by David Burchfield and provide critiques, or evaluations, of, the effectiveness of Burchfield's article and his central argument. Each offers a unique perspective on the persuasiveness and validity of his article. The first critique, written by Sara Carraquillo for an English 112 course at Bowling Green State University in 2000, follows:

Education for All

"I just don't understand," pleads the five-year-old boy. "How does two plus two equal four?"

Mrs. Fredericks, his teacher, feels her frustration rising, but she takes a deep breath and tries again. "Look here at the board Jimmy. See how I've drawn two apples here and two apples over here? Let's count them together. One . . . two . . . three . . . four. See, four. So, two apples plus two apples equals how many apples?"

Jimmy just looks down at his desk as he sinks a little lower in his chair.

"Mrs. Fredericks," interrupts Carmen, "maybe I can help Jimmy." Upon saying this, Carmen gets up from her desk and determinedly marches over to Jimmy's desk carrying four blocks. "Here Jimmy. Let's try using these." She hands him two blocks and keeps two for herself. She asks Jimmy how many blocks each of them has. He answers correctly with two. She then says, "Let's put them together now." They slide all of the blocks to the center of his desk. "Now how many blocks do we have?" Jimmy slowly touches each block and counts out loud as he does so.

"One . . . two . . . three . . . four. FOUR! We have FOUR blocks!"

This scenario demonstrates a classic example of why teachers must strive to develop personal relationships with each of their students. If Mrs. Fredericks had established an in-depth knowledge of Jimmy and his learning capabilities, she would have understood that he learns best while working interactively. Because of this, Jimmy could not grasp the concept of "two plus two equaling four" when Mrs. Fredericks attempted to teach him using visual techniques. The idea that children learn best in varying ways presents itself as a key issue in the article entitled "Teaching *All* Children: Four Developmentally Appropriate Curricular and Instructional Strategies in Primary-Grade Classrooms" by educator David W. Burchfield.

Burchfield, formerly a preschool and elementary-level instructor, as well as an early-childhood grant administrator and consultant, now works as a principal. Because of his vast experience in the field, Burchfield can be considered an authority in the world of education. For the November 1996 issue of *Young Children*, Burchfield composed an efficient article, entitled "Teaching *All* Children: Four Developmentally Appropriate Curricular and Instructional Strategies in Primary-Grade Classrooms," concerning instructional techniques in elementary classrooms. This article targeted parents and concerned citizens. In writing it, Burchfield achieved his purpose: he showed his readers more inventive and productive strategies for reaching each and every child than the methods currently in use.

He suggests four guidelines worth implementing in today's classrooms. These include recognizing the fact that children learn in multiple ways, using the "Project Approach" [a system of educating that is a "real-world, user-friendly guide to organizing purposeful, social, active, and engaging units of study that allow children to be involved in making decisions about the direction, implementation, and evaluation of their learning" (62)], utilizing a workshop for students to enhance their writing skills, and employing several approaches to reading. To make his point effectively, Burchfield relies on numerous credible and current sources, presents examples of how to extend learning to all students, refutes a convincing counterargument, and constructs figures that expand on what he has written. In addition to the tactics used by Burchfield to produce a sufficient argument, his main objective for writing the article remains clear throughout the piece: "To maintain our focus on children" (65).

In writing on the subject of education, David W. Burchfield gathered support from a variety of individuals and sources. For example, not only did Mr. Burchfield accumulate material concerning the four areas of furthering education from books, but also he gained information from a brochure, speeches, and magazine articles. The Galef Institute of Kentucky produced the brochure that Burchfield consulted. For this reason, I believe that one should most definitely consider it a valuable and credible source; the Galef Institute presumably had a committee of qualified professionals that created the brochure. Additionally, David W. Burchfield cited Lucy M. Calkins as another source. Ms. Calkins authored three books from the years 1983 to 1994, each of which Burchfield refers to at some point in the article. Though 1983 may seem rather outdated, one must take into consideration the fact that Burchfield composed his article in November of 1996 and that Calkins had work published in the years of 1991 and 1994 as well. Some of the other sources David W. Burchfield used contained fairly current information. Out of the fifteen or so sources consulted, at least ten had been authored no more than five years earlier (dated 1991). This is remarkably impressive; Burchfield proves that his research is up-to-date and, therefore, trustworthy.

Burchfield continues to substantiate his article by providing insight to the fact that students learn in numerous ways. He refers to Howard Gardner and Gardner's idea pertaining to children and their various understandings; Burchfield writes that "there may be as many as seven 'ways of knowing'" (61). For this reason, it is essential that teachers strive to understand how each of their students learns best. Furthermore, by offering examples of how to guide each student on a personal level, Burchfield continues to strengthen his case. For instance, he suggests several techniques for applying a field trip to the park to a child's classroom work. According to Burchfield, students could create a song about their adventure to the park and what they learned from the experience, draw a picture of what they saw while visiting the park, or conduct an interview with an individual employed by the park, such as a groundskeeper (61). These options all fall into the category of encouraging pupils to learn and discover in an assortment of ways. By permitting students to expand upon the trip in their own manner, Burchfield allows them to reach their full potentials. Burchfield does an excellent job of stressing Gardner's theory and showing educators why it may be necessary to teach each student in a slightly different manner. He also supplies options to educators for connecting with the different types of learners by using specific examples.

As Burchfield writes, he includes a counterargument to further his position. For instance, when approaching the topic of the "Writer's Workshop," he shows its value by stating that it "has spread like wildfire and now affects thousands of classrooms and millions of children" (62). However, some individuals believe that the "Writer's Workshop" is ineffective and, therefore, Burchfield offers evidence against this notion. Mr. Burchfield mentions the classic "story starter" (on the chalkboard) as one of the "least-effective" ways to encourage writing among youngsters (63). In order to maintain the necessity of the "Writer's Workshop" in schools, he comments (in relation to the "story starter") that "such a teacher-driven written command narrows both the choice of topic and the reason to write at all and often leads to a boring product accomplished only to 'get your seat work done,' to please the teacher or to receive external rewards, such as stickers, smiley faces, or grades" (63). Additionally, David W. Burchfield continues to emphasize the importance of writing by using Lucy Calkins' challenge "to allow writing not to be desk work, but 'lifework'" (63). By showing that the conventional technique, the "story starter," is inferior to the "Writer's Workshop," Burchfield makes a valid attempt to suppress any opposition to his standing on the topic.

An additional aspect that strengthens the article "Teaching *All* Children" is Burchfield's inclusion of figures that expand upon what he has written. For example, he provides a figure that lists specific steps for children to use when attempting to read new words. Another figure, or chart, that Burchfield includes contains words that his students frequently use. These devices prove themselves a crucial aspect of Burchfield's article because they add a "picture" to what he has already described. Not only do the figures offer a visual for the reader, but also they clarify exactly what Burchfield means and the point he is trying to make. Besides the obvious advantages to incorporating the figures into his article, they benefit the piece by adding some variety to it as well.

Taking all aspects of the piece into consideration, I believe David W. Burchfield has written a persuasive article concerning the issue of educating today's youth in ways that are conducive to the individual's manner of learning. Burchfield suggests several aspects that educators could incorporate into the everyday routine of teaching primary-aged students. With the experience he has in the field and the current authorities he used to research his topic, he presents an extremely sound case. Moreover, by providing specific examples on how to reach each child on a particular level, using figures to emphasize his points, and providing a rebuttal to any questions of those who disagree with him, David W. Burchfield thoroughly and effectively argues for multiple learning strategies in his article, "Teaching *All* Children: Four Developmentally Appropriate Curricular and Instructional Strategies in Primary-Grade Classrooms."

The following student critique, written by another English 112 student at Bowling Green State University in 2000, Amy Burton, provides an alternative perspective on the effectiveness of Burchfield's article and the validity of its thesis, or central argument. As you read this critique essay, notice how it differs substantially from the above review of the same article, even though the criteria used to judge the article are similar:

Critiquing "Teaching *All* Children"
Why do some children have difficulties in learning, while others do not? And, what can teachers and parents do to help those children with difficulties? David W. Burchfield believes he has the answers to these questions, and he attempts to explain them in his article "Teaching *All* Children: Four Developmentally Appropriate Curricular and Instructional Strategies in Primary-Grade Classrooms."

In his article, Burchfield first states that as schoolrooms continually become more diverse, new teaching methods are necessary. He then offers four new methods to solve the problem; they include knowing multiple intelligences and teaching according to them, using the Project Approach, utilizing the writer's workshop, and developing a balance of reading strategies and cueing systems. According to Burchfield, multiple intelligences means children become gifted in different areas. Examples of the different intelligences include musical intelligence, spatial intelligence, and social intelligence; he concludes children have difficulty in school when they are not taught in their area. The Project Approach then tries to make subjects in school relate to everyday life, and the writer's workshop encourages students to write about the world they live in. Lastly, reading strategies help children form words and, therefore, make it easier for them to learn to read. He believes these methods will encourage, help, and motivate all children.

Evaluating Burchfield's explanations of these methods from a parent's or an elementary school teacher's perspective reveals weaknesses and strengths in the article. Burchfield's weaknesses create an inaccessible and ineffective article. For example, he does not give the credentials of his sources, provide definitions of difficult words, present outside opinions, or offer counterarguments. On the other hand, the article does contain good points that show the article was written passionately and for a good reason; moreover, he has real knowledge of the situation, spent time on research, and has genuine concern for the subject. In spite of these strengths, the article still fails to be effective because of the weaknesses.

Omitting explanations of the credentials of his sources contributes to the failure of the article. Throughout the article, Burchfield states his sources' names without giving the readers any other information about them or their credentials. For example, he contributes his understanding of the different intelligences solely to Howard Gardner (60). In the article, Burchfield credits Gardner for the theory, and then he explains his theory. However, Burchfield does not give any further information about Gardner. For instance, Burchfield never states whether Gardner is a psychologist or sociologist, or if he is well-known, esteemed, or credible. If readers do not know anything about Gardner, how can they believe his theory's reliability? Burchfield makes the mistake of omitting explanations of credentials nine times throughout his article. For instance, he excludes the credentials of DeVries, Kohiberg, Katz, and Chard. Perhaps Burchfield felt that explanations would take too much space, but an intricate explanation would not be necessary; a brief statement would work sufficiently. It would help the paper's credibility and accessibility. By assuming his readers already know the credentials of people discussed, Burchfield does not target one of his core audiences, parents. Parents may not know the credentials of the people discussed; therefore, the language used is inaccessible to them. Leaving out credentials weakens Burchfield's credibility and does not target his core audience.

Similarly, the usage of difficult words weakens the paper's credibility and does not target the core audience. Burchfield does not provide definitions of the most important and difficult words used in his article. For example, Burchfield lists five of the intelligences as "body-kinesthetic, spatial, musical, interpersonal, and intrapersonal" (Burchfield 61). But, he does not give any definitions of these words. Likewise, Burchfield states, "the Galef Institute (1994) has created comprehensive ways of organizing curriculum" (62); Burchfield again does not identify this association, the Galef Institute. Therefore, readers wonder if it is an important organization when given no definition. He also excludes the definition of the "Transformational Curriculum advocated by Rosegrant and Bredekamp" (Burchfield 62).

Available definitions or clarifications of all of these words would have helped readers understand the article more fully; definitions would have made it more accessible. Since definitions are not provided, readers wonder what the words mean and at the same time question the author's credibility. Burchfield may have expected his readers to already know the definitions of these words, but by making this false assumption, he left out his audience. The article was written about children, so consequently, it concerns parents. Also, elementary-school teachers may not even know what some of the words mean. By not supplying definitions, it appears that Burchfield did not even try to target his audience. In the process, he lost credibility and accessibility in his article by not including these definitions.

Through the lack of others' opinions, credibility is lost again. Every opinion given in the article belongs to the author. Several times, he tries to substitute his opinion for fact. For example, when he states the Project Approach is "a user-friendly way to engage children in relevant and meaningful units of study" (Burchfield 65), he does not support his claim with someone else's opinion, like an expert's. He makes the same mistake when he states that the Project Approach is the "most mature, balanced, and practical model" (Burchfield 62). These words are his opinion; he should have backed them up with an expert's opinion or possibly statistics. By not including others' opinions, his article appears biased. He ignores another opportunity to include additional support when he states: "the children would often demand to miss recess in favor of making up the workshop and having the opportunity for written expression" (Burchfield 63). Inserting actual quotes from his students would have been more effective; by not supporting this statement, it appears the author just assumed it. How can readers know for sure if students actually liked these workshops? More quotes would make his paper more effective and credible.

Likewise, counterarguments would have also made the paper more effective. In the article, Burchfield never mentions any counterarguments though several opportunities arise. For example, when he explains the writer's workshop, he states that one-on-one contact between each student and the teacher is necessary. However, he ignores that time may not allow for this. He also ignores if it would be possible for teachers to know and cater to each child's special intelligence area; he never seems to wonder if a teacher could handle having each student in a classroom working on a different activity. He does not interpret all of the consequences of one of his other ideas, posting achievements of students on a poster. He only sees the positive results (motivating children to do well); he never concludes that there may be problems with some students feeling they are inferior. He needs to address counterarguments to improve his argument so it is more believable and effective.

However, even with all of the improvements needed to strengthen the article, it contains some good points. For example, Burchfield states in the article that he has been "a preschool and primary-grade teacher, early childhood grant administrator, consultant, and now a principal" (61). He also used the four methods in his classrooms; "the four curricular and instructional strategies outlined . . . have improved my understanding of children and increased the quality of my teaching and their learning" (Burchfield 61). He believes that children like the new methods, claiming, "The children would often demand to miss recess in favor of making up the workshop and having the opportunity for written expression" (Burchfield 63). Since he has used the methods in his own classrooms, he has first-hand knowledge about how well they work.

Another strength is that it is obvious he put hours of research into the article. He provides detailed explanations and examples for all four methods. For example, in the teaching according to different intelligences method, he provides eight examples. Moreover, the article definitely took him time to research because he used twenty-eight sources in researching it. However, even with so much research, the article still lacked factual evidence; he needed to incorporate more of his research as evidence.

The best point of the article is his genuine concern for the subject. He states that he wants to reach his "goal of helping each child reach his or her potential as an individual" (Burchfield 65). Also, the fact that he has so much experience as a teacher shows that he is dedicated to his career as an educator and interested in helping kids. Similarly, if he really did not care about helping kids learn, he would not have put so much research into an article about it. What really stands out about the article is his sincere concern.

When looking at the article from the critical viewpoint of a teacher or parent, Burchfield's article has more weaknesses than strengths. Burchfield makes mistakes by not supplying explanations of names, definitions of important words, others' opinions, and counterarguments. But, along with those weaknesses are his strengths, including hands-on experience, significant research, and genuine concern for the problem. The strengths highlight the writer's passion and concern about the subject. However, when looking at the article from a critical viewpoint, the weaknesses make an ineffective, unreliable, and inaccessible article. If a parent or teacher wanted to put these methods into action, they would have problems. They would not know any of the possible consequences or difficulties because they are not discussed in the article. Consequently, they would have to read a different article on methods that can help children with learning difficulties.

➤ **Exercise in Examining Student Critiques:** Working in small groups, please answer the following questions:

1. State the thesis of each critique of Burchfield's article.
2. Which criteria did Carrasquillo and Burton use to evaluate Burchfield's article?
3. How did their varying sets of criteria lead to different judgments?
4. How did each writer back up her chosen criteria used to evaluate Burchfield's article with specific examples, or evidence? Would either critique benefit from adding more evidence from the text? If so, where?
5. Which student critique, in your opinion, makes a more convincing argument as to the quality of Burchfield's article and the validity of his argument? Give some specific reasons why you found Carrasquillo's or Burton's review of the article to be more persuasive.
6. What advice might you give each writer in terms of revising her critique? Are there areas in Carrasquillo's or Burton's essays that could be better developed or explained?

➤ **Assignment on Writing a Critique:** Before you begin writing this essay, you should choose an article that is interesting to you in some way, since it could become the basis for a future researched essay. Once you have chosen the article you wish to critique, consider the following steps:

Critically Reading: You must critically read and annotate the text carefully. Make sure that you are thinking carefully when annotating this article. Remember to take the article's genre and purpose into consideration before you try to judge it.

Determining Criteria: After you've critically read the article, think about what basic ideas you used to judge the article. The global qualities on which you judged the article are the criteria that you will need to present in your essay.

Elements of the Critique Essay: Your critique should be a fully-developed essay, at least three full pages long, and should include the following: a clear introduction to the article; a brief summary of the article; several body paragraphs that present an evaluation of the article based upon 3–4 relevant criteria; supporting details, or evidence, from the article to support each criterion; and a conclusion. Finally, do not forget to use proper MLA citation strategies.

Remember that each of these steps in writing the critique is detailed much more thoroughly earlier in this chapter. Refer to the earlier sections as needed.

➤ **Assignment on Reviewing Your Critique's Effectiveness:** After drafting your critique essay, you should find it helpful to compare your work-in-progress to the following list to pinpoint which areas might benefit from revision. Take a close look at these questions to better focus your efforts:

1. How engaging is your essay's introduction? Does it give all the necessary information about the article (title, author, date, and author's thesis)?
2. Is your thesis clearly stated? Does your thesis present your argument regarding the effectiveness of the article being critiqued?
3. Does your summary of the article present adequate background on the article for the reader without overwhelming the reader with too many details?
4. Are the criteria (areas of evaluation) used to critique the article clear? Would additional criteria help you to make a more convincing case to support your review?
5. Is your essay organized according to your criteria? Is each criterion analyzed and backed with concrete, relevant examples (or evidence) from the article itself?
6. How effective is your essay's conclusion? Does it restate your overall opinion of the article's quality and remind the reader of the criteria used to judge the article?

By examining your working draft in terms of the questions above, you should be able to pinpoint more easily where to concentrate your revision efforts. Often, the most significant area needing further development is a more thorough analysis of how the article meets or fails to meet your chosen criteria, using plenty of concrete, specific examples (evidence) from the text.

3   Selecting an Issue: Exploration
Strategies and Audience-Based Approaches

A DEBATABLE ISSUE THAT MATTERS

In searching for a topic for your researched paper, it is important to **choose an issue that is both controversial and significant;** that is, it should generate conflicting opinions, often more than two, and it should matter, not only to you, but to others as well. When you write about debatable and relevant issues, your writing is likely to have an impact on your readers, influencing the way they think or feel. Many of the assignments in this book are already focused for you so that you will not have to spend much time selecting an issue. However, in many instances, you may wish to select your own issue or to focus on one of the issues in this book more specifically to include your own perspective.

This chapter focuses on several ways of selecting and focusing an issue, including **brainstorming, freewriting, clustering, asking questions about a problem, writing dialogues, and role-playing.** All of these methods are based on the idea that the process of selecting an issue begins with identifying what you already know and feel about the topic. Once you understand your own ideas about your topic, you can then move beyond yourself, imagining what others believe and focusing on your audience. Understanding what your audience thinks and anticipating potential points of disagreement will enable you to write a documented paper that will have an impact on your reader.

Begin with Your Own Concerns

To discover issues that are both debatable and relevant, we suggest that you begin by thinking about what matters to you and to your family. Most likely, a great many situations and problems that concern you can be generalized to include others. For instance, look at the following questions about seemingly "personal" situations.

Mothers, Fathers, and Careers: Do you come from a home where your mother has chosen to develop a career or go back to school? Did she find herself having to "do it all"—that is, take care of the house and children, while assuming new responsibilities? How did your father feel about your mother's career? Or, did your family engage in non-traditional gender roles, with your father staying at home and your mother earning the majority of the family income?

Children and Careers: Was it difficult for your parents to find babysitters when you or your brothers and sisters were small? Do you have children and need to find babysitters in order for you to work or go to school? Do you find yourself having to "do it all"—that is, take care of the house and children, as well as go to school?

Older People: Do you have an elderly relative—a grandmother or grandfather? Is your family under pressure about the best way to care for them?

Career Choices: As a student, has it been difficult for you to choose a major because you are concerned most of all with the salary you will be able to earn? Have you ever been torn between choosing what interests you and worrying about whether or not you will be able to earn a living?

Maternity and Paternity Leave: Speaking of career choices, do you think women ought to be guaranteed maternity leaves? Should men be granted paternity leaves?

Domestic Partnerships: Should long-term partners (in either heterosexual or homosexual relationships) receive the same benefits as married couples? Do you think that same-sex marriages should be recognized legally?

Community Service: Have you ever done some form of community service? Do you think that young people ought to do some form of community service after they complete high school? If you have children, do you want them to have experience in community service as part of their education?

Part-Time Jobs: Did you have a job when you were in high school? Did you feel this was a good thing to do? Did it affect your performance in school? Did you feel at a disadvantage because you were young or a student?

Students' Rights: As a high school student, did you ever feel that you were being treated too much like a child? Were there restrictions in the lunchroom? A dress code? Locker searches? Did you think these were fair? Were they necessary? Do you think that adult students ought to be treated differently from younger students?

Transportation: Do you drive to work or school? Do you take public transportation? Who should be responsible for improving public transportation? Are you completely satisfied with your commuting situation?

Think, then, about issues in your own life that you feel are problems. Often, issues of personal concern can suggest possibilities for a paper because they are also of concern to others. The problem of who should pay for child care, the difficulties of providing for the elderly, the rights of women and men in the workplace, or the rights of students—many of these issues can provide you with the beginning of a topic. After all, if the problem is of concern to you, might it also be of concern to others? Does anyone else have an opinion on this topic? Has anyone written about it?

Of course, there might be some topics that will matter only to those personally involved—the question of whether or not the family dog ought to get a haircut, for example (unless you wrote a whimsical essay meant to be entertaining). A topic such as this one is probably too specific to your particular situation and will probably not matter to others. However, you might extend the topic by stating that it ought to be required that all dogs get haircuts once a month, or you might use this debate to discuss the issue of how much money is spent on pets versus resources allocated for the poor. You would not usually want to write about a topic that is of no interest to anyone except for your own family, unless you were writing exclusively for that audience (a family newspaper, for example). Even so, there are many issues that might be equally of concern to your immediate family and to others.

> ➤ **Exercise in Finding an Issue That Matters**: Think about issues with a direct impact on you and your family, using the suggestions and questions above as a starting point. As you consider these concerns (including those related to families, education, or career choices), write down a list of potential essay topics stemming from these issues. Share your responses with several other classmates to generate a more comprehensive list of possible issues to explore.

UNSTRUCTURED METHODS OF FINDING AN ISSUE

Freewriting and Brainstorming

Many students find that writing freely about an issue enables them to understand their own position or feelings about it, particularly if the issue has affected them personally. **Freewriting**, a sort of "stream of consciousness" type of writing, is done when you quickly write down ideas that come to mind about a topic without censoring any information. Ideally, your pen (or your fingers, if you're composing at a computer) should never stop moving during this process, allowing you to generate as many ideas as possible. Jotting down as many words, phrases, or ideas about an issue as possible in the form of a list, or **brainstorming**, can also be extremely helpful. Images that come to mind suggest other images, and frequently students find that they can then generate ideas that they didn't even know they had.

Clustering

Clustering is similar to freewriting and brainstorming, as its aim is to elicit as many ideas as possible. Clustering, however, enables you to group ideas visually and to see possible connections between ideas. To try clustering, place the central idea or topic in the center of the paper and circle it. Around this circled word, write other words that are associated with this central idea and put circles around them as well. Now write other words that are associated with these other ideas and use lines to connect them either to each other or to other words on the page. Clustering helps you to develop details and find connections, which you might not have discovered otherwise. The following figure is a cluster made by a student concerning the issue of whether a screening committee ought to be established to screen books for the high school library.

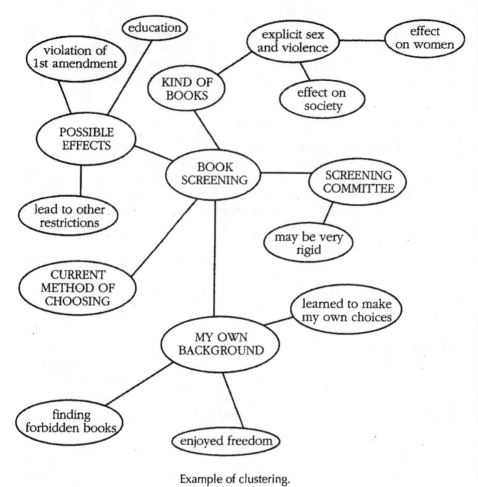

Example of clustering.

Figure 2

Finding a Link

Choosing an issue to write about often involves creating a link between ideas and perceptions within yourself and those just beyond, and that linkage between yourself and the outside world will enable you to say something meaningful. Therefore, we suggest that you not only look within yourself but that you also look beyond yourself to establish links with issues in the world. For example, the issue of whether or not the family dog ought to get a haircut would not, in and of itself, be of interest to the general population. However, if you used a family-related issue to think about other issues related to pet care or public expense for animal care, you might come up with an interesting and controversial issue.

All around you in the media—the newspaper, TV, radio, and Internet—important issues are debated every day. Often these are issues that have endured throughout human history; many of these are issues that have always generated debate. Maybe you will be assigned a general topic by your teacher; perhaps a textbook will offer suggestions. But even if you are not provided with ideas, significant topics can be found all around: issues concerning multiculturalism, women's and men's rights, the function of education, mandatory busing, anti-smoking regulations, seatbelt laws, motorcycle helmet laws, and copyright issues on the Internet, for example. All sorts of debates and controversies are concerned with issues such as these, and they make excellent potential essay topics since they lend themselves to multiple points of view.

Read and Listen to What Others Have to Say

Finding out what others have to say is an excellent way to discover what you, personally, might have to say. The main point is to do something active when you are in the process of selecting an issue. Remember, just because you don't think you know much about a topic doesn't mean that you can't eventually write about it. You may know more than you think. And with a little effort, you can learn more about it. The more you read and listen to what those closest to the issue have to say, you, too, can discover and write about your point of view.

Using a World Wide Web Directory

As will be fully discussed in Chapter 4, another way to find an issue is by searching the World Wide Web (WWW). While it is very easy to get caught up in the plethora of information found on the WWW if you are just aimlessly surfing, many search sites such as Infoseek (http://infoseek.go.com/) and HotBot (http://HotBot.lycos.com/) have indexed small portions of the WWW into directories. The directories on these pages present lists of categories including topics such as Art, Health and Science. If you click on any of these category links, you will be taken to a list of subtopics. If you continue to narrow the topics by clicking on various subtopics, seeking more information on issues which interest you, you can eventually narrow down a topic and, ultimately, find an issue upon which you can write an essay.

For example, you might start your search in the Infoseek directory by following the sample steps outlined below:

1. Click on a general area of interest such as "Education."
2. Once there, you might click on "Colleges" and then "Best Schools."
3. As you look around this page, you don't see anything that looks like it could become a debatable essay issue, so you click on "Surf Education."
4. On the page that appears, you see a promising link entitled "Education problems & issues," so you click on that.
5. On the "Education problems and issues" page, you click on a link entitled, "Center for Education Reform."
6. At this site, you find an article that details the funding inequities among private and public schools. Recalling your own experiences at your public high school and those of your roommate who attended a private high

school, you find that, indeed, there is a debatable issue regarding the inequities surrounding the funding of the nation's schools.

Not every directory search works quite this smoothly, but many do. After some experience with directory searches, you soon will learn which directories contain the items of most interest to you, which directories suit your searching style, and, perhaps most importantly of all, you will learn to recognize when you are "getting somewhere" with your search and when you are not. When one line of searching isn't working for you, try another—as long as you don't give up too easily. Remember also that while you might choose to surf the entire web in search of an essay issue, there is no systematic organization of the web as a whole. Because of this, you could search for hours and find nothing of use. Since directories are organized into categories with many subtopic divisions, the exploration process illustrated above remained very focused and took only a few minutes to complete.

Another benefit of isolating an issue through a directory is that as you move through the various subtopics, you will likely come across related ideas which you hadn't even considered or had even known existed. So, if you find yourself at a complete loss for ideas, a directory search may be just the thing to help you get started.

➤ **Exercise in Searching for Possible Issues Using a Directory:** Choose a broad topic of interest to you, perhaps one related to one of your hobbies, concerns, or career interests (or even your major). Next, using one of the directories on the WWW (Infoseek, AltaVista, and Hot-Bot are just a few possibilities), follow the sample steps listed above to narrow down this general topic and find several controversial issues related to your topic.

STRUCTURED METHODS OF CHOOSING AN ISSUE

Asking Questions about a Problem (What? Who? When? Where? How?)

The five questions journalists frequently ask to generate information about a topic can be applied effectively to the process of discovering an issue for an argumentative essay. Since an argument is concerned with a problem, the questions are focused on discovering as much information as possible about that problem. In Chapter 1, a student named Elisa and her argumentative essay assignment was introduced. Elisa was asked to develop a position about whether or not a screening committee should be established to screen books for the high school library. To help discover ideas and to focus her thinking, Elisa could have framed her questions as follows:

WHAT is the problem? Parents are concerned that some books in the high school library are unsuitable for their children to read. They want to establish a screening committee for the high school library.

WHO finds this a problem? Some parents find the books a problem because they are worried about violence and promiscuity in our society. Other parents worry about the idea of censoring books and about who would be on such a committee. Students find it a problem because they don't want to be restricted in what they read.

WHEN is this a problem? This is a problem when we are dealing with minors, who may be influenced or disturbed by unsuitable books. It can also be a problem when the idea of censorship is extended beyond the high school.

WHERE is this a problem? The situation is focused on the high school, but the question of censorship is much larger than this immediate situation. It raises questions about whether restricting books for high school students is a good idea and whether behavior is influenced by reading.

HOW can the problem be solved? This problem can be solved by understanding that reading books does not necessarily lead to violent behavior and by recognizing that one form of censorship can lead to another. Also, the problem can be solved by recognizing that the screening committee will create more problems than it is likely to solve.

The Topical Questions

In his *Rhetoric*, Aristotle presents the idea of "topics" as a means of discovering material for an argument. Based on these topics, Edward Corbett in *The Little Rhetoric and Handbook* (John Wiley & Sons, 1981) organized questions about these topics according to subject matter, and a few of these sets of questions can help you to choose an issue for a research paper:

Questions About Concepts (e.g., Censorship of Books)
1. How has the term been defined by others?
2. How do you define the term?
3. What other concepts have been associated with it?
4. In what ways has this concept affected the lives of people?
5. How might this concept be changed?

Questions About Propositions (Statements to Be Proved or Disproved)
Example statement: Pornographic literature directly contributes to violent crimes against women.
1. What must be established before a reader will believe the proposition?
2. What are the meanings of key words in the proposition?
3. By what kinds of evidence or argument can the proposition be proved or disproved?
4. What counterarguments must be confronted and refuted or accommodated?
5. What are the practical consequences of the proposition?

You might find that answering these questions will enable you to think of a topic in a new way and discover a point of view that you had not been aware of before.

➤ **Exercise in Using Journalists' and Topical Questions to Explore an Issue**: Choose one of the controversial issues you discovered while completing the previous exercise ("Searching for Possible Issues Using a Directory"). Then, apply the five journalists' questions listed above to help you investigate the issue more thoroughly.

Next, see if you can pinpoint where you stand on your debatable issue by answering Corbett's topical questions, also listed above. To answer his "Questions About Concepts," think of your issue in more general terms. However, before responding to Corbett's "Questions About Propositions," you'll need to adopt a tentative position on your chosen issue.

READER REACTION AND "SO WHAT?"

In selecting an issue that matters, it is essential to anticipate the reaction of your readers, since no one wants to write a boring paper or to tell readers something they already know or already believe. Sometimes students think that the main basis for choosing an issue is whether or not they and their readers have strong feelings about it. Certainly, if you feel strongly about an issue, you will approach it with energy and enthusiasm, and it is a good idea to look first at issues that evoke an emotional reaction. However, having strong feelings is not the only criterion for choosing a suitable issue. To use an outrageous example, probably everyone in our culture would agree that it is not a good idea to allow a person to go out into the streets and shoot people randomly, if that person happens to wake up in an unusually violent mood that day. Unquestionably, if you heard that someone had suggested that everyone should be allowed this kind of license, you would have strong negative feelings about it. In fact, you would probably be outraged or alarmed! Yet, obviously, this topic is not suitable for a paper because the student has not thought about the impact of the paper on its readers. Even if the paper were very well written, even if the student found many arguments in support of the main idea, and even if the student used many secondary sources as evidence, anyone reading the paper would be likely to say, "**So what?** Everyone already thinks that! Only a disturbed person would ever think this is a good idea."

Therefore, unless society changed drastically (or unless you were in the unlikely position of writing the paper for gang members who may think it actually is a good idea to go out and shoot at people from cars), you would not write a paper on such a topic. Similarly, you would not want to write a paper proving that the world was round or that the moon is not made of green cheese because these are not debatable issues. If you found significant evidence to prove that the world is really flat or that scientists have discovered that the moon is really made of green cheese, then the issue would become debatable, and your paper would be important news to many people.

Unless you found such evidence, though, these issues would not be suitable for a researched paper because there is no point in writing a paper about something on which everyone already agrees, or something that everyone already knows about. Such a paper would not matter to anyone and wouldn't be worth the time you spent writing it. The likely reaction to papers on non-debatable or non-controversial topics is "So what?" If you can anticipate a "So what?" when considering a paper topic, you might decide to write about something else.

In choosing issues for your argumentative essays, then, you should choose one that will move your readers to change their minds or at least think about a topic in a new way—one that is sufficiently complex and about which people have different opinions. Fortunately, most important issues in our society cannot easily be decided upon and have at least two sides. Knowing about different sides of your issue helps you frame a more thoughtful position, enabling you to write your paper successfully.

"So What" Can Lead to a Debatable Issue

Sometimes students begin with ideas that are simply statements of fact. They point out that kids usually like sweets or that households consisting of single women with children are often less financially secure than those containing two parents. They might also generate several supporting points for these statements, backed up with solid facts. Yet each of these statements could generate a "So what?" because they are not debatable. Everyone agrees that these statements are true. Yet, each of these statements can be the starting points for issues that are both significant and debatable. The statement that kids usually like sweets could be used to begin exploration of whether sweets should be included in school lunches or whether sweet products should be advertised on television. The statement about single mothers could lead to an examination of reasons for this being the case, perhaps to a position that advocates greater governmental assistance for single mothers than for single fathers. Saying "So what?" about a statement or an issue doesn't mean that you automatically eliminate it. Perhaps it can be refocused into a topic that is both debatable and relevant.

DISTINGUISHING BETWEEN A TOPIC, AN ASSERTION, AND AN ISSUE

Related to the concept of "So what?" is the ability to distinguish between a topic, an assertion about that topic, and a debatable issue within that topic. To help understand the difference between these terms, read the following exchange between two students:

Fred: Have you found an issue for your paper?
Linda: Yes. My paper is about medical research.

Students often refer to their papers as "about" something, or else they say that they are writing a paper "on" something. Yet if you refer to your papers in this way, you may be mistaking a topic for an issue. A **topic** is usually a broad area, and usually no one either agrees or disagrees just with a topic. Note that the words "medical research" are not a statement and make no assertion. The words alone suggest no particular position or point to develop.

Now look at exchange 2:

> *Fred:* Have you found an issue for your paper?
> *Linda:* Yes. I'm writing a paper showing that medical researchers sometimes use animals for medical tests.

You will note here that Linda's second statement is also not an issue, since it cannot divide its readers. Because animals are, indeed, used for medical research, everyone will agree with this statement, so there would be no point in developing an argument about it. This statement is an **assertion**, a statement or a fact that is true. An assertion can be used to support a position, but it is not an issue or a possible thesis for a paper.

Finally, look at exchange 3:

> *Fred:* Have you found an issue for your paper?
> *Linda:* Yes. I'm writing a paper arguing that there should be restrictions on using animals for medical research.

In this exchange, Linda's statement indicates that now she has found an **issue**, since her statement is likely to generate differing opinions or divide her readership. Some readers (perhaps those involved in medical research) might believe that restrictions would hamper medical progress. Others, like animal-rights activists or vegetarians, might argue that the rights of animals ought to be considered more than they are now. Readers might also adapt positions which fall somewhere in between these two extremes—some might, for example, argue that animal testing should be allowed under certain circumstances to ensure that potentially dangerous products do not present safety risks to humans. Of course, with a controversial issue, as with any issue, Linda will have to narrow her focus and define carefully what she means. Does she mean that she is against all use of animals for medical research? Or does she mean that there should be strict rules that limit when or how animals should be used? **An issue for a researched paper, then, ought to be controversial.** Readers should be divided about how they respond to your position. If you think that all readers will agree with you, you should look for another issue.

Phrasing Your Topic as a Question

An idea for helping you decide whether your preliminary choice is a topic, an assertion, or an issue is to see if you can **formulate a question** about it. To some extent, one might say that all research begins with a question, which leads to exploration of possible answers. This underlying question that your thesis statement and your essay's content attempts to answer is called a **research question**. Framing a question related to your chosen issue, then, can lead you to find an issue and understand what additional information you might need. In Linda's third exchange with Fred, she states, "I'm writing a paper arguing that there should be restrictions on using animals for medical research," a statement that focuses on an issue. That statement could be rephrased as the following question, "Should there be restrictions on using animals for medical research?" Note that this question also suggests other questions that can help focus the direction of the paper. Some of these questions might be: When should there be restrictions on using animals for medical research? What should be the nature of these restrictions? Where or in which instances should there be restrictions? Why should there be restrictions on using animals for medical research? Formulating questions can help you decide what additional information you might need to develop your argument.

If we apply the test of formulating a question to Linda's first statement, we can see that it is not an issue. In Linda's first exchange with Fred, she states, "My paper is about medical research." But because this is a topic, not an issue, one cannot rephrase her statement as a question. In the second exchange with Fred, Linda states, "Medical researchers sometimes use animals for medical tests." If that statement were rephrased as a question, it would read "Do medical researchers sometimes use animals for medical tests?"—a question that can be answered by a simple "yes"—and therefore, does not indicate a controversy or suggest a position. One could, of course, move beyond that assertion toward other aspects of the topic that might ultimately lead to the discovery of a controversial issue. One might ask, "Which researchers use animals for medical tests?" or "When do researchers use animals for medical tests?" These are questions that could ultimately lead to the issue-based question, "Should researchers use animals for medical tests?" However, on its own, an assertion cannot be rephrased as a question that will elicit controversy.

➤ **Exercise in Recognizing an Issue and Forming a Research Question:** Decide whether each of the following is a topic, an assertion, or an issue. Then see if you can transform the topics and assertions into controversial issues. Once you have a list of debatable issues, see whether you can ask a research question about each one that could be answered in an argumentative essay.

1. All students at the university are required to take two semesters of writing.
2. Computers at the university.
3. Birth control should be easily available to everyone.
4. Both men and women should be granted maternity leave from their jobs.
5. A college degree has become a requirement for most well-paying jobs.
6. Women are generally paid less than men for the same job.

> ➤ **Assignment on Ensuring Your Issue IS Debatable**: List several possible topics you would like to explore further in an argumentative essay. After reviewing the information about topics, assertions, and issues above, create a list of controversial issues that would generate disagreement or differing opinions among your readers. Finally, phrase a research question you would like to attempt to answer about each debatable issue you've listed.

BEING ACTIVE IN YOUR SEARCH FOR AN ISSUE

If you are having difficulty deciding on a position or finding a topic, remember that it is better to do something actively than to sit and chew your pencil or fingernails, staring at a blank sheet of paper or computer screen. Freewrite, brainstorm, write responses to questions concerned with problems, but don't just sit staring at the wall. Try writing dialogues and envisioning possible advocates in a debate. Browse through a newspaper or magazine. Listen to the news on television or radio; open your eyes to what is happening in your community. Debatable, significant issues are all around you. Searching actively will enable you to find those that are particularly important to you.

PRELIMINARY ISSUE EXPLORATIONS

Considering Your Immediate Reaction to the Issue

To write an argument about any issue, it is important to try to get an overview of what you already may "feel" about it. Of course, part of the value of thinking and reading about an issue is that it can often lead you to change your mind. Nevertheless, when you begin working on an assignment, it is a good idea to assess your first reaction.

How do you find out what you already think about an issue? Talking and thinking about it are good methods. But an excellent way to discover what you already know about an issue is to *write* about it. Realizing the importance of using writing as a means of discovering ideas, the instructor teaching Elisa and her classmates asked the class to write a preliminary response to some questions concerning their own feelings and experiences relating to the issue of book screening in high schools. These are the questions Elisa's instructor assigned:

Think about your own experience as a high school student:

- Did your mother and father monitor what you read?
- Did you ever find books in the school library that school authorities might have thought were inappropriate in some way?
- Did you ever read a book secretly because you felt your parents or teachers would disapprove of it?
- Do you believe that books influence behavior?

- Do you feel it is important that children read or not read certain types of books?
- Do you have strong feelings about monitoring books?

Elisa thought about these questions and then wrote the following response:

When I was a high school student, I read books that my parents and teachers disapproved of all the time, although I was never really forbidden to read any particular book. I think actually that I kind of liked reading something that I thought my parents would disapprove of and that was part of the fun of it. My mother was always telling me that I was reading "junk." She hated all my romance novels and teenage soap opera type stuff. She was always saying I should read "good" literature, although she never told me exactly why.

I remember once finding a book called <u>Peyton Place</u> in my mother's bookcase that I couldn't believe. It was pretty old, written in the fifties, I think, and it was real dog-eared, like it had been really read a lot, some parts over and over. It was pretty easy to find the parts in it that had been read most often, and some of them had some spicy sex scenes, not real raunchy the way books have today, but pretty suggestive for that time. It was funny for me to think that my mother or father used to read these sections, probably over and over again. I also remember the afternoon I "discovered" <u>The Catcher in the Rye</u> in my brother's bookcase. I picked it up and couldn't put it down. But I read somewhere that this terrific book had been banned.

I guess that's why I'm probably basically against book monitoring of any kind. I haven't really been monitored and I would be pretty angry if someone started telling me what I could or couldn't read. Even in high school I felt that way. On the other hand, I never read anything really violent or pornographic with lots of explicit sex and gratuitous violence, and maybe books like that do have a bad influence on society and cause men to think of women as sex objects or have nasty feelings. They might also cause children to become violent, even more violent than they get from watching TV. If I thought that were really true, I think I might be in favor of screening books, even if it did interfere with freedom to some extent.

But I also wonder who would be on the screening committee and how they would decide which books are suitable. Some books that we think are really good literature, like <u>Ulysses</u> and <u>Catcher in the Rye,</u> were banned at one time. I wouldn't want lots of books banned just because someone on the committee felt uncomfortable about them in some way, and I know plenty of people who feel uncomfortable about anything—really uptight types. Next think you know they'd start banning TV shows or movies or dating or whatever, even telling us how to dress.

Elisa looked over her preliminary response and noted a few main ideas: She had never been monitored about what she should or shouldn't read, although her mother had made suggestions and indicated disapproval. She realized that her immediate feeling about monitoring books was that she was probably against it. She noted that, in general, she was against being told what to do and wouldn't like it if the ban on books (one form of censorship) were to carry over into other forms (banning TV shows or telling people how to dress). She was also worried that censoring books could affect really good literature, as it had in the past. Moreover, she felt uneasy about who might be on such a committee and about their criteria for admitting or not admitting books. Despite these concerns, however, Elisa realized that she felt strongly about the possibility that violent or pornographic books could have an adverse effect on women. She discovered that she would be more likely to advocate the screening committee if she felt that there was a direct cause and effect relationship between reading books and committing violent actions.

Actually, at this point, Elisa felt a bit frustrated, because she really hadn't decided how she felt about the issue. She knew that she didn't like being told what to do, and if someone told her absolutely that she was not allowed to read a particular book, she would immediately feel like reading it. On the other hand, she didn't want to be in favor of something that would be detrimental to women. How could she decide what sort of essay to write?

At this stage in the writing or writing-exploration process, Elisa's confusion is to be expected. She had not read anything about the issue yet and had written an exploratory draft based only on her preconceptions about the issue. That exploratory draft had enabled her to see several aspects of the topic and had therefore made her a bit confused. Nevertheless, it also enabled Elisa to start asking important questions about the issue, and asking questions is an important step in developing a position.

Asking Key Questions

Elisa's initial writing enabled her to formulate some **key questions** that she would have to answer before she could take a stand or come up with a position. She could answer these questions both by additional thinking and by outside reading. Here are the questions Elisa felt she needed to answer before deciding what sort of response she would write:

- Can reading books influence behavior? In what way?
- Can violent or pornographic books influence men to feel negatively or violently about women?
- Can pornographic books cause promiscuous behavior?
- Can violent books cause violent behavior?
- Are there other factors to consider?
- Is it likely that a screening committee will be able to make the right decision about which books to include?
- Is the censoring of high school books likely to affect other freedoms?
- Is it possible to arrive at a compromise position?

➤ **Exercise in Asking Key Questions About an Issue**: Choose a debatable issue you would like to explore further in an argumentative essay (this might be an issue you've identified in previous exercises in this chapter). Create a list of key questions related to this issue that you would need to answer in order to adopt a position on your chosen issue.

SHARING IDEAS AND QUESTIONS WITH OTHERS

Sharing ideas and questions with others can also help you understand your assignment so that you can formulate your own position on an issue. Working in a group, Elisa had the opportunity to learn about how some of her peers had responded to the preliminary questions, to see how their responses compared to her own.

Here is James's response to the preliminary questions:

> Although our society is becoming more lenient, there is still a large part of the population that holds onto old-fashioned values who are teaching their kids the difference between right and wrong. My parents always stressed that we go along with family values and not be influenced by radical ideas about morality, so they were very careful to tell us what they felt was suitable or unsuitable for us to read. I think they were right, because it seems to me that people are influenced by what they read. For example, my younger brother's friends all read <u>Sports Illustrated, Car and Driver,</u> and <u>American Guns,</u> and then they beg me to take them to the rifle range and batting cages, and they love to look at and talk about cars. I think they get their ideas about how to behave and about what they like to do, at least some of them, from what they read.
>
> If I had to choose one word to describe how I was raised, the word would be "traditional," and I never was allowed to bring a book or a magazine into the house that my parents thought was unsuitable. I guess I can understand the attraction of some of these "modern" novels, though, but I would worry how they would affect young people, particularly the men. There is so much violence these days anyway, and so much junk on television and in videos, that kids don't need to read about this stuff in books too. If I were a parent, I would want to know that kids in the high school are not reading anything that is going to make them even more violent than they already are. And I certainly wouldn't want my daughter reading books with a lot of sex in them because she might get the wrong ideas.

At first, when Elisa read James's essay, she felt a bit disturbed. Here was a classmate of hers easily accepting a position on censorship without even worrying about loss of freedom or questioning if a relationship really exists between reading and behavior. She noticed that he seemed to accept that connection very easily, but that he never considered that the violence in our society, negative attitudes toward women, or tendencies toward promiscuity could possibly have very little or nothing to do with what people read. In fact, she thought, maybe it is possible that people read violent and pornographic stuff because they have these attitudes already. Then Elisa realized that reading James's response had helped her to understand that the issue of whether or not books can generate violent or demeaning attitudes toward women was really crucial to whether or not she was in favor of the screening committee. Unlike the argument about promiscuity, which she felt was unimportant, the issue of how books could affect men's attitudes toward women was the one she would have to focus on before she could develop her own position.

James's Response: The Concept of Audience

In addition to helping Elisa focus her thinking, James's response also helped her think about the sort of readers or audience she might be addressing in her essay and about what sort of approach would be most likely to convince them of her position. Thinking about how James felt about the issue, Elisa realized that she would have to acknowledge some of his concerns before he would pay attention to anything she might have to say. Otherwise, he would view her simply as an opponent and hold onto his point of view even more tightly. Student writers often forget than no one likes to be told how to think and that most people are not favorably disposed toward someone with a dogmatic attitude. If someone came up to you and said, "Let me show you how wrong you are about this issue, and then I'll tell you how right I am," you would most likely say something rude, and you certainly would not be inclined to change your opinion.

Thus, reading James's response helped Elisa think about her audience, an extremely important concern for writers of argument. The critical role of audience in choosing and framing an argument will occur again and again throughout the remainder of this book.

James's response helped Elisa understand not only her own idea of the issue more thoroughly but also enabled her to gain insight into another perspective on it. Because most controversial topics generate multiple perspectives, it is useful to become aware of as many of them as possible. Elisa gained insight into another perspective on the topic when she read the response of another classmate, Latrice:

> My son is only 5 years old and isn't old enough to go to high school yet. But I know that I wouldn't want him reading some trash he found in the school library. When I send my son to school, I expect that he will get a good education and the right idea about how to behave. I don't send him to school to pick up whatever turns him on, and I know that trashy novels sometimes do appeal to young kids, especially young men.
>
> When I think of a school, I think of a place where someone is in charge of my child. Otherwise I wouldn't send my child to that school. So I think it is a good idea for a committee to make sure that filth and trash don't get into the school library. Kids have plenty else to read without reading that sort of thing in the school. When they get older, then they can decide for themselves what they want to read, and there won't be anyone to stop them. I was raised with strict morals and wasn't allowed to read junk.
>
> I don't let my son watch violence on TV either for the same reasons. If parents don't take care of their kids, the kids will turn out wild.

Reading Latrice's preliminary thoughts on the issue, Elisa learned about how a parent might feel about this issue and recognized that she would have to address the concerns of parents in her essay. She also realized that Latrice had raised two other issues: the responsibility of the school toward upholding moral and behavioral values and the question of age in relation to freedom from censorship. Elisa already realized that, as a high school student, she would have felt angry if anyone had restricted her from reading something that interested her. But didn't her high school restrict her in other ways? She had had to adhere to a dress code, sit in certain areas of the cafeteria, attend classes at certain times, and obey the rules. Maybe the high school did have the right to restrict her because they had assumed responsibility for her during the time she attended. If so, did that mean that they also had the right to restrict what she read?

Elisa also decided that she would talk to her grandmother about some of the issues in her assignment. Elisa's grandmother was a member of a neighborhood yard beautification committee and had experience in working with groups of people. Here is what Elisa's grandmother had to say:

> I don't know much about the effect of pornography or violence. But I do know about committees. I can tell you—they attract some pretty weird people—usually people with an ax to grind of some sort. That guy down the street, McGafferty—he attends every meeting and every time he raises objections to every suggestion that anyone makes. He's got some set idea in his head about what this neighborhood should look like and he's driving us all crazy. I think that a screening committee at the school could probably attract the same kind of people.

Elisa's grandmother helped her think about one of her preliminary questions: whether or not the screening committee would be able to make good decisions. Her grandmother obviously did not think so.

Another person that Elisa talked to was Mrs. Phillips, the librarian at Elisa's local high school. Elisa wanted to find out how decisions were made about whether certain books were ordered and if books were regularly screened for "gratuitous violence" and "explicit sex." This is what the librarian had to say:

> Most of our books are ordered for us because we are part of a state system. But sometimes I will go through a catalog (I receive a large number of catalogs) and see a few books that I think would be particularly helpful. And if the budget allows, I'll order some of these. Sometimes, teachers will specifically request a book, or someone donates a pile of books when they move. But frankly, I can't possibly read all of the books that come in here, and my guess is that some of them might be considered "unsuitable" by some people. And I guess that's a problem. But my feeling is that even really trashy books are less harmful than movies and video, and I'm just glad when students read at all.

The librarian helped Elisa understand how books actually get admitted into a school library. She realized that to a certain extent books were already judged as "suitable" or "unsuitable" on the basis of catalog descriptions. She also realized that the librarian did not seem concerned about "gratuitous violence" and "explicit sex" in books; she worried more about the effects of television, video, and films.

> ➤ **Exercise in Considering Multiple Perspectives on an Issue**: Working in a small group, ask each group member to write a brief response (a paragraph or two) to your research question, or the question that you would like to answer by taking a position on a controversial issue. Then, compare the various responses to your research question, noting similar points of view and opinions that differ from your position.

Understanding the Value Conflicts in an Issue or Assignment

The development of a position usually depends on a person's **values,** which may be defined as abstract ideas or standards of behavior that one considers important. Some common values that many of us probably share are tradition, ambition, security, honesty, responsibility, and freedom of speech. One might ask, then, if we all agree on fundamental values, how can we disagree on so many issues? The answer is that, although people may agree broadly that these values are important, they often disagree about the importance assigned to one value over that of another when controversial issues arise. Values, then, frequently come into conflict. In thinking about her position, Elisa noted that several of her own values came into conflict. On the one hand, she very much valued freedom of speech. Yet she also felt that young people should be safe from harmful influences. Thus, for Elisa, the value she placed on freedom was in direct conflict with the value she placed on security. James and Latrice, however, seemed to have less of a conflict. They did not seem worried about freedom because they felt that security was more important. In times of stress and danger, many of us would also choose security over freedom. If, for example, a gang of killers were loose in the neighborhood and if, in the interest of public safety, a law were passed that no one was allowed out on the street after 10 PM, we might feel that our freedom had been curtailed, but we might not mind very much because we might be more worried about safety.

What Elisa had to decide was whether she viewed books with "explicit sex" and "gratuitous violence" as threatening to safety in some way. Possibly, such books could have the effect of threatening the safety of women or making children more violent, and Elisa realized that these were key issues for her. Thus, Elisa understood that in developing her position, she would have to decide which of her values was more important to her on this issue. Understanding the **value conflicts** relating to an issue or assignment will also help you develop a position for your paper.

AUDIENCE-BASED EXPLORATION STRATEGIES

Role Playing

A helpful method to understand the issues involved in a topic is to **imagine the different people who might be concerned with the topic** in some way.

For example, suppose that at your university, the administration, concerned about the increase of late-night crime in the neighborhood and also about the large dropout rate in the freshman class, has proposed that curfews be instituted in all of the freshman dormitories: ten o'clock on weekdays, one o'clock on weekends. Who might have an opinion on this topic? Certainly, in this case, the administration is likely to be strongly in favor of the curfew, since they proposed it. The students, though, might hold an equally strong opinion that is completely different from that of the administration. Then you might also think about the parents who are often paying the bills. With whom would they agree?

Creating a Character with a Strong Opinion on a Topic-Related Issue

A useful way to understand different positions on an issue is to create a character who would have a strong or even an extreme opinion about it. To do so, imagine that you are at a party where a guest begins speaking in emotionally charged language about an issue relating to the school curfew. Give this person a name, a profession, an appearance. Then, assuming the role of this person, write what he or she might say. For example, you might write something like this:

> My character is named Gary Stevens. He is 45 years old, 5 feet, 10 inches tall, has dark hair with flecks of gray at the temples, is tan, and in pretty good shape, though he has a slight tendency to be overweight. He is wearing gray pants with a white shirt, no tie. He makes a lot of money in the computer business and is sending his daughter to an expensive private college. This is what he has to say at the party:
> "I don't care what students have to say about their so-called 'rights.' As far as I'm concerned, you get rights when you pay for them. That's the way it was for me, and that's the way it is for my daughter. If she doesn't like the curfew, she can go fund herself for college and live on her own too. I'm paying a lot of money for her to have an education and that doesn't include partying all night, particularly in a dangerous neighborhood. I've seen some of the characters who hang around the school at night and they're a pretty rough bunch. My daughter doesn't like the curfew, but she can just put up with it. As it is, let me tell you, she doesn't overwork. Parties and fun—that's all she knows. If she wants me to pay for her education, she can get herself home on time!"

> ➤ **Exercise in Investigating Multiple Perspectives Using Dialogue:** Imagine you are Gary Stevens's daughter. She is at another party on the same evening, and she, too, has a strong opinion on the issue. Write a forceful statement of what she might say about the curfew.

Creating a Brief Dialogue on the Issue

To gain an understanding of your issue, it is helpful to imagine a brief dialogue that might occur among various people with differing opinions about it. If, in your imagination, you can find several points of disagreement among these people, you will know that you have selected a controversial issue that is suitable for a researched paper and the multiple perspectives of differences of opinion generated by that issue. Scripting the discussion will also help you to begin to think about points you might wish to develop or argue against. For example, on the issue of the curfew, you might imagine a university administrator, a student, and a parent stating the following positions:

> *Student:* Having any sort of curfew is ridiculous! At this point in our lives, we are young adults and can make our own decisions.
>
> *Parent:* Just because you are 18 doesn't mean that you are a young adult. According to my definition, an adult is someone who is self-supporting. I don't see you doing that.
>
> *School official:* I think the main point here is safety and fostering good study habits. Having a curfew means that students cannot stay out late when they should be studying.
>
> *Student:* Safety is our own business. If we think that it's not safe to go out, we'll go out in groups or decide on our own to come home early. And, as far as studying is concerned, just because students are actually inside the dorm doesn't mean that they'll be studying. Students can waste time right in their rooms if they want to. It all comes down to whether or not we have the maturity to discipline ourselves. I think we have, and, if not, we will be the ones to suffer.
>
> *Parent:* You can take on that responsibility when you are paying for your own education.

As you can see, one could debate issues related to the curfew for a long time, and in the course of dialogue, many points of disagreement might emerge. These can be stated as questions: Is someone viewed as an adult by age or by economic independence? Does an enforced curfew foster better study habits? Who is responsible for safety—the school or the individual student? Is it the responsibility of the school to foster better study habits? Do parents have rights over their adult children's habits if they are paying for the education? Perhaps you can think of some more.

➤ **Exercise in Writing a Brief Dialogue**: Imagining a disagreement will help you understand extreme positions on issues. Choose one of the issues suggested below and engage in the following activities:

1. Imagine a particular person who might have a strong opinion about the issue. Give that person a name, an age, a profession, and a description.

2. Imagine how that person might feel about the issue. State that opinion in several sentences.
3. Imagine another person or group of people who might have a different opinion. State in general terms what these opinions might be.
4. Write a brief dialogue between these people.
5. List points of disagreement as questions.

Some suggested issues (phrased as research questions) are:

1. Should illegal immigrants to the United States be provided with education and health care?
2. Should high schools censor what books students are allowed to read? Should material deemed "unsuitable" be eliminated from the school library?
3. Should fourteen-year-old boys be allowed to assume the responsibilities of fatherhood if they father a child?
4. Has the women's movement has achieved all of its goals? Is it no longer necessary?
5. Should college students be allowed to sign up for more than five classes, or will they be overburdened with work?
6. Should employers be able to test all employees for drugs?
7. Should those caught selling drugs be subject to capital punishment?
8. Should smoking be allowed in restaurants?

➤ **Assignment on Using Extended Dialogue to Understand an Issue**: Scripting extended discussions between characters with strong positions can also help you explore an issue and develop your own position. Using an issue of your choice, write an **extended dialogue** between two characters who have strong opinions on the subject (you might find it helpful to use the five questions listed at the beginning of the previous exercise to create your two characters). In writing your dialogue, you should observe the following specifications:

1. No one makes outrageous or insulting statements.
2. No one wins; that is, both views seem intelligent.
3. Each character speaks at least twice, for at least half a page at each turn.
4. Each character's words should be planned and carefully structured.

This is thoughtful, deliberate writing, as if each character had revised and edited his or her spoken words for publication, not spontaneous or casual.

Imagining possible participants in a controversy will help you evaluate the relevance of your topic or issue, and writing either brief or extended dialogues will help you decide whether it's controversial. Once you have thought about at least two positions, you can then decide which one you most agree with and perhaps qualify one of the extreme positions. Then you can begin to think about possible directions for developing your own position.

THE ROLES OF AUDIENCE AND PURPOSE IN IDEA GENERATION

The Interplay of Audience and Purpose

The role playing, dialogue approach discussed in this chapter is based on the idea that if you know what your audience already believes about an issue, you will gain a sense of your own position and of what material you ought to include. "Ought to include," however, depends not just on an identified or preferred audience and not just what you think that audience might believe about your issue. In fact, **your purpose in relation to your audience**—what you would have your audience think, do, or even simply consider as a result of your writing—**is just as crucial as the audience itself.**

One purpose of argumentative, academic writing is to establish credibility. As an argumentative writer, you probably want your readers to find you convincing and to be convinced by your writing on an issue, and, in this sense, you might want to eliminate from your consideration those topics/issues on which you have little hope of establishing credibility. Perhaps an issue that comes to mind is one on which you cannot feasibly prepare yourself to speak expertly within the time you have for your project, or perhaps your values and the values of your likely audience are at great odds. **Just as there are many possible positions relative to most controversial issues, so are there many potential goals you might set relative to anticipated readers.** In some instances, you might select an audience for your paper who already hold the same position on the issue that you hold—perhaps the position that "we need more effective sex education in our public schools"—but who disagree as to the best treatment for the problem. In such an instance, you would have a ready audience for a "proposal"-type paper, one that might focus more on analysis and explanation of solutions than on establishing that a problem exists. In other instances and for other issues, you might identify an audience who believes as you do about the existence of a problem, about the necessity of action, and even about the best solution, but they might disagree as to their place within the solution—in other words, about how the solution should be funded or about their own involvement in the solution. In still other instances, you might choose a diametrically opposed audience—an audience whose position is likely to be an exact opposite to yours—and select as your goal only an acknowledgement from your readers of the validity of your position: "We may disagree, but both of our positions have merit."

The point is, many goals and purposes underlie equally valid, controversial, significant researched essays. Chapter 5 identifies several types of argument synthesis essays, each with its specific type or types of purposes in relation to audience. As you consider various audiences with interests in your issue and what those audiences might know or believe, consider also the likelihood of success with selected or target audiences with regard to different purposes. When you have conducted a thorough and realistic analysis of possible issues, audiences, and purposes, you will be prepared to make productive choices for your paper project.

Audience Awareness Questions

An audience-analysis strategy you might find helpful is to use the "Audience Awareness" questions below:

1. As specifically as possible, what sort of reader is my essay intended to address?
   Male or female?
   Age?
   Profession?
   Values relating to the issue?
2. What position on this issue does my reader have?
   What does my reader know about the issue?
   Does the reader hold any misconceptions on this issue?
   Is there common ground that both of us share?
3. What view of the issue do I want my reader to have?
   What evidence can I use?
   Is there any way I can compromise on this issue?

One student, Alexander, chose to write a researched essay about the issue of school uniforms. He chose that topic because when he was in high school, a new ruling had passed requiring all students to wear a specific brand of jeans and a white shirt. The reasons cited for this ruling were that uniforms promoted equality among students, had the effect of focusing students' attention on studies rather than on clothing, and were sufficiently distinguishable from the clothing gang members wore that no student in the school would be in danger of being mistaken for a gang member.

Many of the students, however, were not in favor of wearing uniforms. They felt that the uniforms constituted an infringement on their right to wear what they chose and that the fear of being mistaken for a gang member was exaggerated. Alexander, in fact, had once been a member of a student group that protested the new ruling, and, because he knew a great deal about the opposition, he decided to write an argument in support of uniforms that addressed a group of students protesting the new ruling. This is how Alexander used his Audience Awareness questions to generate material:

1. *As specifically as possible, what sort of reader is my essay intended to address?*
   Male or female? Both male and female students.
   Age? 15–18

Profession? Students

Values relating to the issue? Students hate being told what to do and that includes being told what to wear. They think that parents and school officials are paranoid on the subject of safety. They feel that being free to choose your own clothing is more important than eliminating the threat of being mistaken for a gang member.

2. *What position on this issue does my reader have?*

What does my reader know about the issue? Students tend to think of uniforms as very formal, the sort of uniforms they have in religious schools. They may not know what kind of uniforms the school wants them to wear—informal and comfortable—the sort of clothing kids wear anyway.

Does the reader hold any misconceptions on this issue? They think that the threat of gangs is exaggerated. They don't realize that gangs pose a real threat. They also don't realize how much money school clothes cost and that there are a lot of kids in school who can't afford to dress well. For those kids, a school uniform would be a lifesaver.

Is there common ground that both of us share? I also value individual freedom, but once I understood the advantages of these uniforms, I changed my mind.

3. *What view of the issue do I want my reader to have?* I want them to understand that school uniforms are worth a try. Maybe if they try them for one year, they will see that they are not so bad.

What evidence can I use? Statistics on gang-related crimes, information about the income level at the school, reports from other schools that tried this kind of uniform.

Is there any way I can compromise on this issue? The compromise would be in using the uniforms for a trial and by stressing that these are not uniforms in the traditional sense of the word.

➤ **Exercise in Considering Your Potential Audience**: Using the "Audience Awareness" questions listed above, create a profile of your intended audience. Base your answers to these questions on how your anticipated readers might react to the position you've taken on a controversial issue.

THE GENERAL AUDIENCE VERSUS THE TEACHER

Targeting a specific audience can be useful for generating ideas and for assignments that ask a student to write to a specific individual, group, or population. However, most college essays are not intended for just one person; very commonly, they are addressed to what is termed a "general audience." Who is the **general audience?** Is it your next door neighbor? Your dentist? Your tennis partner? Can you envision a particular person who epitomizes in some way that general audience? One way to think about the general audience for a researched essay is to conceive of it as referring to anyone with sufficient background on and concern for the subject who might read the essay if it were left lying on a table in the college library. A general audience is, therefore, presumed to be a reasonably educated audience that cares about issues and that tends to be persuaded by reason rather than emotion. Individuals within this group might not be familiar with the context and background of the specific controversy you are writing about, but they are concerned that ideas are presented fairly and that credible support is provided.

You should keep this concept in mind if your instructor tells you to "consider your audience" without telling you what sort of audience you should consider. Do not make the mistake of forgetting about audience altogether or thinking that your teacher is your only audience. When students write only to their teachers, they sometimes leave out important information—explanations, definitions, or support—because they think that the teacher doesn't need it. And when students forget about audience altogether, they may assume an inappropriate tone or take an inappropriately aggressive or one-sided position. They may write, for example, a statement such as "Anyone who thinks this is just out of touch with reality," or "These ideas are hopelessly old-fashioned." Because they don't think of their audience as either a real person or as a group of real people, they forget that an outrageous or insulting statement is likely to alienate, rather than persuade, an audience.

Your classmates, too, provide a real and viable audience for your essays, and it is helpful to keep their perspectives in mind while composing your argumentative essays. Often, fellow class members will read your essays at various stages of the writing process (including rough, intermediate, and final drafts) during class activities such as peer evaluation or review. Often, their comments on and reactions to your work in progress are invaluable, allowing you to recognize areas needing modification to avoid confusing or alienating your audience.

➤ **Exercise in Recognizing Your Audience:** Examine the following paragraphs from a student paper concerned with whether further government legislation is needed on behalf of women's rights in the workplace. Can you find areas in the paper where the student seems to have forgotten about audience? Can you determine the audience for whom this paper was written?

Equal Opportunity Effort

In today's job market it appears that there is not equal opportunity for women. Men continue to dominate in areas of high pay and executive positions, and some leftist groups and radical feminist organizations attribute this to sex discrimination. These groups then scream that we need additional affirmative action programs by the government to give women more advantages than they already have. I do not see this as necessary and those who are in favor of increasing these programs are really advocating reverse discrimination and unfair practices. Affirmative action is just another form of discrimination.

Today, over half of the female population are in the work force. Women are working in jobs once thought to be exclusively for men. But women do not hold prestigious positions at these jobs.

In the past, people thought that affirmative action programs would help women advance. The Equal Pay Act of 1963 guaranteed equal pay, no matter the sex, for jobs of equal skill level. Title VII of the Civil Rights Acts of 1964 prohibited discrimination in private employment on the basis of race, color, religion, national origin, or sex. In 1965, Executive Order 11246 was passed, which carried forward a program of equal opportunity in government employment. Executive Order 11375 further amended 11246. It states that the policy of equal opportunity applies to "every aspect of Federal employment policy and practice" (Executive Order 11375).

You would think that these acts would be enough. But they do not seem to be. Now, because women are not advancing as far as they could in the workplace, various radical groups are screaming for more legislation. Don't they realize that legislation doesn't work?

UNDERSTANDING YOUR POSITION ON INDIVIDUAL RIGHTS

A general issue that will have an impact on your position on many controversial issues is that concerning individual rights—that is, how strongly you feel that each individual ought to be able to enjoy his or her individual rights as opposed to feeling that individual rights must be secondary to the well-being of society as a whole. One extreme position on this topic is that each person in society must be given his or her individual rights under all conditions, that each person counts as an individual above all else. Another extreme position is that the rights of society are much more important than the rights of the individual, that in every society, each individual must give up as many individual rights as necessary for society to function successfully. A moderate position lies somewhere in between.

When laws are passed, an individual might feel as if his or her rights are being infringed upon. Thus, you might say, "I don't need a law requiring me to wear a seatbelt, because I always wear one anyway." Someone else might say, "Others are not as responsible as you and they must be required to do what is necessary. Our society can't afford to care for those who are severely injured in automobile accidents." In another instance, you might say, "I shouldn't be required to justify the deductions on my tax form. I am an honest person and would not claim anything unnecessary." The government might say, "You may be honest, but there are many who aren't. We have to require proof from everyone in order for our society to function. And if you wish the protection of our government, you must obey its laws."

In order for you to argue a position on significant, debatable issues, you need to examine how many individual rights you are willing to give up in order for society to exist. Almost everyone agrees that obeying red and green signals is necessary for traffic to function smoothly and would support a law requiring all motorists to do so. But probably few would be in favor of a nightly curfew in order to deter criminals who operate during the evening hours. Thinking about where you are willing to compromise will help you develop a position.

➤ **Exercise in Thinking about Individual Rights**: Laws requiring motorists to obey traffic signals and wear seatbelts are designed to help society function more safely; they concern the welfare of society. Yet there are probably other "laws" that could be passed that might also make society safer, although some of them might inhibit individual rights more than you would recommend. For example, a law requiring all minors to be accompanied by an adult after certain hours might contribute to child safety; yet at this time, this law does not exist and many would probably be against passing it.

Would you be in favor of such a law? Or would you feel that it would be too much of a restriction on individual freedom? Think about what other "laws" could be passed in the interest of public safety. Write some of these down and compare them with possible "laws" devised by your classmates. Which ones would you support? In thinking about these "laws," try to determine your position on individual rights versus your concern with public well being.

EXPLORATORY DRAFTS AND ESSAY PROPOSALS

As Chapter 6 shows in more detail, the types of audience and purpose exploration that have been described in the preceding paragraphs can be grouped together into what we call exploratory drafts and essay proposals.

While exploratory drafts could consist of relatively random, stream-of-consciousness thought, we suggest that you write exploratory drafts with a very specific goal in mind—to figure out who your audience is and what you want them to get from your writing. Thus, you might want to write an exploration of your own preconceptions or an audience dialogue after a small amount of reading on your issue, as Elisa did, or you might want to read much more intensively and even take extensive notes, *then* do some exploratory writing. Exploratory drafts can help you to focus your thinking. Exploratory drafts, you see, are a means of writing your way into knowing.

Like exploratory drafts, essay proposals can help you focus your thinking about an issue you've tentatively selected to write about. They enable you take a closer look at your issue to determine where you really stand on the issue and why. Writing a proposal also encourages you to consider your audience and how they might respond to your stance. Writing instructors often require proposals so they might help guide students toward productive issues and away from those that could be problematic.

4 Finding Information

Perhaps the single most useful resource for completing academic research is your college library. Your library is not just the brick and mortar building which houses books and journals; it is a network of information whose resources often spread well outside the building and the campus. In addition to their own collections, some libraries have formed partnerships through which students at one institution can borrow books from another. Many libraries also provide students with free access to web-based research databases, electronic journals, and other research services.

USING BOOKS FOR RESEARCH

When many people begin researching a topic or issue, they immediately think that this means finding books. Many students have grown accustomed to stacks of library books, using the resources found within their high school libraries to conduct all of their academic research.

The value of a good book cannot be underestimated. Books have the length, breadth, and substance needed to give readers a solid background on a topic. Although books may seem prohibitively long for use as sources in college-level researched essays, it is not always necessary to read entire works in order to use them as sources. For instance, you might choose to skim a book for a relevant chapter, look at its Table of Contents, or peruse the index to determine a book's usefulness as a credible source for a potential essay.

Although books are able to explore topics more comprehensively than articles, you should be aware that for researched essays which focus on current, debatable issues, the information found in books is sometimes outdated. In general, it takes a year or two for authors to write a book, and another year or so before the book is published and distributed. You should also be aware that the sources upon which the writers of the book relied could have been books, thus extending the cycle of outdated information. So while a book published only a year or two ago might appear to contain current information, that information might, indeed, be much older. While books may be useful to gain historical perspective or for general reference, when you are writing an essay about a current issue, a journal or magazine article might be more up-to-date.

Despite these limitations, the information in books written by reputable authors is generally reliable (though one should always critically analyze information before using it), and most people are familiar with (and quite comfortable with) strategies for finding books. Most college libraries maintain an electronic catalog of their collections, allowing fast and accurate searches by author, title, subject, or keyword. As Figure 3 illustrates, college libraries often offer many different search options.

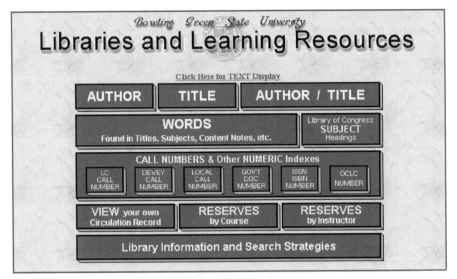

Figure 3

Finding a Book

If you know specifically what book you're looking for, the most direct way to find it is by conducting an author search or a title search. These searches will quickly tell you whether a particular library has the book you are looking for.

However, most folks doing research do not have a specific source in mind as they research. They are usually interested in finding relevant information pertaining to a subject, topic, or issue, rather than a particular book by a particular author. Thus, most researchers have to resort to other types of searches that look for information in different ways.

Keyword searching and subject searching are a bit more complicated than author or title searching. Subject searches only look within the book record in the actual Library of Congress subject headings for the word or words you stipulate on the database search screen. Conversely, keyword searches look for your words in the subject heading, title, and content notes of book records. For instance, while you may not know the exact Library of Congress subject heading needed to find information on "Internet Censorship" using a subject search, a keyword search using these terms will probably yield something of value. In short, if you're not sure of the exact subject heading, try a keyword search instead.

When searching for books, one should also keep in mind the likelihood of different library search catalogs working differently. You can usually combine and exclude different keywords from your search, allowing you to narrow or expand what you're looking for. For example, the library at Bowling Green State University allows searches to be more clearly defined using the terms "AND," "OR," "NO," and the symbol "*," also known as **Boolean terms**. As can be seen in Figure 4, various combinations of these terms and keywords will yield various search results. While Boolean terms are widely used, it is best to check how your library catalog handles searches before delving too far into a book search.

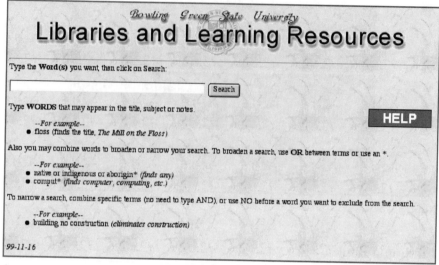

Figure 4

> ➤ **Exercises in Finding Books:**
>
> 1. Suppose that you have decided to explore the topic of "veganism" with a goal of finding an issue for your researched essay. What types of useful information might you expect to find about this topic in books? How would you go about searching for books on this topic? Try several different searches, using different combinations of terms. What do you find?
> 2. Complete the interactive library tutorial found at http://www.bgsu.edu/colleges/library/infosrv/tutorial/tutor1.html. While this tutorial is designed specifically for Bowling Green State University, the concepts it reinforces are used in libraries nationwide. As you complete the tutorial, note any questions you have and bring them to the next class.

USING PERIODICALS FOR RESEARCH

Generally speaking, a periodical is a publication distributed at regular intervals such as daily, weekly, or monthly. Newspapers, magazines, and professional journals are examples of periodicals you might consider as potential research sources.

The information found in current periodicals is relatively up-to-date because the publication and distribution processes do not take long. The more current information available in periodicals is well suited to the shorter arguments assigned in college, that is, writing assignments that do not require large amounts of overview or historical information. And periodicals may also provide so-called "background" or historical information, both in recent publications (which may, in fact, take a historical approach) and in the archived periodical collections that college libraries typically compile—in bound volumes or on microfiche. As you familiarize yourself with your college library or conduct a specific source search, you may benefit from learning which periodicals your library archives (maintains back issues for) and for which years.

Newspapers

The differences among various types of periodicals can be important when determining what types of information you need. Generally, newspapers such as *The New York Times* and *The Washington Post* are printed daily and cover world, national, and local news. Local and campus newspapers such as *The Putnam County Sentinel* or *The BG News* focus primarily on local and campus issues, making them ideal sources for information on these types of issues. Newspapers also carry investigative stories and feature articles. Newspapers typically print many articles that are short and to the point, making them useful if you don't need a lot of detailed information about a single issue.

Popular Magazines

If the information found in a newspaper doesn't fit your needs, there are many types of popular magazines that offer specialized information for particular audiences. For example, there are popular magazines geared toward news enthusiasts, bicyclists, gourmet cooks, and amateur woodworkers as well as almost every other group imaginable. Popular magazines cater to the specific interests of readers, offering a variety of information in which their perceived audience—sometimes called a "target demographic"—might be interested. One type of popular magazine is a news magazine such as *Time*. This type of magazine offers in-depth coverage of select national and world news as well as lengthy feature stories for the news enthusiast. Likewise, the health magazine *Fitness* provides in-depth information about exercise, diet, health, and sports.

While popular magazines don't usually have as many articles as newspapers, the information offered is usually more detailed, offering readers more information on a particular topic. Because this information is intended for a rather general audience, however, articles in popular magazines are typically not "scholarly"—not marked by the detail, backing, or authority academics and professionals expect in support of serious arguments. Thus, ordinarily you should not rely heavily upon them in academic researched essays.

Professional and/or Scholarly Journals

For more technical information, professional journals usually contain the most recent research pertaining to a particular profession. The information in journals is usually heavily scrutinized by a panel of people within the profession before it is published. However, since journals are usually published for individuals in a particular field, the language or jargon can sometimes be difficult for someone outside the profession to understand. While it may be difficult to decipher some of the information found in journals, many journal articles can be read by non-professionals (including students) with the help of a dictionary. Spending extra time reading professional or scholarly articles is worth the effort since these types of periodicals are usually the most reliable for researched essays.

Regardless of which type of periodical you use, the credibility of a periodical's information typically corresponds to the reputation of the periodical itself. When determining the value of information, regardless of source, one should always practice the critical reading strategies discussed in Chapter 2. For example, one would probably **not** use an article about the safety of the latest Hollywood diet printed in a tabloid magazine such as *The Weekly World News* as a research source. Articles in such publications are not based on rigorous research, nor do these types of periodicals have a reputation for reliability or integrity. Along the same lines, one could rely heavily on the credibility of an article on the same topic printed in the *Journal of the American Medical Association.*

➤ **Exercises in Using Periodicals for Research:**

1. Suppose that while browsing the periodicals at your local bookstore you ran across several articles on veganism in the following periodicals. What might you expect each to focus on? How useful might each be in your researched essay?
   - Article in the journal *The New England Journal of Medicine*
   - Article in the tabloid *The National Enquirer*
   - Article in the popular magazine *Vegetarian Times*
   - Article in the newspaper *The Columbus Dispatch*
2. Imagine that you are searching for information on the following topics/issues. Which type(s) of periodicals would provide the most appropriate information for each topic/issue?
   - Gulf War Syndrome
   - The current political climate in Mexico
   - A proposed tuition increase at your college
   - MP3 technology
   - ADD/ADHD in elementary school children
   - Police brutality
   - Job prospects for someone in your field of study

Finding Periodicals

Because any given library could have access to hundreds of periodicals, most use several types of indexes to help library users find the information they're looking for. Indexes are often specialized to allow researchers to locate information in a specific subject area. For example, Bowling Green State University offers its patrons access to many research databases. As can be seen in Figure 5, a categorical listing of the literally hundreds of databases available at a single library can make navigation through these databases much faster and more precise.

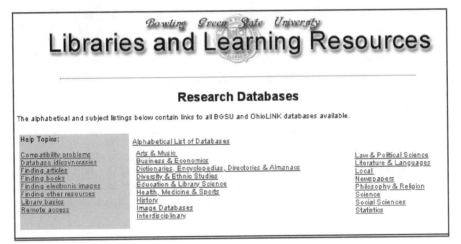

Figure 5

Deciding which database to search for the articles you are seeking can be daunting, so, unless your topic is very discipline-specific, you should start your search in one of the "Interdisciplinary" databases such as Lexis-Nexis Academic Universe, Periodical Abstracts, or SIRS Researcher. Once you have picked an index to search, finding information is relatively simple. As you can see in Figure 6, indexes such as Periodical Abstracts often allow you to search in the same ways online catalogs allow you to search for books—by author, title, subject, or keyword.

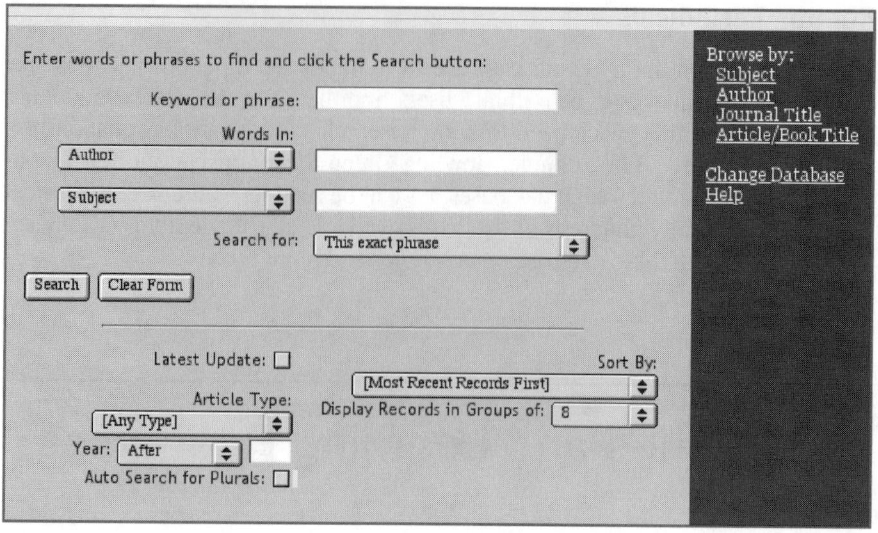

Figure 6

> ➤ **Exercises in Finding Periodicals:** Access an interdisciplinary database such as Lexis-Nexis Academic Universe. Conduct a search for information on veganism. Note the number and kinds of resources that are found. Now conduct the same search using a discipline-specific database such as the Science Citation Index.
>
> 1. How do the results of this query differ?
>   a. What does this tell you about some of the possible differences between these two databases?
>   b. From this observation, what can you assume about databases in general?
> 2. Conduct the exact same search using at least two more databases. What do these results tell you?
> 3. Now, repeat steps 1 and 2 using your own research topic.

USING ONLINE RESOURCES FOR RESEARCH

Chances are that you have heard about the tremendous amount of information available on the World Wide Web (WWW). This information can be credible or completely lacking in credibility because literally anyone has the opportunity to put almost anything on the web for anyone to view. So—while you can rely on your library to filter out many unreliable sources when searching for books and periodicals—when using the web, *you* are the only filter.

The good news is that the web contains a great deal of information; the bad news is that you must be very critical when deciding which information to believe and which to dismiss. When considering a web-based source as support for an academic assignment, you would do well to carefully evaluate the source before relying on it. Don't forget the analysis strategies you learned in Chapter 2.

The bad news also is that unlike your library, no one keeps track of the millions of web pages. There is no comprehensive WWW index. Do not despair, however. Web companies such as AltaVista, Yahoo, and Excite offer ways to find specific information on the web—you just have to figure out how to use the tools they provide.

Finding Online Resources

The two basic types of information-finding tools on the web are search engines and directories; often, both types of tools can be found at the same search site. The search engine tool usually consists of a box that allows you to type in your search request or query. A directory usually looks like a list of categories such as news, health, and business. While often found on the same pages, these two tools operate in vastly different ways.

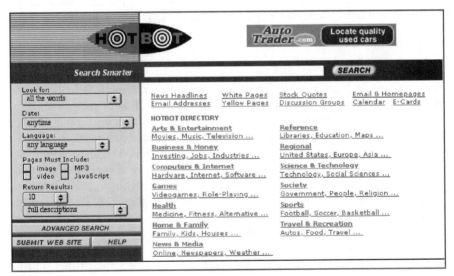

Figure 7   (http://hotbot.lycos.com)

➤ **Exercise in Finding Online Resources:** Look at the image above taken from a popular search engine/directory.

    1. Where is the search engine on this page?
    2. Where is the directory?

Directories and Search Engines

Directories (also called Internet Guides, Indexes, Tables of Contents, etc.) are online categorized lists of other web sites. Companies such as Infoseek, HotBot, and Yahoo employ people who manually index web sites. They examine individual pages, often create short descriptions of what the pages offer, and place the pages into the appropriate categories, along with other valuable sites. For example, the Infoseek directory contains a "Money" category that has sites related to things such as stocks and bonds.

Search engines, on the other hand, find information for you by using automated indexes created by software called "crawlers" or "spiders." Spiders and crawlers are constantly, automatically browsing the WWW and cataloging web pages. Using the full text of web pages, the spiders and crawlers look at the words within the web page to determine how and where the page will be cataloged. It might be helpful to imagine the spiders and crawlers making their own index written in an arachnid language that we can't understand. Their index is so huge (it might encompass up to fifty percent of the entire web) and so complicated that only they can understand it—which is why we must construct very specific queries. When you request specific information through a search engine, the spider or crawler combs through its catalog and presents you with the information it finds based on what you have requested.

A Learning Analogy

Another way to look at the differences between search engines and directories is to think of the WWW as a huge *unsorted* collection of recipes that you received as a gift. When you first moved away from home, your mother thought it would be great to put together a collection of your favorite family recipes. She contacted all your relatives, who then copied recipes on individual cards and sent them back to your mother. The response overwhelmed your mother. There were so many different recipes coming from so many different people that she didn't quite know how to organize them, so all the recipes were just tossed into a great big box and given to you. There were probably thousands of recipes in that great big box, just as there are probably millions of pages on the web.

Though you appreciate all of the recipes, you can't imagine that no one thought to put them into some type of order for you and voice your complaint to your brother. He feels sorry for you and one day starts rummaging through the millions of cards. He tries to make some sense out of things by going through each card and categorizing them. Initially, he creates stacks based on the type of food each recipe makes. He makes stacks of entree recipes, dessert recipes, etc. When recipes don't quite fit into any of the food categories, he puts the cards in people categories: Cousin Terry's recipes in a stack, Uncle Jamar's recipes in a stack, etc. When he can't figure out from whom the recipe came or into what food category a recipe fits, he starts creating stacks based on major ingredients. There are now additional stacks in which the main ingredient is tofu, apples, chocolate, etc.

This is sort of how directory designers create web directories. They sift through the plethora of information on the web and methodically categorize various web sites. While their categories are often more precise than the recipe categories here, the purpose behind the directory is the same—trying to create some type of order out of an incredible amount of unorganized information.

As your brother is categorizing all of these recipes, you notice that Penny, your three-year-old sister, has been watching intently. Penny is pretty precocious, and you begin to realize that if you show her a word or set of words, she will rummage through that big box of recipe cards and emerge with cards which contain those words. You experiment with this a bit and find that while she always finds recipes that contain the words you ask for, you don't always get what you want. She can recognize the words, but she doesn't have the ability to understand what the words mean. For example, when you asked for "rosemary chicken" she retrieved the chicken pot pie recipe your Aunt Rosemary contributed. So, while Penny is precocious, she is unable to read your mind—she can only retrieve what you ask for.

Search engines work more or less in the way precocious Penny works. That is, software "spiders" sort through parts of the web and retrieve pages that contain what you have asked for. Although it is possible to refine your searches on web search engines by asking for information using the strategies discussed later in this chapter, sometimes these types of searches prove to be more fruitful than at other times.

Deciding on a Search Strategy: Directories versus Search Engines

Now that you have a basic understanding of the differences between directories and search engines, you might be wondering when you should use which one in your essay research. The answer lies primarily in how specific your topic is. In general, if your topic is broad (or if you are still searching for a topic), you might start by using a directory. As you click through the various categories, you will gradually narrow the topic.

For example, suppose one day you have a craving for that wonderful turkey meatloaf your friend Carlotta makes. Do you try to find it using the directory (your brother's stacks of cards in various categories) or the search engine (your sweet sister, Penny)? Since you know very specifically what you are looking for, you decide to put Penny to work. You show her the words "turkey meatloaf" and "Carlotta" and turn her loose in the refrigerator box. Soon she emerges from the box with the recipe for "Carlotta's Turkey Meatloaf."

Having located the main course, you rummage through your pantry for something to go with the meatloaf. The only substantial things you find are three wrinkly potatoes. You decide that you will see whether there is a recipe that will help you make something out of these meager ingredients. Since your search will be pretty general, you decide to search through the stacks of cards (the directory). While you don't know exactly what is in each pile of cards, there is a stack of side dish recipes and a stack of recipes in which potatoes are one of the main ingredients. You begin to search through the potato stack and *voila*—there is a recipe for "Grandpa Lawrence's Potato Salad."

As you can see, search engines and directories both have their benefits. If your topic is already very narrow, you will probably have better luck using a search engine to quickly get you to the specific information you need (like Carlotta's meatloaf). If your topic is large or only loosely defined (you need a recipe that uses potatoes), a directory may help you focus more manageably.

Once you learn how to conduct effective queries (which will be discussed in the next section), using a search engine is usually the most efficient way of finding information **if** you know what you are looking for. Keep in mind, though, that by going directly to a specific piece of information, you might miss other related information that could be useful to your research. (Similarly, researchers using the so-called "serendipity method" traditionally have wandered through a general area in the library, looking in book titles and tables of contents for ideas that might spur their thinking or bring them additional sources.)

➤ **Exercise in Deciding on a Search Strategy:** Imagine that you are trying to find information on the following topics. For each, determine whether you would you use a search engine or a directory and briefly explain why.

1. The evolution of the hybrid automobile engine
2. Osteoporosis
3. Today's business news
4. A recipe for pineapple cake
5. The soothing effects of classical music
6. Possible side effects of LASIK eye surgery
7. The topic you are currently exploring for an essay assignment

---

Searches Using a Directory versus Using a Search Engine

Though the previous analogy to recipe cards is a bit far-fetched, it helps to show the vast differences between search engines and directories and the different ways each can be used. It may help to now shift from the highly improbable scenario of a toddler looking for recipes to a very real scenario of a student searching for essay resources.

Using a directory is somewhat like surfing a very narrow segment of the web—sometimes you wander around quite a bit before finding what you want. Although web sites in a directory are categorized (in theory making it easier to find what you want), you can never be sure that the category you would expect a web site to be in is the same category the directory's editors decided upon.

One way to get around the various categories of directories is by conducting your own searches using a search engine. While this may seem to be the most direct way to get to very specific information you want, narrowing your search appropriately can be difficult. If your search is not done properly, you could end up with a screen full of information that has very little to do with what you are searching for. To make this process less complicated, let's look at some examples:

Example 1:

Suppose that you have found some background information on veganism and have decided that you would like to write an essay arguing that if every person in the world would adapt the vegan lifestyle, we could end world hunger.

You decide to try looking up information in the www.altavista.com directory. Your search starts under the "Health" category. From there, you click on "Alternative." At this point, you are uncertain whether to look under "Fitness and Nutrition," "Life Issues" or "Change." You decide to go to "Fitness and Nutrition," and from there, click through to "Nutrition and Healthy Eating," and then to "Food and Nutrition Information Center." However, this page doesn't give you the information you want, so you go back to the "Alternative" category and click to "Change." However, you find nothing there either. This process of dead-end searching goes on for quite some time until you finally realize that you were looking in the wrong place for information. Remember that when you already have a narrow topic, using a search engine is usually the most efficient way of finding specific information.

Example 2:

You are interested in writing a research essay about some aspect of alternative medicine, but are unsure exactly what you want to focus on. Since you really need to get going on this essay, you decide to try finding some information in the www.altavista.com directory.

Your search starts under the "Health" category. From there, you click on "Alternative." There you see what could be an interesting site, "Why Did Laughter Evolve?" You read the article there and find what seems to be some credible information arguing that the person who controls a group's laughter is the most powerful in that group. It also addresses the various benefits of laughter, a subject that you find interesting. Although this is not at all what you had thought of writing about, there might be an argument about medicinal laughter in there.

But, where do you go from here? This is the only article on the topic of medicinal laughter you've found so far, and to make your essay credible, you'll need much more source support. Since you now have a very narrow topic, it looks like it's time to go to a search engine.

As the above examples illustrate, directories and search engines are very different tools. If you use the "wrong" one, your research attempts could dead end. Therefore, the first step in conducting productive WWW research is selecting the right online search tool.

Making a Directory Do What You Want It to Do

As we have previously mentioned, the art of using a directory is much like surfing the Web—you click on the links that you want to visit, and you're taken to that page. Sometimes you find what you're looking for, and sometimes you don't. Since an editor controls the sites in the directory that are available to you (much like the designer of a web site decides what will be linked to an individual page), you are limited by what that person has chosen to include.

Making a Search Engine Do What You Want It to Do

Making a search engine do what you want it to do is much more complicated. The reason for the complication is that you are in charge of asking the search engine for the information you want. The process of creating an appropriate set of directions or query can be a bit tricky because while a good query can get you all of the information you need, *you* must construct that query. An important thing to keep in mind is that all search engines work a little bit differently. Some search engines use only very simple commands like + and − signs. Others allow you to construct very complex searches through which you can request pages with certain domains, such as words that are "near" what you are searching for. These options can be useful, but they can also be incredibly confusing. We suggest that you stick with learning a few basic commands on one search engine and then progress to more complicated search techniques as they become necessary.

Which Search Engine Should You Use?

Ah, good question. There are many differing opinions regarding which search engine is "best." Some are bigger, some are faster, and some are easier to manipulate. While there is a more complete list later in the chapter, the following search engines are especially useful when searching for information for your researched essays:

HotBot	<http://hotbot.lycos.com/>
Infoseek	<http://infoseek.go.com/>
AltaVista	<http://www.altavista.com/>
Yahoo	<http://www.yahoo.com/>

We suggest that you try a few search engines, and when you find one that you're comfortable with, use it. Learn its intricacies so you can construct effective queries. Regardless of which search engine you use, remember that even the largest only covers about fifty percent of the WWW, so you'll never see "everything." However, you'll probably see enough to get the information you need.

BASIC SEARCH TECHNIQUES

(Adapted from <u>www.searchenginewatch.com/facts/math.html</u>)

The key to finding information using a search engine is the same as for finding information using a research database: asking for what you want in the correct way. While many people are comfortable using the Boolean terms previously mentioned (AND, OR, NOT), these terms aren't recognized by all search engines. Likewise, these terms have to be used in the proper order with your keywords or you won't get the results you want. Almost all search engines, however, recognize some simple mathematical symbols that allow you to construct rather complicated queries. If you become adept at asking for specific keywords in combination with the appropriate mathematical symbols, the search engine will most always be able to find what you are looking for.

Be Specific

Remember that the more specific your search is, the more likely you will find what you want. Don't be afraid to tell a search engine exactly what information you are looking for. For example, if you want information about the medicinal benefits of laughter, try a phrase search for exactly that. A search on HotBot using the phrase "medicinal benefits of laughter" yields several relevant sites. You'll be surprised at how often this technique works; however, don't stop here. Phrase searching sometimes works, but you will usually need to refine your query to make it truly effective.

Using the + Symbol to Add

Sometimes you want to make sure that a search engine finds pages that have all the words you enter, not just some of them. The + symbol lets you do this.

The + symbol is especially useful when you do a search and then find yourself overwhelmed with too much information. Imagine that you had begun your search for information on medicinal laughter by simply searching like this:

laughter

If so, chances are that you would probably get many off-target results, including pages of jokes. Because your goal is to find web pages with references to both "laughter" and "medicinal" on the same page, you could search this way:

+medicinal +laughter

Note that if you want all of the pages to contain all of the words, you must include the + symbol before *each* term that must be included. (Remember these terms can appear *anywhere* in the page, not just in the title.) If a term is not preceded by the + symbol, that term will be seen as optional to the search. If all terms are preceded by the + symbol, only pages that contain all the words will appear in your results. Here is another example:

+veganism +world +hunger

This search would find pages that contain all three terms. Such a search would be helpful if you wanted to narrow down a search to pages that mention veganism and world and hunger, rather than on the United Nation's plan to end world hunger.

Using the - Symbol to Subtract

Sometimes you want a search engine to find pages that have one word on them but not another word. The - symbol lets you do this. For instance, if you want pages that deal with veganism, but don't want to be overwhelmed with pages dealing with using animals for clothing, you could search this way:

+veganism -clothing

Searching in this fashion tells the search engine to find pages that mention "veganism" and then to remove any pages that also mention "clothing."

In general, the - symbol is helpful for focusing results when you get too many that are unrelated to your specific topic. Simply begin subtracting terms which are not related to your research, and you should get more directed results.

Using Quotation Marks for Phrase Searches

Now that you know how to add and subtract terms, we can move on to phrase searches. While adding and subtracting terms are effective query tactics, a phrase search can be a much better way to get the specific answers you are looking for. For example, remember above when we wanted pages about medicinal laughter? We entered both terms like this:

+medicinal +laughter

This particular query retrieves web pages that contain both words somewhere, but there's no guarantee that the words may necessarily be in the same phrase or even near each other. You could get a page that mentions laughter in the opening paragraph, but ends up being a promotion for the movie *Patch Adams,* which you don't want. So, while all the words you added together would appear on this page, it still might not be related to what you are looking for.

Doing a phrase search helps avoid this problem. A phrase search lets you tell a search engine to give you only pages where the terms appear together in exactly the order you specify. You do this by putting quotation marks around the phrase, like this:

"medicinal laughter"

When you place quotation marks on both sides of your query term, only pages that have all the words in the exact order shown above will be listed. The answers should be much more on target than with simple addition.

Combining Symbols

Once you've mastered adding, subtracting and phrase searching, you can combine symbols to easily create targeted searches. A very detailed search for our vegan topic might look like this:

+veganism + "world hunger" –clothes

When we ran this query on HotBot, this search yielded fifty-eight relevant web sites.

Getting Even More Specific

If you find that you need to perform even more specific searches, check out your search engine's "Help" feature. There you can find engine-specific instructions on how to best perform complex searches using that specific search engine.

➤ **Exercises in Basic Search Engine Techniques:**

1. Log on to http://www.snap.com. Using the search engine, construct a query to find information on herbal medicine using various combinations of phrase searches, adding and subtracting terms. Note the number and kinds of pages that are found. Now conduct the exact same search using the search engine found at http://www.hotbot.com
   - How do the results of this query differ?
   - What does this tell you about some of the possible differences between these two search engines?
   - From this observation, what can you assume about search engines in general?
   - Conduct the exact same search on at least two more search engines. What do these results tell you?

2. Log on to http://altavista.com and find information on conducting an advanced search using this search engine. Using AltaVista's advanced search techniques, construct a unique query for each of the following issues which would yield very specific results:
   - Information on legislation that limits tobacco advertising
   - Information on gender inequalities in the elementary classroom
   - Information on early release programs for nonviolent criminals
   - Information on Internet addiction in teenagers
   - Information on welfare reform in your state

Directory and Search Engine List

The following is a list of popular search engines and directories. Each is a little bit different, so keep experimenting with different search engines until you find one that works for you.

AltaVista	http://www.altavista.com
Britannica Online	http://www.britannica.com
Ask Jeeves	http://www.askjeeves.com

Direct Hit	http://www.directhit.com
HotSheet	http://www.hotsheet.com
Excite	http://www.excite.com
IWon	http://www.iwon.com
FAST Search	http://www.ussc.alltheweb.com
HotBot	http://hotbot.lycos.com
LookSmart	http://www.looksmart.com
Lycos	http://www.lycos.com
Go / Infoseek	http://www.go.com
GoTo	http://www.goto.com
MSN Search	http://search.msn.com
Google	http://www.google.com
Netscape Search	http://search.netscape.com
Northern Light	http://www.northernlight.com
Open Directory	http://dmoz.org
Snap	http://www.snap.com
Yahoo	http://www.yahoo.com

News Sites

The following is a list of popular sites where you can find the current news. Browsing through news stories can often help spark ideas for essays as well as provide ample source material. Some of these sites focus on different types of news, so keep looking until you find what you're looking for.

ABC News	http://abcnews.go.com
CBS News	http://cbsnews.cbs.com
HotBot News Search / NewsBot	http://www.newsbot.com
CNN Online	http://www.cnn.com
Hotwired	http://www.hotwired.com
MSNBC	http://msnbc.com/news
Excite NewsTracker	http://nt.excite.com
NewsDirectory.com	http://www.ecola.com/news
1stHeadlines	http://www.1stheadlines.com
NewsHub	http://www.newshub.com
NewsTrawler	http://www.newstrawler.com
Fox News	http://www.foxnews.com
Northern Light's Current News	http://www.northernlight.com/news.html
The New York Times on the Web	http://www.nytimes.com
The Washington Post	http://www.washingtonpost.com
Time	http://www.time.com/time
USA Today	http://www.usatoday.com

> Exercise in Finding an Issue:

1. Log on to one of the News Sites above and begin surfing it for a possible topic. Remember that the best topics might not present themselves as argumentative at first. Create a list of five topics that you found interesting that might, indeed, be developed into an issue for your next essay.
2. Pick one of the topics from the list of five. Log on to a different news site above and search for information related to that topic. Print out at least two articles that somehow add information to the topic.
3. After reviewing the two articles you have printed, determine a possible argument that could be made regarding this topic (no matter how unlikely the argument may be at this point). Be prepared to report this possible thesis to your class.
4. Now formulate a very narrow search that will help you find information supporting an argument on this issue. Remember to add, subtract, and use multiple terms to get the best results possible.

FIELD RESEARCH

Thus far, we have concentrated on collecting other people's research; that is, all of the outside information sources mentioned in this chapter have been written by people other than you. While it makes sense to support your own assertions with those of other people, there are times when collecting research yourself also makes sense. For example, you are unlikely to find a published survey on the perceptions of veganism on your campus or a published interview with your family doctor documenting her views on veganism. If these types of information are important to your research, you may have to go out and conduct primary research on your own. This type of field research can help you find answers to the exact questions you are asking as well as bolster your credibility as a researcher. If you do decide to embark on field research, you need to be aware that you assume a great deal of responsibility to protect your subjects. You must always assure that your research causes no harm to those whom you are researching.

Before embarking upon field research, you should also make sure that you are following any specific rules that your institution may have regarding it. For instance, at Bowling Green State University, interviews and questionnaires must be proposed and approved through the Human Subjects Review Board (HSRB) *before* you can proceed. The approval process takes time, so be sure to factor it into your essay's timeline. Check with your instructor to see if your institution has similar regulations.

[The following field research sections—"Observation," "Interviews," and "Questionnaires"—are excerpted by permission from John Trimbur, *The Call to Write*. New York: Longman. 1999. 549-565.]

OBSERVATION

Observation has an important advantage over other research methods: it gives you direct access to people's behaviors. Let's say you've done some background research on how men and women interact in conversations, and you want to test some of the findings in the published literature. Interviewing or surveying wouldn't give you very reliable information because even if people were willing to be honest about how they behave in conversations, it's not likely that they would be accurate. In contrast, by going to the school dining hall over a period of several days, you could observe what men and women, in fact, do when they talk and what conversational patterns emerge.

The Process of Observation

Planning

These questions can help you guide your planning. You can use them to write a proposal that explains the role of observation in your research plan.

- Does the line of research you're pursuing seem to call for observation? What research question or questions are you addressing?
- How, exactly, can observations help you answer your research question?
- What kinds of observations would be most useful? Who and what do you want to observe? What are the best times and places for these observations? How many observations should you do?
- What should your observations focus on? What exactly do you want to record in your field notes? What method or methods will you use to record your observations?

Remember that you may need to request permission to observe, as well as permission to use any recording devices.

Conducting Observations

When you arrive at the place where you'll do your observation, look for a vantage point where you will be able to see what's going on and yet won't be obtrusive. Consider whether you want to move periodically from one spot to another to get a number of different perspectives on the activity or place you're observing. Make sure any equipment you've brought, like a camera or tape recorder, is ready to use.

Researchers typically develop their own system of taking field notes. Nonetheless, a few suggestions may be helpful. Begin writing down the basic facts—the date, time, and place. Keep your notes on one side of the page. Depending on your research questions, here are some things to consider:

- **The setting.** Describe the overall size, shape and layout of the place. You may want to sketch it or draw a diagram. Note details—both what they are and how they are arranged. Pay attention to sounds and smells, as well as what you can see.
- **The people.** Note the number of people. What are they doing? Describe their activities, movement, and behavior. What are they wearing? Note the ages, races, nationalities, and genders of the people. How do they seem to relate to one another? Record overheard conversation in quotation marks.
- **Your response.** As you observe, note anything that is surprising, puzzling, or unusual. Note also your own feelings and reactions, as well as any new ideas or questions that arise.

Analyzing Your Notes

After you've finished your observation, read through your notes carefully and, if you want, type them up, adding related points that you remember. Then make sure you analyze your notes from the standpoint of your research questions:

- What patterns emerge from your notes? What do your main findings seem to be? What, if anything, surprised you?
- What research questions do your notes address? What issues remain to be addressed?
- Do your observations confirm what you have read? How will you explain any discrepancies?
- What should your next step be? Should you go back to the library? Should you conduct further observations? If further observations are needed, what form should they take?

INTERVIEWS

Interviews are often an essential part of capturing the personality and opinions of a person. The types of interviewing you do depend largely on the kind of research question you're raising and the sources it leads you to. Interviews with experts and key participants within your research focus can provide you with up-to-date information and analysis, as well as a deepened understanding of your issue, and can make a significant contribution to a research project. The setting of your interview may vary, depending upon demographic and time constraints. While in-person interviews have some significant advantages over the other types (including more spontaneous discussion and immediate feedback), telephone, mail and e-mail, and online (e.g. IRCs (Internet Relay Chat), MUDs (Multi User Domains), and MOOs (MUD Object Oriented)) interviews can also be viable settings.

The Interview Process

Planning

The following considerations can help you get started in planning interviews.

- **Conducting background research.** The first step, as in any research, is to get an overview and basic information about your topic. At this point, you are likely to be formulating questions to guide your research. Consider how interviewing can help you answer these questions. What do you hope to find out?
- **Choosing interview subjects.** The nature of your research question should suggest appropriate subjects to interview. Does it make sense to interview an expert on the topic? Or does your research seem to call for interviews with a number of people involved with the issue you're investigating? Are the subjects you're considering likely to provide the information you're looking for?
- **Preparing interview questions.** Use the notes from our background research to prepare interview questions. Interviewers normally use open-ended questions to get their subjects talking—phrasing questions in such a way that the natural answer is "yes" or "no" generally leads to a dead end. How open-ended your interview questions are, of course, depends on your research question and your subject. If you are interviewing an expert on your topic, your questions should likely be precise and seek specific information. When you have come up with a list of questions, organize them so that one question leads logically to the next.

Setting Up the Interview

Whether the person you plan to interview is a stranger, a friend, or a relative, you'll need to set up an interview. Generally this means writing a letter or making a phone call, both to ask for permission and to set a time. Introduce yourself and your purpose. Be honest about what you're doing—many busy people are happy to help students with assignments. However, be prepared to be turned down. Sometimes busy people are just that—busy. If someone seems too busy to meet with you in person, try asking whether you could interview him/her by telephone, mail or e-mail—or whether they know someone else you could interview. Above all, be polite. Be sure to schedule the interview far enough in advance of the due date of your research project to allow you to follow up with more questions if necessary or with further research if the interview leads to areas you had not previously considered. And, if it's appropriate, ask the person you're interviewing if there is anything you should read before the interview.

Conducting an In-Person or Telephone Interview

For in-person and telephone interviews, the interview itself is a crucial moment in your research. To get an in-person interview off on the right foot, arrive promptly. Make sure that you dress appropriately and that you bring your questions, tape or video recorder (if you have permission to record the interview), a pad and pens, and any other materials you might need. For telephone interviews, make sure you call at the time agreed upon.

Because in-person and telephone interviews are really conversations, the results you get will depend in part on your flexibility as a listener and a questioner. The person you're interviewing will be looking to you for guidance, and it is quite likely that you'll be faced with choices during the interview. Let's say you are interviewing someone about why she attends your college, and she says, "I came because they've got a really good computer science program, I got a good financial aid package, and I didn't want to go very far from home. You know what I mean?" She then pauses, looking at you for direction. You've got a choice to make about which thread to follow—the student's academic interests, her financial situation, or her desire to stay near home.

After the Interview

Especially with in-person and telephone interviews, plan time immediately afterward to review the results of the interview and to make further notes. Transcribe your tape, if you recorded the interview, or print out hard copies of email or online interviews. Make sure that you have noted direct quotations and that you've written down pertinent information about the interview (such as the time, date, and location).

Analyzing the Transcript

Material from an interview can be used in many different ways in a research project. It can be central to the final report or can provide supplementary quotations and statistics. The ideas you had ahead of time about how you would use the interview might be changed by the interview or by other aspects of your research process. To help you understand what use to make of the interview, write responses to these questions:

- What are the most important things you learned? List what seem to be the main points.
- What, if anything, surprised you? Why?
- What does the interview contribute to your understanding of your research question? How does the information relate to what you've already learned about your topic? If information, opinion, or point of view differ from what you expect, how would you account for this?
- What questions does the interview raise for further research? What sources does it suggest you consult?

A Final Note on Interviews

Make sure you thank the people you interview—a note or email message is a nice touch. And, when you've finished your paper, send them a copy along with a letter or email thanking them again.

> ➤ **Exercise in Interviewing:** Work with a partner. Interview your partner about why he or she decided to attend your college. Before the interview, think about the questions you want to ask, how you want to conduct the interview—in person, by telephone, online, or via email—and how you want to keep track of what's said. Write a paragraph or two about the interview experience. What sorts of questions were the most effective? Did any ideas and topics come up that you had not expected? What decisions did you make during the interview about threads to follow in the conversation? What, if any, were the advantages and disadvantages of the interview setting you chose? What problems, if any, did you experience in recording information?
>
> Compare your response to the interview process with those of classmates. What generalizations can you, as a class, draw about interviewing?

QUESTIONNAIRES

Questionnaires are similar in many ways to interviews, except they obtain responses from a sizable group of people rather than from just a limited number. Questionnaires can also target a particular group of people. For example, questionnaires might be used to find out why students at your college have chosen to major in biomedical engineering, or the reasons employees at a particular company do or don't participate in community service activities. Or questionnaires can survey the beliefs and opinions of the "general public," as is the case with those conducted by political pollsters and market researchers on everything from people's sexual habits to their religious beliefs to their product preferences.

While interview questions are generally open-ended, questionnaires tend to use multiple-choice, yes/no, and other "closed" sorts of questions. In a sense, they sacrifice the depth of an interview for the breadth of data provided by a survey.

Deciding whether you should design and distribute a questionnaire depends largely on what you're trying to find out. If, for example, you've read some research on the television viewing habits of college students and want to find out if students at your school fit the patterns described, it makes sense to survey students about their habits rather than interview three or four students. The multiple results you get are liable to give you a more accurate picture.

The Process of Designing and Conducting a Survey

If a questionnaire seems appropriate to your research project, you'll need to decide whom you will survey, prepare a questionnaire, conduct your survey, and then compile and analyze the results.

Getting Background Information

The process for designing a survey is similar in certain respects to designing interviews. Namely, you'll begin by researching your topic to get an overview and background information. Then you'll need to determine whether a survey is the most appropriate method to address your research question. Does it make sense to gather information on the opinions and habits of a number of people instead of talking to a few in depth or doing other forms of research? At this point, before you expend the time and effort it takes to design and conduct a survey, make sure that a questionnaire is likely to provide you with the information you're seeking.

Selecting Participants

To be sure that they can generalize from the results of their surveys, professional researchers try to obtain responses from a sample of people that is representative of the population they're investigating. If, for example, you're surveying students who major in bioengineering or employees of a particular company, it should be easy enough to send questionnaires to these specific groups. In other cases, however, you may need to choose people within the population at random for inclusion in the survey.

If your results are to be meaningful, you'll also need to include enough participants in your survey to give it credibility. Keep in mind that, regardless of how you conduct your survey, not everyone will participate. In fact, as pollsters are well aware, it's generally necessary to survey many more people than you can expect to receive responses from. Often as few as ten percent of the questionnaires mailed out will be returned. A good rule of thumb is to aim for forty percent and, if you don't get many responses the first time, to do multiple distributions.

When you write up your findings, any generalizations based on your survey should be limited to the population that survey was representative of. You could not, for example, make generalizations about American voters as a whole based on a survey of students at your college. Be sure that you discuss any potentially relevant information on survey participants, such as information on age, gender, occupation, and so on.

Designing the Questionnaire

The results of your survey will depend to a large extent on your questionnaire. There are some considerations to take into account in designing a questionnaire:

- Include a short introduction that explains the purpose of the survey and what you will do with the results. Point out that survey participants' opinions are important. Ask survey participants to complete the survey and give an estimate of the time it will take.
- Make sure the questions you ask focus on the information you need for your research. There is a temptation in designing a questionnaire to ask all sorts of things you're curious about. The results can be interesting, to be sure, but asking more questions than you actually need can reduce your response rate. In general, keep the survey brief in order to maximize returns.
- Design the questionnaire so it is easy to read. Make the visual design suggest to the participants that it won't take long to fill out. Don't crowd

questions together to savespace. And leave plenty of space for open questions, reminding survey respondents that they can write on the back.

- At the end of the survey, write a thank-you and explain where or to whom the survey should be returned.

Types of Questions

Questions can take the form of checklists, yes/no questions, multiple-choice questions, ranking scales, and open questions. Each type works somewhat differently. Usually you will want to combine the types of questions to give you the particular information you need. You will also need to consider the most effective and logical order to present the questions on the survey. Surveys typically begin with the least complicated or most general questions in the beginning and open-ended questions at the end.

Here are examples of the most common types of questions designed for a research project investigating whether the political attitudes and involvement of students at the researcher's college supported or refuted claims in published literature that students today are generally apathetic when it comes to politics.

Checklist

Which of these political activities have you participated in? Please check all that apply.

_____ voted in national election
_____ voted in state or local election
_____ campaigned for candidate
_____ worked for a political party
_____ attended a political rally or demonstration
_____ belonged to a political organization or advocacy group
_____ other (specify):

Yes/No Questions

Are you a registered voter?

_____ Yes
_____ No

Multiple-Choice Questions

How would you describe your political views?

_____ left-wing
_____ liberal
_____ moderate
_____ conservative

_____ right-wing
_____ none of the above/don't know

Ranking Scales

Please rank the following items according to their importance as national priorities. (Use 1 to indicate the highest priority; 7 for the lowest.)

_____ strengthening the economy
_____ reducing crime
_____ balancing the budget
_____ improving education
_____ improving the health care system
_____ improving race relations
_____ reducing poverty

Likert Scale

Likert scale questionnaire items gauge the degree of agreement with particular statements of opinion. Researchers typically design a sequence of such items.

Please indicate the degree to which you agree or disagree with the following statements. Enter the number that best expresses your view on each item.

1—Strongly agree
2—Agree
3—Not Sure
4—Disagree
5—Strongly Disagree

_____ It is important to be well-informed about current political events.
_____ There's no point in getting involved in politics because individuals can have little influence.
_____ Voting in elections is a responsibility, not just a right.
_____ The political system is controlled by politicians and lobbyists.

Open Questions

Open questions call for brief responses. Such questions are more time-consuming and difficult to tabulate than closed questions, but they can often yield information that other types of questions will not.

What, if anything, has motivated you to be interested in political affairs?

_____
_____
_____

What, if anything, has posed obstacles to your being interested in political affairs?

_____

_____

_____

Conducting the Survey

Your questionnaire can be distributed in various ways—in person, by mail, by telephone, or online through listservs, newsgroups, or Web sites. Your choice of how to conduct the survey will depend on your choice of a sample population, on your deadline, and on your resources (mail surveys, for example, can be quite expensive because you'll need to provide stamped, self-addressed envelopes).

Compiling, Analyzing, and Presenting Results

Compiling results amounts to tallying up the answers to each question. This is a fairly straightforward procedure for closed questions such as checklist, yes/no, multiple-choice, ranking, and Likert scale items. For open questions, you might write down key words or phrases that emerge in the responses and tally number of times these (or similar) words or phrases occur. Keep a list of answers that seem of special interest to use in your research report as quotations.

Researchers present the results of closed questions as percentages in the text of their reports. In addition, you may want to design tables, charts, graphs, or other visual displays of your results to complement the written report.

Remember that your results do not speak for themselves. You need to analyze and explain their significance to your research project. The following questions can help you begin such an analysis:

- What patterns emerge from responses to individual questions? What patterns emerge from responses across questions?
- How would you explain these patterns? Try to think of two or more explanations, even if they appear to be contradictory or mutually exclusive.
- What is the significance of these explanations for your research? If the explanations seem contradictory, can you think of ways to reconcile them? If not, on what grounds would you choose one over the other?
- What tentative claims might you make based on your analysis of the results? How would you justify such claims?

➤ **Exercise in Generating and Evaluating Questionnaires:** Work together in a group of three or four. Your task is to design a pilot questionnaire that surveys student opinion about some aspect of the academic program or student services at your college. You could focus on, say, orientation for new students, required first-year courses, tutoring, or something else that interests you. Begin by listing the kind of information that you want to get from the survey. Then write five to ten questions that seem likely to give you this information. Test your questionnaire by administering it to ten to fifteen classmates. Once you've gotten their responses, evaluate your questionnaire:

• Did you get the information you were looking for?
• Is each question worded in such a way that it provides the information you anticipated?
• Should you word any of the questions differently to obtain the information you're seeking? Should you delete any of the questions or add new ones? Explain your answers.
• Compare your group's experience to that of other groups. What conclusions can you make about questionnaire design?

➤ **Exercises in Conducting Field Research:** Work together in a group of three or four.

1. One by one, share your essay issues with each other. Discuss the types of evidence each person will need to gather in order to construct a convincing argument.
2. Together, determine what types of field research might be most beneficial for each person's issue and who might be interviewed and/or surveyed.
3. Individually, develop a plan and timeline for conducting this research. Factor in the time it may take for your research apparatus to be approved (if necessary), timeline for distributing, collecting, and tabulating results, timeline for interpreting data, etc.
4. Individually, write the questions you would like to ask your research subjects.
5. Together, review each person's questions and discuss changes that might be made, questions that might be added/deleted, etc.

5   Argumentation and Synthesis

THE ELEMENTS OF ARGUMENT

When some people hear the word "argument," they think of a heated exchange, an emotionally charged disagreement such as the following:

> *Louisa:* It's perfectly obvious that we need a woman for the job. Our department has hired only men for the last twenty years.
>
> *Nick:* Women can't do a job like this. They have to be able to think clearly, without getting emotional. Hire a woman? That's a joke!
>
> *Louisa:* You know, that's really a sexist remark! How can you say such a thing to me?
>
> *Nick:* Look, let's get serious here. Everyone knows that women can't compare to men when it comes to keeping their heads. Any woman who took this job would be an emotional basket case in two weeks.
>
> *Louisa:* Did anyone ever tell you what a jerk you are? Well, if not, let me be the first!
>
> *Nick:* You're just mad because you can't face the truth about your own sex! Typical female reaction!

The above dialogue is the sort of exchange we often associate with the word "argument," and indeed, we do use the word in everyday speech to refer to this kind of angry discussion. However, when the term "argument" is used in reference to a researched paper, it means an essay that develops a reasoned position—a thesis statement or claim that aims to convince the reader that its ideas are true, or at least worth considering. The word "argument" in this context implies that reasons will be used logically to support a main point. We use arguments when we write about the important issues of our culture in order to make decisions, to explain and analyze situations, to predict potential consequences, to convince readers of our positions, or to propose solutions.

Some people think of argument as a specific genre of writing, but in actuality, most writing may be considered a form of persuasion in that writers usually try to convince their readers of something. Whenever you write for someone other than yourself, which is most of the time, you want your reader to feel that what you have to say is important and worth reading, which takes at least some persuasion. But to have even more of an effect on a reader—to persuade your readers to adopt your point-of-view on a controversial issue or to at least re-consider their objections to your viewpoint—you need to be able to build thesis-driven arguments backed by sound evidence. Even a common opinion such as "My roommate is difficult to live with" can be considered an argument; however, in order to convince the housing staff to relocate either you or your roommate to another dorm room, you would have to prove your claim by citing evidence (he blasts his radio during inappropriate hours, leaves dirty dishes around the room, has a terrible temper, etc.). You would also have to establish that you are a believable person whose word is reliable, that you don't complain about every roommate you have, and that you don't exaggerate or falsify information.

Thus, without the skills of being able to assert a **thesis** and back it up with solid **evidence,** it is unlikely that you will be able to convince others of your viewpoints.

The first half of this chapter, then, focuses on the important characteristics of a successful argument (the second half focuses on argument *synthesis*). In particular, you will learn the following about argumentative writing:

1. To understand the role of reason and logic in building convincing argumentation.
2. To become aware of three approaches to argument as presented in the writings of Aristotle, Stephen Toulmin, and Carl Rogers.
3. To develop convincing arguments by knowing how to effectively analyze your audience's expectations, consider all sides of a debatable issue, and use evidence in support of your position.

THE PURPOSE OF ARGUMENTATIVE WRITING

The importance of effective argumentation has been evident since ancient Greece and Rome, where persuasion was first seen as the art of promoting a speaker's ideas in a way that engaged listeners and activated support. Being able to convince others demanded communication skills that few had mastered at that time; thus, persuasive skill was often used as a means of eliciting power. While oratory persuasion was first heralded by ancient rhetoricians (those who specialized in the study of using language effectively and persuasively), especially in the political arena, the writings of Aristotle, Cicero, and Quintilian carried the importance of effective argumentation on to written discourse as well.

Today, scholars still use the theories and strategies offered by these ancient rhetoricians to create and promote complex written arguments in researched essays. However, while the importance of persuasion still reigns, the purpose behind arguing has changed. The purpose of argumentation has shifted from the quest of power to the quest for new inquiries, where new understandings, new "truths" (ideas that a given community can agree upon and accept as true or factual), and new perspectives are valorized as a means for learning—a means of participating in our society's intellectual forum. Additionally, in order to generate new inquiry, writers must learn more about their own values and "truths," which often change and mature over time. Hence, as Linda McMeniman so eloquently sums it up in her 1999 text *From Inquiry to Argument,* "Argument, then, is an honorable and productive activity that seasons our own perspective and makes a reasonable contribution to our society" (8).

A common college or university assignment, the argumentative researched essay requires you to read widely on and think critically about an important and controversial issue, formulate your own unique position on that issue, and present your position in such a way that your readers will take your views seriously. In fact, many college instructors assign such essays specifically to assess critical reading and thinking skills. Now that you better understand the purpose of argumentative writing, the rest of this chapter will focus on helping you to write persuasive prose effectively, so that you can complete researched essay assignments with confidence.

Understanding Key Terms and Concepts Related to Researched Writing

The first step in grasping argumentative strategies is to learn the terminology involved in the process of building persuasive positions on controversial issues. Once you have researched and read widely on any given issue, you will need to formulate your **thesis** on the controversy, also called a **main or central argument, position,** or **proposition.** A thesis clarifies your position on an issue by investigating, explaining, and/or proposing problems, causes, and solutions. An argumentative thesis also can promote a value, something you consider important or good for our society. In order for your thesis to be persuasive, you will need to back it up with **supporting arguments,** also known as **reasons** or **points,** that help further your position. When attempting to convince your audience of your supporting arguments, you will need to use **evidence,** or **backing,** obtained from a variety of sources—from your own experience, from what is regarded as "truth" within a given community, and from facts, statistics, authorities, and case studies. Such evidence can be found in published materials of all kinds, and it also can be generated through field research. Remember, though, the goal of writing a documented, argumentative essay when presenting your evidence. As stated in Chapter 1, this goal is not simply to show how much information you have found. The evidence should be used purposefully to convince your reader of your own thesis and supporting arguments.

It is also important to understand that most of the issues explored in researched papers are concerned with **conflicts in values,** that is, a variety of differing and complex opinions on what people feel is important or best for society. Unlike the issue of whether or not one's roommate is too difficult to live with, issues concerned with conflicts in values usually do not boil down to a simple pro versus con argument. Most of the time, *all* sides have some merit (which is why issues are considered controversial). Additionally, a pro versus con or "all or nothing" mind-set can lead writers to oversimplify complex controversial issues and to overlook possibly more thoughtful arguments that discuss some negotiation or compromises between viewpoints. Furthermore, issues concerned with conflicts in values usually cannot be easily supported by simple physical facts. Writing an argument about a complex social or political issue involves considerable thinking and substantial support; thus, for your position to be convincing, you most likely will have to use outside sources to explore background material, define terms, or establish criteria or standards for analysis.

Furthermore, because all sides of a controversy usually have at least some merit, your readers will expect you to anticipate and address their concerns with your thesis. Doing so will show your readers that you have considered all sides of the controversy before coming to your own conclusions on the issue. Remember that establishing credibility with your readers is essential to persuading them.

However, even if you do not fully sway those readers who strongly oppose your position, you will gain their respect by acknowledging their **opposing arguments,** also known as **counterarguments.** It's important to note that you cannot just mention that you are aware of potential counterarguments; you must also address their concerns by *refuting* them, by *accommodating* them, or by *compromising,* in a **rebuttal** aimed at convincing the opposition to see your side of the issue. When *refuting* a counterargument, you argue that, while others have a certain concern with your thesis or a supporting argument, you have evidence that either proves or suggests the contrary. When *accommodating* an opposing argument, your rebuttal will be focused first upon making concessions, or agreeing that the opposition has a valid concern, and then upon arguing that while the opposition has a reasonable issue with your thesis, you think that your position is still more logical, more convincing, more sensible, less costly, more effective, etc. Finally, in a *compromising* approach to a potential counterargument, your rebuttal would suggest a view or proposal somewhere between your position and an alternative position. An instance of argumentative compromise might consist of admitting that your ideal solution to a problem is not likely to be enacted and calling, therefore, for a reduced measure with better chance for acceptance.

Now that you have been introduced to the basic terminology involved in writing a thesis-driven, argumentative essay, let's take a closer look at the strategies involved in using these concepts.

FINDING A POSITION

Beginning with a Topic

As introduced in Chapter 3, "Selecting Issues," you can sometimes initiate your search for an essay beginning by exploring issues that matter to you personally. Many times, you can discover an important societal issue by looking at your personal or familial situation, since problems that concern you or a family member might easily concern persons outside your family. The heated dialogue at the beginning of this chapter, for example, involved two people arguing about whether a woman ought to be hired for a particular job at a particular firm. They also argued about the stereotypical view of women as emotionally unstable. Although the argument concerned specific persons and a specific situation, the issues of giving women equal standing in hiring practices and the effects of unflattering female stereotypes are of importance to everyone. That "argument" was really concerned with the broader issues of women's positions in society, gender discrimination in the workplace, and the related issues of affirmative action and equal opportunity.

Controversy and the Concept of Audience

When you think about a "target" audience for a researched paper, you might become somewhat confused. An argumentative paper should be based on a controversial issue, something that divides your readers. However, suppose you were a member of a club aimed at halting the use of animals for medical research, and you decided to write a paper arguing this same position. If members of that club read your paper, they would all agree with you. So, does that mean that this issue is not a suitable one for a researched paper?

This is a complicated question, but perhaps the most plausible answer can be found by examining the controversy in relation to all affected communities.

As in the above scenario, writing to your club members on a position that everyone agreed with and supporting that position with information everyone already knew would only lead the members to all nod their heads, but they would not have learned anything or changed their minds about the issue. Thus, the more suitable question to ask when determining the validity of an issue for a given audience is: can I persuade this audience on this issue? If the answer is no (as in the case of the club mentioned above, since there would be no controversy on the stated issue within that given community), the next step is to either: 1) keep the same audience and present some new information or a new perspective on the issue so that they learn something; or 2) reevaluate your choice in audience so you can persuade readers from opposing viewpoints to consider your position.

For example, instead of trying to convince your club of something they already believe in—to join together to halt the use of animals for medical testing—you could try to promote a vegan lifestyle within your club that respects animal quality of life issues, but takes that respect even further into diet and clothing choices. Conversely, you might want to stay focused upon putting a halt to medical research on animals, so you could alter your audience (and purpose) choice to instead target those who support animal testing, those who might be able to fund your club's cause, or those you may be able to convince to become future members of your club.

No matter which route you take, you should select an issue that generates controversy within a given community or communities in our society. If it is unlikely that you will change your readers' minds, then you might consider showing them a new way to think about the issue, presenting a perspective based upon newly available evidence, or changing your audience and purpose to allow a chance for significant impact on your readers.

Transforming a Statement into an Issue

Sometimes, even a general statement with which everyone seems to agree can be transformed into an issue by using a qualifying statement and a careful definition. For example, think about the following statement:

> Nuclear weapons are evil.

Upon first reading it, most people would probably agree with this statement. They recall the horrors of nuclear explosions, the ghastly, deformed victims of Hiroshima, and the possibility of world destruction. This statement, though, could be turned into a controversial issue if it were phrased as follows:

> Although most people regard nuclear weapons as simply "evil," some people argue that they have served as a deterrent to another world war. Therefore, due to their role in preventing world war, nuclear weapons should not be considered entirely evil.

Notice that the "although" part of the statement refers to what people generally think about this issue, while the thesis consists of an arguable statement with which some people will disagree. Many arguments begin with an "although" clause, which presents the current situation, the ideas that are generally believed, or the situation that presently exists. Using an "although" clause helps you focus your argument so that you do not write about something that everyone already believes and, at the same time, shows readers that you have considered alternative, or opposing, viewpoints before asserting your thesis. The "although" clause presents the position that people generally think of nuclear weapons as bad; nevertheless, some people (including the writer in this case) argue that there is something that might be considered good about them since they seem to have served as a deterrent to additional world wars.

➤ **Exercise in Considering Multiple Audiences:** For each of the following controversial issues, independently generate a list of all potential audiences who might be interested in, involved with, or able do something about the issue at hand. Who might be concerned with the following issues?

1. Ritalin as the most common treatment for ADD and ADHD
2. Using SAT and ACT scores as a measure of future academic success in college
3. The portrayal of women in the media
4. The downloading of MP3s off the Internet
5. Police brutality
6. Internet censorship

Next, in small groups, discuss, combine, and condense your audience lists for each; then, try to come to an agreement on the best audience to target for each issue. Be prepared to defend your group's choice in a class discussion.

Establishing Common Ground Between Writer and Reader

In order for a thesis or claim to convince an audience, the writer and the audience must share values, principles or beliefs that can serve as a bridge between them. Additionally, those writers who are successful in bridging differing viewpoints on any given controversial issue are able to show their readers that they are educated on all sides of the debate. For example, a university student who works out frequently in the gym might write a letter to the editor of the school newspaper arguing that working out five times a week is the best way to prevent students from gaining the "freshman fifteen" and to help students maintain a healthy lifestyle. He might point out that students should take advantage of the student recreation center because it is free to all students and offers weight training, cardiovascular training, and a variety of other recreational sports, such as racquetball, archery, and wallyball. He might also suggest that working out five times a week doesn't take as much time as many might believe, since just 20 minutes of aerobic exercise is enough—which is less time than most spend watching a favorite TV sitcom.

By making the above points, the student writer bridges differences of opinions his readers (fellow college students) may have. He does this by choosing to write about an issue of concern to most students; by making the issue seem to concern any who are committed to healthy living; and by appealing to those who may be concerned with monetary issues, the potential monotony of exercise, and time constraints.

> ➤ **Exercise in Bridging Differences of Opinions:** For each audience and situation cited below, work in small groups to decide how awareness of common values could be used to bridge differences of opinion and create a convincing argument. Collaboratively write a short persuasive paragraph for each.
>
> 1. *Audience:* Your economics professor.
>   *Situation:* You want an extension on a researched paper.
> 2. *Audience:* A high-school principal.
>   *Situation:* You want students to have a chance for input in meetings concerned with establishing a new computer lab.
> 3. *Audience:* Parents of teenagers at a local high school.
>   *Situation:* You want parents to fund a party for students at the beginning of the year.

THE ROLE OF REASON AND LOGIC

No matter which audience you choose to target when writing any given essay, you must note that any college researched paper is written for a rational audience, people who base their decisions on reason and logic, not on prejudice or mood. Similarly, if a political candidate tells you he or she is the best person for the job, you will expect that person to support that claim with convincing reasons (e.g., he or she has had plenty of experience in similar work, has an excellent record, or plans to work hard). You would not expect that person to say, "Vote for me because I wear terrific-looking suits, or because I have a cool haircut." Rational audiences expect reason in the arguments in order to find them convincing.

The most common types of reasoning used to convince readers are *inductive* and *deductive* reasoning. Although both strategies are discussed in more detail later in the chapter, here is a brief distinction between the two: The inductive essay is reasoned by starting with a particular situation and moving on to making a generalization based upon that situation. Induction is based upon inference, in which the writer essentially claims that what is true of one instance can be held to be true in other similar instance, or that examining the evidence of a specific situation can lead to a general assertion or conclusion about an issue or circumstance.

Conversely, the deductive essay is reasoned by starting with a generalization and moving on to make an assertion about a particular situation. Deduction is based upon deducing, in which the writer essentially claims that a rule, classification, or definition held to be true for any given general group, class, or category can also be applied to specific situations, or that examining the general rules surrounding an issue can lead to a similar conclusion about a specific facet of that issue. While the choice of reasoning is left completely up to the writer, most writers find that one kind may work better than the other depending upon the issue, their goals, or their targeted audience. Sometimes, too, writers decide that one type of reasoning works best with their individual writing style. Still others believe that a mix of the two is most effective.

Therefore, it is important for college writers to understand how reason works in an argument. Not only does the argumentative thesis have to be reasonable in order to engage a rational audience, but the writer must also present a progression of logical reasons that support the thesis in order to convince readers that the main argument is valid. Because reason and logic are essential in persuasive prose, writers often look to models that provide strategies for appealing to readers through the use of reason and logic. The discussion that follows will examine three approaches to reason as explained by Aristotle, Stephen Toulmin, and Carl Rogers.

ARISTOTLE'S APPROACH TO REASON

In his *Rhetoric*, the Greek philosopher Aristotle defined three ways a writer or speaker can appeal to an audience: through *ethos* (Greek for "character"), which refers to the trustworthiness or credibility of the writer or speaker; through *pathos* (Greek for "emotion"), which refers to the emotional appeal of an argument; and through *logos* (Greek for "word"), which refers to the logical appeal of an argument—in particular, the quality of the reasoning and supporting evidence. Ethos, pathos, and logos are all important, but logos or reason is particularly so, since no rational audience can be convinced by an argument that is not reasonable.

Deductive Reasoning: The Syllogism and Enthymeme

Deductive reasoning is based on the principle that a conclusion about a specific situation may legitimately be drawn from previously accepted truths for the category under which that situation falls. The following exchange is an example of deductive reasoning, otherwise known as reasoning from generalities to particulars:

> Maria: I heard on ESPN the other night that all basketball players could stand to work on their free-throwing.
> Anna: But what about Jeff Hornacek and John Stockton, who play for the Utah Jazz? They represent some of the best free-throwers in the NBA.
> Maria: Since they said that all players could stand more practice at this skill, that includes Hornacek and Stockton.

In this exchange, Maria's conclusion that even Hornacek and Stockton need to continue practicing their free-throws was reached deductively because it was based upon the rule that all basketball players could stand to work on their free-throwing skills. Thus, deduction provides a structure for reasoning, one that can be best seen in a syllogism.

Recognizing the importance of connecting the thesis, its support, and its underlying assumptions, Aristotle created a three-part structure called a **syllogism,** which consists of three statements: a *major premise*, a fundamental truth, belief, or value; a *minor premise*, a particular example of the major premise; and a *conclusion*, a statement which uses the information in the two premises to assert that what is true of the major premise is also true of the minor premise. A famous syllogism is the following:

> All people are mortal (major premise).
> Ricardo is a person (minor premise).
> Therefore, Ricardo is mortal (conclusion).

The above syllogism is both valid and true because both the major and the minor premises are true. However, note that the following syllogism is valid, but not true:

> All students like rock music (major premise).
> Jonathan is a student (minor premise).
> Therefore, Jonathan likes rock music (conclusion).

The major premise, "All students like rock music," is not true; although many students may like rock music, not all of them do. Therefore, although the syllogism is valid in that it fulfills the proper form for a syllogism (as illustrated above), it cannot be considered true.

Here is a paragraph taken from Elisa's paper from earlier in this book that uses deductive reasoning:

> The First Amendment to the United States Bill of Rights states that "Congress shall make no law respecting an establishment of religion or prohibiting the free exercise thereof, or abridging the freedom of speech." That amendment, fundamental to the concept of a free society, may be regarded as a guarantee against censorship, implying that citizens of the United States have the liberty of reading anything they choose. By censoring what students are able to read, the proposed screening committee would deprive students of their rights as citizens.

Here is the deductive or syllogistic pattern of Elisa's paragraph:

> Censorship is forbidden under the Bill of Rights (major premise).
> The screening committee is a form of censorship (minor premise).
> Therefore, the screening committee would be forbidden under the Bill of Rights (conclusion).

Elisa's pattern of deduction is valid and logical because her major premise, minor premise, and conclusion all are logically connected. Whether we agree that her conclusion is *true*, however, as in the example of Jonathan and rock music, depends upon our positions on at least two issues: whether local school boards may enact regulations where Congress may not, and whether the screening of books for minor students is in fact "abridging the freedom of speech." These possibilities for alternative interpretations, of course, are what make Elisa's issue controversial.

It's important to note, too, that while syllogisms can help provide the framework for your reasoning, they should not appear in this form within your argumentative essay. Instead, you can use them as a starting point to ensure that your reasoning is both valid and true; then, once you are sure of your reasoning, you can translate your reasoning into formal, written argumentative discourse.

The Enthymeme

The **enthymeme** is an abbreviated version of a syllogism which leaves the major premise unstated and uses a "because" clause. An enthymeme may be defined as an incomplete logical statement that is based on the acceptance of the unstated major premise and will not be valid without it. Here is an example of how a syllogism may be stated as an enthymeme:

Ricardo is mortal because he is a person.

This claim is both valid and true because all rational people accept the major premise or underlying assumption that "All people are mortal."

The syllogism and enthymeme are based on the idea that there are truths that all reasonable people will accept, such as the principle that all people are mortal. However, as the world has become more complicated and as many different cultures interact, we have come to realize that there are many so-called "basic" principles that some people believe in but others do not. Some people might believe that it is important for all people to work hard; others might feel that working hard is a waste of energy. Some people think that marital fidelity is important, yet others might disagree. Therefore, for the essays you write in college, it is important to understand that absolute principles are very few; thus, you must anticipate potential questions and objections from your audience. For example, Elisa's paper is based on the following enthymeme:

The screening committee would be forbidden under the Bill of Rights because it is a form of censorship.

As discussed above, some people may feel that Elisa's reasoning is both valid and true, but others might question it. They might say that the censorship forbidden in the Bill of Rights pertains to adults, not to children under the age of eighteen, and a school has the right to protect its children. Others might say that the censorship forbidden under the Bill of Rights does not include any form of speech that might cause harm to a particular group, such as pornographic materials. In this example, the major premise, "Censorship is forbidden under the Bill of Rights," would not be as absolutely accepted as the premise "All people are mortal."

Understanding that most major premises are not absolute will help you anticipate the objections of your audience. Elisa might make a more convincing case in her argument against the screening committee if she realized that some people might not view the committee as a form of censorship, and others might feel that censorship is permissible for children under the age of eighteen. By showing that such a committee would actually be a form of censorship, through demonstrating that one form of censorship can easily lead to another, or by making the case that high school students need to be treated like adults, Elisa may be able to establish common ground between her opinions (or values) and those of her audience.

➤ **Exercise in Establishing a Common Ground Between Writer and Audience:** For each audience and debatable issue cited below, work in small groups to decide how awareness of common values shared by each potential audience could be used to write a convincing argument. Take notes on your discussion and be prepared to discuss your decisions with the class.

1. *Audience:* Parents.
   Situation: You want all parents to decide, for the sake of their children's development, that one of them needs to stay at home until their children are at least of school age.
2. *Audience:* People in abusive relationships.
   Situation: You want all people in abusive (verbal, emotional, and/or physical) relationships to get out of these relationships regardless of the circumstances.
3. *Audience:* Parents of teenagers and the administration at a local high school.
   Situation: You want the parents and administration to agree to the distribution of birth control devices at school.

➤ **Exercise in Understanding Syllogisms and Enthymemes:** For each of the following enthymemes, work in small groups to identify the unstated major premise. Then rewrite each enthymeme as a syllogism. Finally, discuss the accuracy or truth of these assumptions.

1. Sophie would not be a good tour guide because she is easily annoyed.
2. Mrs. Smith is a terrific speaker because she uses lively examples.
3. *Misery* is a great movie because it kept me on the edge of my seat.

4. The multicultural movement is a threat to national strength because it emphasizes differences between groups instead of similarities.
5. The women's movement has threatened the stability of the family because it takes women out of the home.
6. Participation in sports is good for kids because it teaches them team spirit.
7. Alphonse is not a good teacher because he has no patience.
8. You should buy this hair product because it will make your hair look shinier.

Inductive Reasoning

Inductive reasoning is based on the principle that a conclusion may legitimately be drawn from incomplete evidence—in fact, since it is impossible for everyone to have experienced *everything*, this is a very common form of reasoning that we use all the time. The following exchange is an example of inductive reasoning, otherwise known as reasoning from particulars to generalities:

> *Maria:* I'm going over to Smith's market to pick up some fresh fruit for lunch.
>
> *Anna:* Oh, don't go to Smith's. I've gone there four times this week, and every time, they were out of really fresh fruit. All they had left were some wormy-looking apples.

In this exchange, Anna's conclusion that Smith's is not a good store for fresh fruit was reached inductively because it was based on several visits, although not on visits occurring every day. But because Anna feels that her four visits provide sufficient evidence for her conclusion, she cautions Maria against going there.

Most of the information we have about everyday life we have obtained through induction. Although we have not seen every alligator in the world, the few we have seen, either live or in pictures or films, have lived in wetlands. Therefore, we believe that alligators live in wetlands. Similarly, we believe that all cats meow and birds sing, although surely we have not seen every cat or bird ourselves.

In order to evaluate a conclusion reached by induction, you have to feel that your sample provides an adequate, representative sample. (This, of course, also pertains to statistics that are derived inductively.) If you say, "All women doctors are incompetent. Let me tell you about this awful woman doctor I went to," you are basing a conclusion on an inadequate sample (only one woman doctor). Additionally, if you ask people to fill out a questionnaire relating to a campus issue but distribute it only to a small segment of the affected population, any conclusions you might base on the responses might be invalidated by non-representativeness of your sample.

Many scientific conclusions are reached inductively through controlled experiments under laboratory conditions. In fact, the relationship between smoking and lung diseases was reached in this way. But unlike Anna, who based her conclusion on only four visits (and, after all, maybe Smith's was out of fresh fruit only during those visits), the scientists who conducted the experiments concerning the relationship between smoking and lung disease used thousands of subjects and repeated the study many times to ensure that the conclusions were valid. When we use inductive reasoning to reach a conclusion, we have to be careful that our experience has really been adequate (sufficient examples or cases to make a reasonably accurate prediction for a general population) and representative (adequately sampling all significant categories or "demographics"). Many unfair stereotypes are formulated because people generalize hastily from very limited experience. Most importantly, using generalizations in your own writing will not convince rational audiences; they will only hinder your credibility with your readers.

➤ **Exercise in Thinking about Induction and Deduction:** Independently examine the following statements and decide whether they are based on inductive or deductive reasoning. Then decide whether these statements are well-reasoned. Afterwards, discuss your observations in small groups:

1. Jewel is one of our most reliable and careful employees. In fact, since he joined the firm five years ago, he has never made a mistake on the job. Because he has made numerous mistakes this week, I think he may be sick or having personal problems.
2. People who are interested in lizards usually like other reptiles as well. Ricardo has a large lizard collection, so I think he will also like this iguana.
3. Students who have completed the program in geography at UCLA usually have excellent training in statistics. Josephine is a graduate of that program, so it is likely that her statistical skills are excellent.
4. Dutch students are required to study many European languages. Frans is Dutch, so he probably speaks German and French.
5. Louisa is very athletic and works out at the gym every day, so she will probably be able to learn to roller blade very easily.
6. Clifton is very interested in basketball, so if you wish to sell him that TV, display the television set when a game is on.

THE TOULMIN SYSTEM

The British philosopher Stephen Toulmin has developed an informal system of logic that takes into consideration the reaction of a potentially skeptical or hostile audience. Toulmin's system presumes that an audience might begin by opposing the writer's claim; such an audience might pose many questions and objections before accepting it. This acceptance, Toulmin feels, can occur only if the writer first establishes common ground with the reader and gains the reader's trust. Whereas formal logic is based on the structure of the syllogism and presumes that the first premise is one that all will accept, Toulmin's system admits that most major premises are not absolute, certainly not as absolute as the premise that "all people are mortal." Toulmin, therefore, feels that it is necessary to include another term, the "backing," which, as its name suggests, provides support for the major premise in an argument. Toulmin thus acknowledges the importance of establishing the truth of both a first principle and the claim that derives from it. He also pays greater attention to the importance of qualifying and clarifying all statements in an argument in order to take into account potential objections of the audience.

Components of Toulmin's System

There are six elements in Toulmin's system. The first three correspond to the major premise, minor premise, and conclusion of a syllogism. Toulmin refers to the major premise as the **warrant,** the minor premise as the **grounds,** and the conclusion as the **claim.** An example of a conclusion, or **claim,** in the Toulmin system would be, "Schools should require students to wear uniforms." The **grounds** in Toulmin's system correspond to the minor premise in a syllogism—which you will remember is a specific example of the major premise—but they consist not just of one statement, but of all the information and evidence that can be used to support the claim. Thus, for the claim that "Schools should require students to wear uniforms," the grounds might consist of information from educators about how uniforms enable students to focus on studies rather than on clothing choices or statements from police about gang-related incidents based on the wearing of certain types of clothing. Unlike the minor premise, then, the grounds consist not only of the reasons for the claim but of all the supporting evidence as well.

The **warrant** is like the major premise of a syllogism—that is, it consists of a general statement from which the grounds and the claim follow logically. An example of a warrant is the statement, "Schools should institute policies that foster student learning and contribute to student safety." Toulmin, however, recognizes that most warrants are not self-evident or universally accepted. Seeing that, he has created a fourth element called the **backing,** which has the function of supporting the warrant. For the warrant, "Schools should institute policies that foster student learning and contribute to student safety," the writer might provide statements from educators on why it is important for schools to establish standards of conduct, law enforcement officials about the dangerous climate in many schools today, and parents about their ideas on instituting their own policies.

Toulmin's system contains two additional components, **qualifiers** and **conditions of rebuttal. Qualifiers** limit the absoluteness of a claim by suggesting that it is true only under certain circumstances. Qualifiers enable writers of academic argument to restrict their claims by using expressions such as "very often," "sometimes," or "probably." Qualifiers can also explain circumstances in which the claim may not be completely true. The claim that "Schools should require students to wear uniforms" might be qualified as follows: "Schools should require students to wear uniforms when disproportionate emphasis on clothing distracts students from learning or when threat of gang violence constitutes a threat to student safety."

The sixth element in Toulmin's system, the **conditions of rebuttal,** indicates instances in which the claim or warrant might not be true or other objections that the audience might have. In the example about school uniforms, an audience might argue that school uniforms are too restrictive and make everyone look exactly the same. Therefore, the claim might include the following conditions of rebuttal:

> Schools should require students to wear uniforms as long as administrators allow some flexibility and choice.

Toulmin's system has the advantage of anticipating audience reaction and acknowledging the importance of qualification. It acknowledges that for both the warrant and the claim, readers are likely to bring up exceptions and recognizes that successful writers of argument must anticipate them. The following model shows the six elements of Toulmin's system:

Enthymeme: Schools should require students to wear uniforms because they foster student learning and contribute to student safety.

Claim: Schools should require students to wear uniforms.

Qualifier: In areas where disproportionate emphasis on clothing distracts students from learning and where gang violence constitutes a threat to student safety.

Grounds: Information about successful institution of uniforms; incidents of in-school, gang-related violence in relation to clothing choices; testimony by educators and parents about the undesirable effects on learning as a result of students' concerns with clothing.

Warrant: Schools should institute policies that foster student learning and contribute to student safety.

Backing: Statements from educators about why it is important for schools to establish standards of conduct and ensure safety.

Rebuttal Conditions: Unless the uniforms are so restrictive that they inhibit self-expression.

The Syllogism and the Toulmin Model: A Comparison

The Aristotelian syllogism and Toulmin's system are similar in many ways. The three main elements in both systems correspond to one another—that is, the major premise, minor premise, and conclusion in the syllogism are similar to Toulmin's warrant, grounds, and claim. There are, however, differences between them as well. In the syllogism, the *major premise* is an accepted idea that does not need to be proved (e.g., all people are mortal), whereas in the Toulmin system, the *warrant* (schools should institute policies that foster student learning and contribute to student safety) needs to be established in order to link the claim and the grounds. The *backing* supplies this support for the warrant.

The importance of qualifying the claim is also given greater emphasis in Toulmin's model through the qualifier and the conditions of rebuttal. The *qualifier* indicates that claims are not static, and the *conditions of rebuttal* anticipate audience objections, further limiting the absoluteness of the argument. Thus, Toulmin's model is less formal and rigid than Aristotle's concept of the syllogism.

➤ **Exercise in Understanding Toulmin's Approach to Argumentation:** Read a newspaper or magazine article that takes a stand on a debatable issue and respond in writing to the following questions:

1. What is the argument concerned with?
2. What is the writer's thesis or claim?
3. What grounds does the writer use?
4. What is the warrant implied in the claim?
5. What reasons does the writer use to convince his or her audience?

ROGERIAN ARGUMENT

In his work with patients, psychologist Carl Rogers developed a form of argument that is useful to understand in the context of argumentation. Rogers noted that although many people can be convinced by reason, many resist rational proof because they need to feel that their own point of view is understood, and only then will they be able to consider new ideas. Rogers thus has a concept of audience as defensive and fearful, an audience that does not easily tolerate challenges to its own views but can be convinced if it does not feel threatened.

Writers who agree with Rogers' view of audience and wish to use his model believe that they will not have the desired effect upon their audience if they adhere to the standard form of argumentation—that is, the structure in which the thesis is presented at the beginning of the essay. For a fearful audience, direct statements of new ideas are more likely to generate resistance than compliance. To convince an audience such as this, Rogerian argument advocates postponing the statement of the thesis and using the beginning sections of the essay to indicate to the audience that the writer understands their position and to generate sympathy and understanding. Writers of Rogerian argument indicate to their readers that they understand their opposing points of view. Rogerian writers, then, restate any opposing point of view and indicate those aspects of it they agree with. Then, having gained the audience's confidence and trust, the writers can then state their own thesis or claim, and at that point, the audience might be more willing to accept it.

Rogerian Argument: Structure and Tone

Writers who decide to use Rogers' model will use a different structure for their papers. Instead of stating the thesis directly, in the first or second paragraph of the essay, they will defer the thesis statement and use the beginning of the essay to establish common ground between reader and writer. The conclusion in a Rogerian argument may also be somewhat different. Writers who use traditional argumentative forms will often reaffirm the claim in the conclusion. In a Rogerian argument, the conclusion may call for additional discussion on the issue or for a further exchange of ideas. Therefore, the writer of a Rogerian argument hopes that the audience will, at the very least, consider his or her argument seriously because the writer did give serious consideration to any opposing arguments within his or her essay.

You may never write a true Rogerian argument; after all, it is difficult to establish a common ground with *all* possible readers. Nevertheless, Rogers' concept of empathy can help writers establish a sympathetic tone that acknowledges the existence of multiple perspectives. Writers who understand the importance of establishing common ground between writers and readers and who assume a respectful, qualified tone are more likely to win the trust of their audience, even if they use a traditional form of argument other than Rogers' model.

➤ **Writing Assignment on Using Rogerian Arguments:** On your own, write a brief Rogerian argument responding to one of the following scenarios. Afterwards, compare your arguments and discuss your strategy in small groups.

1. A mother is worried about allowing her fourteen-year-old son to join a backpacking club. Write a Rogerian argument to help her understand why this might be a beneficial experience for her son.
2. Your roommate does not want to go to the dance that the school is holding at the beginning of the year because he or she is afraid of not knowing anyone there. Write a Rogerian argument to help him or her understand why it might be a good idea to go.
3. One of your friends says that he or she will never use a computer. He or she says that writing by hand and then typing has worked well in the past and can continue to work in the future. You suspect that for some reason, he or she is afraid to use a computer. Write a Rogerian argument helping him or her understand why it is important to know how to use a computer.

FACTS, VALUES, AND POLICIES IN ARGUMENTATIVE WRITING

Annette Rosenberg (*The Structure of Argument*, New York, Bedford Books, 1994) points out that most arguments are either claims of fact, claims of values, or claims of policy. Actually, many argumentative essays could be considered to be all three. A **claim of fact** aims to convince a reader that something is true, as in Louisa's statement (at the beginning of this chapter) that the firm had not hired any women. A **claim of values** attempts to prove that something is right or wrong, just or unjust, effective or ineffective. Louisa was not aiming to prove simply that no women had been hired in the firm; she was asserting that this condition was not right or desirable. A **claim of policy** usually attempts to show that a policy, rule, custom, or law either is or is not desirable. In the argument between Nick and Louisa, Louisa was arguing that the current hiring policy was unfair, while Nick was arguing that the policy was based on what he felt was a valid reason: women are emotionally unsuited for such a job.

You will note, though, that neither Louisa nor Nick was particularly convincing in their argument (although most of us would agree that Nick began the argument with outrageous statements). Neither of them had examined both sides of the question, neither had produced substantial evidence, and neither of them made us feel that they had thoroughly researched the issue or had thought seriously about it. Moreover, since they were both so short-tempered and resorted immediately to extreme statements, neither of them made us feel that they knew what they were talking about.

> ➤ **Exercise in Asserting Claims of Fact, Values, and Policy:** Working in small groups, brainstorm a list of 5–10 issues that could be developed in argumentative essays. Then, determine whether the arguments underlying each issue are claims of fact, claims of values, claims of policy, or a combination of any of these.

DEVELOPING AN ARGUMENT THAT IS CONVINCING

Unlike Louisa and Nick, you need to be as convincing as possible when you write a researched paper so that your readers will consider your ideas seriously. The following four strategies will help you to develop a position convincingly:

1. Establish authority or a credible "writing self" so that your reader trusts you and will pay attention to what you have to say.
2. Be aware of your reader or audience and indicate that you have considered both sides of the question.
3. Understand the implications and consequences of your position.
4. Use evidence effectively in support of your position.

Establishing Authority or a Credible "Writing Self"

There are some people who on a personal level can convince anyone of anything. They have natural charm and convincing mannerisms that make people believe them. Their ways of speaking, their expressions and tone of voice, their body gestures—their entire beings—create the impression that they are honest and informed. These people are convincing, even those who deliberately attempt to deceive or know little about their subject. If they choose to misuse this talent, they make very successful swindlers.

On the other hand, there are people who have great difficulty convincing anyone of anything. These people can't make up their minds about what they really think and go back and forth between alternatives. Because of their own indecision, they don't inspire confidence. Then there are those who seem overly sure of themselves, so sure that they are abrasive in their manner. These people attempt to dictate what people ought to think without acknowledging that other people may have valid ideas, too. Often they are poorly informed about their subject and simply assert their ideas without proof or evidence.

A **credible writing self** is neither indecisive nor overconfident; it is one which readers will believe and trust. In creating a credible writing self, you are aiming to convince your readers that you have considered different facets of the topic, that you know what you are talking about, and that you are honest, informed, and reasonable.

Using a Reasonable Tone

If you look at television advertisements, you will note that most of the people advocating the products seem to be reasonable, coherent, and thoughtful. After all, we tend to believe people who seem to be in control of themselves and distrust those who seem out of control or hysterical. In writing an argument for a researched paper, then, you should aim for a forceful but measured tone. You should indicate that you feel strongly about an issue, but you should avoid inflammatory rhetoric, which can create the impression that you are about to "freak out."

In the following excerpt from the article "You New Women Want It All" (the entire article can be found in Ch. 7, pp. 247), author Donald Singletary attempts to show the misread signals which may result between women and men because of their differing perceptions regarding the role of the "new woman" in today's society in light of the women's liberation movement and the sexual revolution. He asserts that while men have interpreted this "new woman" to be one who wants to take charge of her own destiny by not relying on men to get what she wants out of life, women have confused men by sending them signals indicating they still want to be taken care of by men. Note that Singletary asserts, rather than substantiates, his position:

> Women, I honestly think, believe it is easy for men to approach them. If that
> were true, I would be dating Jayne Kennedy and Diahann Carroll. Talking
> to a woman for the first time, especially without an introduction, is always a

crap shoot. For men, it is worse. It is tantamount to walking down a dark alley knowing a psychopath with a big baseball bat and little mercy is in there. Approaching someone means you have to bare yourself and lay some of your cards on the table. That's not easy—particularly with the "new woman" who waltzes into a room like it's the set of *Dynasty*. Thumbs up if she likes you; to the lions if not.

(Essence, July 1985)

Several of the terms used here, in particular "crap shoot" and "psychopath," are exaggerated, used to inflame rather than explain. Singletary is implying that all women are unapproachable, yet demand attention upon entering a room full of men. If you think about these associations, you know they are not valid and do not logically strengthen Singletary's position, especially when you consider his female audience. In this section of his article, Singletary neither uses a measured tone nor develops his position with good, solid evidence. Therefore, we tend to dismiss his ideas. He has not projected a writing "self" or persona that we are inclined to trust.

On the other hand, Singletary does use a more reasonable tone later in his article, and because of this, he is able to raise reasonable questions about the debate surrounding how the woman's liberation movement and sexual revolution should affect women's relationships with men. This improved "writing self" acknowledges good will on both sides of the controversy:

Liberation. Independence. They're words that imply hard-won, new-found freedom. Freedom from the shackles of the past. That should include the freedom to look at relationships in a new light. Taking one or two bad experiences into each relationship thereafter is not being liberated. It is being shackled, weighed down, by your past. Understanding that the changes that took place for women also changed the perspective of many men is important. It means that realignments in relationships are necessary.

(Essence, July 1985)

In this later excerpt, Singletary uses less-exaggerated word choices and leaves out any unnecessary and unflattering generalizations about women and their relationships with men. Thus, if the author's intent is for women to examine their own relationships in light of the women's liberation movement and sexual revolution, he is much more likely to convince women to do so within the later portion of his article. Unfortunately, because of his uneven tone earlier in the article, some readers may never get to his more effective tone and more persuasive reasoning, since it may have turned them off enough to stop reading the article entirely.

Establishing Authority Through Knowledge

Using a reasonable tone and appearing trustworthy are important ways of creating a credible writing self. Another is to establish authority by being knowledgeable about and in control of your material. Advertisers are well aware of this; they know that an authority (a famous person, for example) or even someone who seems to be an authority (an actor dressed up to like a doctor, for example) can be more convincing than the average person can. We all recognize that those who have attained high status in their fields command authority simply by the use of their names. However, how do you establish authority, or present a believable "writing self," if you are a college student writing about an issue that is relatively new to you?

One of the most important points to remember is that those who have attained high status within a given community did not do so overnight. Their names do not just magically hold authority; those who are considered experts in their fields earned that status by widely reading research within their field and adding to their discourse community by getting their own research published. Therefore, even if you are not considered an expert in the field you are researching, **you can establish authority by knowing your subject well.** Only when you thoroughly understand your issue will you be able to write about it with conviction. It is therefore important that you examine the background of your issue, define your terms, and read pivotal research on your issue, including several sources that can give you alternative points of view. Backing your claims on the issue with the research of those who are experts in the field will lend you credibility, thus making your arguments more believable for your readers.

The Authority of Personal Experience

As a student, you are probably not yet a recognized expert in any field, and so your name on an essay or a reference to yourself within the essay would not help to make your argument more convincing. However, for some topics, your personal experience may serve to establish you as knowledgeable, simply by illustrating your personal investment in the topic. In the following opening paragraphs, for example, Anna Quindlen, in her essay arguing against capital punishment, indicates her familiarity with a series of murders committed by Ted Bundy. She also emphasizes her role as a mother who views the killing of young women with particular horror. Thus, although she is not an acknowledged expert in the field of criminology, Quindlen establishes authority by stressing her personal associations with the topic:

> Ted Bundy and I go back a long way, to a time when there was a series of unsolved murders in Washington State known only as the Ted murders. Like a lot of reporters, I'm something of a crime buff. But the Washington Ted murders—and the ones that followed in Utah, Colorado, and finally in Florida where Ted Bundy was convicted and sentenced to die—fascinated me because I could see myself as one of the victims.
>
> The death penalty and I, on the other hand, seem to have nothing in common. But Ted Bundy has made me think about it all over again, now that the outlines of my 60s liberalism have been filled in with a decade as a reporter covering some of the worst back alleys in New York City and three years as a mother who, like most, would lay down her life for her kids.
>
> (Anna Quindlen, excerpt from "Life in the 30s—Death Penalty's False Promise: An Eye for an Eye." *The New York Times,* Sept. 17, 1986. Copyright 1986 by the New York Times Company. Reprinted by permission.)

Thus, in the beginning of this article, Quindlen's references to her early awareness of the Bundy murders, her days as a reporter in New York City, and her involvement with her children show that her own life experiences have qualified her for reflecting on this issue and formulating a position.

Be Aware of Your Audience

Identifying with Your Opponent: The "We" Attitude

You are more likely to convince your reader of your position if you **indicate that you are aware of alternative viewpoints** and can even identify with them to some extent. Note the difference in acknowledging an opposing position in the following two exchanges:

Scenario 1

Steve: Did you get a doctor's appointment for next week?

George: No. The doctor I usually see was on vacation and the only appointment they had for that time was with a woman doctor. I'm not going to a woman doctor! They're never as good as men!

Steve: Why not? Are you living in the Dark Ages? Women are just as good doctors as men.

George: Well, you can say what you like, but I'm still not going.

Scenario 2

Steve: Did you get a doctor's appointment for next week?

George: No, the doctor I usually see was on vacation, and the only appointment they had for that time was with a woman doctor. I'm not going to a woman doctor! They're never as good as men!

Steve: I understand how you feel. I used to feel that way myself, even though it was kind of a sexist position. But I've learned that there are many really fine women doctors, and Dr. Smith is particularly good. She has top medical credentials, excellent experience, and a terrific way of putting people at ease. I'm going to her myself.

Now at this point, George might still say, "Well, you can say what you like, but I'm still not going." Some people won't change their minds no matter what. But, then again, he might also say this: "Okay, maybe I decided too quickly. If she's that good, and you've used her yourself, maybe I'll give her a try."

Thinking About Your Audience: An Example

In the following excerpt, Vera Elleson points out that although most of us were raised to be competitive, some aspects of competition are undesirable. Notice how Elleson indicates to her readers that she, too, shares the competitive spirit. She does not simply lecture to her readers or show them that their thinking is faulty:

> We can have an impact—on the setting in which we work, our friends, family, co-workers, and profession. Each of us must begin with ourselves. Most of us have been acculturated to a competitive mode of behavior. We must

recognize how we view and interact with others. It is time now to change what is not positive and growth enhancing. Each of us should pause and ask, "Do I put others down or fail to support others in my attempt to get ahead? Do my competitive strivings interfere with my own emotional well-being, with the development of trust between me and others, and with my personal or professional effectiveness?" How often do educators move others by setting them against each other in a vicious struggle for a position at the top? Or do they work cooperatively with students, each learning from and teaching the other?

(From Vera Elleson. "Is Competition a Cultural Imperative?" *Education Digest*, Nov. 1984.)

Using "we" instead of "you" lets readers know that the writer understands their position. It is also a good idea to acknowledge others' positions before presenting your own. Let your readers know that you have already considered alternative positions and then cite reasons why you don't believe those positions to be valid (or as valid as your own position).

➤ **Exercise in Thinking About Your Audience:** Think about a controversial issue you're considering writing about for an argumentative essay. Determine at least two extreme opposing positions. Then formulate your own position (which might be a compromise between extremes). Working in groups of three to five, discuss how you might acknowledge an opposing or alternative position in a researched paper:

Example

Topic: Smoking in the workplace
Issue: Should smoking be allowed in the workplace?
One Extreme Position: Smoking should be outlawed in the workplace because it is a health hazard.
An Opposing Extreme Position: Smoking should not be outlawed anywhere because people have the freedom to do as they please with their own health.
Compromise Position: Smoking should not be allowed in certain areas in the workplace, or workers should be given smoking breaks during which they can go outside to smoke (since secondary smoke affects others as well as the smokers).

Acknowledging an Opposing Position: Sample Paragraph

Those who smoke might feel that forbidding smoking in the workplace is an unnecessary restriction of individual freedom and that whether or not people decide to smoke is their own business. They might also argue that if the government passed a law against smoking in the workplace, they could then pass laws restricting all sorts of other activities. However, although I share this concern about the dangers of restricting individual freedom and recognize that, for some people, smoking is an important part of their lives, I still advocate forbidding smoking in the workplace except in designated, restricted sections or by allowing workers breaks in which they can smoke outside. Unlike many activities that only endanger the person involved, smoking in the workplace poses a threat to the health and comfort of everyone around, not just to the smoker.

Analysis of Sample Paragraph

1. Those who smoke might feel that forbidding smoking in the workplace is an unnecessary restriction of individual freedom and that whether or not people decide to smoke is their own business (first acknowledgement of an opposing position).
2. They might also argue that if the government passed a law against smoking in the workplace, they could then pass laws restricting all sorts of other activities (second acknowledgement of opposing position).
3. However, although I share this concern about the dangers of restricting individual freedom (third acknowledgement—indicating that you share these concerns), and even recognize that for some people, smoking is an important part of their lives (fourth acknowledgement), I still advocate forbidding smoking in the workplace except in designated restricted areas or by allowing workers breaks in which they can smoke outside (main position).
4. Unlike many activities that only endanger the person involved, smoking in the workplace poses a threat to the health and comfort of everyone around, not just to the smoker (reason for position).

Using Rebuttal Paragraphs Effectively to Refute, Acknowledge, or Compromise with an Opposing Position

Although it is unlikely that you will be able to sway all audiences to accept your position, you can make a stronger case for your stance on an issue by convincing those holding alternate viewpoints that your argument has merit and is worth considering. An effective approach to take when writing an argumentative essay, therefore, is to address the major concerns of your opposition by including rebuttal paragraphs. As you'll recall from the beginning of this chapter, rebuttal paragraphs are usually written using one of three argumentative strategies. First, they might *refute* the opposition's stance by providing evidence disproving their concerns. Next, they could *accommodate* an opposing argument, conceding that although the opposition has a valid concern, the writer's position is still more rational for a number of reasons. Finally, rebuttal paragraphs might *compromise* between both positions, proposing an acceptable middle ground. Many times, rebuttal paragraphs employ several of these strategies. For example, you might first acknowledge the validity of a concern voiced by an opposing position, then refute this concern using evidence found in your research. In addition to the sample paragraph provided earlier which acknowledges an opposing position, several more rebuttal paragraphs written by student writers are offered below to help you understand how effective counterarguments work:

Sample Rebuttal Paragraph: Refuting an Opposing Position
(Written by Sharon Lewandowski for a researched essay in English 112 at Bowling Green State University.)

> Though there are many benefits of providing protection and shelter to animals in zoos, there are many people who do not agree with keeping animals in captivity. One argument that many people have is that there is little empirical evidence that much is learned from visiting zoos, an opinion expressed by Randy Malamud in his article, "Reading Zoos: Representation of Animals in Captivity." It is pointless to have animals on display, he argues, if nothing is gained for the animal or the education of people. However, Malamud's idea is simply not true. There is an educational value to being able to walk into a zoo and show a child many different animals. The educational function of a zoo is accomplished by allowing anyone to see exotic animals. Especially to a child, this leaves a lasting impression. Viewing live animals increases the awareness of the necessity to save these animals and their habitats so they can return home (Gavzer). Zoos not only educate the people who come to visit, but also they dedicate about fifty-two million dollars to conservation education programs and teach more than 12 million people a year (The Collective Impact). If the only learning experience people get out of visiting zoos is realizing how important it is to save these animals and that they are living creatures who have the right to live, then zoos are doing their jobs well. Zoos are in this fight for the long run. They want to help animals win the battle of survival. The existence of zoos is very important and provides an invaluable opportunity to educate the public.

Sample Rebuttal Paragraph: Compromising with Opposing Position
(Written for a researched essay in an English 112 class at Bowling Green State University, by Andrew Barnes.)

> Concerned administrators and parents have a valid point when they say that the Internet has many sites not appropriate to a school environment, including pornography. Yes, sites that are inappropriate for children to view are out there on the Web and easily accessible. At this point, there is nothing that can be done to eliminate the existence of such materials, only measures to keep kids from accessing them. This issue is an important one in this nation, and even President Clinton has said violent images "warp young perceptions" (Thomas 1). There are a great deal of harmful sites for young eyes, even those that do not contain pornographic images. Hate groups, militias, bomb recipes, and cults abound in the realm of cyberspace. It is also true that "the Internet has given every half-wit his day in the court of public opinion" (Skinner 2). Anyone can make a web page with his or her own

opinion, and some are illegal and very inappropriate for students to view in school. However, there is something that we can do about this problem. There are specially designed programs that filter content viewed and control what can be accessed over the school's Internet connection. Among them are Web-Sitter, Net Nanny, Bess, and many more that are less known. Michael Martinez, a reporter for ABCNews, agrees, "there's plenty of filtering software that will block out questionable websites" (2). By taking these measures to protect our children, we can dispel the myth that the Internet is evil or a bad idea. Perhaps Martinez puts it best when he states, "the Internet itself isn't good or bad in and of itself" (2). This simply means that at home, parents should be responsible for knowing and approving of what their kids view online, and at school, administrators are responsible for installing filter software, allowing kids to use the Internet as a valuable resource for learning.

> ➤ **Exercise in Writing Counterargument and Rebuttal Paragraphs:** Consider a debatable issue that interests you or that you might explore in an argumentative essay and write a possible thesis statement which reflects your position on the issue. Next, try to speculate about what those holding another position on the issue might argue: what might be their main concern? With the opposition's major concern in mind, write a counterargument (or rebuttal) paragraph that either refutes, acknowledges, or compromises with your opponent's position.

Understanding the Implications and Consequences of Your Position

The Complex Nature of Problematic Issues

Social, ethical, or political dilemmas of our culture usually have no easy answers, no clearly marked right and wrong; by definition, an issue for a researched paper is likely to be complex. To take an intelligent stand on a complex issue, then, means that we have to **acknowledge this complexity** and indicate that we are aware that there are no simple answers. Although on some issues, those about which you have especially strong opinions, you might be able to take a clearly defined, emphatically-stated stance, sometimes **your position on a complex issue might be a compromise between two or more extreme stances.** For example, some people believe that abortion is wrong under any circumstances and therefore believe that no abortions should be allowed. Others believe that women should have access to abortion whenever they wish and that abortion should be allowed freely. An alternate position on this controversial issue might involve finding middle ground between these two extremes.

However, whether you take a strong position on one side of an issue or develop a position that is a compromise between extremes, you should be aware of the consequences and implications of your position and realize that **any posi-**

tion is likely to favor some groups over others. There are very few policies, legal solutions, plans for living, or schemes for reform that are going to please everyone. Society is diverse, people have different goals and needs, and any policy that is favorable to one group is probably going to be unfavorable to another. Thus, in developing a position, you should consider what effect(s) that position is likely to have and on whom each effect is likely to be most significant.

To illustrate this point, let us examine the proposal, discussed a page or two back, that smoking should not be allowed in the workplace because it constitutes a health hazard. Then let us consider why smoking in the workplace is considered a complex issue and what differences in opinion one might encounter. Finally, let us consider the consequences and implications of a position on this issue.

When first thinking about the issue of potentially banning smoking in the workplace, one might feel that it is not complex at all. It is well known, after all, that smoking is dangerous to people's health, and there are many statistics showing the relationship between smoking and second-hand smoke and a variety of lung diseases, such as lung cancer and emphysema. When one thinks about these statistics, forbidding smoking in the workplace seems like a reasonable idea since the consequences seem completely positive: improvement of people's health. A logical conclusion might be that everyone would be in favor of such a proposal.

If you think about human nature, though, you will realize that the solution is not that simple because people do not always do what is good for them. You might then consider whether you think that society ought to take on the role of protecting people from themselves. Perhaps society ought to regulate any behavior that is dangerous to people's health. Maybe other unhealthful habits, such as drinking coffee or eating too many sweets, should be forbidden at work by law as well? If you believe that smoking should be forbidden at the workplace on the basis of being unhealthful, why not include other health-endangering habits as well?

➤ **Exercise in Thinking About Consequences and Implications:**
Write a one-two page essay responding to the following question: Should something that is dangerous to people's health be outlawed? Why or why not? Then compare answers with your classmates.

In responding to the above exercise, you have probably come to the conclusion that a position that advocates outlawing anything that is dangerous to people's health would be considered extreme in our society. Some of you may have decided that what a person does is his or her own business, and that people should have freedom to engage in any behaviors they wish, even those which are injurious to health, as long as these behaviors do not harm others. Eating too many sweets, not getting enough sleep, or even drinking alcohol, as long as the drinker is not also a driver, does not endanger anyone else's health except that of the person who is engaging in that activity. Many of you may feel that in a free society, what a person does to affect his or her own health is usually only that person's personal business.

Others of you may have responded in terms of consequences—you may have pointed out that it would be impossible to enforce a law that restricted all behaviors injurious to health. If we remember Prohibition during the 1920s, and if we recall what we know of human nature, we will realize that a policy forbidding all unhealthful habits would result in numerous people breaking the law, and that unless we had a society in which people were under constant surveillance (as in George Orwell's *1984*), such infractions would be difficult, if not impossible, to detect.

Now let's return to the smoking issue. Here are two extreme positions:

1. Smoking should be forbidden everywhere because it is dangerous to health.
2. Smoking should not be restricted because what people do to endanger their own health is their own business.

However, what makes the smoking issue additionally complex is the fact that smoking doesn't endanger only the health of smokers; it also affects those around them who are breathing the smoke-filled air. This adds another dimension to the argument—the idea that smoking affects others as well. This perspective suggests the idea that if smoking also endangers the health of nonsmokers, then it does not fall into the category of being simply a personal habit. Moreover, what adds even further to the complexity to the issue is the question of how to define a workplace. Should people whose homes double as places of business, for example, be required to maintain a smoke-free environment? Should a guest in a hotel room be forbidden to smoke in the privacy of his or her room because a maid will come in to clean? The other problem would be enforcement, particularly since many workers would be reluctant to report coworkers who violate a non-smoking policy.

Thus, in thinking about such a complex issue, one might decide on a compromise position—forbidding smoking in the workplace except in restricted areas and allowing workers to take "smoking breaks" in these restricted areas only.

Even when you develop a position that seems to be a compromise, however, you will often discover that the position benefits one group more than another. For example, requiring smokers to do their smoking in a restricted area probably gives greater consideration to the rights of nonsmokers. In thinking about the consequences and implications of a potential position for your researched paper, then, you might think about the following questions:

1. What is the area of controversy?
2. Can I state two extreme positions concerning this area of controversy? Do I believe in one of the extreme positions? Can I develop a position that is a qualification or a compromise?

3. Who is likely to benefit from my position or proposal? Who is not likely to benefit? Is one group likely to benefit more than others?
4. Can I predict the consequences and implications of my position? Is it likely that my ideas can be implemented or enforced?

➤ **Exercise in Analysis:** Skim through one or two areas in your reader to locate a controversial issue. Then, for that issue, see if you can determine at least two extreme positions and a possible compromise between them. Write these positions and your compromise position in complete sentences. Then think about the consequences and implications of these positions. Who is likely to benefit from each one? Is one group likely to benefit more than others? Can these ideas be implemented or enforced? Why or why not? If so, how?

Using Evidence Effectively

When you cite reasons for your position, you must support them with **appropriate, accurate, and relevant evidence.** This evidence can be drawn from a number of sources, including examples from experience, the statements of authorities, and statistics.

Experience as Evidence: Real and Hypothetical

A number of positions suitable for a researched paper can be substantiated by examples drawn from your own life or from the lives of other individuals. If you choose an issue of concern to students or to those in the field of education, you may indeed find that you can cite relevant examples based on your own experience or that of other students. Or you might decide to use a hypothetical example to illustrate your point. In his essay, "The Case for Torture" (*Newsweek*, 1982), Michael Levin develops the point that although our society is against torture, there are some extreme cases in which even the most gentle person will be in favor of it. To introduce his position, Levin creates the hypothetical example of a terrorist who has hidden an atomic bomb on Manhattan Island. He then asks whether or not torture should be used to locate the bomb, and then moves on to other cases, not quite as extreme, to similarly illustrate his point. Citing examples from your own experiences, the experiences of others, or creating appropriate hypothetical examples as illustrations can be an effective way of providing support.

The Statements of Authorities

Showing that authorities in the field agree with your statements is another effective method of gaining support for a position. Of course, these experts should be acknowledged authorities in their field (simply having one's name in print does not automatically indicate expertise), and their statements should be sufficiently current so that they are relevant to the situation under consideration. For example, the detrimental effects of secondary smoking have only been firmly acknowledged in the last several years, so if you were writing about the issue of smoking in the workplace, it would be important to cite a recent medical expert on that topic. Stuart Hirschberg points out that expert testimony usually:

1. points out a causal connection,
2. offers a prediction about the future, or
3. offers a solution to a problem.

For example, on the issue of smoking in the workplace, the expert might:

1. show the connection between smoking and secondary effects (causal connection),
2. point out that it would be impractical to ban smoking altogether (offer a prediction about the future), or
3. propose to ban smoking in the workplace except in restricted sections (offer a compromise solution).

(From Stuart Hirschberg, Strategies of Argument.
New York: Macmillan, 1990. 63–65.)

Also, by briefly identifying an author's credentials, or why he or she is considered an authority in a given field, you can strengthen the major points of your argument. Providing your audience with expert opinions corroborating your position and validating your claims lends credibility to your stance on an issue, adding to the value of your own reasoning. Remember, too, that you must choose your sources carefully in order to obtain the most current and valid information by the most knowledgeable and influential authors. For more suggestions about how to characterize and introduce credible sources in your researched essays, be sure to read the section in Chapter 7, pages 240–241, "Introducing and Characterizing Source Material with Transitions."

➤ **Exercise in Determining the Authority of an Author:** In the library or online, find several sources which might be used to find information on the issue of whether or not it is ethical or humane to keep animals in zoos. Then, answer the following questions about the authority of each source you found addressing this issue:

1. What are the author's credentials? Is any information given about the author's education or expertise in his or her field?
2. Has the author researched the topic thoroughly, and does he or she provide a bibliography which lists credible sources consulted?
3. What is the reputation of the source in which the author's work is published? Is it an academic or scholarly journal? A tabloid magazine? A website with affiliations towards a particular group or in support of a certain agenda? How does the source's reputation affect the author's credibility and the value of his or her research?
4. Which of the sources would you choose to include in your researched essay and why?

Statistics as Evidence

Statistics can be an extremely forceful way of supporting a position. However, it is important to realize that statistics can also be misleading if they are not current or representative of the population they intend to describe. For the issue concerning secondary smoking, the statistics revealing the effects of second-hand smoke on non-smokers have only recently been published, so if you were writing about this topic, you would have to be careful that you used only the most current studies. In citing statistics, it is also important that you use only those published by reliable sources (large, well-known scientific institutions or government agencies such as the U.S. Census Bureau or the Centers for Disease Control are just two examples).

What can be particularly misleading about statistics is the extent to which they actually represent the general population. For example, if you questioned students in one particular class about their feelings concerning required courses, you might find that they were all in favor of them and conclude that students in general have positive feelings about required courses. Yet this one class might have been special in some way and may not be representative of the general population of students at the university. Moreover, some statistics can be misleading because of erroneous sampling methods. One common error is sampling results from a self-selecting population. For example, if, after a departmental exam, you posted a large sign that said, "Please fill out this form to express your feelings about the final examination," it is likely that only the students who had negative feelings would respond voluntarily. (The others probably did not have strong enough feelings to bother filling out the form.) You might then conclude that students in general hated the final examination, but this may not have been the case at all since you were not using a representative sample. To obtain meaning-ful statistics in this situation, you would have to question a random sample of students who represent a wide range of distinguishing personal characteristics (men and women, majors and non-majors, etc.). Statistics can be an extremely effective means of support, but it is important to think about what they mean when you include them as evidence.

➤ **Exercise in Evaluating Statistics:** Access the website <u>www.stats-usa</u> <u>.gov</u> on the WWW. Click on the link, "State of the Nation," and scroll down the page, noticing the different types of statistics pertaining to eco-nomic trends in America. Then, see if you can find relevant statistics in-cluded in this site to support or dispute the following claims:

1. Personal income has continued to rise for most Americans in the last year.
2. New home sales in the U.S. have fallen dramatically in the last six months.
3. Retail e-commerce sales have exhibited steady growth in the last several months.

SYNTHESIS

As you read in the previous section, no matter which approach you choose to employ when writing an argumentative essay, establishing a credible writing self, being aware of your targeted audience(s) and their opinions surrounding the issue at hand, understanding the implications and consequences of your po-sition on the controversy, and using evidence supporting evidence effectively are all essential components of well-written and *convincing* persuasive prose. How-ever, while you may have read extensively and completed exercises on better un-derstanding your own position and the perspectives of potential readers on par-ticular controversial issues, more needs to be said about how you can establish yourself as a credible researcher and writer though the use of appropriate, accu-rate, and relevant evidence.

Although citing real-life experiences, statements of authorities, and statis-tics as evidence are necessary in backing your claims—so that your writing is credible and persuasive—there is a preferred strategy in academia for demon-strating your authority on the issue and for using your source support to do so. This preferred strategy is called synthesis.

WHAT IS SYNTHESIS?

According to *The American Heritage College Dictionary* (third ed.), *synthesis* is "the combining of separate elements or substances to form a coherent whole," and the verb *to synthesize* means "to combine so as to form a new, complex product" (1377). To illustrate, while a cook will blend separate ingredients (e.g., olive oil, balsamic vinegar, garlic, cilantro, basil, and oregano) to create just the right balance of harmonious flavors for a house Italian dressing, a successful researcher-writer will gather resources on the issue he or she is researching and use the information found to link the work of each author to one another and to his or her own thinking. The writer will use the material he or she has gathered to create a discussion that supports his or her own views. Thus, just as the cook synthesizes different simple ingredients to create a new, more complex, synthesis dressing, the writer synthesizes several published sources to support his or her own complex argument in a synthesis essay. The basic task of writing a synthesis is to identify constituent elements of interlocking source materials and combine them into a single, unified, and unique piece of writing.

Stated another way, a well-written synthesis is a representation of well-respected, published opinions on any given issue that illustrates a reasonable consensus of authorities on that issue. While there certainly must be disagreement in order for an issue to be considered controversial, what you will be interested in finding as you conduct research for your essay are areas in which noted, respected authors knowledgeable about the issue find *consensus.* As a writer, you can determine a relative representation of consensus on these specific ideas or assertions by researching your issue extensively enough to at least suspect consensus and to find the most powerful, published voices on each side of the controversy. Doing so will enable you to better understand all of the complexities surrounding the issue and help you to come to a conclusion as to where you stand on the issue.

In short, in the context of a writing assignment, a synthesis is your own written discussion on an issue in which you present and discuss your research in terms of how it supports your well-defined and guiding thesis. It is important to note, too, that written synthesis assignments are not limited to composition classes. Throughout college, you will most likely be assigned many synthesis essays. For example, the following non-composition class assignments call for synthesis:

> *Biology:* Over the course of the semester, we have read a textbook and several periodicals on human reproduction, both natural and technology-assisted. In a 6-8 page paper, reflect on what you have read and assert an informed opinion on whether or not you believe that the advantages of fertility treatments outweigh the physical, economic, and social disadvantages.
>
> *Psychology:* This semester you will be assigned many readings on the structure of the human brain and its functioning in relation to consciousness, perception, motivation and learning, sleep, dreaming, memory, drugs, glands, and personality. You are to pick one of these functions to research further (outside of the required course readings) and write a 10- to 12-page paper on what you believe to be the most promising research trend within the area you choose.

Note that although neither the word "synthesize" nor the word "synthesis" appears in either assignment, the instructors expect students to gather and read sources, formulate an opinion on what they read, write an essay supporting that viewpoint by discussing relevant research that will back their claims, and discuss the similarities and differences in sources' views. Thus, the instructors are asking for synthesis essays. The instructor who created the Biology assignment, for example, probably expects more than "I read four sources who agreed with fertility treatments and two who disagreed; therefore, I agree that the advantages of fertility treatments outweigh the disadvantages." By *comparing* and *contrasting* the views of multiple sources in regard to specific advantages and disadvantages, however, analyzing the relative strengths and weaknesses of the arguments made, you can form and present your own, original conclusions based on the conclusions of all your sources, illustrating an informed (if relative) consensus of opinion in your synthesized response to the assignment. Likewise, the instructor who created the Psychology assignment undoubtedly expects student responses to represent and take into account the views of multiple sources on several criteria as the student supports her/his claim about the "most promising research trend." These sources won't all agree with each other, make the same arguments, or even use the same terminology, but *in combination, their ideas can be proposed as grounds for belief in your (i.e., the synthesizer's) argument.* In order to complete such assignments successfully, you will need to know how to synthesize what you read to support your own original opinions.

Distinguishing Between Synthesized Argumentative Essays and Informative Essays

Often, student writers assume that they are simply to summarize the ideology of the authors they read when writing researched essays (you might recall the earlier discussion of Malcolm and his misunderstanding of a researched essay assignment in Chapter 1). However, unless your instructor specifically asks for a literature review, most likely he or she would rather you read widely on the assigned issue and then discuss critically your sources' and your own views on the issue than merely restate what you read. When you synthesize rather than merely reproducing what your sources have said, it helps your instructors see that you can do more than regurgitate the facts and will allow them to evaluate how critically you have assessed your research findings. Therefore, even though your entire Biology or Sociology lecture class may be assigned the same researched essay, your unique insights and opinions would distinguish your essay from the essays of your classmates. You, the writer, are the most important source in any synthesis essay. No matter how much research material you gather and include in your essays, it is your voice and convictions that should dominate your written discussion.

Although your voice needs to be the driving force behind your synthesis essays, you will not be able to compose persuasive or successful discussions without an in-depth, critical reading of the outside sources important and relevant to those discussions. Thus, the success of your synthesis essays will be dependent upon how critically you read the related research **before** you begin writing. Consequently, your best bet for producing a convincing synthesis is to carefully read sources to better understand the issue at hand—and your stance on it—and to evaluate each source for its usefulness to your discussion. Therefore, as the writers of *The Allyn & Bacon Handbook* (second ed.) put it so well, because writing a synthesis demands solid critical reading and writing skills, it "represents some of the most sophisticated and challenging writing you will do in college" (Rosen and Behrens 53).

THE PURPOSE OF SYNTHESIS IN ACADEMIC WRITING

In the previous Argumentation section, you learned that you can establish authority by knowing your subject well. But to know your subject well, you will need to do extensive reading within your research focus. Few of us would expect to become fluent in French after listening to just one "Teach Yourself French" audio cassette; indeed, it takes plenty of time and effort to even begin to understand the fundamentals of a foreign language. Similarly, it would take more than reading just one article on the controversy surrounding smoking in public before you could take an informed stance on the issue. Granted, reading a single source on a subject is the first step to better understanding it; however, a single source only provides you with one author's (or group of authors') perspective. Each additional source you read will offer another perspective and evidence to support that perspective. The more widely you read on your subject, the more thorough your knowledge of that subject becomes—and the more prepared you will be to write!

As you read multiple sources on your subject, you should be creating dialogues between yourself and your sources and among the sources themselves. You should note differences of opinions, how some sources support the views expressed in other sources, how some sources bring up points with which you agree, or how some sources bring up points which you find offensive or inaccurate. This internalized dialogue is the first step to synthesis. Getting these relationships between the sources' ideas and your own position down on paper in a purposeful way that supports your thesis is the next step. While the rest of this chapter provides more in-depth guidance on the steps to writing effective synthesis essays, it is important for you to understand at this point that ultimately, synthesis is the vehicle you need to organize source support within academic arguments.

Although several close, critical readings of relevant sources are essential when planning to write a synthesis, you will still need to be selective when choosing information from each source to use as support within your essay. It is simply not possible or advantageous to cite every author who has been published on your specific issue or to discuss every point they may have included. Thus, you will need to select from each source the information that best allows you to fulfill the purpose of your essay. What point(s), exactly, you want to make in your essay will affect your claims, the evidence you select to support your claims, and the way you organize your evidence.

HOW DO YOU SYNTHESIZE?

As discussed, engaging in careful and extensive reading of relevant research and creating a dialogue between you and your sources are critical to creating an effective synthesis. While, as with most writing strategies, there is no one "right way" to synthesize, there are some basic guidelines that can assist you in blending evidence from multiple sources into one unified argument. This section provides a process for writing a synthesized argument and exercises to help you practice your evolving synthesis skills. Keep in mind that synthesizing ideas involves selection and judgment, and no two writers are going to do it the same. There will always be some variation in which sources and ideas from those sources are chosen to support similar claims, how the source support is used (summarized, paraphrased, or quoted), and how the synthesized argument is organized.

Steps for Writing a Synthesis for a Specific Research Focus

1. Read your writing assignment carefully, paying close attention to the research requirements and suggestions for choosing an issue.
2. Research your issue widely, making sure that you are only choosing credible sources (refer to Chapter 2 for tips on evaluating sources).
3. Read each source to get a general impression of the content, using annotation, notetaking, outlining, or summarizing as necessary. Identify the main idea and supporting points of each source, as you would in preparing to write a summary.
4. Reread each source, this time to start assessing what is being said, rather than just understanding the content. Make evaluatory annotations.
5. Determine points of similarity and contradiction among your sources by examining the Questions for Identifying Relationships Among Sources below.
6. Decide on your position on the issue and which supporting arguments of your own you would like to convey to your readers.
7. Locate in each source the information that you can use to support each of your claims.
8. Draft synthesis note sheets (explained on pages 167–171) by summarizing, paraphrasing, and quoting relevant evidence from the sources.
9. Draft your synthesis essay, using the synthesis note sheets and the synthesis strategy for paragraph development (explained on pages 172–175) and drawing on your knowledge of basic argumentative strategies.

Questions for Identifying Relationships Among Sources

Consider the following questions for each source you consider using in your re-searched essay.

1. Does the source agree with any of your other sources?
2. Does the source provide clarification for another source through the use of background information, definitions, or additional details?
3. Does the source provide any examples, or other evidence, for points made by another source?
4. Are there cause and effect relationships between any of your sources?
5. Does the source disagree with or contradict any of your other sources?

➤ **Exercise in Identifying Relationships Between Sources:** In small groups, read the following excerpts from student synthesis essays and dif-ferentiate and discuss the types of relationships (as identified in the above "Questions" section) illustrated between the sources in each example.

1. In fact, I conducted an interview with Amy Konkler, who worked at a tanning salon, and she stated that "tanning beds are much safer than the sun because they regulate the type of rays your body is exposed to." Karl Newmann, M.D. also supports the idea that the sun is more dangerous than tanning. He explains, "tanning machines emit the UV-A and UV-B rays, which are the tanning rays of the sun, but not the UV-C rays" (1).

2. Joan Connell agrees that violence on television has definitely become an issue. She states, "In 1980 the most violent show registered only 22 incidents of violence per hour" (4). She then provides a table of car-toon ratings for 1992. Some of the most violent cartoons contained as much as 109 violent acts per hour (4). . . . For an example of the vio-lence in cartoons today, all you have to do is watch an episode of *Beavis and Butthead.* Kevin Baker, author of "Beavis and Butt-head Are Dead, But Comedy Lives," explains, "They torture animals, harass girls, they like to burn stuff and they sniff paint thinner" (1). . . . Be-cause of this increase of such cartoon violence, William Phillips, a writer for *Parenting,* believes that "Children under the age of seven are particularly at risk for imitating cartoon violence, since they have difficulty distinguishing between televised fantasy and reality" (1).

3. Some might argue that mastectomies are not the answer because there are preventative drugs for cancer. They say the "drugs could save many women from more dramatic cancer-fighting measures: mastectomies, chemotherapy, and radiation" (Warren 1). Peter Howe, a writer for *The Boston Globe,* also agrees that mastectomies are not the answer. He states that "the saving of those 18 lives [referring to Lynn Hartmann's study] is clearly important, but the 621 women who probably would have survived without prophylactic mastectomy paid a price that would be considered unacceptable in the future . . . .

Advances in the use of cancer preventing drugs such as tamoxifen should be developed as easier options" (2). He has a good point, but tamoxifen has side effects just like any other drug you take. For instance, "tamoxifen markedly increased the risk of uterine cancer and blood clots in the lungs and large veins"(Warren 2).

4. The destruction of humanity that has been caused by the sanctions is sufficient reason for their discontinuance. Since the introduction of the sanctions in August of 1990, it is estimated that 567,000 Iraqi children have died as a consequence, and this number continues to grow (Zaidi 1485). The best estimates of the total mortality due to sanctions, adults and children, indicate that 1.8 million have died (CASI 19).

5. . . . in a recent survey that I conducted in which there were 58 respondents, 83% believed that the sanctions against Iraq should be maintained. Considering the obviousness of the situation as it has been presented in this analysis, why is it that the majority seems to offer their support? To answer this question, I recently shared correspondence with Dr. Don Jelfo, a professor of Political Science at Cuyahoga Community College. Dr. Jelfo . . . explained that "The popular rationale amongst those who support sanctioning is that they are a necessary evil required to contain Saddam Hussein and prevent him from inflicting damage on his own people and neighboring countries. The United States is considering the past aggressiveness of the Iraqi guard under Saddam against Kuwait and rebellious factions within Iraq, therefore assuming a protective role."

*Excerpts 1–3 in the previous exercise were taken from BGSU student-writer Jennifer Allison's English 112 essays, written in 1999 (essay titles: *"Is Tanning in a Sunbed Really That Bad for You?," "Are Cartoons Really Appropriate for Children?," and "Would You Consider a Mastectomy?")*

**Excerpts 4–5 in the previous exercise were taken from BGSU student-writer William Swindell's 1999 English 112 essay, *"Everything the United States Does Not Know, We Learned in Kindergarten."* His essay can be found in its entirety at the end of Chapter 6.

> **Assignment on Recognizing Relationships Between Sources:** Reread the "Questions for Identifying Relationships Among Sources" section to remind yourself of the possible relationships. Next, read through all of the sources you have found while researching the issue you are writing about and begin annotating your sources, noting the relationships between each of your sources and your own viewpoints on the issue.

Synthesis Note Sheets

Synthesis note sheets provide a useful means for writers to generate their own theses, supporting claims and topic sentences for paragraphs. Additionally, they assist writers in ensuring that they have ample source support to back their claims. Thus, the benefits of using synthesis note sheets are plentiful. Once you assemble the synthesis note sheets, you can 1) decide which claims/points are the strongest, 2) see at a glance how related ideas from different sources interact and whether or not you have enough support for your claims, and 3) achieve with relative ease true synthesis that is organized according to your claims (not source-by-source summaries). Take, for example, the work of Justin, who used synthesis note sheets as a prewriting strategy when assigned the essay from which the following passage has been excerpted:

> To many, old age is a depressing topic. No one wants to experience the fee-
> bleness of body and the social neglect that we assume comes with old age.
> Yet old age is a universal condition that awaits us all. In a well-organized
> essay, using at least four outside sources, consider the following question:
> What can be done so that the aged in our society can live a more fulfilling
> life? As part of your paper, you should demonstrate awareness of some of
> the problems of the aged in today's culture. Make sure that you narrow
> your topic so that you can adequately develop your ideas.

After examining his own feelings and experiences with the topic in preparing to write this paper, Justin noted that one of the key terms in the assignment
was the word "fulfilling." In order to decide what constitutes a fulfilling life, he
decided he had better include a definition of that term. In his research, he found
several definitions he might wish to use in his paper. He recorded them on Synthesis Note Sheet 1.

As Justin read about his topic, he kept finding information about problems
that many have encountered after deciding to retire. He learned that although
some people looked forward to retirement as a time of freedom, a time when
they would no longer have to work long hours, most found it a time of stress.
Justin discovered that many old people suffered a loss of identity, a lack of
meaningful activity, and a deadly isolation from the mainstream of society when
they retired. Consequently, he created Synthesis Note Sheet 2 to record some of
the source support he found on this facet of the topic.

As he continued to work on his paper, Justin noted that his assignment specified that he illustrate awareness of some of the problems the elderly currently
face. Therefore, he created Synthesis Note Sheet 3 to record the specific problems faced by the elderly which he found in his research.

Synthesis note sheets help you to complete essay assignments in many
ways. They can assist you in the following: breaking down all parts of both the
assignment and the issue at hand in order to flesh out all subtopics, determining
your own stance on the issue, developing and backing your supporting arguments for your stance, and organizing each portion of your essay (organization
strategies will be discussed further in Chapter 6).

See p. 284

Synthesis Note Sheet 1

Subtopic/Claim: Defining what is meant by "fulfilling."

Possible Topic Sentence: Older people have the potential to lead as productive, fulfilling lives as younger people do by staying mentally and physically active.

Note/Quote/Paraphrase with in-text citation (author's last name & p.#):	*Reason for Using:*
1. "Life at any stage" requires a challenge (Tuan 145).	To show that the needs of the old are the same as those of any human being.
2. "The secret of success, found so often among those who have bridged their three-score-and-ten in health, serenity, and happiness, pertains to their ability to remain curious and concerned. They possess the common denominator of being self-educable, self-sufficient, and aware of all that is taking place around them" (Perera 112).	To show the need to progress, to work at something.
3. "Most older Samoans explain their longevity by the fact that they keep busy every day" (Holmes 8).	To show that other societies also value productivity.
4. "One pressing need of people in all stages and walks of life is to be useful" (Blau 16).	Other support for this definition.

Synthesis Note Sheet 2

Subtopic/Claim: Retirement should be rethought.

Possible Topic Sentence: Engaging in a more active retirement is one important way for older people to remain happily involved in society and alleviate feelings of worthlessness.

Note/Quote/Paraphrase with in-text citation (author's last name & p.#):	*Reason for Using:*
1. Early retirement is wasteful (Mead 25).	Negative idea of retirement.
2. "Retirement! What a distressful word! It smacks of retreat, withdrawal, seclusion from circulation" (Perera 112).	Retirement means isolation.
3. "For many, the word 'retirement' in the United States means a shift from a busy, active life, to one of idleness and boredom" (Jones 57).	Retirement has negative connotations.

Synthesis Note Sheet 3

Subtopic/Claim: The present condition of the elderly in our society.

Possible Topic Sentence: Currently, many older people face an increasing risk of feeling idle, lonely, or powerless as they age.

Note/Quote/Paraphrase with in-text citation (author's last name & p.#):	*Reason for Using:*
1. Advanced industrial society has resulted in enforced idleness for the old (Blau 21).	One problem of old: idleness.
2. "I see no human beings. My phone never rings. I feel sure the world has ended. I'm the only one on Earth. How else can I feel? All alone" (Percy 1).	Another problem of old: loneliness.
3. "For the mast majority it is almost tautological to say "old and poor'" (DeBeauvoir 6).	Another problem: power.
4. "Often, they feel as if they have no function in life. Their roles as earners are lost with retirement" (Jones 17).	Another problem: uselessness.

In fact, as Justin constructed his synthesis note sheets, he came to the realization that he needed more synthesis note sheets to narrow his information even further. He recalled that there was a great deal of information concerning the financial uncertainty that many of the aged face. Thus, he decided to create Synthesis Note Sheet 4 to address this concern alone.

Synthesis Note Sheet 4

Subtopic/Claim: The present condition of the elderly in our society: financial problems.

Possible Topic Sentence: Financial uncertainty and instability may also lead to a reduced quality of life for the elderly.

Note/Quote/Paraphrase with in-text citation (author's last name & p.#):	*Reason for Using:*
1. "For the mast majority it is almost tautological to say "old and poor'" (DeBeauvoir 6).	Support from social commentator.
2. "At a time in their lives when they need more, rather than fewer services, older people suffer drastic drops in income" (Percy 1).	Support from authority (senator).
3. "Social security payments have increased over the years, but they are not linked to the cost of living or adequate to keep retirees out of near poverty" (Kuhn 41).	Member of Gray Panthers.

Next, as he read over his synthesis note sheets and the problems that many elderly encounter, Justin came to the conclusion that before he could come up with some viable ways to help the aged live more fulfilling lives, he needed to know why these problems exist in the first place. Hence, he constructed Synthesis Note Sheet 5.

Synthesis Note Sheet 5

Subtopic/Claim: Causes of problems.

Possible Topic Sentence: Fear and lack of preparation for old age in American are rooted in our dominant ideologies promoting independence and self-reliance.

Note/Quote/Paraphrase with in-text citation (author's last name & p.#):	*Reason for Using:*
1. The situation is due to the following combinations of (1) a particular set of values, (2) a particular level of technological development, and (3) a particular form of social organization (Holmes 20).	Causes.
2. In American society, the fear of dependency is so great that an individual who is not self-reliant is an object of hostility (Hsu 216).	Causes linked to values.
3. Democracies are societies on the move, and they have little time for ceremony or convention (Smith 28).	To show causes as rooted in democracy.

As Justin created the synthesis note sheets for the research information he found on these issues surrounding the elderly, he noted that at least some of the problems were preventable if one prepared adequately. He thus chose to focus on the argument that in order for each of us to live a more fulfilling life as an old person, we will have to prepare for it when we are younger. He determined that part of this preparation would have to be establishing financial security since it is hard to live any kind of life, much less a fulfilling one, without adequate means of support.

As he formulated his ideas further, Justin figured that although one could secure financial stability on an individual basis, it would probably be better if the government had some programs as well, programs reinforcing or supplementing social security. Moreover, he concluded another form of preparation would involve developing interests, activities, and involvement with others before retirement that could be continued later in life.

The key to a successful old age, Justin resolved, was in preparing for it, not denying that it was ever going to happen, as so many do. That meant increased awareness for everyone. Once he decided on this preliminary thesis,

Justin was ready to refine his main points, begin considering opposing arguments and how to address them, and complete additional synthesis note sheets where appropriate.

Therefore, Justin discovered through his research on the issue and his use of synthesis note sheets what it means for the elderly to live a fulfilling life and what problems are currently preventing many older people from living better lives. He also found out what causes these problems to exist and what his opinions are regarding the plans which need to be implemented in order for most people to avoid these same issues when they, too, grow older and face retirement.

➤ **Exercise in Understanding the Use of Synthesis Note Sheets:** In small groups, look back over Justin's research process, synthesis note sheets, problem prevention suggestions, and tentative thesis and decide whether you believe he needs to create more synthesis note sheets. If so, which subtopics/claims still need to be covered? If not, why do you feel he has enough to go on? Additionally, discuss how well each subtopic or claim is supported. Do any need any more, less, or different kinds of support? Be prepared to explain your answer. Finally, generate some possible opposing arguments or concerns some of Justin's readers might have and consider how he might address each concern to positively influence readers.

Synthesis Strategy for Paragraph Development

Once you have completed your synthesis note sheets, you may wonder how you are to use them when writing your essay. What follows is one highly useful method of using sources to support your claims. While this strategy may seem a bit rigid or forced at first, once you have internalized the strategy, you will find that it ensures that your claims are the focal points of the discussion and that you are connecting your source support to your points in a way that enables your readers to easily see the relationships between your claims and evidence.

Remember that while a true synthesized argument in defense of a writer's thesis is supported by *at least* two different sources and connected together to support one idea, **your idea,** do not misinterpret this as meaning that two citations in a paragraph automatically constitutes synthesis. A supporting argument paragraph (or a discussion consisting of two or more consecutive and highly related paragraphs) is not synthesized unless it is backed by evidence from two or more sources that are closely related in your text, relevant to your claim, *and* representative of the state of relative consensus on that same claim. Notice that "synthesis" means more than showing readers that you could find more than one person to agree with you.

The following model illustrates one method for synthesizing sources at the paragraph level:

- Each synthesis paragraph (or set of paragraphs if the discussion warrants it) should begin with a **reason** that explains why your thesis is valid. The reason should serve as your topic sentence that will guide the discussion taking place within the rest of the paragraph.
- Once you have offered your reason in your topic sentence, you will need to provide **evidence** from one of your sources that helps to illustrate or support your reason.
- Next, you will need to **explain** what the evidence means and/or how it supports the reason you have provided in your topic sentence in your own words.
- For synthesis to occur, you now need to incorporate more evidence from additional source(s) that further substantiates your reasoning.
- In order for the additional evidence to be smoothly integrated, you must provide **connections** between the information showing the relationship of one piece of evidence to another. This can be done through the use of verbs and transitions that help make those connections clear for the reader (refer to Table 3: "Verbs and Transitions That Can Help Synthesis," on pages 284 in Chapter 8).
- Every time new evidence is presented, you should provide an **explanation** of how it furthers your reason.
- Finally, you need to wrap up you paragraph or section by developing your idea more fully, providing some **discussion** of how all of the information in the paragraph fits together as well as **connections** explaining how the information in the paragraph furthers your argument by helping to prove your thesis is valid.

If we break a synthesis paragraph down into its pieces, it might look like this:

1. Reason why the thesis is valid;
2. Evidence from a source that supports this reason;
3. Explanation of how/why the evidence supports the reason;
4. Connection to a second piece of evidence from a different source;
5. Evidence from the second source supporting this reason;
6. Explanation of how/why this second piece of evidence supports the reason; (steps 4-6 can be repeated several times, using different sources);
7. Discussion of how all of the evidence presented in the paragraph fits together;
8. Connection explaining how all of the information in the paragraph furthers your argument and/or helps prove your thesis.

Suppose that you were writing an essay supporting the position that the media does not affect youth as detrimentally as many critics believe. Here's an example of how a synthesis paragraph might be put together using the method described above:

1. **Reason why the thesis is valid:** Critics have been all too eager to attack the media as the source of our nation's ills. However, the majority of these attacks have provided little in the way of scientific support.

2. **Evidence from a source that supports this reason:** Indeed, as Keith Meilke, author of "On the Relationship Between Television Viewing and Academic Achievement," asserts, "most treatment of this issue fails to reflect the rigor of a serious search for truth" (324).

3. **Explanation of how/why this evidence supports the reason:** In fact, some attacks on the media not only fail to include the necessary support for their claims but engage in a flagrant denial of the research results we do have.

4. **Connection to a second piece of evidence from a different source:** And these attacks are not limited to one segment of the media. In fact, any media source that appears to have contact with youth is subject to criticism. But even these claims' staunchest supporters must admit that their attacks lack a credible scientific foundation.

5. **Evidence from the second source supporting this reason:** For example, Dr. Elizabeth Brown and Professor William Hendee, authors of the article "Adolescents and Their Music," are supporters of the argument that media can adversely affect teens. However, they also note that "the evidence of possible effects . . . [of media on teens] has so far been anecdotal and circumstantial" (409).

6. **Explanation of how/why this second piece of evidence supports the reason:** By the authors' own admission, the best support for these attacks appear to be limited to specific stories of youth who've gone bad because of their exposure to the media. However, as anyone in the scientific community will know, anecdotes and stories, no matter how horrific and popular, are not adequate foundation for an argument that makes generalized claims.

7. **Discussion of how all of the evidence presented in the paragraph fits together:** All of this appears to suggest that many of the attacks traditionally waged against the media have been reactionary appeals rather than factually supported claims. Without scientific support, claims that the media incite violence and contribute to moral decay are little more than inflammatory opinion. These claims do the easy job of fingering the media as the culprit but fail to *prove* anything at all.

8. **Connection explaining how all of the information in the paragraph furthers your argument and/or helps prove your thesis:** As anyone familiar with the art of argument knows, it is this last job of proving something that is the hardest and most important. Anyone can make a claim, but the search for truth requires concrete evidence, and this, most critics

lack. In spite of these weaknesses, though, the attacks continue to surface and be met with popular support.

When all of these pieces are put together, the synthesis paragraph looks like this:

Critics have been all too eager to attack the media as the source of our nation's ills. However, the majority of these attacks have provided little in the way of scientific support. Indeed, as Keith Meilke, author of "On the Relationship Between Television Viewing and Academic Achievement," asserts, "most treatment of this issue fails to reflect the rigor of a serious search for truth" (324). In fact, some attacks on the media not only fail to include the necessary support for their claims, but engage in a flagrant denial of the research results we do have. And these attacks are not limited to one segment of the media. In fact, any media source that appears to have contact with youth is subject to criticism. But even these claims' staunchest supporters must admit that their attacks lack a credible scientific foundation. For example, Dr. Elizabeth Brown and Professor William Hendee, authors of the article "Adolescents and Their Music," are supporters of the argument that media can adversely affect teens. However, they also note that "the evidence of possible effects . . . [of media on teens] has so far been anecdotal and circumstantial" (409). By the authors' own admission, the best support for these attacks appear to be limited to specific stories of youth who've gone bad because of their exposure to the media. However, as anyone in the scientific community will know, anecdotes and stories, no matter how horrific and popular, are not adequate foundation for an argument that makes generalized claims. All of this appears to suggest that many of the attacks traditionally waged against the media have been reactionary appeals rather than factually supported claims. Without scientific support, claims that the media incite violence and contribute to moral decay are little more than inflammatory opinion. These claims do the easy job of fingering the media as the culprit but fail to prove anything at all. As anyone familiar with the art of argument knows, it is this last job of proving something that is the hardest and most important. Anyone can make a claim, but the search for truth requires concrete evidence, and this, most critics lack. In spite of these weaknesses, though, the attacks continue to surface and be met with popular support.

Keep in mind that this development technique is only a way to get started. There is little doubt that an entire essay following this format would quickly bore the reader, as it offers little variation. Therefore, as you become comfortable with developing synthesis paragraphs, you should work to create more varied paragraph structures to help keep your reader engaged.

> ➤ **Exercise in Reinforcing Synthesis Skills:** Find two or more sources that present views on the same issue (this could be an issue you are researching for a potential essay). After reading and thinking about the information provided, take a stance on the controversy and write one paragraph in which you assert a reason (for believing in a certain way about the issue). Offer support for this reason by using the method outlined above. Be certain to strive for synthesis by illustrating the relationships between your sources' views and your own view (i.e., the reason on which your paragraph is based) *as well as* the relationships among your sources' views. Remember, too, to let your own voice be heard.

Ensuring That Your Voice Is Heard

[Adapted from Leonard Rosen and Laurence Behrens. "Do Not Become Invisible in Your Papers." *The Allyn & Bacon Handbook.* 2nd edition. Needham Heights, MA: Allyn & Bacon, 1994: 53-55.]

When writing an argumentative synthesis essay, always avoid allowing your sources to dominate the discussion. You should be the lead singer in each performance, with your sources employed as the backup singers. With this in mind, remember that a synthesis should draw on your insights first, then the insights of others. Thus, sections or major arguments within your synthesis essay should be organized according to *your* claims, not according to your sources. A paper organized as a string of summarized sources is not a synthesis, because it makes no attempt to create dialogues among the views represented in the essay (yours and your sources').

For example, in the context of a paper on fertility treatments, a discussion organized as source summaries would leave the writer invisible. The instructor assigning the synthesis essay would not need to read much further than an opening statement such as the one that follows to know that the writer may not be the lead singer in the ensuing essay:

"Several researchers have discussed the topic of fertility treatments."

This statement focuses more upon the writer's research than the writer's own ideas and should raise a red flag that the outside sources will be taking the lead in the essay that follows. Consequently, the writer needs to better illustrate that he or she has critically read and assessed the related reading material, has come to his or her own conclusions on the issue, and has a clear sense of purpose. A more effective setup for the issue might read as follows:

"Many couples today are faced with the heartbreaking problem of infertility, which is most often diagnosed after a woman is not able to conceive by natural means after trying for at least one full year. To help them combat infertility, many couples decide to rely on technology. The most common techniques for assisted reproduction, or fertility treatments, are the administration of a number of various drugs or the procedure of in-vitro fertilization. While many childless couples look forward to what such treatments can do to help them start a family, there are several downsides to these options. Therefore, after researching this controversial and emotional issue carefully, I have come to believe that the use of assisted reproduction techniques should be seriously reconsidered, for several reasons."

In this revised essay introduction, the writer's purpose and position are clear, and we can sense that in the rest of the discussion that follows, the outside source materials will not overshadow the writer. Therefore, in order for your readers to be guided by your voice and for them to recognize and pay heed to your arguments, you will need to be conscious of the danger signs that your voice is being overshadowed by your source materials.

Danger Signs That Your Voice Is Being Overshadowed

1. Your paragraphs are devoted wholly to the work of the authors you read.
2. Virtually every sentence introduces someone else's ideas.
3. Virtually every sentence needs to be cited.
4. The impulse to use the first person "I" never arises.

If you detect any of these danger signs cropping up in your essay, you will need to reexamine your thesis and all supporting claims, ensuring that they are tied to your essay's own original purpose and not based solely on source summary. To prevent this overshadowing from occurring in the first place, let us remind you that the main goals in writing a synthesis are to create and participate in a discussion governed by your own views on a controversial issue—a discussion in which you draw on source information to contribute to an argument that you design and control.

6 Planning the Researched, Argumentative Synthesis Essay

Academic writing assignments vary from class to class, from instructor to instructor, from discipline to discipline, and so forth. Of these types of assignments, this chapter focuses specifically on planning for documented, argumentative synthesis essays. It also gives directions and samples—as part of the planning for these kinds of essays—for essay proposals and exploratory drafts. You may not need or want to use every process strategy described in this chapter for every academic essay you write, even though they very likely would be beneficial if you used them. However, for the researched and assigned-source essay assignments listed in this chapter, these strategies are indispensable. Please give them your best attention and consider carefully the rationales for completing them.

As earlier chapters in this book have maintained, carefully constructed researched-writing projects take advantage of pre-thinking, including one's own preconceptions as well as the perceptions of others. Well-planned researched writing also takes advantage of recursive planning and of informed cycles of revision. The time you spend on essay planning activities won't eliminate the need for revision. However, this time and effort may help you avoid some missteps and establish a big-picture consciousness (of your whole potential essay) as you write. The bottom line is that as your essay drafting and revising progresses, your "planning" will undergo parallel evolution. Planning, then, isn't something writers do just once. Instead, effective writers plan, re-plan, and continue planning through the end of a writing project. Whether scripted as a formal outline, a chart, or even just a list of notes, the important thing is that you have a plan and that it is flexible, changing to reflect new ideas and revised thinking.

APPROACHING YOUR ASSIGNMENT

Planning Your Time

Sometimes, when students are presented with a writing assignment, they read it through but remain removed from it until the last night, when the pressure mounts to begin writing. All of us know that terrible, last-minute feeling of panic. We stare at the blank page and nothing comes to mind as the hours tick away into the night. Some people experience this inability to write because they suffer from writer's block. These people find that any writing assignment causes them to panic. But most of us experience inability to write because we have not thought seriously about the assignment; we have not involved ourselves in the topic by asking questions, thinking, talking, reading, and writing about it so that we can develop a position over a period of time. When you involve yourself in a topic, your mind perks away at it even when you don't realize it. Then, when you begin to write, you find that you have more to say about your subject or issue than you had anticipated. To avoid last-night writer's block, we suggest that you plan your times as follows:

1. **List all of the activities you will engage in when you write your paper.** These could include talking with someone about the issue, brainstorming, researching, reading, summarizing and comparing sources (perhaps on synthesis note sheets), writing early drafts, revising, and printing the final draft.
2. **Estimate the time you think you will need for each of these activities.** Then decide when and where you will actually complete these activities so that you can have enough time.
3. **Add up the total.** If possible, add at least an hour to each estimate.

Making a Plan

While most writers have their own individualized preferences for handling a writing project, establishing a plan that includes all necessary tasks and the deadlines for each task can help them stay focused and pace their project, allowing them to finish the project as comfortably (and with as little stress) as possible. To illustrate, Elisa (our model student from earlier chapters) had two weeks to write her paper; here is the time management plan she came up with:

1. Read the assignment and write an exploratory draft.	Monday—in class
2. Share draft with other students and discuss ideas.	Wednesday—in class
3. Read and summarize the assigned essays.	Saturday—all day at home
4. Brainstorm and come up with a brief outline.	Sunday (1-5 PM)—at home
5. Write a first draft.	Monday (6-11 PM)—computer lab
6. Go to Writing Center on campus and get feedback on draft.	Tuesday (1-2 PM)
7. Use feedback to revise draft.	Tuesday (9-11 PM)—computer lab
8. Meet with instructor to discuss draft.	Wednesday (9-10 AM)—instructor's office
9. Revise draft according to instructor's feedback.	Thursday (1-6 PM)—computer lab
10. Find out about documentation style requirements and have a peer review my draft.	Friday—in class
11. Revise draft according to any helpful peer advice. Edit draft for style and correctness.	Saturday (start at 11 AM)—computer lab
12. Proofread draft.	Saturday (10 PM)—computer lab
13. Print final draft.	Saturday (11 PM)—computer lab

Although the paper was due on Monday, Elisa wanted to finish it by Saturday, in case she came across difficulties she hadn't anticipated. Again, you may be saying, "It's impossible to plan ahead like this. Elisa is unreal." Such planning certainly is difficult for any of us. However, when you receive your next assignment, you might think about what sort of plan you might aim for, one that actually works for you. An "Essay Writing Time Management Form," which you might find useful as a starting point for establishing your own plan, follows:

Essay Writing Time Management Form		
Type of Activity	*When?*	*Where?*
Reading assignment		
Brainstorming		
Writing exploratory draft		
Reading sources		
Developing preliminary topic		
Writing a proposal		
Creating an outline		
Writing first draft		
Getting feedback on first draft		
Writing second draft		
Revising second draft		
Editing second draft		
Proofreading final draft		
Checking documentation		
Printing and copying		

Before you begin implementing the plan and writing your essay, first immerse yourself in your issue by doing the following activities:

1. Think about the purpose of the assignment.
2. Clarify key terms.

3. Consider your immediate reaction to the issue.
4. Ask key questions.
5. Share questions and ideas with classmates.
6. Try to understand the value conflicts in the assignment.
7. Read and compare some opinions on the issue.

These activities will enable you to get involved in your topic so that you will be able to develop a position.

➤ **Assignment on Planning Your Writing Project:** After reading your assignment carefully—noting requirements, suggested timeline, etc.— generate a plan for completing your project. Feel free to use Elisa's plan or the Essay Writing Time Management Form as a model.

Understanding the Purpose, or "What Am I Expected to Do?"

You might remember that Elisa was assigned to write an essay on the topic of potential censorship (screening) of books for her high school library by a screening committee of concerned citizens. To try to understand the purpose of her assignment, Elisa reread it several times, looking for terms that would indicate to her what she was required to do. As she read, she noted the terms "develop a position" and "formulate an opinion." Elisa decided, then, that she was being asked to take a position in the controversy over whether the screening committee ought to be formed. The other part of the assignment Elisa noted was that she had to decide the extent to which such a committee would be consistent with the values stated in the United States Constitution. Thus, as an important first step in beginning her paper, Elisa carefully considered the **overall purpose** of the task.

You also should consider the "to do" terms—sometimes called the "command verbs"—in your writing assignments. It's not a bad idea to underline or highlight such terms as you encounter them in an assignment to make sure you don't forget a key requirement and to give yourself a reminder to check into any requirement you don't understand. Commonly used command verbs in college writing assignments include "analyze," "explain," "support," "define," "distinguish," "evaluate," "document," and "synthesize." Other key commands in writing assignments take the form of a short phrase, such as "show the relationships between." Once you have determined all the key "to dos" in your assignment, you are ready to begin thinking about where and when (in your essay) to address each of them.

Clarifying Key Terms in the Assignment

The **key terms** in an assignment help you decide which terms or concepts need additional clarification or definition. These key terms, as distinguished from the command verbs described above, relate to the *content* of your essay or issue instead of relating to your methods (for example, analysis or evaluation) of writing. In looking over her assignment, Elisa focused on the terms she felt she needed to define: "unsuitable," "explicit sex," and "gratuitous violence." Although she had heard of some of these terms before, she decided that she would have to figure out what these terms meant to her in the context of this assignment before she could decide if she was in favor of the screening committee (her purpose, or focus, in her essay). She was not sure about the meaning of the word "gratuitous," so she looked it up in the dictionary and discovered that it meant "not required, called for, or warranted by the circumstances." She also looked up the word "explicit," just to make sure she understood it, and found that it meant "plain in language, distinctly expressed, clearly stated, not obscure or ambiguous." The word "unsuitable," she decided, was a matter of interpretation she would have to think about—she knew the definition. Also, Elisa noted that she would have to find out what the First Amendment actually said in order to use it to bolster her position on book screening.

EXPLORATORY DRAFTING

Sometimes, writing what you believe about an issue or what you think others might believe is a very productive way to move toward a more formal draft of your assigned essay. Exploratory drafts are being reintroduced here because there are many different kinds of exploratory writing you can do, and productive exploratory writing can be done at virtually any stage in a writing project. Thus, you might want to write an exploration of your own preconceptions or an audience dialogue after a small amount of reading on your issue, as Elisa did in Chapter 3, or you might want to read much more intensively and even take extensive notes, *then* do some exploratory writing as Molly does on the next page. Regardless of when you fully explore your issue, exploratory writing must be done or you risk missing your audience or losing your purpose in the final draft. In short, if you explore your audience and purpose fully before drafting, you will be better prepared to write on the issue you are addressing because you will gain a better sense of your own position and the information you will need to include in order to reach—and, hopefully, persuade—your readers.

"Who Do I Want to Read My Essay?" and "What Do I Want Them to Get from It?"

Two things you must always consider when writing are the audience to whom you are writing and the purpose of the writing itself. In other words, ask yourself, "Who do I want to read my essay, and what do I want them to get from it?" Writing about these issues in an exploratory draft can help you clarify your thinking regarding these inevitable questions.

For example, suppose that you are writing an essay arguing that your community hospital needs to institute a program to inform patients of the healing benefits of laughter. The essay would be approached very differently depending on whom the essay is written for and what the desired outcome is. If the argument is directed toward the staff at the hospital, the purpose may be to convince them that medicinal laughter is a valid form of treatment. The focus may need to be on reassuring them that there is clinical research touting the benefits of medicinal laughter. However, if the argument is written to try to sway a large insurance company to donate money to implement such a program, the focus may need to be on the potential for shorter hospital stays due to medicinal laughter that would, in turn, save the insurance company money.

As you can see in the above example, it is not enough to merely come up with a debatable issue—you must always consider the audience and purpose. In fact, you may not have even realized that there could be more than one audience and purpose had you not done some initial exploration. Since the audience and purpose of an argument are not always obvious based on the thesis alone (as can be seen above), it is well worth your time to adequately explore your audience and purpose before getting too far into the writing process, hence the need for an exploratory draft. You might find it helpful to refer back to this initial exploration frequently throughout the writing process to make sure that you have not strayed from your intended audience and purpose.

SAMPLE EXPLORATORY DRAFT

The following exploratory draft was one of the first steps in the writing process of Molly Brooks, an English 112 student at BGSU in 2000, whose final draft will be featured in Chapter 8. After engaging a small group of her classmates in an extended dialogue to help her focus her intended audience and purpose, she drafted the following:

Exploratory Draft

I have decided to explore the controversy of prohibiting smoking sections in restaurants for my researched essay. I believe that my intended audience is anyone who has their own opinion regarding the topic and also anyone who could do something about it (such as the owner of a restaurant).

Some of my readers may possess values related to this topic such as the rights of smokers and non-smokers. Each reader may have a different opinion, perhaps depending on their smoking or non-smoking status. One might say that non-smokers should have their rights granted over smokers, yet another may disagree by arguing the opposite.

Because smoking has become a major issue in America, my audience should have a fairly good background on my topic. Tobacco sales are rocket-high, and there is an enormous amount of people dying from lung cancer. These two facts should give my audience a good understanding of the effects of smoking and may help them decide whether or not smoking should be permitted in restaurants. I feel that my readers need to become more aware of the effects that smoking has on non-smokers (second-hand smoke). Perhaps being informed of exactly how harmful smoking is to others will help people see why it shouldn't be permitted in restaurants.

For my essay, I want my readers to understand exactly why I believe there should not be smoking sections in restaurants. I will achieve this by providing four strong reasons: second-hand smoke affects non-smokers; it is very disturbing when trying to eat; some non-smokers are allergic to smoke; and it violates the rights of "innocent" non-smokers. I think that if those who read my paper understand how disturbing and unhealthy smoking is in restaurants, they may express their opinion to restaurant owners to change their restaurants to strictly non-smoking.

While giving my reasons as to why smoking should be prohibited in restaurants, I will also acknowledge a few counterarguments. One of these counterarguments is that banning smoking from restaurants violates smokers' rights because they are being told that they cannot do something that is perfectly legal. Another counterargument that I plan to address is that if non-smokers don't like smoke in the air while they are trying to eat, they can go elsewhere. Restaurant owners may also be concerned that they will lose smoking customers if they ban smoking from their restaurants. Hopefully, by showing that I at least acknowledge reasons behind permitting smoking in restaurants, those who disagree with me will be more likely to change sides on the issue.

Overall, I hope that my researched essay informs readers of the real danger behind allowing people to smoke while others are trying to enjoy a meal. It would be great if enough people realized the negativity of smoking sections in restaurants so that maybe these sections would be banned in every restaurant across the country.

➤ **Exercise in Examining Audience and Purpose:** In small groups, examine the sample exploratory draft above and discuss the following:

- Who is the intended audience?
- Is this the best audience to target? Explain your answer.
- What is the purpose behind her argument?
- Do you believe her purpose to be realistic? Explain your answer.
- Which reasons does she provide to support her position? Are there any others that could be added to support her position? If so, which reasons?
- Which counterarguments does she plan to address? Does she forget any? If so, give other opposing views she should consider.

➤ **Assignment on Exploratory Drafting:** First, type your research question and answer it with your tentative position, or thesis, on the issue. Next, complete the following three components of the exploratory draft:

1. Imagine several different people who have different viewpoints about the issue, and write an **extended** dialogue between these people (see example in Chapter 3, "Creating a Brief Dialogue," page 94).

2. After completing the dialogue, consider each possible audience affected by the issue and your position on it. Decide toward whom you should gear your essay by determining who you need to persuade in order to fulfill the purpose of your argument.

Based upon your tentative thesis, answer the following:
- Specifically, who should be your intended audience? Explain why.
- What do your readers already know about the issue?
- What more do your readers need to know about the issue?
- What values do your targeted readers possess?
- What common ground do you and your readers share?
- Which position do your readers have on this particular issue?
- How does their position differ from yours?
- Which counterarguments will you have to address?
- How do these considerations of your audience affect the way you'll need to approach the issue within your essay?

3. Now that you have explored the issue and decided on your targeted audience, you need to determine what you hope to accomplish in your essay. Explore your purpose more fully by answering the following:
- What do you want your readers to get from the essay?
- How will you achieve this effect?
- What reasoning may be most effective?
- What evidence may be most effective?

WRITING AN ESSAY PROPOSAL

Like exploratory drafts, essay proposals can help you focus your thinking about an issue you've tentatively selected. Essay proposals usually consider such aspects of the writing situation as audience and purpose, and they typically are created prior to the drafting of the essay itself. The proposal helps you take a closer look at your issue to determine where you really stand and why. It also encourages you to consider your audience and how they might respond to your stance.

You might write a proposal for various college writing assignments because they often act as permission-seekers or feedback-getters. In the business world, you might submit a proposal to introduce to your employer or a potential client a project you hope to complete or an idea you'd like to try. In your composition class, you may be asked to submit writing proposals to suggest (and preview) essays you'd like to write. In both of these cases, proposals allow you to formalize your thinking and ask others what they think about your idea(s). College instructors often require proposals for significant or complex projects, such as major researched essays, because the proposal-feedback process allows them to guide students toward more successful writing.

SAMPLE ESSAY PROPOSAL

The following essay proposal was a direct result of Molly Brooks' exploratory draft. This fill-in-the-blanks proposal allowed Molly to communicate to her instructor what she was hoping to accomplish in her essay and also allowed her instructor to comment on the issue and approve her plan.

Name: Molly Brooks

1. Describe the problem or phenomenon you plan to write about:

Smoking in restaurants

2. Research question (Pose a question you would like to answer to help direct your research):

Should there continue to be smoking sections in restaurants?

3. Discuss the approach you plan to take in answering your research question:

I'll take a position on the issue, give four reasons as to why I think smoking should be banned in restaurants, provide counterarguments, and refute them.

4. Indicate your tentative answer to your research question in a complete sentence (working thesis):

There should not be smoking sections in restaurants.

5. List at least 4 possible arguments/points/reasons to support your thesis:

1. Second-hand smoke affects the health of non-smokers.

2. The smell of smoke is very distracting while trying to eat.

3. Some non-smokers are allergic to smoke.

4. Smoking violates "innocent" non-smokers' rights.

6. List some possible counterarguments to your reasons/points or thesis:

1. It also violates smokers' rights when they're told that they can't smoke in a restaurant.

2. If non-smokers don't like smoke in the air while they are eating, they can go elsewhere.

7. List some possible refutations/concessions to the above counterarguments:

1. Yes, but the right of those who aren't doing anything potentially harmful to others is more important.

2. Non-smokers shouldn't be forced to leave a restaurant because someone else can't wait to light up.

8. List two people you might be able to interview about the issue. Also, describe their relationship to the issue and the kinds of information you hope they would be able to provide.

    1. A manager/owner of a restaurant that prohibits smoking. S/he could give me reasoning as to why smoking isn't permitted in their establishment.

    2. A smoker and a non-smoker. Both could give their opinion on the issue.

9. Describe your potential survey and the respondents. Describe their relationship to the issue and why their opinions/answers would be valuable to your essay.

I could give a survey to 30 people, regardless of whether they smoke or not. I'm sure almost everyone has gone into a restaurant that offers both smoking and non-smoking sections, so almost everyone could provide their opinion.

10. Describe your intended audience. Remember that it should be someone (or a group of people) who can do something about the arguments you present.

My intended audience could be managers/owners of restaurants who could convert their restaurants into strictly "non-smoking." Another audience could be non-smokers who could be persuaded to protest the restaurants they visit in an effort to get smoking banned.

➤ **Assignment on Writing a Proposal:** Complete the following tasks in order to propose your research path and issue focus to your instructor:

1. State your research question in a complete sentence.
2. Indicate your answer to your research question in the form of a working thesis.
3. List three to four points/reasons to support your thesis.
4. List at least two possible counterarguments to your reasons/points or thesis.
5. List some possible refutations/concessions to the above counterarguments.
6. Describe who should be interested in reading your essay besides your instructor. Think about groups of people who would support your thesis/argument, those who would not, and those who might not be on either side. Hence, describe the audience(s) you plan on addressing in your paper and where one might expect to read your paper if it were published.

7. List two people you might be able to interview about the issue. Also, describe their relationship to the issue and the kinds of information you hope they would be able to provide.
8. Describe whom you might survey for views on this issue. Explain their relationship to the issue and why their opinions/answers would be valuable to your essay.
9. List other information you will need to support your argument. In which types of sources will you most likely find this information—books, popular magazines, professional journals, online articles or websites, or elsewhere?

THE STRUCTURE OF ACADEMIC ARGUMENT

As you think about beginning to draft your assigned essay, you may find it less intimidating if you understand the form an academic argument usually takes and plan the sequence of ideas you are going to develop. One characteristic of researched writing you should realize is that the more complex your paper is going to be and the more sources (and source ideas) it incorporates, the more planning you will probably need to do. Your synthesis note sheets and prewriting such as summaries, character dialogues, and exploratory drafts will be an immense help to you as you begin to plug ideas about your issue into an essay plan.

Most students come to college with an awareness of one or more common essay structures or forms. The question is: will a form you have used in the past work for the essay you are about to write? The form and structure for a researched paper, like that for any text, depends on what you are trying to accomplish. Form must follow content, not the other way around. However, over many years, the classical form of argumentation has come to be accepted, and it is important for you to be aware of it in planning your paper. But once you understand it, you are then free to modify it to suit your own purposes.

The Classical Argumentative Structure

A classical argument usually contains the following sections:

1. **Introduction.** In this section, which may consist of only one or two paragraphs, you introduce your topic, indicate why it is important, and present your position. This section also gives your audience its first acquaintance with you as a credible writer whose perspective is trustworthy.
2. **Background information and definitions.** In this section, you place your position within a cultural context, perhaps by showing that it has aroused current interest, that it generally stimulates controversy, or that it has not been understood adequately. This section might include personal experience that is relevant to the issue and might define important key terms.

3. **Acknowledgment of opposing points of view.** In this section, you summarize alternatives to your position on the issue in question. Such a summary indicates that you understand other positions; in fact, you may concede that certain aspects of opposing or alternative arguments have merit. You may also point out weaknesses in alternative positions. A discussion of other, understandable positions leads naturally into the presentation of your main arguments. It also establishes you as someone who has researched the topic thoroughly and shows that you realize that the issue is complex.

4. **Presenting your main position.** This is usually the longest and most substantial section of your essay. In this section, you present your position or claim, present one or more reasons, and support your reasons logically, either with evidence (examples, facts, statistics, data) or with statements from authorities, analogies, and illustrative examples.

5. **Conclusion.** This section summarizes your main argument and perhaps suggests what action, if any, your readers ought to take. Perhaps it indicates why the issue is important or postulates possible implications of a policy or situation. In general, the conclusion provides readers with a sense of closure on the issue.

It's important to note that while most formal arguments include all of these sections, they might not be handled in exactly this order. As you read and work through the remainder of this chapter, you will learn strategies for determining how to best organize your academic, argumentative essay.

PLANNING THE OVERALL DESIGN OF YOUR PAPER

You understand argumentative form, and you have a great many notes. Now is the time to plan the preliminary structure of your paper. Begin by reading over all of your notesheets and notecards and thinking about your approach to the issue you will be writing about. Reread your position statement (from your exploratory draft and/or essay proposal, if you have written one or both) so that you are sure you have a clear purpose in mind for your paper. Some students find it helpful to read this position statement aloud, or they keep it on a separate sheet for easy referral. If you keep your position statement (thesis statement) handy, you can glance at it as you write each of your main points and ask yourself the following questions: "How does this point relate to my main position? Is it a supporting argument? Is it an example? Is it an opposing argument (counterargument)? Does this idea pertain to my overall conception of the issue?"

Finding Your Main Points

Question, Response, and Reader Expectations

In a researched paper—as in most types of academic writing—**formulating a position implies a question,** whether or not it is stated specifically in question form. To illustrate, if your position argues that "Human cloning should be banned permanently and world-wide," the implied research question asks, "Why should there be a universal and permanent ban on human cloning?" If your position asserts, "School newspapers must be censored, at least somewhat, by a responsible adult," the implied research question asks, "Why should school newspapers be censored, at least somewhat, by a responsible adult?"

Thus, the position statement sets up an expectation for the reader that the body of the paper will respond to an implied research question and provide an answer and a justification. For example, if you take the position that "Human cloning should be banned permanently world-wide," the body of your essay would probably establish that the potential problems associated with the legalization of cloning outweigh the possible medical advances and cite evidence supporting that claim, such as a lack of successful and extensive scientific research, potential identity problems a clone would endure, and the ethical and moral dilemmas surrounding the practice of cloning itself. Because the body of your paper should answer your research question, you would need to select sources (and portions of those sources) that are likely to provide some of those answers. Then, as you read, you would begin making connections and inferences about the information you find. These connections and inferences would help you to select the main points of your paper.

> **Assignment on Finding Your Main Points:** Follow the steps below to help you find your main points:

1. Reexamine your position.
2. Ask what questions are implied in that position.
3. Decide what evidence will help you answer your questions and provide support.
4. Evaluate the source information you have found and jot down some main points. You will now be able to decide if the information you have gathered will provide the evidence you need to back your position.

If you find that you must modify your thesis because you are unable to answer the questions it implies or because the act of reading has led you to change your mind about your position, you should then repeat this sequence.

Modifying Your Position: Working Through the Sequence

When you begin locating your main points, you may decide to modify your thesis or position statement. For example, Clifton, a freshman enrolled in an introductory history course, was assigned to develop a position on some issue having to do with Abraham Lincoln. In thinking about his topic, Clifton realized that like most American students, he had been raised with the idea that Lincoln was the epitome of wisdom and goodness, a true humanitarian. However, Clifton did not wish to write a paper detailing what he suspected most potential readers already knew or thought was true about Lincoln, so he decided to approach his research with the idea that perhaps Lincoln was not as much of a humanitarian as everyone thinks. Through his course, Clifton had learned that political concerns were important factors in the Civil War, and he hoped that he could focus his paper to show that Lincoln was as much concerned with politics as he was with freeing the slaves. He thus began looking through the information gathered in his preliminary research, hoping to present the following claim:

> Everyone thinks of Abraham Lincoln as a great humanitarian, as the President who was primarily concerned with freeing the slaves. Yet, that position is somewhat of an exaggeration. Although Lincoln has the reputation for being concerned with slavery purely on moral grounds, his humanitarian views, by modern standards, would be considered moderate, at best. In his campaign against slavery, Lincoln was motivated by political and social concerns.

When he was ready to write, Clifton then went through the four steps outlined in the assignment above:

1. He **reexamined his position** and decided that he still wanted to write about it. He thought it would have a strong impact on his readers if he could show something about Lincoln that few had considered before.
2. He **asked questions that were implied in his position.** In looking over his thesis statement, Clifton decided that some of the questions his paper had to address included, "Why do I say that Lincoln was a moderate by modern standards? What do I mean by a 'moderate'? Which political and social concerns influenced Lincoln's behavior?"
3. He then decided that **the information he needed to answer these questions** might be concerned with a definition of what is meant by modern humanitarian views, a discussion of Lincoln's political affiliations, or perhaps an analysis of the political situation during Lincoln's term. In order to establish that Lincoln was not as interested in freeing the slaves as he was on settling political differences, Clifton thought he needed some statements Lincoln might have made that would provide support and establish justification.
4. Finally, he **evaluated his source information** and jotted down some main points contained within that information. Once he reexamined this information, he would then be able to see whether it would sufficiently back his thesis and fulfill the purpose of his essay.

These are the main points Clifton decided to develop from his notes:

1. Lincoln was a member of the newly formed Republican party, which was strongly against continuing slavery in new territories. Lincoln was expected by party members to adopt a strong antislavery campaign as his party platform. Lincoln was strongly in favor of a united America. He

viewed slavery as a divisive force splitting the North and the South. Therefore, he was against slavery because of its effect on the Union.

2. Because he was so strongly in favor of the Union, Lincoln wanted all citizens in society to feel as if they had the opportunity to advance. He felt that slavery would prevent workers from obtaining employment, reinforcing class distinctions in the South.

3. England, an important source of income for American products, was objecting to importing from a slave-owning country.

4. Lincoln denied being a Whig, meaning that he did not hold ultraliberal views.

Clifton then reread his main points and looked back at his position statement. He discovered that he actually had very little information on the first part of his position (Lincoln's humanitarian views were moderate by modern standards) and realized that if he wished to develop that point, he would have to find additional information on Lincoln's actual position on slavery. He also realized that even if he found additional information on this topic, he would then have to explain what he meant by saying "moderate by modern standards." Therefore, he had to decide either to drop that part of his position statement or modify the statement in some way. He decided that the more efficient direction to take would be to revise his position as follows:

> Although Abraham Lincoln has the reputation for being against slavery purely on moral grounds, he was also motivated by political and social concerns.

Thus, Clifton modified his position when he began the process of noting his main points. Structure can influence purpose just as purpose can help to determine structure. Note that Clifton's original thesis idea contained the more surprising assertion having to do with Lincoln's "moderate humanitarianism." His modified thesis, absent this assertion, may not be quite as exciting for readers as the original thesis, but because the original thesis did not seem feasible to Clifton—at least in the time remaining to finish his researched essay—he probably was wise in choosing as his focus the most significant argument he could effectively make in the time at his disposal.

ARGUMENTATIVE GENRES

Although many textbooks, including this one, give suggestions about patterns of essay organization, the truth is that when you know a great deal about an issue and your purpose for writing, you usually do not think about organization so mechanically; instead, the best mode of organization often becomes clear because it is inherent to the issue and the argumentative genre of your essay. Therefore, it is often useful for students to think about how their issue fits into a particular genre. For example, if your issue lends itself to the taking a position genre, you can make sure that you follow the basic structure of that type of argument. Also, you may recall various types of argumentation you have learned elsewhere in your education that could be used to help you approach and organize your essay. Some of these argumentative genres include:

1. **Arguing a position.** You might be for or against one side of a controversial issue, or your position might be a compromise. An example of a "taking a position" essay would be an essay that tries to sway an audience of non-Greek students to consider rushing, or joining a sorority or fraternity, for a variety of reasons.
2. **Proposing a solution.** If your issue can be framed as a problem in need of a solution, you might discuss plausible solutions and then argue that one is more feasible, suitable, or effective (or combinations thereof) than the others. For example, a student-writer may argue that the declining number of Greek students on their campus is becoming a problem and propose a solution to the Panhellenic Council and/or Greek Life office to combat the issue.
3. **Speculating about causes.** Perhaps the causes of your issue need to be fully explored. If so, you might speculate about several causes and then argue that one is more plausible than the others. For instance, a student-writer might try to find out why students are not as interested in joining fraternities and sororities as students in the past; then, once all the possible causes have been examined, the essay could focus upon the most influential cause of this decline that might best lead to some insight on how to address it.
4. **Evaluating single items or alternatives.** In this argumentative genre, you might argue for or against relative values for single or multiple items, concrete or abstract. By way of example, a student-writer considering joining a sorority in order to meet new people and make new friends might examine all possible options for meeting new people on and off campus. After evaluating all the options, she decides that she can meet new people just as easily at campus-sponsored events. Therefore, she argues to her readers that the cost of a sorority is not worth it because those considering rushing can meet other students just as easily—at no cost to them—by attending the campus-sponsored activities.

These typical argumentative genres are often used in combination with each other as well as in combination with other rhetorical devices such as:

- Comparison and Contrast
- Definition
- Description
- Example and Illustration
- Classification and Division

> ➤ **Exercise in Testing Genres:** For the following list of campus issues, try to determine which argumentative genres outlined above would provide the best strategy for approaching a writing assignment where you must argue something about these campus-related issues:

- A poor parking situation
- Athletes getting preferential treatment
- Lack of food variety in cafeterias
- Lack of entertainment
- On-campus versus off-campus living

> **Assignment on Testing Genres:** Considering the issue you would like to explore for your next essay, determine which of the argumentative genres outlined above would best suit your issue and purpose for writing.

USING SYNTHESIS NOTE SHEETS TO ORGANIZE INFORMATION

A useful strategy for organizing information around a particular aspect of an issue is to use the synthesis note sheets discussed in Chapter 5. These sheets include information from several sources that you can incorporate into your paper with relative ease. While engaged in some writing projects, you may not know exactly how you are going to use each piece of information in your notes (if, indeed, you eventually *do* use each piece of information in your final paper) until you actually begin to write the paper. In other projects or with other topics, you may determine early on how you will use each piece of information, and it is a good idea to jot these ideas down in the "Reason for Using" column of the synthesis note sheets before you forget them.

While it should now be apparent that synthesis note sheets can help you as you gather information, they can also be used as a device to help you plan your paper. Recall Justin and his assignment:

> To many, old age is a depressing topic. No one wants to experience the feebleness of body and the social neglect that we assume comes with old age. Yet old age is a universal condition that awaits us all. In a well-organized essay using at least four sources, consider the following question: What can be done so that the aged in our society can live a more fulfilling life?
>
> As part of your paper, you should demonstrate awareness of some of the problems of the aged in today's culture. Make sure that you narrow your topic to a particular issue, so that you can adequately develop and support your ideas.

Remember that Justin prepared the following synthesis note sheets as he explored his issue. The sheets have already helped him focus his ideas about dealing with old age; now, he will use them to help him organize his essay.

Synthesis Note Sheet 1

Subtopic/Claim: Defining what "fulfilling" means.

Possible Topic Sentence: Older people have the potential to lead as productive, fulfilling lives as younger people do by staying mentally and physically active.

Note/Quote/Paraphrase with in-text citation (author's last name & p.#):

Reason for Using:

1. "Life at any stage" requires a challenge (Tuan 145).

To show that the needs of the old are the same as those of any human being.

2. "The secret of success, found so often among those who have bridged their three-score-and-ten in health, serenity, and happiness, pertains to their ability to remain curious and concerned. They possess the common denominator of being self-educable, self-sufficient, and aware of all that is taking place around them" (Perera 112).

To show the need to progress, to work at something.

3. "Most older Samoans explain their longevity by the fact that they keep busy every day" (Holmes 8).

To show that other societies also value productivity.

4. "One pressing need of people in all stages and walks of life is to be useful" (Blau 16).

Other support for this definition.

Synthesis Note Sheet 2

Subtopic/Claim: Retirement should be rethought.

Possible Topic Sentence: Engaging in a more active retirement is one important way for older people to remain happily involved in society and alleviate feelings of worthlessness.

Note/Quote/Paraphrase with in-text citation (author's last name & p.#):

Reason for Using:

1. Early retirement is wasteful (Mead 25).

Negative idea of retirement.

2. "Retirement! What a distressful word! It smacks of retreat, withdrawal, seclusion from circulation" (Perera 112).

Retirement means isolation.

3. "For many, the word 'retirement' in the United States means a shift from a busy, active life, to one of idleness and boredom" (Jones 57).

Retirement has negative connotations.

Synthesis Note Sheet 3

Subtopic/Claim: The present condition of the elderly in our society.

Possible Topic Sentence: Currently, many older people face an increasing risk of feeling idle, lonely, or powerless as they age.

Note/Quote/Paraphrase with in-text citation (author's last name & p.#):	*Reason for Using:*
1. Advanced industrial society has resulted in enforced idleness for the old (Blau 21).	One problem of old: idleness.
2. "I see no human beings. My phone never rings. I feel sure the world has ended. I'm the only one on Earth. How else can I feel? All alone" (Percy 1).	Another problem of old: loneliness.
3. "For the vast majority it is almost tautological to say 'old and poor'" (DeBeauvoir 6).	Another problem: power.
4. "Often, they feel as if they have no function in life. Their roles as earners are lost with retirement" (Jones 17).	Another problem: uselessness.

Synthesis Note Sheet 4

Subtopic/Claim: The present condition of the elderly in our society: financial problems.

Possible Topic Sentence: Financial uncertainty and instability may also lead to a reduced quality of life for the elderly.

Note/Quote/Paraphrase with in-text citation (author's last name & p.#):	*Reason for Using:*
1. "For the vast majority it is almost tautological to say 'old and poor'" (DeBeauvoir 6).	Support from social commentator.
2. "At a time in their lives when they need more, rather than fewer services, older people suffer drastic drops in income" (Percy 1).	Support from authority (senator).
3. "Social security payments have increased over the years, but they are not linked to the cost of living or adequate to keep retirees out of near poverty" (Kuhn 41).	Member of Gray Panthers.

Synthesis Note Sheet 5

Subtopic/Claim: Causes of problems.

Possible Topic Sentence: Fear and lack of preparation for old age in American are rooted in our dominant ideologies promoting independence and self-reliance.

Note/Quote/Paraphrase with in-text citation (author's last name & p.#):	*Reason for Using:*
1. The situation is due to the following combinations of (1) a particular set of values, (2) a particular level of technological development, and (3) a particular form of social organization (Holmes 20).	Causes.
2. In American society, the fear of dependency is so great that an individual who is not self-reliant is an object of hostility (Hsu 216).	Causes linked to values.
3. Democracies are societies on the move, and they have little time for ceremony or convention (Smith 28).	To show causes as rooted in democracy.

As Justin reviews his synthesis note sheets, he might realize a need for his essay to show how dealing with old age is a problem in need of a solution. It is also clear that to present a feasible method of dealing with the problems of aging, Justin will have to explore the causes of the problem. He will also need to define key terms as they come up in his essay.

While it may seem that all of these discovery steps happen in a very orderly fashion, with each step yielding a specific, fruitful result, this is not often the case. Keep in mind that writing is a circular process. You may often have to write, rewrite, think, and re-think before your essay comes together.

➤ **Assignment on Using Synthesis Note Sheets:** Using Justin's note sheets as a model, begin generating your own synthesis note sheets for your essay by examining your supporting reasons for your thesis (you may have outlined these on your essay proposal) and the evidence you have found that can either support or contradict those reasons. Although you may complete these sheets any way you like, we suggest that you word process them and save them on a disk so that you can cut, paste, and revise your source evidence more easily.

YOUR MAIN POINTS: CONSTRUCTING A PLAN OR OUTLINE

As was noted in Chapter 5, Justin has already determined a working thesis, and we can see that he has ascertained the basic argumentative genre of his essay. He can now use the synthesis note sheets to construct an outline for his argument. For some writers, the word "outline" is a dirty word since, for them, the idea of creating a structure in advance means limiting possibilities. For other writers, writing an outline is a useful way of creating the paper. It helps them to construct logical relationships between ideas, which sometimes involves discovering new ideas in the process. For these writers, outlining forces consideration of the overall meaning of the paper, which may only have been vaguely formulated before. It also helps to determine the order in which ideas are presented so that the paper's main purpose is more easily conveyed. They see an outline as flexible, as easily changed as one's ideas.

Whether or not you use an outline is your own decision. However, before reading about various methods of outlining, please give careful consideration to these general principles:

1. **There is no one way to plan a paper.** There are many forms of outlining and planning. You should use the one that works best for you.
2. **Outlines are flexible.** Just because you have indicated a particular order in your outline does not mean that you have to stick with it. Your outline will probably change as you write your paper. In fact, some writers write an outline *after,* rather than before, they write their papers because doing so helps them find gaps in their logic or areas that need further development. Other writers write an initial tentative outline to get them started; then, they constantly revise and reshape their outlines as they draft their essay.

Jotting Down Ideas

While jotting down ideas about a topic at random has been suggested earlier in this book as an effective means of deciding upon a focus for a paper, jotting down ideas in the order you wish to discuss them is also an easy, informal way to plan a paper. As an example of how jotting down ideas can serve as a planning method, look at Justin's tentative plan:

> *Working Thesis:* Living a more fulfilling life in old age requires financial and educational preparation, on both governmental and individual levels.
> *Introduction:* Short sketch of old people sitting on a park bench, feeling useless. Indication that this is a problem. Then state position to suggest a partial solution.
> **Problems of the old in contemporary American society.** (This establishes that the issue is an important one.) Not only physical and financial problems, but enforced idleness leads to feelings of worthlessness and loss of identity.

Definition of a "fulfilling" life as one in which there is a feeling of being needed, of being as productive and independent as possible.
Preparation can help people live a more fulfilling life in their later years.
Financial preparation—government programs, increased emphasis on retirement programs in private industry, attention drawn to the need for preparation.
Preparation by developing interests outside one's job, interests that can occupy one's lifetime.
Using old people to fulfill the needs of others. Government programs in which old people work with children or teenagers. Reeducating society to view old people as a resource to enrich society, not as a burden.
No program will work unless society stops thinking of old age as a taboo subject. Need for group rethinking on the topic.
Of course, these problems will not be easily solved. Even with the best preparation, old people can become sick or disabled. This is a complex topic.
Conclusion: Important to keep thinking about this issue.

As Justin jotted down his ideas, he noticed that the preparation he was advocating could be accomplished in two ways: the government could generate it, or each individual could initiate it. Therefore, he regrouped his ideas as follows:

Introduction: Short sketch of old people sitting on a park bench, feeling useless. Indication that this is a problem. Use thesis statement to suggest a partial solution.
Problems of the old in contemporary American society (reinforcing claim). Not only physical and financial problems, but enforced idleness leads to feelings of worthlessness and loss of identity.
Definition of a "fulfilling" life as one in which there is a feeling of being needed, of being as productive and independent as possible.
Preparation can help people live a more fulfilling life in their later years.
Government programs:
  Financial:
  Increased emphasis on retirement programs in private industry.
  Attention drawn to the need for financial preparation.
  Cultural:
  Government programs to sponsor activities for older citizens.
  Programs using old people to fulfill the needs of others, working with children or teenagers.
Individual preparation:
  Financial awareness.
  Development of interests that can be continued after retirement.
Reeducating society to view old people as a resource to enrich society, not as a burden. No program will work unless society stops thinking of old age as a taboo subject. Need for group rethinking on the topic.
Of course, these problems will not be easily solved. Even with the best preparation, old people can become sick or disabled. This is a complex topic.
Conclusion: Important to keep thinking about this issue.

> ➤ **Assignment on Jotting Down a Plan:** Keeping your thesis, purpose, and main points needed to fulfill your purpose in mind, generate a tentative plan for your essay. You can either outline your plan or jot it down in a similar manner as Justin.

INCORPORATING YOUR SYNTHESIS NOTE SHEETS

Once you decide on a form for your main ideas, you can then incorporate your synthesis note sheets into your plan. While the information on the individual sheets sometimes leads to individual paragraphs, the ideas each sheet contains might be split up into more than one paragraph. Conversely, while planning and writing the essay, you might find that an idea that originally had an entire sheet to itself works better when combined with ideas from another sheet. In short, do not force your writing to be governed by the synthesis note sheets. Rather, keep revising your perceptions of how the ideas can best go together, using the synthesis note sheets to help you find the information you need. Here is an example of how Justin did it:

> **Introduction:** Short sketch of old people sitting on a park bench, feeling useless. (Present statistics on the elderly.) Indicate that this is a problem— establish importance. Use thesis statement to suggest a partial solution.
> **Problems of the old in contemporary American society:** Further establishes importance. Not only physical and financial problems, but enforced idleness leads to feelings of worthlessness and loss of identity. *(Use Synthesis Note Sheet 2.)*
> **Definition of a "fulfilling" life as one in which there is a feeling of being needed**, of being as productive and independent as possible. *(Use Synthesis Note Sheet 1.)*
> **Preparation can help people live a more fulfilling life in their later years.** Government programs. Financial. *(Use Synthesis Note Sheet 4.)*

Below is a paragraph from Justin's paper, which he generated by combining information recorded on Synthesis Note Sheets 1 and 3. This paragraph is concerned with establishing that the problems of the elderly are not only physical and financial but psychological as well. The notes in the margins indicate how Justin incorporated ideas from the synthesis note sheets into his own position.

In addition to enduring physical and financial hardship, many of the elderly also suffer a loss of a sense of purpose in life, which creates feelings of uselessness and loneliness. Furthermore, "Advanced industrial society has resulted in enforced idleness for the old" (Blau 21), which results in the elderly feeling as though they "have no function in life" (Jones 17).	*Notesheet 3* *Notesheet 3* *Notesheet 3*

Since they are no longer earners, no longer a part of
the growing, developing part of society, many of them
feel as though their lives are over. According
to Blau and Perera, a fulfilling life means
that one is working at something, facing new
challenges, and feeling useful. However,   *Notesheet 1*
the elderly in this society are considered
marginal, no longer necessary to society (16; 112).

Note that Justin used both direct quotation as well as summary and paraphrase. Also, note how quotation marks and source references were used.

Incorporating references from his note synthesis sheets helped Justin work through a first draft of his paper with relative ease. But remember that the purpose of constructing a plan is to help you; there is no "best" way to do it, and the plan is not an end in itself. Therefore, you can include anything in the plan that will help you get a better notion of an effective structure for your paper.

> ➤ **Assignment on Incorporating Your Synthesis Note Sheets:** As you can see by looking at Justin's example, as he incorporates his synthesis note sheets, he is synthesizing his source information with his own ideas. Now it is time for you to start doing the same. Gather all of your synthesis note sheets generated at this point. Using the synthesis strategy for paragraph development explained in Chapter 5, begin composing your first synthesized body paragraph for your essay. Next, share that paragraph with your instructor. Finally, using your instructor's suggestions, craft your remaining synthesized supporting arguments.

USING CLUSTERING AND TREE DIAGRAMS TO PLAN

Clustering, which is also a tool we use to discover ideas, can be a way of mapping the structure of a paper. Where jotting down ideas or outlining are basically linear designs (top to bottom), clustering for structure enables you to move horizontally or all over the page. You can then see that some ideas are subordinate to others, while some are "superior" or independent. See Chapter 3 (page 78) for a sample **cluster diagram.**

A **tree diagram** is another form of planning. It has the advantage of enabling you to show levels of generality and specificity without necessarily dividing ideas into parts. It gives you a visual map of your ideas that can help you understand the relationship of the parts to the whole. See the tree diagram on the next page, which relates to Justin's thesis statement (repeated below), to get an idea how to construct one.

Working thesis: Living a more fulfilling life in old age requires financial and education preparation on both the governmental and individual levels.

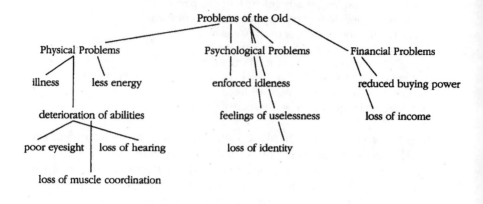

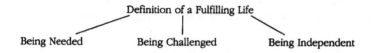

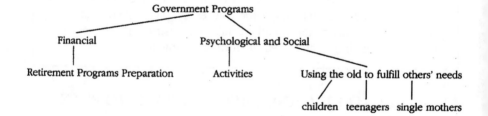

Tree Diagram. What Can Be Done so that the Aged in Our Society Can Live a More Fulfilling Life?

Figure 8

An Important Qualification: In reading about models and methods of organization in this chapter, you might have formed the idea that successful writers always use various methods of organization consistently, always keep information organized, and generally write papers in a methodical fashion. Yet as anyone who writes papers frequently will attest, writers often are less disciplined than they would like to be. Many writers are involved in several research projects at the same time, and they jot down notes not only on carefully constructed notesheets but also on whatever they happen to have, wherever they happen to be—on the backs of envelopes, in the corners of shopping lists, and so on. Sometimes, if writers already know a lot about their topics, they can plan a great deal of their paper before beginning to write or search for information. In other words, although you may find that one of the models presented here is a good one to imitate because it enables you to organize information efficiently and coherently, you may also find that another method is more comfortable for you. It is up to you to find the method that works best for you.

> ➤ Exercise in Generating Questions from Thesis Statements:

   1. Read the following position statements. In small groups, formulate a question for each that you would expect the body of the paper to answer. Then, if you know at least something about the topics, discuss subpoints that could serve as support.
      a. Eighteen-year-old citizens need further preparation in order to vote wisely.
      b. Fast-food establishments generate excessive waste.
      c. Young people ought to be required to perform a year of public service
      d. President Kennedy's reputation as a statesman is based more on his personal charisma than on his accomplishments as President.
      e. American undergraduates should be exposed to some form of intercultural experience as part of their education.
      f. Women are still being socialized to think of careers as secondary to marriage.
      g. Computers are going to change our concept of privacy.

   2. Examine the above position statements again. For those issues you know something about, decide how you might use history, causality, definition, analysis, or comparison to develop related ideas.

Back to the Beginning and Knowing How to End

Writing the Introduction

More pencils probably are chewed over the writing of an introduction than over any other section of a paper. Writers often have problems with introductions because they try to write them first, before they really know what they want to say. If you are having difficulty writing an introduction, an approach that works for many writers is to stop trying to write the introduction and save it for last, after you have written the rest of the paper. Usually, once you have clarified your thinking, your introduction will not be such a problem to write. Another point to keep in mind is that often the second, rather than the first paragraph, turns out to be the true beginning of a paper because the first paragraph turns out to be more of a warm-up. It's a good idea, then, in working on an introduction to take a look at the second paragraph as a possibility. Remember, too, that introductions can be longer than just one paragraph.

Another especially useful strategy for writing an introduction is to begin your essay by stating what is generally believed, followed by your thesis (indicating what is actually the case). Andrew G. Kadar, in his article, "The Sex-Bias Myth in Medicine," uses this strategy to lead up to his claim that despite current notions of the superior medical attention that men receive, it is actually women who receive the better care:

> "When it comes to health-care research and delivery, women can no longer be treated as second-class citizens." So said the President of the United States on October 18, 1993. . .
>
> The list of accusations is long and startling. Women's-health-care advocates indict "sex-biased" doctors for stereotyping women as hysterical hypochondriacs, for taking women's complaints less seriously than men's, and for giving them less thorough diagnostic workups. A study conducted at the University of California at San Diego in 1979 concluded that men's complaints of back pain, chest pain, dizziness, fatigue, and headache more often resulted in extensive workups than did similar complaints from women. Hard scientific evidence therefore seemed to confirm women's anecdotal reports. . . .
>
> In fact, one sex does appear to be favored in the amount of attention devoted to its medical needs. In the United States, it is estimated that one sex spends twice as much money on health care as the other does. The NIH also spends twice as much money on research into the diseases specific to one sex as it does on research into those specific to the other, and only one sex has a section of the NIH devoted entirely to the study of diseases afflicting it. That sex is not men, however. It is women.
> "The Sex-Bias Myth in Medicine." (from Andrew G. Kadar.
> *Atlantic Monthly* Aug. 1994: 66-70.)

In beginning his article, Dr. Kadar spends several paragraphs establishing that most people believe women receive inferior health care. Having done this, his claim makes a strong impression on his readers and leads directly into the support he will cite in the article.

In another example, Elena begins an essay affirming the benefits of the multicultural movement by citing those who criticize it:

> In his recently published book *The Disuniting of America*, Arthur Schlesinger Jr. refers to "huddling" among new immigrants as "an understandable reaction for any minority group faced with new and scary challenges" (175). Schlesinger sees huddling as natural, but unfortunate, if it lasts too long, because it exaggerates differences, intensifies resentment and drives each race further apart. Moreover, according to Schlesinger, when people choose to maintain their ethnic and cultural bonds, they are less likely to assimilate easily into American culture. However, although there are instances where ethnic pride is taken to an extreme and sometimes offends people, multicultural awareness promotes enlightenment and open-mindedness. Multiculturalism thus leads to better racial and cultural relationships through cultural awareness.

Starting with an opposing viewpoint or with what is generally believed is one of the most efficient ways of beginning an essay, and many academic writers use this technique for every essay they write. Other possibilities for the introduction are as follows:

1. **The topic, the issue, and the controversy.** Readers need to know what issue you are going to write about and why that issue is controversial.
2. **Your position or thesis.** Readers also should be told where you stand on this controversy. State your position clearly in the introduction or, for longer papers, within the first several paragraphs.
3. **The significance of the issue.** Readers need to know why an issue is important or significant.
4. **Background of the issue.** Use the introduction to present relevant background material and define important terms. However, more detailed background and definitions should be discussed in the body of the paper.
5. **Attracting your reader.** The introduction is a good place to interest your reader in what you have to say. Establishing the significance of your issue is a good way of doing this. Another technique is to challenge a prevailing view, present a new piece of information, or use an illustrative example or quotation.

For more tips on handling introductions, see "Improving Introductions" in Chapter 8 (pages 281–282).

Writing the Conclusion

Conclusions are also difficult. After grinding away at a paper, researching, writing, rewriting, restructuring, and refocusing, the temptation is to say, "Well, that's all I have to say, so good-bye." Don't give in to that temptation, though. Conclusions are also important. They focus the reader's attention back to the problem addressed in the introduction and, most importantly, emphasize why what you have been discussing is significant. Here are some possibilities for conclusions:

1. **Returning to something in the introduction (framing).** Often, you have introduced your issue with a statement of a particular problem or an illustration of a situation that needs to be addressed. If your introduction contains this material, you might wish to return to it in the conclusion. Returning full circle to the introduction can provide your essay with unity.

2. **Postulating the implications of your position.** You might conclude your researched paper by showing how the issue you have discussed will have an impact on society as a whole, thus placing the issue in a wider context. A paper arguing against restricting smoking in public buildings, for example, might refer to the wider context of individual rights or suggest that if smoking is restricted, other individual liberties could be threatened as well.

In the following example, Peter Rose uses his conclusion to state that ethnocentrism will have the effect of causing fragmentation in society.

> Ranking others according to one's own standards and categorizing them into generalized stereotypes together serve to widen the gap between "they" and "we." Freud has written that "in the undisguised antipathies and aversions which people feel toward strangers with whom they have to do we may recognize the expression of self-love—of narcissism." In sociological terms, a function of ethnocentric thinking is the enhancement of group cohesion. There is a close relationship between a high degree of ethnocentrism on the part of one group and an increase of antipathy toward others. This relationship tends to hold for ethnocentrism of both dominant and minority groups.
>
> (From Peter Rose. *They and We: Racial and Ethnic Relations in the United States.* New York: McGraw Hill, 1990.)

3. **Illustrating your position with an anecdote.** You might help your reader experience the significance of your position by concluding with an illustrative anecdote or description. For example, an essay arguing in favor of affirmative action policies to provide women with equal opportunity might cite the example of a particular woman who is now successfully launched in a career or the opposite situation of a bright woman who has remained in a dead-end job due solely to lack of opportunity. A paper arguing in favor of restricting smoking in public buildings could conclude with a description of a smoke-filled restaurant, where it is difficult even to see, let alone taste, the food.

In the following example, James Fallows uses an anecdote in his conclusion to reiterate his point that new immigrants, like those in the past, are interested in assimilating to American culture:

> Most of the young people I met—the rank and file, not the intellectuals who espouse a bilingual society—seemed fully willing to give what in Fuchs'

view the nation asks. I remember in particular one husky Puerto Rican athlete at Miami Senior High School who planned to join the Navy after he got his diploma. I talked to him in a bilingual classroom, heard his story, and asked his name. He told me, and I wrote "Ramon." He came around behind me and looked at my pad. "No, no!" he told me. "You should have put R-A-M-O-N-D."

(From James Fallows, "The New Immigrants."*Atlantic Monthly* Nov. 1994. 62-89.)

Of course, in using an anecdote in your conclusion, you have to be careful not to be silly or obvious. Clever use of this type of conclusion, though, can be extremely effective.

4. **Summarizing.** The most common form of concluding an essay is to summarize your main points, reminding readers why the issue and your position on it are important. Be careful, however, not to simply restate your main points in the same manner as you presented them in your essay. Try to reinvigorate your approach by using fresh language.

In the following example, Arlene Skolnick uses her conclusion to summarize the main point of her essay—that the state of the American family is strongly connected to economic conditions:

However great the difficulties of the present appear, there is no point in giving in to the lure of nostalgia. There is no golden age of family life to long for, no past pattern that, if only we had the moral will to return to, would guarantee us happiness and security. Family life is always bound up with the economic, demographic, and cultural predicaments of specific times and places. We are no longer a nation of pioneers, Puritans, farmers, or postwar suburbanites. We must shatter the myths that blind us and find ways to cope with our present, the place where social change and family history have brought us.

(From Arlene Skolnick. "The State of the American Family." *Embattled Paradise: The American Family in an Age of Uncertainty.* New York: Basic Books, 1992.)

For more tips on handling conclusions, see "Improving Conclusions" in Chapter 8 (pages 293–294).

➤ **Exercise in Examining Introductions and Conclusions:** Skim through two or three articles in your course reader. Analyze the strategies employed by the authors in their introductions and conclusions. Discuss the strategies employed and assess the effectiveness of each in small groups.

> ➤ **Assignment on Writing Introductions and Conclusions:** Look back through the suggestions for writing introductions and conclusions. Begin writing the introduction and conclusion for your essay using the suggestions as a guide.

ARGUMENTATIVE SYNTHESIS ESSAY ASSIGNMENTS AND SAMPLE ESSAYS

The following assignments are included to help guide you through the processes involved in completing an argumentative, researched essay. The first assignment—the assigned, multiple source essay—is geared more toward the researched assignments where some, if not all, of the source information is provided for you by your instructor or a course reader. The second assignment is one that requires you to *independently* and extensively research an issue in order to find ample, relevant, reliable, and credible sources on your own.

Assigned, Multiple Source Essay Assignment

> ➤ **Assignment on Writing an Assigned, Multiple Source Essay:** The assigned, multiple source essay is a written discussion of your own ideas about the subject matter of four or more sources, where you use and synthesize ideas from the sources you've read to support and illustrate your own argument (thesis). An effective multiple source essay revolves around your thoughts but exhibits thorough familiarity with the sources you read.
>
> **The Assignment**
>
> Using the sources your instructor and course reader has provided, build and defend an argument on a controversial issue. Be sure to make your paper truly argumentative, rather than just bombarding your audience with hordes of quotes from your sources. The main voice in the essay should be your own. A typical problem students have with this assignment is allowing the sources to take over the essay, thus failing to show the relationships between the various sources. Remember that you are the lead singer in this performance; do not let your back-up singers take over the show.
>
> Your paper should have a strong central argument, or thesis. This thesis should be narrow enough for you to fully develop your argument. Your argument should be one that reasonable people might disagree with, not something that is a matter of consensus.

You should use quotes and paraphrases from your sources to show the various positions on the issue and to defend your argument, or your position on that issue. Be sure that your sources provide support for all sides of the argument. Discuss the strengths and weaknesses of each side, or point of view, defending your position against the strongest counterarguments offered by your opposition.

This essay will be evaluated according to how well you integrate information from the readings to support your thesis.

Essay Components

In essence, you must include the following in your essay:

1. *Introduction:* Introduce the topic and issue in an interesting way. Consider using questions, anecdotes, statistics, and scenarios that are relevant to your topic to capture your readers' attention. Give your readers a reason to read on! You should also give an overview of the issue at hand by briefly introducing readers to the different viewpoints related to your research question.

2. *Summary of your argument:* This is where you'll want to set up the parameters of your essay which inform your readers of your thesis—the main argument you will be supporting throughout the essay—and purpose. What precisely is the point you are trying to make? How do you intend to go about it?

3. *Arguments:* Each argument you make to support your main point/thesis should be clear to your readers. Remember that analysis of your thesis is vital throughout your essay—all points you make should relate directly back to your thesis. Each argument should be developed in its own paragraph(s), and all arguments should be developed with an appropriate balance between direct quotes, paraphrases, and your own ideas in your own words. Think about which sources support your arguments. Your thesis and arguments must have essential connections with the sources you use/cite. Be sure to show relationships between ideas, rather than writing one paragraph about each source.

4. *Counterarguments/rebuttals:* Think about which sources contradict your arguments. When these sources bring up reasonable problems with your argument(s), you should address them in a rebuttal. Either refute these counterarguments, make concessions to what they are bringing up, or suggest a compromise that might be acceptable to all parties.

5. *Conclusion:* Remember that this is the last glimpse your readers have of your essay; therefore, it must be strong. How will you approach it? With what message do you want to leave your readers? Do not present any new information in your conclusion; wrap-up your points in

a "fresh" way. You might consider closing with a "call to action" or conveying some other memorable message to your readers

Note: Keep in mind that **metadiscourse** and **transitions** are essential to your readers' overall enjoyment of your essay. They "walk" your readers through your points, one-by-one. They illustrate the connections between both your ideas and the ideas presented in your sources.

Format
Your essay should be approximately 1000-1500 words (4–6 pages), typed, and double-spaced, using the MLA format for both your essay and Works Cited page.

A Final Note on Audience

Remember to write for a target audience and keep this specific group of readers in mind as you develop your position and decide on the most convincing supporting arguments to persuade them to consider your point of view on a controversial issue. Also, as you synthesize source material in your essay, bear in mind that your readers have probably not read the sources you are synthesizing. Since your audience does not have an "insider's view," you will have to make a concerted effort to be as clear and concise as possible when showing the connections between your ideas and the ones from your sources.

SAMPLE ASSIGNED, MULTIPLE SOURCE ESSAY

The following essay was written in 2000 by Sarah Duncan, at that time a student in English 112 at Bowling Green State University, to fulfill the assignment above. For this assignment, students were given several readings, including some on websites, from which they could gather information for their essays.

U.S. Government Cannot Censor the Internet

Imagine living your life afraid to speak out that you were gay. What if homosexuality simply wasn't acceptable in your hometown, not to mention within your family? This situation is all too common among teens of this generation. Jeff Walsh was one such young man who couldn't bring himself to reveal the news he had been keeping a secret. At the age of 23 with the support of fellow gay peers online, Walsh came out and shared his homosexuality with this friends and family. The Internet became an outlet for him, a place to talk with other homosexuals who often felt alone and depressed as well ("The Plaintiffs").

Unfortunately, gay sites like the one Walsh visited and those that are similar are in danger of being blocked from Internet users because of new online censorship laws that some states are trying to pass. Their purpose is to shield minors from harmful material located on the Web, but their efforts have stirred a huge controversy because the government should not be allowed to censor the Internet.

One reason why the Internet should not be regulated by the government is because it can be a way for people to share and discuss information as shown in the previous example about Walsh. There are many people in the world that have problems and are seeking advice, yet they do not have the courage to disclose their information to their family and friends. After encountering several questioning youth similar to himself, Walsh created *Oasis Magazine*, an online resource for gay kids who desperately needed to express themselves and improve their self-esteem by chatting with others ("The Plaintiffs"). If the laws are passed, then Walsh's site will be censored because it is about homosexuals, and it will be blocked from Internet users simply because it contains the word "gay." The computer will automatically assume that it is inappropriate for minors, and its content will not be considered at all. Since the creation of *Oasis Magazine* in December 1995, Walsh says, "I can count on one hand the number of letters I have received from people who opposed the site. By contrast, I've received far more from parents of queer youth, thanking me for producing the site and noting how much it has helped their children" ("The Plaintiffs").

About two years ago, a survey was conducted that illustrated the need for online resources for gay youth. Over 2000 kids participated, and the results stated that 68% of them said being online has helped them accept their sexual orientation; and of that percentage, 51% said being online was crucial to helping them feel better about themselves ("Recent Online Survey"). Another statistic stated that 40% of gay youth who thought of killing themselves said that when they feel suicidal, they go online to find someone with whom to talk ("Recent Online Survey"). "For many queer and questioning youth, Oasis is what keeps them alive," said Walsh. "Considering the high risk of suicide among this demographic, this law would actually endanger the lives of the very youth it is hoping to protect" ("Recent Online Survey"). Obviously his site is helping kids reveal their sexuality and cope with being viewed differently, which means something has to be done so these sites aren't blocked from other potential refugees who are looking for a way to seek help and information.

A second reason why the government should not place restrictions on the Web is because adults can be deprived of valuable information if the sites are censored. This reason is similar to the previous one because in both cases, a key word or phrase deemed by the government as being harmful to minors is located somewhere on the site. This makes it potentially dangerous if a person of less than 18 years of age views it; therefore, the site is censored and blocked to all users. For example, if the censorship laws are passed, all sites involving any kind of nudity or sexual conduct—including sex education, AIDS awareness, gay and lesbian issues, and descriptions of prisoner rape in a human rights document—will be blocked ("Publishers Join"). Other examples are those sites with sexual advice columns, discussion boards on gynecology, and Web sites for bookstores and art galleries. This also means that art and literature cannot be freely expressed online, resulting in the censoring of some of Michelangelo's work as well as some verses from the Bible because they express sex or nudity.

Walsh asserted his frustration with censorship when he said, "As a former newspaper reporter, I understand that many people are concerned about the vast, unregulated content on the Internet. There are many online sites that a parent might find inappropriate for their child. But the answer is not blocking all sites with sexual content without regard for context" ("The

Plaintiffs"). Dr. Marty Klein, a Licensed Marriage and Family Therapist who lives in California, is afraid that if Michigan's censorship law is passed, he will not be able to educate people about healthy sexual expression and practices which can be valuable to many adults. His free Web site entitled SexEd.org allows visitors to ask questions about masturbation and female orgasm ("ACLU Challenges"). The Internet has become a popular medium for the widespread distribution of material and should be a great resource for adults to obtain information. Important information cannot be kept from adults simply because there is a risk that a minor may come across it.

Another reason why the government should not censor the Internet is because it is not possible to escape the inappropriate sites from other countries by only restricting sites from U.S Internet servers. For example, 40% of the Internet content originates outside of the United States ("ACLU Challenges"). This means that censorship laws in the United States would be ineffective because nothing would stop a minor from catching a glimpse of a French pornography site or a bomb-making site created by the Russians. Sure, they would be blocked from viewing harmful American sites, but there is a great opportunity for them to access inappropriate foreign material. The Child Online Protection Act is an example of one law that will be ineffective if it is passed. The U.S. Government's own Justice Department declared that minors will still be able to locate harmful material on foreign sites, non-commercial sites, and through chat rooms even if it is passed ("Appeals Court"). Many countries around the world are struggling to develop a universal Internet regulation law so it is impossible to obtain harmful foreign material. For example, France prohibits material that expresses racial hatred online, yet Canada does not (Olson 162). It is not uncommon for the hate sites to reappear on another country's Internet server that allows them. By transferring servers, the sites have escaped censorship and are now available for all Web browsers, including minors, to see (Olson 163). Basically, there cannot be total control until every state in the country and every country in the world adopts the same laws for regulation. Until then, all efforts toward censoring the Internet will be ineffective.

In addition to the reasons explained previously, another reason the Internet should not be censored is because it is unconstitutional to do so. Free speech is protected under the First Amendment of the Constitution of the United States, and if online censorship laws are passed, that right would be violated ("ACLU Challenges"). If there are no free speech restrictions in newspapers and on televisions, then there shouldn't be any on the Internet. The Communications Decency Act (CDA) was one censorship law that was passed and later found unconstitutional ("Supreme Court"). The Supreme Court ruled in Reno vs. American Civil Liberties Union that the act was an unconstitutional restriction on free speech. In a 7–2 decision, it was agreed that the CDA places an "unacceptably heavy burden on protected speech" and "threatens to torch a large segment of the Internet community" ("Supreme Court"). Steven R. Shapiro, Legal Director of the national ACLU, said, "This is one of the most important free speech cases in many, many years. The Courts today recognize what Congress did not—that free speech cannot flourish under the shadow of censorship" ("Supreme Court"). Besides violating free speech, censorship is also unconstitutional in another way. The Interstate Commerce Clause of the of the U.S. Constitution is also infringed ("Publishers Join"). For example, New Mexico signed the SB 127 bill into law, which meant that all sites harmful to minors should be blocked. This law, however, is unconstitutional because it restricts free speech in other states and in other countries. SB 127 is a New Mexico law seeking to limit communications outside of its boundaries which is illegal ("Publishers Join").

Supporters of the censorship laws would argue that children cannot be under constant supervision; therefore, there is a need for government regulation of harmful sites. They argue that children can get into trouble and can be victimized on the Internet. However, there are ways of restricting Internet access to minors without concealing valuable information and denying Americans their right to free speech. Parents can take steps to limit their children's accessibility to inappropriate material. One of the most important things parents can do is take time to explore the Internet with their child and see what their interests are. It is important for the parents to be involved in their online surfing and guide them to sites that will not harm them in any way. Another good idea for parents is to advise the children not to give out personal identification of any kind unless it is brought to the parents' attention and they agree that it is safe. Parents must warn children to never set up a meeting with anybody they meet online and not to respond to any offensive e-mails or chats. It is a good idea to set the computer up in a family room or another place that is out in the open so the children can be more easily monitored ("Tools & Tips"). Perhaps parents should also consider installing filters to effectively screen out inappropriate material ("ACLU Challenges").

President Clinton addressed the issue of parental involvement at an event back in July of 1997. He affirmed, "And, finally, we must recognize that in the end, the responsibility for our children's safety will rest largely with their parents. Cutting-edge technology and criminal prosecutions cannot substitute for responsible mothers and fathers. Parents must make the commitment to sit down with their children and learn together about the benefits and challenges of the Internet. And parents, now that the tools are available, will have to take upon themselves the responsibility of figuring out how to use them" ("Remarks by the President").

In the last four years, at least 25 states have considered or successfully passed online censorship laws ("ACLU Challenges"). Groups like ACLU continue to challenge the government's right to restrict the Internet, struggling to keep cyberspace free. The U.S. Government should not censor the harmful material to minors on the Web because that phrase is too broad, and it includes many sites that are not offensive in the least. Their efforts will also be ineffective, and the censorship laws are simply unconstitutional. Parents should be given the responsibility of restricting their children's Internet use, not the United States Government.

Works Cited

"ACLU Challenges Michigan State Cyber-Censorship Law, Citing Commerce Clause and Free Speech Rights." American Civil Liberties Union Freedom Network. 13 Feb. 2000. http://www.aclu.org/news/1999/n062399a.html.

"Appeals Court to Hear Arguments in Second Battle Over Federal Internet Censorship Law." American Civil Liberties Union Freedom Network. 13 Feb. 2000. http://www.aclu.org/news/1999/ni10299a.html.

Olson, Elizabeth G. "As Hate Spills Onto the Web, a Struggle Over Whether, and How to Control It." *Perspectives: Technology and Society.* Ed. Dianne Fallon. Madison, WI: Coursewise Publishing Inc., 1999. 162–163.

"Publishers Join Court Fight Against New Mexico Internet Censorship Law." American Civil Liberties Union Freedom Network. 13 Feb. 2000. http://www.aclu.org/issues/cyber/censor/newmexico.html.

"Recent Online Survey Shows Need for Minors to Access Online Resources." American Civil Liberties Union Freedom Network. 13 Feb. 2000. http://www.aclu.org/issues/cyber/censor/newmexico.html.

"Remarks by the President at the Event on the E-Chip for the Internet." Office of the Press Secretary. 13 Feb. 2000. http://www.whitehouse.gov/WII?New?Ratings/19970716-6738.html.

"Supreme Court Rules: Cyberspace Will be Free! ACLU Hails Victory in Internet Censorship Challenge." American Civil Liberties Union Freedom Network. 13 Feb. 2000. http://www.aclu.org/news/n062697a.html.

"The Plaintiffs, Their Sites, and Their Statements." American Civil Liberties Union Freedom Network. 13 Feb. 2000. http://www.aclu.org/issues/cyber/censor/newmexico.html.

"Tools & Tips for Parents: Take the Trip Together." 13 Feb. 2000. http://www.americalinksup.org/parentstips/index.html.

Researched Essay Assignment

> **Assignment on Writing a Researched Essay:** This essay is quite similar to the assigned, multiple source essay except for the fact that none of the sources you will use to support your ideas in this essay will be provided for you, and you will be required to develop your thesis/arguments more fully. This is also another synthesis essay; therefore, this assignment demands that you write the essay <u>based</u> on your ideas, but <u>supported</u> by the outside sources you locate. You will be responsible for the following:

1. researching and reading widely on a social problem or phenomenon,
2. establishing your claim/viewpoint on this problem/phenomenon,
3. creating relationships between the views expressed by your various sources, and
4. blending this source material with your own thoughts to create a meaningful and effective argument.

The Assignment

For this assignment, you are to focus on a social problem or phenomenon that exists in the U.S. on the national, state, or local level. An example of a problem might be on the increasing violence in public schools. An example of a social phenomenon might be the American television viewers' obsession with shows that offer us a peep hole in which to watch "real life" as it is happening (e.g., *The Real World, Road Rules, Survivor, Big Brother*, etc.). In your paper, you will first have to identify/explain the social problem or phenomenon. Then, in the bulk of your essay that follows, you will have a choice as to how you proceed. You may:

1. try to determine the cause of the social problem or phenomenon,
2. explore solutions to the social problem or phenomenon,
3. take a stand that the social problem or phenomenon really doesn't exist or that it isn't as severe as some people believe,
4. argue that the social problem or phenomenon is a great deal more serious than what most people perceive and that it needs immediate attention for several reasons, or
5. combine a couple approaches (e.g., first consider the causes of a problem, then propose a solution that best solves the most influential cause).

No matter what route you take, remember that this should be an **argumentative** essay. That is, you must try to convince your readers that, in spite of some opposition, your perspective on the social problem or phenomenon is the most logical, reasonable, and/or sound.

The goal of this essay is not only to develop information gathering and processing skills but also to weave the conclusions of the research into an original essay, complete with an arguable thesis. Because interviews and surveys can also serve as outside source support, you might consider writing about a current, localized issue for or about an audience who is easily accessible for this type of research. For example, your issue could be as localized as deficiencies in the university's financial aid program, or it may extend into your home community, county, or state. Whichever issue you choose to address, be sure that it is reasonable and controversial—and that conducting interviews and surveys will not be exceedingly difficult if you choose to do so.

The researched essay will be graded on the quality of the research, the clarity and accuracy with which the information is presented, and the intelligence with which sources are used to support your own original and relevant argument.

Which issues would be suitable for this assignment?

Almost any issue can be researched for this paper. However, in some instances, the easiest way to create an avenue for the use of survey and interview data is to particularize/localize your argument (as mentioned above). For example, if you wanted to look at problems Planned Parenthood encounters, you could very easily go to a local Planned Parenthood and structure your paper around controversies that have affected that particular branch. Not only would you be able to get brochures and pamphlets (materials which would be available at any Planned Parenthood), you could also interview employees and volunteers there and survey local residents who may have taken advantage of the services that Planned Parenthood has to offer. There are local branches and/or representatives of just about any national organization you can think of—use this assignment to see what is in your area.

If you don't want to go to the trouble of going to a local city council meeting or visiting the Democratic Headquarters in your hometown, why not pick something on campus? Young Republicans, Lesbian and Gay Alliances, Christian Coalitions and Earth Day Activists abound. If you're not quite so politically or civically minded, why not focus on an issue directly related to college students? Is there something you could investigate about dorm assignments? Charge cards? Library accessibility? Possible preferential treatment of athletes? Advisor policies? The possibilities are endless.

Last but definitely not least, you could investigate a social problem or phenomenon within the media. For example, is there a problem with the depiction of a particular ethnic group, gender, or other minority in a movie? Does the popularity of the X *Files* and movies such as *Independence Day* and *Men in Black* signal a certain distrust of the government? Did the media overstep its bounds with the Clinton scandals?

A Note on Audience

Remember that, in general, you are writing your essay for a college-educated, academic audience; however, you will specify your own specific audience and purpose in your research proposal and exploratory draft. Keep this audience in mind while writing your essay. Who is most likely in the position to do something about your argument?

Additionally, don't forget that you must fully explain the credentials of your sources when you use them in your paper to better set up the credibility of the authors, interviewees, and survey respondents for your readers. Remember that the more credible and reliable your research is, the more believable you will be to your audience. For example, when including quotes from your interviewee, you must tell us exactly who that person is and why that person is relevant to the topic at hand. Also, if you conduct your own survey, you must let us know that, as well as the scope of the study. Keep in mind, too, that asking 30-50 residents how they feel about the current construction hassles in your hometown can help you suggest that public opinion is pulling one way, but you cannot claim, on the basis of your survey alone, to know the mind of all residents. Finally, please realize that for non-college issues, students—including your roommates—are most likely not authorities on the problem/phenomenon.

Format

Your researched essay should be approximately 6–8 full pages in length, word-processed, and double-spaced, using the MLA format in both the body of the essay and the Works Cited page.

SAMPLE RESEARCHED ESSAY MODEL

The following essay, written in 2000 by William Swindell, was submitted as a "final" draft for the above researched essay assignment, in English 112 at Bowling Green State University.

Everything the United States Does Not Know,
We Learned in Kindergarten

Those of us that have kept an eye on the lessons adorning the walls of our elementary school classrooms will no doubt remember the famous poster entitled, "Everything I Need to Know I Learned in Kindergarten." This poster, a clever piece of work, reminds us that, regardless of how complicated life may become, we will always be able to reduce matters to the worthy principles that accompany the better side of human nature. Be nice. Play fair. Clean up your own messes. Even the most radical among us will have a tough time removing such well-founded principles from our conception of proper behavior. Unfortunately, an emergent characteristic of nations seems to be that these principles, although treasured on the micro-level of society, need not be adhered to. In this respect, some nations are worse than others, such as the United States.

To illustrate the assertions above, I will examine the current treatment of the nation of Iraq by the United States government, specifically the effects of economic sanctions imposed upon Iraq following the Persian Gulf War. These sanctions, adopted to prevent Iraq from re-arming itself, have reduced the once prosperous nation to a people crippled by poverty.

I offer three reasons to demonstrate that the United States government has forgotten what it learned in kindergarten, and thus should drop the economic sanctions currently imposed upon the people of Iraq. First, the United States simply is not being nice. The sanctions have desecrated human life, amounting to the destruction of an entire society. Second, the United States is not playing fair. The US government has imposed standards upon the Iraqi government to which no other nation on the planet is held. And lastly, the United States is not cleaning up its own mess. In fact, it is making matters much worse, as it is painfully evident that the sanctions have not and will not lead to the effect that the US government purports to desire.

To adequately grasp the current state of affairs in Iraq, adequate background information is necessary. The first act of tragedy was written when Iraqi president Saddam Hussein invaded neighboring Kuwait on August 2, 1990. Four days later, on August 6, economic sanctions were imposed upon Iraq by the United States-led coalition, reducing its imports to virtually nothing (Strock 1A). Because the sanctions failed to have any effect on the

Iraqi occupation of Kuwait, the United States and its allies launched Operation Desert Storm, an operation lasting from January 15 to February 28, 1991 (Zinn 586). At the conclusion of the war, the sanctions remained in place, with the purpose of persuading the Iraqi government to disarm itself to a degree that would satisfy the United Nations' hired weapons inspectors.

To make a long and sad story short, these weapons inspectors played for a while and then were forced out of Iraq, never finding the proof that would have pleased the United States and its remaining allies into removing sanctions. Because post-war Kurdish rebellions had flared in northern Iraq, no-fly zones were erected, to protect the Kurds from reprisals and to better allow the allied air powers to exert themselves over Iraqi forces, if necessary. A proud people, the Iraqi army rebelled when possible, but they only succeeded in drawing additional US and British air attacks down upon themselves, resulting in a great deal of death and destruction for the Iraqi citizenry. To lessen the human disaster that was unfolding due to the harsh economic sanctions, the "oil for food" program was implemented, with limited success, on April 14, 1995 (Haliday 65).

The United States has adamantly refused to allow any easing of the current sanctions until weapons inspectors are once again permitted to resume their task inside the Iraqi border. The inspectors are understandably considered spies from Iraq's perspective, and the Iraqi government will not allow them admittance into the country. Some nations that originally supported the allied coalition, such as France and Russia, have since dropped out of it, and the United States and Britain are now the enforcers of the sanctions—although it is clear that the United States is the primary enforcer. The role of the United States is evidenced by this reasonable conjecture: If the United States withdrew its support for sanctions, Britain would do likewise, but not vice-versa. This is the current state of affairs. Consumed by a game of "which government can act the least mature," the US blindly stands its ground while the Iraqi people have no choice but to sit back and watch politics do its work.

The destruction of humanity that has been caused by the sanctions is sufficient reason for their discontinuance. Since the introduction of the sanctions in August of 1990, it is estimated that 567,000 Iraqi children have died as a consequence, and this number continues to grow (Zaidi 1485). The best estimates of the total mortality due to sanctions, adults and children, indicate that 1.8 million have died (CASI 19). Those who support sanctions believe that they are clever, pointing out that these numbers are inexact and, as such, should not influence our policy. This inexactness, however, is understandable. The World Health Organization estimates that five to six-thousand children die every month in Iraq, so it is difficult to be critical of statisticians who are unable to meet US demands for precise accuracy (CASI 20).

The validity of the estimated number of Iraqi children deaths is established in the following exchange that occurred between Lesley Stahl and her guest Madeline Albright (then the US ambassador to the United Nations) on *Sixty Minutes*, May 12, 1996. In that exchange, Stahl asked, "We have heard that half-a-million children have died. I mean, that's more children than died in Hiroshima. Is the price worth it?" To this question, Albright staunchly replied, "I think this is a very hard choice, but the price— we think the price is worth it" (CASI 18). With mind-numbing coldness, Albright reveals the US position on the sanctions, but it is more important to note that she does not dispute the death of half a million Iraqi children. The United States cannot plead ignorance.

While many of the aforementioned deaths are directly attributable to starvation, much of this starvation has resulted from the deterioration of the Iraqi medical system following the imposition of the sanctions. In a comparison of available hospital records from 1990 and 1991, the *New England Journal of Medicine* recognized the following pattern: "a reduction in admissions, an increase in the total number of deaths, and a twofold or threefold rise in the hospital mortality rate. The decline in admissions was thought to be due to extreme transportation difficulties caused by a lack of fuel" (Asherio 328). The sanctions have brought about a non-availability of medical supplies, worsening sanitary conditions due to poor water treatment, and a lack of electricity that has corroded the much-needed medical care that is available to Iraqi citizens. The deterioration of Iraqi medical services is clear, as indicated in Table 1, below (CASI 7).

Table 1

	Major surgical operations	Laboratory tests	Drugs and supplies budget	Ambulances (Baghdad)	
1989	15,125	1.49 million	$500 million	350	(1990)
1996	4,417	.5 million	$25-50 million	21	

The effects of the US sanctions are horrific. Placing no value on human life, the US is building its ego upon the graves of children. Former UN Assistant Secretary-General and Humanitarian Coordinator in Iraq Denis Halliday was most blunt when he said, "We are in the process of destroying an entire society. It is as simple and terrifying as that. It is illegal and immoral" (66). It is clear that the Iraqi sanctions have created a humanitarian crisis, the cost of which exceeds that of any benefit the US might be driving at—namely, a completely disarmed Iraq.

The United States does not have, humanitarian issues aside, a good reason to maintain sanctions against the Iraqi people. The US demands that the independent nation of Iraq, in order for sanctions to be eased, admit weapons inspectors into their nation to ensure that they have completely disarmed. Because Iraq has resisted this proposition, the US delights in painting Saddam Hussein as a militaristic madman willing to sacrifice the lives of his people for weapons with which he can one day conquer the planet. Those who accept this fictive portrayal without question are merely obedient pets of the US government and media. We laugh at the image of an adult pointing a rifle at a small child with a peashooter and saying, "put it down or I'll shoot," but this is the sad reality of what the United States does in its affairs with Iraq. How much would it take to persuade the US to disarm itself completely, and why should we expect that Iraq would be any more willing to do so? The media demonize Saddam as a killer of his own people, completely overlooking the fact that the United States is asking Iraq to submit to a vulnerable position not required of any other nation on the planet. If the United States demands that Iraq disarm, I counter with the rational request that the US lay down its own weapons. Unfortunately, I speak as a rational idealist, and world history has shown that politics does not often associate itself with rational thought.

The fact of the matter is that the United States cites Iraq's invasion of Kuwait as sufficient reason to request that Iraq disarm itself. The Iraqi army surely did invade Kuwait. However, other countries have in recent years invaded independent nations without the United States showing much concern. For example, Indonesia invaded East Timor, Israel invaded Lebanon, South Africa invaded Mozambique, and the US itself invaded Grenada and Panama (Zinn 583). Each of these invasions should be viewed as equally wrong by the moral giant that is the United States. However, these nations maintain today a formidable military force that is not questioned. This contradiction causes me to ask: Why is Iraq being treated differently in its invasion of Kuwait? (The reality, of course, is that Kuwait has oil, but this is to be kept a secret, because we all know that the US does not trade blood for oil.) How can we expect Iraq to ignore the ability of its neighboring nations— many of them with long-lasting hostility toward Iraq—to invade Iraq's borders? For example, according to the Foreign Policy Association of New York, Israel is reported to be working on a thermonuclear weapon. Furthermore, Israel has made it clear that it would respond to a chemical-weapon attack with nuclear force. In addition to this, the armed forces of Saudi Arabia and Egypt have greatly benefited from US arms sales, creating a military stronghold surrounding Iraq (FPA 51). As I have been unable to justify the US sanctions against Iraq in terms of human life, I am likewise unable to find political justification. Quite simply, Iraq has been singled out and is being asked to submit to an unreasonable position.

The United States persists in upholding sanctions against Iraq in the apparent belief that these sanctions will force Iraq to submit to weapons inspections and subsequent disarmament. However, after all that has transpired up to this point, is there reason to believe that this will happen, or will continuation of the sanctions result only in further destruction of humanity? I have often heard that the definition of insanity is doing something over and over while expecting to get different results. According to this proposed definition and the evidence relating to the Iraqi sanctions, the United States government is insane. The sanctions have failed, and it is past the time to recognize this, put an end to the sanctions, and repair (to the extent possible) the damage they have wrought.

In the near-decade since economic sanctions have been imposed against Iraq, the Iraqi government has moved no closer to submitting to the will of the United States. In all objectivity, it appears that the United States wishes to annihilate the Iraqi people, to destroy the problem and thus do away with the need for a proper solution—something that the US government has been unable to provide. Although Kuwait and its oil would be safe as a result of Iraq's destruction, allowing—in fact, causing—this destruction is not good foreign policy. The sanctions are, in fact, worse than useless because they are hardening an antagonism within the Iraqi people. In a recent letter to the editor of *The Independent*, Dr. Audrey Stevenson writes of his experience as a British citizen during World War Two: "My experience of being bombed during the Second World War did not make me want to throw out Winston Churchill—quite the opposite. But it did give me a profound and increasing dislike of the perpetrators of the bombings, namely the Nazis. Why should the Iraqis be different?" (Stevenson 6). The analogy Dr. Stevenson presents is chilling in several respects. How different, for example, can the current conditions in Iraq be from the conditions of pre-World-War-II Germany under the Versailles Treaty (Halliday 66)? Indeed, this is a scary situation. The sanctions are hopeless and are backfiring, yet the political leaders of the United States continue to cling to their sinking ship.

Despite the suffering of humanity, the injustice of the US position, and the obvious failure of the sanctions as a practical measure, there has been no relief for the Iraqi people. In addition, the American public is woefully uninformed, even deceived, about the reality of the situation. For example, I recently conducted a survey in which, out of 58 respondents, 83% reported that the sanctions against Iraq should be maintained. Considering the evidence presented in this analysis, one might ask why the majority seems to support these sanctions. To answer this question, I recently corresponded with Dr. Don Jelfo, a professor of Political Science at Cuyahoga (OH) Community College. When asked to shed light on why the sanctions remain in place, Dr. Jelfo responded, "The popular rationale amongst those who support sanctioning is that they are a necessary evil required to contain Saddam Hussein and prevent him from inflicting damage on his own people and neighboring countries. The United States is considering the past aggressiveness of the Iraqi guard under Saddam, against Kuwait and rebellious factions within Iraq, and therefore assuming a protective role."

The common reason offered by Dr. Jelfo, though, is flawed in several respects. First, it is important to realize that the threat posed by Iraq, before Desert Storm and certainly after, has been exaggerated by the United States with the cooperation of the media. It is commonly agreed that the Iraqi army was defeated only four days after the Gulf War began (Struck 1A). On the basis of this performance, looking at the matter in terms of politics rather than humanitarianism, it is pointless to maintain sanctions out of fear of the Iraqi military. Further, as historian Howard Zinn writes, "It was given the name Desert Storm. The government and the media had conjured up a picture of a formidable military power, but Iraq was far from that. The US Air Force had total control of the air, and could bomb at will" (Zinn 584). By depicting the Iraqi army as a greater threat than it was and is, the United States facilitates its task of "selling" the war and subsequent sanctions to the public. Aside from hyperbolizing the military threat Iraq represents, the media has delighted in portraying Iraq as an aggressive nation whose leadership is concerned only about militaristic schemes. The reality, instead, is that the nation of Iraq is as good as or better than most other nations with respect to war and peace. Muhammad Hallaj, a retired professor of Political Science, plainly points out that "Iraq has neither threatened nor attacked any Middle Eastern States not involved in territorial disputes with it." Hallaj goes on to suggest, "That Iraq has not been involved in nearly as many wars as the United States since World War II does not seem to moderate America's perception of Iraq as aggressive and warlike" (67). The largest threat that actually exists in Iraq is not measured in weaponry at all and is being built through the efforts of the United States: the animosity that has understandably arisen among the Iraqi people against the West. To my knowledge, animosity of such magnitude has never, in world history, culminated peacefully.

Let us now address the claim that the sanctions are protecting the Iraqi people from Saddam Hussein's brutality. It is true that the Iraqi military did forcibly put down Kurdish uprisings in the wake of Desert Storm (Struck 1A). This action took place in much the same way that the US forcibly put down its own little rebellion in the 1860s, although this nation no doubt looks upon this instance more favorably than the Iraqi action against the Kurds. Trading human life to maintain a nation is far from a novelty in world history, and this is precisely what the Iraqi military sought to do. In addition, I fail to see how the deliberate starvation of 22 million people, most of whom do not care about missiles or oil, has protected them. The matter reduces simply to the fact that in causing (to date) the deaths of 1.8 million Iraqis through sanctioning, the US loses its right to claim attempted protection of the Iraqi population. I cannot help but imagine that if we were able to survey the Iraqi citizenry, Saddam Hussein would clearly emerge as a more agreeable force in their lives than the United States of America.

It is time to quite "protecting" the Iraqi people and the countries neighboring Iraq. How long do we expect to maintain this protection that we claim is required? Even if we do manage the unlikely admittance of weapons inspectors and eventual Iraqi disarmament, surely we don't expect we will be able to maintain such an unnatural state indefinitely. Sooner or later, we will have to give the Iraqi leadership—most likely Saddam Hussein—its freedom, and the longer we delay, the worse it is going to be, for both the US and Iraq.

As illustrated by the past decade's occurrences in Iraq, the question of whether government's evolution has been beneficial to humankind has no obvious answer. For myself, I prefer the nomadic hunting and gathering lifestyle that blessed our species before the advent of the senseless, heartless patriotism residing at the root of the destruction inflicted upon the Iraqis. Life above all else! This is the principle that governments and kindergartners everywhere should adhere to. In our society at present, one ruthless killing is condemned as an act of murder, but millions of ruthless murders, sponsored by a flag, are condoned as necessary acts of war. I would blissfully give up driving and walk to my places of business with a lighter conscience, rather than to have knowingly caused the death of a single individual so that my oil and gasoline are cheaper. Generations from now, only a few lines of an American history textbook will be devoted to the casualties of Iraq, similar to the few lines devoted to the forced march of Native Americans into the Pacific. And our children will skim these few lines, glance proudly into the upper corner of the classroom, and whisper to themselves, "with liberty and justice for all." It is past time to put an end to the use of human lives as political pawns, so that we once again may remember the sacredness of human life that we learned, and practiced so well, in kindergarten.

Appendix A

"Iraqi Sanctions Survey"

Those surveyed: 25 male residents and 33 female residents in the city of Bowling Green, Ohio.
Age: All respondents were over 18 years of age.

Question 1: Are you concerned about the consequences of the US-endorsed sanctioning of Iraq?   YES   NO   27% responded that they were concerned
73% responded that they were not concerned

Question 2: Do you believe that the nation of Iraq is a threat to the world?
   YES   NO   92% responded that Iraq is a threat
8% responded that Iraq is not a threat

Question 3: Do you believe that the US should maintain economic sanctions on Iraq?   YES   NO   83% responded that sanctions should be maintained
17% responded that sanctions should not be maintained

Works Cited

Asherio, A. "The Gulf War and Infant and Child Mortality in Iraq." New England Journal of Medicine 328 (1993): 931-936.
Campaign Against Sanctions on Iraq (CASI). "Starving Iraq: Humanitarian Crisis We Can Stop" March 1999. 29 Nov. 1999 <http://www.ex-parrot.com/casi/briefing/pamp_ed1.html>
Foreign Policy Association. "Third World Arms Bazaar: Disaster for Sale?" New York: Great Decisions 23 (1990): 48-57.
Hallaj, Muhammad. "Is Saddam a Threat to the Middle East?" World & I Sept. 1998: 66-71.
Halliday, Denis. "Iraq and the UN's Weapons of Mass Destruction." Current History Feb. 1999: 65-68.
"Iraqi Sanctions Survey." Unpublished survey. Conducted by William R. Swindell. December 3, 1999.
Jelfo, Dr. Don. Personal interview. December 1, 1999.
Stevenson, Audrey. Letter. The Independent. 22 Dec. 1998, sec. B:15.
Struck, David. "The Persian Gulf: The Other Side of Victory." The Baltimore Sun 28 July 1991: 1A+.
Zaidi, Sarah. "Health of Baghdad's Children." The Lancet 346 (1995): 1485-1487.
Zinn, Howard. A People's History of the United States. New York: Harper's, 1995.

7   Working with Information

INCLUDING SOURCE MATERIALS IN YOUR WRITING

In Chapter 2, summarizing was discussed primarily as a means for grasping the main ideas of an entire piece of writing, rewriting the key points of something you have read in order to make an accurate and reasonably complete representative of the author's text—yet doing so in a more condensed form. In this chapter, we will consider summarizing primarily as it might apply to single source ideas you wish to use within your own documented writing. Alongside this discussion of summarizing, you will find discussions of paraphrasing and of using direct quotations, the other two conventional ways of including source materials in your writing.

All of these methods of including source materials in your writing, however, carry with them a responsibility for acknowledging the sources in which you found the information. Thus, let's consider next the questions of *why* documentation is both expected and the right thing to do, and *what* you must document in order to meet your responsibility as an academic author. Your writing handbook or style manual can show you the specific techniques currently accepted as conventional for documenting academic writing.

ACADEMIC HONESTY AND PLAGIARISM

Much of your college education will involve learning what others have written or said and then integrating those ideas into your own thinking. In academic writing, any ideas or language not credited to another are assumed to be creations of the author. You are undoubtedly aware that you are expected to do your own writing in college classes and that serious consequences may follow if you submit someone else's work as your own or allow someone to submit your work and take credit for it. You may not be aware, however, that "borrowing" even a small chunk of material created by another person and including it in your own writing can also be labeled "academic dishonesty," specifically plagiarism, if you fail to acknowledge the source from which you have borrowed. You must realize, therefore, that standards for academic honesty in writing do not technically distinguish between "large" and "small" borrowings without attribution. You either have acknowledged the sources of borrowed materials—both words and ideas—or you have not. The derivation of the English word "plagiarism," from the Latin word for "kidnapping," helps clarify why plagiarizing another person's originally created words or ideas—like kidnapping—can be treated as a very serious offense.

As long as you are conscious of your responsibility for acknowledging your sources, you can write with confidence. Inadvertent omissions of a citation may occur as you are learning where and how often to cite to distinguish your ideas and words from those of your sources, but as long as you work closely with your instructor and make good-faith efforts to document appropriately, you will soon have the hang of it and have nothing to fear. Remember, too, that good notetaking procedures clearly label which materials are attributable to specific sources. As you write your paper from your notes and/or outline, then, you need only cite as indicated in your notes/outline to fulfill at least your most basic responsibility for documentation. An introductory guide to plagiarism-free writing follows.

What Responsibilities Do Authors Address when Citing Source Materials in Their Writing?

1. *Attribution*: giving appropriate credit to the originator/s of ideas and words
2. *Accuracy*: representing others' words, ideas, and positions as realistically as possible
3. *Credibility*: representing the factuality or authoritativeness of source-ideas appropriately
4. *Reader convenience*: making it as easy as possible for readers to follow up on words or ideas cited.

What <u>Must</u> Be Acknowledged?

1. *Any direct quotation that may be attributed to a specific source:* Remember that reproductions of another's exact wording, even if cited, still require quotation marks.
2. *Paraphrases of another's ideas or words:* A *paraphrase,* sometimes called an *indirect quotation,* is by definition a reproduction of another's idea/s in your own words. Paraphrases do not require quotation marks but <u>do</u> require documentation of the material's origin. Any groupings of exactly reproduced source-words in your text constitute *quotations,* not *paraphrasing,* and should appear in quotation marks, plus citation.
3. *Summaries of another's ideas or words:* A *summary,* a compilation of several ideas attributable to a single, external source, also is by definition comprised of your own words, also must be cited, and also—as with paraphrases—must show with quotation marks any groupings of source words.
4. *Arguable assertions*: When possible, any controversial or arguable (not undeniably factual) assertions presented in your writing should be cited. Citing such assertions helps to meet your responsibility for attribution and helps readers recognize the potential credibility or truth of your assertions.
5. *Statistics, charts, tables, and graphs from any source*: Cite/credit all graphic material, even if you yourself create the graph.
6. *Co-authored or collaborative works*: Cite all "co-created" or collaborative ideas and words, including those contained in works for which you may claim some but not exclusive credit.

What Need Not Be Acknowledged?

1. *Common knowledge*: If a wide spectrum of readers is familiar with an idea or its truth is generally accepted, you need not cite it. Quotations, paraphrases, or summaries attributable to a specific source, however, should still be cited if at all possible—no matter how widely known.
2. *Facts available from a wide variety of sources*: If a number of textbooks, encyclopedias, or almanacs (general-reference sources) include an idea you wish to use in your text, you need not cite it. You can still increase your credibility, however, by citing; most statistics should be cited.
3. *Your own ideas, discoveries, or words* (excluding, of course, words based upon another's words or ideas).

Final Tips on Citing Source Materials

Computer-based or Internet materials cannot be generally categorized as "common knowledge," nor does the absence of clear authorship for computer-based materials in any way detract from your responsibility for acknowledging them as sources. For information regarding the documentation of online sources, you should consult an up-to-date writing handbook, a current style guide, or—for the very latest documentation conventions—online style guides such as the one provided for *The Scott, Foresman Handbook*. The current address for the Scott, Foresman "citations manager" is http://occ.awlonline.com/bookbind/pubbooks/hairston_awl/chapter4/deluxe.html. For advice on handling difficult or unusual cases, be sure to consult with your instructor. And as a general guideline, when in doubt, cite!

➤ **Exercise in Citing Source Material**: Decide whether or not the following potential sources for a researched essay would need to be cited. Explain your reasoning, using the citation rules explained above:

1. An article in the *New World Encyclopedia* which states that The Declaration of Independence was signed in 1776.
2. A study in the *New England Journal of Medicine* proposing that most cancers are linked more closely to environmental factors than heredity.
3. Statistics in the *Cleveland Plain Dealer* indicating an overall decrease in violent crime during the last five years.
4. A documentary on the History Channel which reports that by the age of sixteen, Napoleon had reached the rank of officer in the French military.
5. Information about censorship in public libraries posted on the American Library Association's home page.
6. A personal web page whose author claims that the death of Princess Diana was caused by the British government and the CIA.

SUMMARY

Although summarizing, paraphrasing, and direct quotation of source materials are all acceptable ways of introducing such materials into your writing, we can discriminate between the three methods by examining the purposes for which each technique is more suited. **Summarizing,** for example, is best used when our purpose is to relate the general idea or ideas of a substantial "chunk" of writing and to do so in relatively few words. When we summarize, we use our own words—not the words of the source—yet it is still important that we *portray the original author's meaning as accurately as possible.* **Paraphrasing** typically would be used when our purpose is to convey a point-by-point representation of a source's ideas, the idea/s in a single source sentence, or, at most, two or three closely contiguous (next to each other) sentences in the source text. When we paraphrase a source idea, just as when we summarize larger chunks of text, we use our own words—not the words of the source. **Direct quotation** of a source typically is reserved for source passages so precise in their wording, so uniquely appropriate, and/or so striking that we believe no summary or paraphrase could be nearly as effective. All three representations of a source idea—summary, paraphrase, and direct quotation—must be cited when used in another person's writing. Direct quotations also must be placed within quotation marks (with the exception of the special block-quotation format).

Examine the excerpted paragraph below from Hilary Cosell's "Ms. Givings" (pages 260–268):

> And of course success meant other things, too. It meant freedom from economic and emotional dependence on men. It meant you were a special person, a brave and strong pioneer out there fighting the good fight. Hacking your way through the jungle to beat a path for successive generations of women to follow. It made you superior to women without success, several cuts above them. It was proof that you were USDA Prime, while the others were some inferior cut of person. Hiding behind traditional femininity and clutching the very chains that bound them.

If you were writing a paper in which it would be useful for you to cite Cosell's 1985 thoughts about the tension between "traditional feminism" and success, you might summarize this paragraph as follows:

> In the mid-1980s, Cosell described the benefits of "success" for women as promoting independence, developing a sense of the pioneering spirit, paving the way for future women, proving one's superiority, and breaking the cycle of "traditional femininity" (262).

Please note that the sample summary attempts to represent all the main ideas of seven sentences in one sentence—although you may summarize larger passages from source materials in more than one sentence—and that it both quotes exact wording reproduced from the original and cites the entire summarized passage. One of the skills you may need to practice consciously in your documented writing before you perfect it is to use quotation marks any time you reproduce in your own writing any words or phrases that are unique to the source material being cited. In fact, you also must be aware that even single words from outside sources often are placed within quotes to distinguish that word as the unique terminology or usage of a specific author.

A final and important point to remember is that summarizing is not just another way of showing off our research; a paraphrase of each of Cosell's seven sentences or a block quotation of her entire paragraph would, in most cases, strain the attention-span of your reader inappropriately and tend to "fluff up" your writing. In argumentative academic writing, the argument you are making is yours, not your sources'; thus, you should use only as many words in reporting source-ideas as are beneficial to your argument. Don't become so fascinated with the words of your sources that you repeat every word or every sentence. Summarizing can help.

PARAPHRASE

As stated previously, academic writers typically **paraphrase** when their purpose is to convey a point-by-point representation of a source's ideas. Paraphrasing is similar to summary in that both use *your words* to represent other persons' ideas, but it differs from summary in its scope—paraphrasing being more of a sentence-by-sentence representation. Paraphrases could be the same number of words, in fact, as the original text they represent, but this would be an accident, since you place no emphasis in paraphrasing on a word-for-word representation of the source material. For this reason, paraphrases have often been called "indirect quotations," and we might think of a paraphrase as something halfway between a summary and a direct quotation. In paraphrases, as in summaries, *you must try to represent the authors' meanings as accurately as you can determine them.* As you practice summarizing and paraphrasing others' published writing, you may want to review the critical reading suggestions in Chapter 2.

Paraphrases or indirect quotations often represent the original source's ideas with a "that" statement, as in the following example:

> Cosell said that for women in the 80s, professional success had additional benefits.

As a developing academic and, later, professional writer, you will benefit from awareness that your only goal in paraphrasing isn't to avoid using the original author's words without quotations, which would be plagiarism. If that were the case, academic writers could eliminate all concerns about plagiarism simply by using direct quotations every time they used a source idea in their writing. Instead, we represent source ideas through paraphrase because the specific ideas within one or more source sentences are important enough to have a one-for-one representation within our writing, but our overall writing purpose is better served by representing that idea in our own words than by using the author's words.

As you read in Chapter 5, documented academic writing quite commonly is a **synthesis** or amalgamation of various source perspectives on the individual points we are making in an essay. To create writing with a consistent "voice" and argumentative focus—two key criteria for successful academic writing—we must avoid overdependence on sources for either the wording or the argumentative "slant" within the essay. To put it another way, if you cite ten different sources in a researched essay, and if each of those sources has a different voice, tone, or manner of approaching the issues, your essay is much likelier to be readable and coherent if you represent sources' ideas in your own words as much as possible. Moreover, if you paraphrase as you take notes from sources or place short paraphrases within an intermediate outline, you will understand your source material much better than you would if you relied exclusively on rote quotations. This increased understanding, too, leads to much more effective argumentative writing.

➢ **Exercise in Paraphrasing Source Material:** Imagine that you have been assigned a researched paper in which you wish to paraphrase (and cite) several assertions from the David Burchfield article, *Teaching All Children: Four Developmentally Appropriate Curricular and Instructional Strategies in Primary-Grade Classrooms*" on pages 59–67. Consider each of the excerpts below and rewrite them in your words. Try to convey the original author's meaning as faithfully as possible. Use direct quotes sparingly, if at all.

Example:
Original—"If we truly adopt the belief that children are different and unique; if we expand our view to include a broader concept of intelligence and then accept the idea that there may be as many as seven 'ways of knowing' and understanding what we learn, dramatic implications consequently result for the whole scope of teaching and learning" (61).
Paraphrase—Burchfield asserts that educators must learn to recognize various learning strategies children exhibit and adjust their methods of teaching to encompass those differences which make children "different and unique" (61).

1. "No longer can we conduct themes or units of study with our students by simply sequencing for a period of a week or two teacher-directed activities that seem to go in no specific direction. Nor can we narrowly focus our unit study solely on reading, writing, and math or demand that most or all children do the same thing at the same time" (61).
2. "There may be some non-negotiable activities, experiences, and, projects that are built in by the teacher over the course of the unit of study. The powerful motivators for the children, however, are that they are involved in decisions about the course of the study, the topic at hand is relevant, and the children are actively and socially involved in making sense out of the concepts and skills" (62).

3. "Ironically, perhaps the least-effective way to encourage meaningful, relevant, and child-sensitive writing is the typical 'story-starter' on the blackboard (which many of us experienced in school ourselves during an occasional creative writing lesson). Such a teacher-driven written command narrows both the choice of topic and the reason to write at all and often leads to a boring product accomplished only to 'get your seat work done,' to please the teacher, or to receive external rewards, such as stickers, smiley faces, or grades" (63).

4. "The writer's workshop taps a powerful desire on the part of the child to express relevant and significant ideas. In fact, it is my experience that children, when allowed to write from their earliest years in school, choose to write more than read, quite possibly as a result of the basic human need for expression and the yearning we have in this life to truly be heard. The writer's workshop is an age-appropriate place for the individual to flourish while both learning to write by writing and making sense of significant ideas" (63).

DIRECT QUOTATION

When you are working with information, you sometimes wish to write down the exact words of a source rather than a summary or a paraphrase. Here are some instances when you would be likely to use a direct quotation:

Forceful Style of Quotation: If the style of the quotation is so unique that its power would be lost if you paraphrased or summarized, you might choose to use the source's words in addition to the idea. For example:

> Although the students were not especially interested in American history, all of them found inspiration in Patrick Henry's famous saying, "Give me liberty, or give me death!"

Please note that the above quotation is not cited since an educated person in our society can be assumed familiar with the quotation's attribution to Patrick Henry (common knowledge). Then note the less effective paraphrase of this remark:

> The students were inspired by Patrick Henry's statement in which he indicated that he must have liberty or else he would prefer to die.

Authority of the Quotation: If the main importance of a quotation is that it was spoken by a particular authority or famous person, you would probably choose to use direct quotation rather than a paraphrase or summary because it would lend authority to your own position. For example:

The well-known behaviorial researchers Masters, Johnson, and Kolodny similarly point out that "school age children are also exposed to obvious gender-role stereotypes on television" (378).

Report of First-Hand Experience: If you are discussing someone's first-hand experience, you would probably wish to use direct quotation for the sake of reliability. For example:

Airline crash survivor John Rondell claimed that "the smoke filled the cabin immediately after takeoff" (A5).

Wording We Wish to Question, or to Which We Wish to Draw Attention: If an author relates his or her ideas in a particularly distinctive or expressive manner, we may want to use a direct quote to reproduce the impact of the author's wording for our readers. For example:

Cosell's style is very direct and, at times, staccato, as when she writes: "To win a man and then keep him. By softness, passivity, dependence, nurturing, peacemaking."

Punctuating Direct Quotations

Whenever you quote directly, be sure to enclose all quoted material within quotation marks and to punctuate as follows:

1. **Commas and periods are placed inside quotation marks,** unless you are documenting a source that has no page numbers. Thus:

   The professor stood up quietly and said, "I do not expect to continue at this position."

   Peter Singer states that "according to one estimate, 15 million children under five die every year from the combined effects of malnutrition and infection" (428).

2. **Semicolons and colons are placed outside of the quotation marks.** For example, here is the original:

   Many young adults are confused about what direction they should take. Young women, in particular, are still unclear about their goals and are often torn between the desire to raise a family and the lure of professional ambition (Baker 19).

Here is an example of how this material could be quoted using a semicolon:

   Baker discusses the confusion young adults often experience in deciding "what direction they should take"; in particular, he focuses on young women's difficulty in choosing between family and career (19).

Here is an example of how this material could be quoted using a colon:

> Baker focuses on two choices that cause young women "to be unclear about their goals": their interest in family life and their desire for professional success (19).

3. **Question marks and exclamation marks are kept within quotation marks if they are part of the original quotation.** For example:

> Professor Begley asked, "What is the meaning of life?" [The question mark is part of the original quotation, so it is placed inside the quotation marks.]

> Didn't the students feel uncomfortable with that question about "the meaning of life"? [The question mark is part of the whole sentence, and thus it is placed outside the quotation marks.]

4. **Single quotation marks are placed inside double quotation marks for a quote within a quote.**

> Professor Jones claimed that he would "never respond to Professor Begley's question about 'the meaning of life.'"

5. **An ellipsis should be used when part of a quotation has been omitted.** For example, here is an original quotation:

> Television is also a powerful force in the gender-role socialization of young children because it provides a window to the rest of the world. The fictionalized world of Saturday morning children's cartoons is filled with gender stereotypes: the heroes are almost all males, and the females are shown as companions or as "victims" needing to be rescued from the forces of evil. Even award winning children's shows such as *Sesame Street* have been criticized because women were seldom shown employed outside the home and male figures predominated.
>
> (From William Masters, Virginia Johnson, and Robert Kolodny. "Gender Roles.")

Here is an example of the use of an ellipsis:

> Masters, Johnson, and Kolodny assert that "television is also a powerful force in the gender-role socialization of young children. . . . Even award winning children's shows such as *Sesame Street* have been criticized because women were seldom shown employed outside the home and male figures predominated."

Ellipsis points are created using three spaced periods (although if you are also concluding a sentence, you'll need four spaced periods, as shown in the example above). When using ellipses, it is important that they not be used in a manner which might distort or change the writer's meaning.

6. Square brackets are used whenever you need to substitute or add words to a quotation.
For example:

> Masters, Johnson, and Kolodny indicate that "gender-role socialization of young children [occurs] because [television] provides a window to the rest of the world" (45).

When you copy quotations directly, be sure you are using the author's exact words and punctuation, including any mistakes or misspellings. To avoid inadvertent plagiarism (that is, failing to appropriately distinguish material taken from a source from your own words or ideas), be sure to use quotation marks at the beginning and the end of the quoted material. Remember, even two consecutive words copied from one of your sources should be enclosed in quotation marks to indicate that they are not your own.

➤ **Exercise in Quoting, Paraphrasing, and Documenting Sources:** Choose a print source material (e.g., a journal article, book chapter, or website) containing relevant information that you might consider using for a researched, argumentative essay. Then, after reading the source material carefully, decide on several key pieces of information you might want to cite in your potential essay and write the following:

1. A summary of the source material
2. Several paraphrases of the original source material
3. A few distinctive quotes from the source material

Be sure to introduce and provide proper documentation for each summary, paraphrase, and quotation.

RECORDING SUMMARIES, PARAPHRASES, AND QUOTATIONS IN YOUR NOTES

Despite the common availability of copy machines, writing down notes in the form of summary, paraphrase, and quotation is still an important part of the research process. Students sometimes think that if they photocopy a sufficient amount of material that they do not have to take notes. Simply photocopying a source, however, does not give you the opportunity to consider meanings or to select material that you wish to include in some form in your own writing. **Writing down notes** enables you to interact with the text, helping you understand and remember what you read. This section will give you suggestions on methods of recording information from sources into your notes, so that you can then incorporate them effectively into your paper.

Too Much or Too Little?

Understandably, students often are concerned with saving time, and they sometimes wonder whether they will be more efficient if they write only a few notes, rather than many. More notes, however, typically work better than fewer notes. Often, when you begin taking notes, you may not be quite sure of your issue, and you may refocus your thesis later to include aspects you hadn't considered in the beginning. Therefore, **when in doubt, take more notes than you think you might need.** As you work, you might discover that you need them after all.

Recording Your Notes: Notecards versus Note Sheets

Over the past two decades or so, a popular method of teaching students to record notes for a research paper involved using notecards, and many students trained in this method may still prefer using them. Notecards are very easy to sort by topic or subtopic, and because they provide only limited room for writing, they can aid students in breaking down a topic into manageable parts. If you are comfortable using notecards and find them an effective method for recording information, please continue to use them.

In the experience of many writers and teachers, however, taking notes usually requires more room than a notecard provides, and, in fact, one efficient notetaking process includes jotting down ideas as they occur, right next to the note. For both of these reasons, you might require more writing room than a notecard allows. You might also find that notecards are easy to lose, although you could lose a notebook as well. In general, a notebook with detachable pages in a ring binder could be your best option for taking notes. An inexpensive softcover folder with fasteners to hold the paper is easy to carry around and allows for rearrangement of information as needed. It is also helpful if the folder has side pockets as well, for additional storage of information or computer disks. You might also prefer to take notes using your computer's word processing program. One advantage to this strategy is the "cut and paste" option which allows you to rearrange information easily as your ideas for an essay's content and organization continue to evolve.

Two types of sheets may be useful to you in taking notes, the Source Note Sheet, which may be used for recording notes about a single source, and the Synthesis Note Sheet—discussed in Chapters 5 and 6—which is used to organize information about one aspect of a topic and may include notes from several sources.

The Source Note Sheet

A Source Note Sheet is used to record notes about a single source. It includes a summary of the source and contains information from only that source. A Source Note Sheet helps you to record your notes easily and can also be used to prepare your bibliography since these sheets can be alphabetized. On the next page is an example of a Source Note Sheet. You can use your computer to prepare a form for this sheet and work directly at the computer as you take notes. If you prefer to work in hard copy, you can make copies of your Source Note Sheets and fasten them into your notebook.

In creating a Source Note Sheet, you begin with the author's last name so that you can easily alphabetize the sheets to create your bibliography. Note that there is also a section for a brief summary of your source, so that you can remember its overall purpose. This is particularly useful if you are writing a paper in which you have to compare different points of view on an issue (in other words, argument synthesis papers). Note also that there is a space allotted for writing down the page number, a very important piece of information. Too many of us have spent wasted hours in a library hunting for a source for which we forgot to write down a necessary page number. If you remember to include this information as you take notes, you can save yourself a great deal of time.

In the section marked "Note" on the Source Note Sheet, you can either paraphrase an idea you want to remember or write it down as an exact quote. If it is an exact quote, remember to put quotation marks around it so that you can document it properly when you write your paper.

Note also the section of the Source Note Sheet marked "Idea about Note." As you read, you get ideas that you cannot pursue immediately. You may think to yourself, "This would provide a good argument against that other article I read." So you might write, "Compare with _____ article." Or you may think, "This is a good example of _____." As you read, many of these ideas will occur to you, but later, when you have finished reading, you may have forgotten them. Using this space to jot down ideas as they occur to you can help you avoid losing these potentially fruitful thoughts.

Source Note Sheet

Author: Donald Singletary

Title: "You New Women Want It All"

Journal Information (if appropriate): Essence

Publisher (if appropriate):

Date and Place of Publication: July 1985

Pages: 95-99

Short Summary:

In this short, humorous article, written from a man's perspective, Singletary accuses modern young women of wanting all the advantages of being liberated women but also wanting many of the advantages of being traditional women. He uses many examples from the dating scene, in which women will take the initiative in approaching a man and selecting a restaurant, but then want men to pay.

Page Number	Note	Idea about Note
3	Years ago, men chose women who could cook, take care of a house, and raise children. Women chose men who would make good providers.	Use to show that roles haven't changed much.

> **Exercise in Using Source Note Sheets:** After carefully reviewing the completed Source Note Sheet above, create your own version, referring to the sample as a guide. Then, finish your Source Note Sheet using information taken from a potential source for your researched essay. If you've already gathered several sources, you should complete a Source Note Sheet for each one.

The Synthesis Note Sheet

The Synthesis Note Sheet, discussed in Chapters 5 and 6, is useful for organizing notes around a particular aspect of an issue or topic. It includes enough information from each source so that you will be able to incorporate it into your paper with relative ease. Justin used several Synthesis Note Sheets in Chapter 5 to organize his notes for his paper concerning old age.

If you use Synthesis Note Sheets and include direct quotations, be sure to enclose them in quotation marks within your notes, so that you can remember to document them properly if they are included in your paper. Summaries or paraphrases based on sources, should you include them in your notes, also need to be appropriately identified as to the source from which they derive, although obviously you should not place them within quotation marks.

INCORPORATING SOURCES SMOOTHLY INTO YOUR TEXT: AVOIDING THE "CROUTON EFFECT"

Students who have had little experience using outside sources in a paper sometimes have difficulty incorporating their sources smoothly within their text. They seem to just sprinkle them in, like croutons in a salad, with the result that the quotations sometimes don't blend in. The reader crunches on them from time to time and may enjoy the flavor, but the information from outside sources always stands out in a way that might distract the reader's attention. Unless you deliberately wish to create an interruption or distraction, you should aim for a smooth blend of quoted material within your own prose.

To take an obvious conversational example, suppose you had used your lunch hour to see your instructor about whether she plans to assign a paper at the end of the semester. Your instructor responds to the question as follows:

> "I have given the matter considerable thought and have decided that I will not assign a paper at the end of the semester."

You then meet a friend who asks where you were during lunch. You would be unlikely to respond like this:

> I went to see the instructor and asked whether she was planning to assign a paper at the end of the semester. The instructor said that there would be no paper assigned. "I have given the matter considerable thought and have decided that I will not assign a paper at the end of the semester."

Note that the quoted material in the example directly above is simply thrown in at the end like a crouton onto a salad, that it repeats information the student (you) has already said, and that it fails to blend in smoothly with the student's own words. If you answered in this way, your friend would probably look at you strangely. Yet, many students present quoted material in just this way because they are unaware that such material should be integrated (incorporated) into their own prose. They think that quoted material, above all, should be used to support their own statements, and, of course, this is partly true. But it is also important that it be blended.

To avoid the "crouton effect," try to include quoted material as part of your own sentences. If you include summary and paraphrase as well as direct quotation, you will achieve a smoother effect than if you use only direct quotation. For example, in the conversational sample above, you would be more likely to respond:

> I went to see the instructor. She said that there will not be a paper assigned at the end of the semester.

This summarizes the instructor's statement. Or, if you wished to quote exactly:

> I went to see the instructor, who said, "I have given the matter considerable thought and have decided that I will not assign a paper at the end of the semester."

Below are some possibilities for incorporating quoted material smoothly into your own text. The following excerpt from *Time* magazine, concerned with the issue of whether all-male clubs ought to be allowed, is used to illustrate these ideas:

> Yet amid the antique rugs and deep leather chairs, the clubs do furnish a setting for the exertions of professional life: back slapping, ego massage, and one "contact sport"—making business connections. In short, though they offer relaxation, the clubs are places of business too. Meal tabs and an-

nual dues that can run into the thousands of dollars are often picked up by a member's employer as a business expense.

(From Richard Lacayo. "Storming the Last Male Bastion, the Supreme Court Ushers Women into the Private Club." *Time* 4 July: 1988: 43.)

Here are several ways to incorporate the preceding material into a paper:

Incorporating Essential Words and Phrases Into Your Text

Read closely the following example:

> Allowing male-only clubs places businesswomen at a disadvantage since their function is not only recreational. As a recent article in *Time* magazine points out, in addition to being places of relaxation, "the clubs are places of business too" (Lacayo 23).

Please note the placement of the page number and the reference to the author's name. One of the prime functions of systems of documentation is to enable readers to locate your source. Note also the strategic use of "points out." This expression is an example of what writing teachers call "verbs of attribution"—a single verb or short verbal phrase that introduces a statement from a source.

Incorporating Most of the Text by Using an Ellipsis

Sometimes the section you wish to quote contains material that is not essential to your main point. In this case, you may leave out the nonessential piece, but you must insert an ellipsis (three spaced dots) to show that you have omitted something. Here is an example of how to use an ellipsis in this way:

> Most businesses recognize the importance of clubs for "making business connections. . . . Meal tabs and annual dues that can run into the thousands of dollars are often picked up by a member's employer as a business expense" (Lacayo 43).

Please note that current MLA conventions call for a period after the word "connections"—ending a sentence in the quoted material—then the three spaced periods indicating omitted material. If a section of quoted material is omitted from within a sentence, just the three spaced periods should indicate the omission.

Long Quotations

For a quotation more than four lines long, use a block indented ten spaces and do not use quotation marks. Double-space between your words and the quoted material, double-space the quoted material, and do not indent the first line of the quoted paragraph. Place the citation reference after the last mark of punctuation. Here is an example:

The unfairness of male-only clubs is pointed out in a recent *Time* magazine article:

> Yet amid the antique rugs and deep leather chairs, the clubs do furnish a setting for the exertions of professional life: back slapping, ego massage, and one "contact sport"—making business connections. In short, though they offer relaxation, the clubs are places of business too. Meal tabs and annual dues that can run into the thousands of dollars are often picked up by a member's employer as a business expense. (Lacayo 43)

TRANSITIONS AND FRAMING OF SOURCE MATERIALS

Transitions: Relating Ideas Effectively

As writers, when we craft sentences and paragraphs to explain our thoughts and convictions on a particular issue, we want to make sure that all of our ideas progress smoothly and logically. One way that we can make sure that these connections between the various parts of our essays are clear and easily followed is by using **transitions**. Transitions enable readers to follow the discussion or argument inherent to a piece of writing by using words, phrases, sentences, or paragraphs to connect ideas and relate them to one another. For instance, when writers connect their supporting points to a central argument or thesis using complete sentences at the beginning of a paragraph, we refer to these transitional sentences as **topic sentences**. Writers may also use transitions when they connect a new thought or idea to a preceding sentence or paragraph. For example, writers might choose to show a relationship between a point being made and a previously stated idea by using a transitional word or phrase such as "similarly," "consequently," or "as a result." Using transitions ensures that our reasoning is clearly understood by our readers by guiding them through each point in our argument and showing them how these ideas are related.

Using Transitions to Make Clear Connections

Transitions have many varied and specific functions which improve the clarity of our writing, starting with the logical connections of ideas (both our own and from sources) within and between sentences and paragraphs. The following list demonstrates some of the various ways we can use transitional words and phrases effectively to improve and clarify the connections we make for our readers in our writing.

Transitions are often used to:

- **express points of consensus** (similarly, likewise, in the same way) *Example*: Test scores have finally started to rise for fourth-grade students taking the Ohio Proficiency Tests; **similarly**, student performance on these exams has continued to improve nationwide.
- **note areas of contradiction** (conversely, on the other hand, on the contrary)

Example: The water quality of Lake Erie is now considered to be safe and free from harmful contaminates. **On the other hand,** regular testing is still imperative to maintain these conditions.

- **show a sequence of ideas** (additionally, furthermore, not only, . . . but also, finally)

  Example: Visitors to the Smithsonian museums in Washington, D.C. are often dismayed by the deteriorating conditions of the buildings. **Furthermore,** policymakers are lobbying for increased funding to renovate these national treasures.

- **express a causal relationship** (therefore, consequently, as a result)

  Example: Many credit card companies are eager to extend thousands of dollars in credit to college students; **consequently,** many young adults find themselves mired in debt before they graduate.

In addition to the suggestions above, more comprehensive lists of transitional words and phrases can be found in your college writing handbook. Adding these "connectors" to your writing helps to clarify for your readers how the various ideas in your sentences, paragraphs, and argument as a whole relate to one another, so it is definitely worth the effort to include transitions in your writing.

Introducing and Characterizing Source Material with Transitions

Another way we use transitions in our writing, especially in argumentative, researched writing, is by introducing quoted or paraphrased material with clear connections to previous sentences and ideas. Framing the quotations and paraphrases we choose to include in our essays helps to substantiate our claims by identifying these sources and letting our readers know why we've decided to include them. We might characterize, or frame, these sources in many different ways, such as identifying the author(s) by status or position, assessing the authority of an author or an idea, or referring to previously-conducted research.

To illustrate, suppose you wanted to provide support within a researched essay for the position that tobacco companies should be liable for the medical expenses of long-term smokers. An excellent way to frame a stellar quote endorsing your stance on this issue would be the use of a strong transitional sentence or phrase reminding the reader of your position on this issue and clearly linking credible source material to your stance or thesis. Frames might appear before, after, or in the middle of cited material. Below are several examples of quotations "framed" by transitional phrases that link the quoted material to the writer's main point:

- Dr. Lentner, a member of the American Medical Association, agrees that the tobacco companies are at fault, asserting, "measures should be taken to ensure restitution for these unwitting victims suffering from long-term health problems."
- Those who began smoking before the tobacco companies posted warning labels on their product are "entitled to receive full compensation result-

ing from this inexorable lack of disclosure," contends noted legal scholar Anne Kellett.

- "Long-term smokers are more likely to suffer from sprains and broken bones than non-smokers," reports an influential study conducted by the United States Army.

Along with using clear transitional phrases to introduce cited material, you can add variety and interest to sentences containing quotations and paraphrases by choosing different verbs of attribution instead of relying on just one or two mundane verbs (e.g., "says" or "said"). When selecting a verb of attribution to introduce cited material, be sure to choose the appropriate verb for a given context. For instance, the verb "disputes" implies contentiousness on the part of the author, but the verb "comments" indicates a more subdued tone. In addition to the verb choices used in the examples above, some additional suggestions for verbs of attribution may be found in your college writing handbook and in Table 1 below:

Table 1

Verbs of Attribution			
acquiesce	concede	maintain	relate
acknowledge	concur	mention	remark
add	continue	note	stress
affirm	declare	observe	suggest
caution	dispute	offer	summarize
claim	emphasize	persist	urge
comment	explain	reiterate	warn

The Benefits of Framing Quotations and Paraphrases

By framing all quotations and paraphrases, we accomplish several goals. Primarily, we are able to provide our readers with clear connections between source materials and the positions we have taken on issues. Also, by introducing all quoted and paraphrased materials through framing, we can clearly establish why we have chosen to use a particular source. For example, our "frame" for a quotation or paraphrase might note the source's expertise in the field. Finally, by framing borrowed material with transitional phrases, we avoid "floating" or stand-alone quotations, quotations merely dropped into our writing without explanation.

Avoiding Floating or Stand-Alone Quotations

Suppose, for example, you wanted to use an interesting quote by a respected music historian to support the claim that the Beatles are the most influential rock band in history. If you wrote the following sentence using the quoted material, you would create a floating quotation:

> "The Beatles have had an immeasurable influence on many pop and rock music bands during the last few decades."

However, if you rewrote the sentence to include a transitional phrase to frame the quoted material, you could avoid the floating quotation and identify the source as well:

> According to Audrey Graham, rock historian and contributor to *Rolling Stone* magazine, "The Beatles have had an immeasurable influence on many pop and rock music bands during the last few decades."

Notice that by providing a transitional phrase to introduce the quoted material, you can both establish the credibility of the source for your readers and better connect this source information to your own ideas, thus validating your stance. Transitions used with quoted and paraphrased material help to link these sources both to your own ideas expressed throughout the supporting paragraphs of your essay and to other source material as well (for more information about showing relationships between sources, please refer to the "synthesis" section in Chapter 5).

➤ **Exercise in Recognizing and Eliminating Floating Quotations**: The following floating quotations need to be introduced. Try to frame each floating quotation using transitional words or phrases:

1. "Commercially sponsored research is putting at risk the paramount value of higher education—disinterested inquiry. Even more alarming . . . universities themselves are behaving more and more like for-profits companies" (by Eyal Press and Jennifer Washburn in "The Kept University" from *Atlantic Monthly*).
2. "Only by alighting somewhere—and staying put—do we stand a chance of finding out who we are, where we are, and what we are going to do about it" (by Stephanie Mills in "The Journey Home" from *Sierra* magazine).
3. "But despite their star status, the Park Service's health is deteriorating, with pollution, overuse and encroachment by commercial and environmental threats all requiring attention against a backdrop of political maneuvering and budgetary constraints" (by Thomas Ciemins in "Parks in Peril" from *E Magazine*).

4. "To the recording industry, Napster enables users to create the world's biggest bootleg collection, robbing song creators and performers of crucial royalty payments. To its fans, Napster is the greatest radio station in the world, a place to pick up new music for nothing and a community at which to talk about music with others with similar tastes" (by Jefferson Graham in "Caught Between Rock and a Hard Drive" in *USA Today*).

5. "School-to-Work programs will decrease our basic freedoms. Obviously, programs that standardize education, that direct what young people can study, that move toward compulsory education, and that limit people's access to jobs will undermine the development of strong individuals who understand democracy, can think freely, and are responsible citizens" (by Larry and Susan Kaseman in "Taking Charge" from *Home Education Magazine*—online version).

METADISCOURSE: THE SUPERCONNECTORS OF EXPOSITORY WRITING

As we write—especially as we write argumentatively—one of the most effective measures we can use to make our reasoning logical and understandable to our audience is to imagine each reader asking, "Why are you telling me this?" To make sure that our reader is, indeed, able to comprehend the purpose and direction of our writing, we need to use "superconnectors," or metadiscourse, to connect each major point we'd like to make to relate our argument back to our thesis.

The term **"metadiscourse"** might best be explained by looking at the smaller words within it. One of the meanings of the word, "meta," according to the third edition of the *American Heritage Dictionary*, is "Beyond; transcending; more comprehensive." The term "discourse" is defined as "a formal and lengthy discussion of a subject, either written or spoken." Metadiscourse, then, is the process in which we momentarily pause from the subject of our writing to remind our readers of our argument's central assertion and reaffirm how each supporting idea or reason proves that assertion to be correct (in our opinion).

The use of metadiscourse in argumentative writing allows us to provide a clear framework in which to outline and organize our ideas for our audience. These superconnectors keep the writer's supporting ideas focused and allow the writer's argument to progress smoothly and logically.

Metadiscourse: Creating Meaningful Links Between Ideas

Why is metadiscourse so important to coherent writing? Just as transitions provide words, phrases, and sentences to help writers make clear connections between ideas expressed in the sentences and paragraphs of an essay, metadiscourse allows writers to create links among the various parts of an essay and show relationships between these parts and the argument as a whole.

For example, think of the last time you read an article, essay, or chapter from a book which failed to hold your interest because the supporting ideas of the writing seemed unclear, and the main idea remained uncertain. As a reader, you were probably reluctant to continue making the effort to understand the material and soon gave up trying! Using metadiscourse conscientiously helps us to avoid "losing" our readers by giving them a road map to guide them through the main ideas discussed in our writing and how they relate to one another and our thesis.

Using Metadiscourse to Improve Comprehension

To better understand just how crucial metadiscourse is to clear, effective argumentative writing, let's consider how vital these superconnectors are in everyday conversations. Suppose, for example, you're returning a borrowed movie to a friend, and your friend asks you what you thought of it. "It was great," you gush, thinking of all the action-packed scenes. "The part where he realizes he's being chased by an army of federal agents is so suspenseful. The looks on their faces when he escaped once again! I couldn't even watch when he crept though that dark, underground tunnel, knowing that those bloodhounds were coming in the opposite direction. Not to mention the part when. . . ."

However, as you continue to summarize the movie with these random thoughts, you notice that your friend's attention span is waning, for she has already seen the film and knows the details of the plot. Quickly, you refocus your comments about the movie, connecting these various reactions and ideas to one central assertion. You then continue, "What I'm trying to say is that the film was so exciting because there was never a dull moment," backing up this opinion with specific scenes from the film which you think will best illustrate, or prove, this main point.

In the example above, the speaker recognized that her listener failed to grasp her main point. Therefore, she rephrased her discussion of the film to link her major points back to her primary assertion (that the movie was continuously exciting). Similarly, when we write argumentatively, we strive to use language which clearly identifies for our audience the essential points being made to uphold our central argument or thesis and how these points both relate to each other and to the argument as a whole.

Connecting Major Parts of an Essay with Metadiscourse

Successfully relating supporting paragraphs to one another to promote an overriding thesis is one crucial function of metadiscourse in argumentative writing. When we use metadiscourse to create these overview sentences—linking major points of an essay with our controlling idea, or thesis—we keep our argument organized and our audience informed. For example, an argumentative essay might have the following thesis:

> **Thesis**: Though controversial, the National Endowment for the Arts should continue to receive government funding because it allows artists the finan-

cial resources to create, promotes public awareness and appreciation of art, and advocates art education from preschool through adulthood.

If the writer, during the course of writing the essay, wanted to develop each of these supporting points without losing his or her focus or the audience's comprehension of the central argument, he or she would need to use metadiscourse. When these superconnectors are placed at the beginning of each paragraph, introducing a new, supporting idea for the thesis, they act as topic sentences. To continue with the above example, the writer of this argumentative essay might sustain his or her thesis (that the NEA should receive government funding) by leading the audience through each supporting argument using the following topic sentences:

Topic Sentence for Supporting Point #1: First, without the financial support provided by the National Endowment for the Arts, many artists could not afford to continue their work.

Topic Sentence for Supporting Point #2: Not only does the National Endowment for the Arts give artists needed financial support, but also the funding it receives leads to public support for the arts by encouraging more widespread appreciation for the arts.

Topic Sentence for Supporting Point #3: Lastly, the National Endowment for the Arts champions lifelong learning in the arts by investing in teachers, artists, and educational organizations.

➤ **Exercise in Writing Qualified Thesis Statements and Topic Sentences**: Consider the following list of topics and decide what position you might take on each one in an argumentative essay. Then, try writing a qualified thesis statement and several topic sentences to express your position and the reasons supporting your stance for each topic:

1. Cloning animals for medical research
2. Homeschooling children as an alternative to public education
3. Censoring Internet materials to protect public library patrons
4. Banning automobiles from the National Park System
5. Tracking students according to how well they score on standardized tests

---

The Paragraph As Metadiscourse

Metadiscourse in longer, more complex, or researched essays may consist of an entire paragraph which provides an explanation of what the writer intends to accomplish in the paper. In addition to using metadiscourse to improve the connections between and within supporting paragraphs and our controlling idea or thesis, writers also use metadiscourse to establish or remind their readers of the sequence and content of their argument overall. When metadiscourse is used in the form of a transitional paragraph (as opposed to just a transitional word, phrase, or sentence), the writer creates a forum in which he or she may speak directly to the individual reader and acknowledge the reader's goals, preferences, and expectations.

To better explain how an entire paragraph of metadiscourse can provide clear direction for an argumentative essay, let's consider the following paragraph written by Randy Hermiller during the spring semester, 2000, in an English 112 class at Bowling Green State University. Randy's central assertion, or thesis, is that improvements need to be made in several key areas to improve airline safety. To strengthen his stance on this issue, he realizes that before he can argue whether or not airline safety is being appropriately addressed, he must explain to his readers (who may know nothing about the airline industry) which agencies are responsible for airline safety:

> In order to adequately grasp the current issues concerning air safety, sufficient background information is necessary. The first thing to know is that air travel safety basically rides in the hands of the pilots and the air traffic controllers. The main responsibility falls in the hands of the pilots. It is their job to fly the plane, which can be a very difficult task in the event of a rain or snowstorm. The air traffic controllers also share an equal amount of responsibility in the safety of the jet. It is their job to ensure that the jet is not going to hit anything in the sky. They are also liable for ensuring that the plane has a clear runway to land on. In addition, the air traffic controllers are also accountable for guiding the planes in and out of severe weather. Another important player in the airline industry would be the Federal Aviation Administration, better known as the FAA. They manage all safety operations that take place with the airline industry and are responsible for making rules and regulations to aid in the safety of the passengers and the crew aboard the airliners. Also there is a government funded agency called the national Transportation and Safety Board, or better known as the NTSB. Their job is to oversee the FAA in making sure that safety precautions are being taken; they are also the people who investigate accidents of all types of transportation such as trains, airplanes, ships, and automobiles. Many people would assume that with these two government agencies in place, airline safety would not be an issue in the United States, but sadly, it is. Now that an adequate background of the aviation industry has been presented, we can observe what makes it so unsafe.

The Vital Functions of Metadiscourse

Metadiscourse performs many important functions to better lead readers though the various components of an argumentative essay. First, superconnectors serve as **signals of anticipation** for possible reader objections—argumentative objections, or objections stemming from impatience if the writer's ideas are not presented clearly. The sample paragraph above anticipates specific objections while forecasting the direction and the significance of the ideas that follow. In this example, Randy anticipates readers' objections by outlining the various agencies responsible for safe air travel to lay the groundwork for his argument before defending his position that they are not attaining the imperative safety standards. Similarly, writers might use superconnector expressions such as, "Some readers might be thinking there's no connection between _____ and _____," or "Before proceeding, we must . . ." to address readers' concerns before launching into the argument and its supporting points.

Superconnectors, or metadiscourse statements, perform other important functions, such as providing **signals of reiteration**, as when we interrupt the flow of our writing to remind the reader of a critical distinction. We might write, for example, the phrase, "as previously mentioned, stalking is an escalating crime in America," to reintroduce a pivotal concern in our argument. Effective metadiscourse also offers **signals of amplification**, as when an author writes, "We cannot overstate the importance of green plants to our environment." Lastly, they present **signals of relation**—relating specific pieces of information to each other, relating this information to the writer's central argument, and relating debatable statements to the value-systems of readers. For instance, at the end of a paragraph about euthanasia, an author might appeal to his or her reader's sense of fairness by writing, "What would you think if your parent were in this position, hopeless and helpless?"

All of these functions of metadiscourse present the writer with options to strengthen his or her argument by acknowledging the reader's objections or expectations, a strategy which makes it possible for the writer to reach the goal of any argumentative essay—persuasiveness to the reader.

The Role of Metadiscourse in Coherent and Logical Argumentative Writing

The frequent use of superconnector expressions, or metadiscourse, allows our readers to better follow our argument, and, consequently, increases the likelihood that they will agree with us or at least be more sympathetic to our concerns. By acknowledging our readers' curiosity and their desire to see relationships between ideas, we can encourage readers to consider our point of view on an issue. Making our position and the ideas supporting that position clear to readers through the effective use of metadiscourse gives our writing the power to help readers see where we're going with our argument and arrive at the destination (or a better understanding of our stance on an issue) along with us.

Readings on the Sexual Revolution

You New Women Want It All!
Donald Singletary

A: Why is it always *sex, sex, sex?* Can't a man talk to me as a professional?
B: All men want to do is talk business; there's no romance.

Donald Singletary, "You New Women Want It All!," *Essence,* July 1985. Reprinted by permission of the author.

A: These guys are together all day at work; now they come in the club and they're still over there in a group talking to each other.

B: Damn, I can't even come in here to have a quiet drink with my girlfriend without men coming around to hit on us.

A: I feel that as a woman today I can have just as much freedom as a man. That means a casual affair is okay.

B: I don't understand men. They want to jump into bed as fast as they can. They don't want any commitment.

In each of the above, statements A and B were made by the same woman at different times. In the second example they were made in the same evening.

Imagine eating in an expensive restaurant. You pick up a shaker and it reads: "salt or sugar." Or picture the announcer's voice at the beginning of a boxing match: "In this corner we have the liberated woman. And in the *same* corner we have the woman who wants to be 'kept.'" Let's place the man in the role of referee: How does he judge this fight? Yes, it is confusing, isn't it? Not to mention annoying. It is *very* annoying. What we have here are examples of mixed messages, conflicting signals. And to put it bluntly, it is the women who are sending the confusing signals and the men who are getting confused. Not to mention angry.

In the last few years—since women began their quest for greater personal independence, better jobs and pay comparable to men's and the right to make decisions about what they do with their bodies—men have struggled to understand this "new woman." The signals that we are getting are that women want to take charge of their own destinies. They want to compete alongside men for the fruits of success in society. They no longer wish to rely on men for the things that they want out of life. Instead they have opted to get it themselves. Although these changes do in fact create some anxiety among men, many feel that they will ultimately free men from some of the traditional male responsibilities society has imposed upon them. Ideally, this should mean men no longer have to carry the full burden of financial support, decision making and being the aggressor in romantic pursuits. Right?

Wrong! That's one message women send. But there is another message that says, "I'll have my cake and eat yours too."

A perplexed former coworker of mine once said, "You would think that a woman making, say, $35,000 a year could go out with whoever she wants—even the guy in the mail room. But no, she wants somebody who makes $45,000 a year! Why? Because she's still looking to be taken care of."

For this man and for many others, the assumption is that once a woman has the necessary financial security, the need to form relationships on the basis of what a man earns is gone.

Not so.

It's what some of us call the "my money, *our* money" syndrome. Here's a typical example: A man and woman meet through a mutual friend. Both single, they begin chatting about themselves. They are both professionals, make approximately the same money, and each has attended a good college.

SHE: *You're very nice to talk to. It's so refreshing. A lot of men these days can't deal with an independent woman. They seem to always want the upper hand, and if you are making the same bread, they become insecure. I think they still expect women to be impressed with what they do.*

HE: *That's true. I even see that in some of my own friends. But I like a professional woman, not one who's dependent on a man.*

SHE: *That's me. Hey, why don't we have dinner sometime? I know a great little place.*

They go out to dinner at an expensive restaurant that *she* chooses. *At last,* he thinks, *a woman who doesn't wait for the man to take the initiative, an independent woman! Wow, I never thought I'd be taken anyplace like this by a woman.*

The check comes, and she waits patiently for *him* to pick it up. Thank goodness our hero has his American Express card up to date. I know guys who've had to excuse themselves from the table and dash out into the streets in search of a bank cash machine. In fact, I've been one of those guys. It's tough. You have to run out in the bitter cold (it's *always* cold) without your coat because you don't want the waiter to think you've left without paying. As one of my cronies put it, "Women want it all today, from soup to nuts—and the man has to pay for the meal."

No one is suggesting, least of all me, that women *have* to pay or date "dutch." But when one professes her liberation, as did this woman, the man has the right to expect her to follow through. The emerging new woman has not only created confusion for men; she has created some problems for women as well. At least one of them, as you might expect, is a paradoxical one. Now that women have more money and more mobility, there don't seem to be any men around. There is, they say, a shortage of men. Not *any* men, mind you, but those with the "right stuff." In conversations between women and men, women and women, coast to coast, the question, "Where are all the men?" always rears its head.

I defy you to find one man, one *real* man, who actually believes there is a shortage of men. Yes, I know what the statistics say. But what I and other men see is quite different. We see women who talk around as if they couldn't care less about a man. Women don't have time.

One of my own former girlfriends once told me that she was having a difficult time deciding on what to do with her new status. She had recently passed the New York bar and had gotten a new job. "I don't know what I should be: a socialite, a hard-boiled attorney, or sort of work out a blend of my professional and social life," she mused. Curiously, none of the choices included me, so I asked, "Where do I fit in?" She stared blankly for a moment, as if she'd come home and discovered she'd forgotten to buy catsup. Then she said, "You know, Donald, sometimes I think you really have a place in my life, and sometimes I think if you walked out the door and never came back, it wouldn't faze me at all."

I had to ask.

Had it not been about nine below zero (it's *always* cold) that February night, I would have left right then. (I have since garnered lots more pride.)

Women sit at tables in fours and fives wondering where all the men are, while the men sit a few feet away at the bar. The women almost never initiate anything. Believe me, if there were only ten eligible women in New York, I'd have two of them. If I didn't, it wouldn't be because I didn't try.

It is baffling to men why women are not more aggressive. One has to assume that they are simply not interested. Here are some examples of what "eligible" men are saying.

> Women don't have time for you these days. I swear, making a date is like making a business appointment. Everybody's got calendars and datebooks.

> While women are in their twenties, they party like crazy and tell you not to pressure them into relationships. Then all of a sudden they hit 30 and uh-oh! Everybody races the clock to get married and make that baby. What are we, sperm factories? I'm supposed to get married so *you* can have cut crystal?

> It's *quality* I'm looking for, not quantity. I don't care how many women there are out there, it's quality I want. By the time you weed out the workaholics, the ones so bitter about their past lovers that they hate every man, the ones that want you only for your money/prestige, the druggies (yes, women do that too) and star seekers (noncelebrities need not apply) and ones who want fathers to their children, the margin really narrows.

> I'll believe women are liberated when one walks up to me, says, "Hey, good-lookin'," buys me dinner, pats me on the cakes and suggests we go to her place for a nightcap.

It's ironic. Women are always telling me that men are intimidated by independent, assertive women. Where are they? On a recent *Donahue* show dedicated to single men, one man posed this question: "How many women out there would drive two hours to pick me up, take me out and spend $100, bring me back home and leave?" Yes, I'm certain some have done it. Just as I know there are some readers who have figured out the number of angels on the head of a pin. However, although the number of miles and dollar amount might seem exaggerated, the routine is one that is typical and expected of men.

I remember once being headed out the door at about 9:30 on a Saturday night when the phone rang. It was a woman I dated once in a while, and she invited me out that night. Already headed elsewhere, I respectfully declined. "Well, excuse me," she said, obviously miffed. "I guess I have to book ahead."

I remember that I really had something to do that night. I think it was open-heart surgery or something, so I explained that to her. She wouldn't have cared if it really had been open-heart surgery; she felt rejected, humiliated.

I hate to tell you this, but whenever you ask someone out, there is a possibility they will say no. Men know it, they live with it. I'll never like it, but I have gotten used to it.

Oh, you thought we had it easy, huh?

Women, I honestly think, believe it is easy for men to approach them. If that were true, I would be dating Jayne Kennedy *and* Diahann Carroll. Talking to a woman for the first time, especially without an introduction, is always a crap shoot. For me, it is worse. It is tantamount to walking down a dark alley knowing a psychopath with a big baseball bat and little mercy is in there. Approaching someone means you have to bare yourself and lay some of your cards on the table. That's not easy—particularly with the "new woman" who waltzes into a room like it's the set of *Dynasty.* Thumbs up if she likes you; to the lions if not.

I'm certain that it's easier for many men. And I'm equally certain that I've fooled lots of women with my cool, sophisticated façade. It comes with years of practice and experience.

What men are seeing and hearing from women, either directly or indirectly, is that there is a very bad problem with self-image. I'm not quite sure why. It seems contradictory. There are more women than ever before who are well educated, have lucrative careers and are well dressed and good-looking.

Therein may lie the problem. Women are insecure not only about the shortage of men but also about the increasing number of what they see as competition—other women.

I've said it myself. A women walks into the room and I'm introduced to her and I think, *Okay, you went to a good school, you've got a good job and look good. So what? So do most of the women in this room. In fact, so do most of the ones I meet.* Increasingly, there is nothing exceptional about being young, gifted and cute. It has, in many circles, become a given. Male friends of mine often say, "Why do women place so much emphasis on what they do professionally?" That automatically sets up a false criterion that men fall prey to. It creates a value system that emphasizes material things. Women, of course, are not solely responsible for that. Throughout history men have shown off their uniforms, three-piece suits and jobs since shepherding paid top dollar. However, at the same time, our criteria for women were based largely on hair, ankles, calves—you get the picture.

Nowadays we find ourselves asking more questions about education, career goals and so on. These are valid questions for anyone to ask, mind you, but they are not by any means the sole criterion for what makes a good human being, let alone a good relationship. It does, on the other hand, keep the mind beyond the ankles, which is a step in the right direction.

Years ago men chose women who could cook, take care of a house and raise children. Women chose men who would make good providers. Today more and more men do their own cooking and cleaning, and are becoming closer to their children. Women, on the other hand, are becoming more self-supporting. This sounds to me like a marvelous opportunity for people to find some other reasons for relationships and shed some old ones. However, that does not seem to be happening.

It becomes extremely difficult to decipher the signals. One says, "I want a man who's sensitive, caring, spiritual and warm." The other says, " I have this list of things that I feel I should have. I want a man who can help me achieve them and move up in society."

There is a curious side to the pursuit of Mr. Right Stuff. When women settle for less, it is *far* less. I'm not talkin' triflin' here. But for some reason, Brother Rat seems to capture their attention. The story has become a tired soap opera.

I knew a woman, a professional, good school, good job, condo, the whole ball of wax. She could never find a guy good enough. She always broke off the relationships, saying that the men would feel bad because she made more money; their fragile egos would be crushed. She went out with a good guy. A professional, a nice person. They were to be married. At the last minute she shifted gears and decided she wanted more time as a career woman. She left him. She spent her days bemoaning the fact that she had nobody. Then she met a rogue. Not the charming, sophisticated, Billy Dee Williams type, but a sleazy, coke-dealing, never-had-an-honest-job type. She let him move into her apartment; he spent her money and left her in debt with a great loss of self-esteem. Yet at a given opportunity, whenever he came through town, she would take him in for a few days, and yes, lend him money.

Figure it out.

I have spent nearly all my adult life in the communications business as a writer, journalist, and media specialist, and ten years in corporate public relations. None of these things, however, prepared me for the biggest communications gap of all—that between men and women.

It happened so suddenly. Things hadn't changed very much for decades. Then came the middle sixties, while the Black movement was in full fury, and eventually people began questioning, challenging, their sexual roles. Age-old ideas about love, marriage, sex, family and children began to change for women—and for men as well.

When women were fragile little princesses (they never really were, but they played the part), it was a lot more palatable for men to play the role of Prince Charming. There is, at least among college-educated, professional women, little impetus for a man to feel he has to sweep you off your feet as you stand together, pinstripe to pinstripe, Gucci to Gucci, M.B.A. to M.B.A. But there you stand, waiting for him to open the door and take you to dinner. During the day he holds the door at work and she's furious. At night she stands in place until he opens it.

What's a guy to do?

How does one approach the new woman? Should he be forward? more aggressive and to the point? Or should he be more subtle? Should he try to appeal to her intellect through conversation? Or should he be more romantic? Can he assume she is more sexually liberated or that she is seeking only a "meaningful relationship?" How do you separate platonic friendships from romantic inclinations? Who pays the bill? Does the fact that she's "career-oriented" mean that she doesn't want to have time for a relationship?

Women are facing a backlash from men that will rival the white backlash of the seventies and eighties. And, like the white liberals in the sixties, the disenchanted men are the "nice guys"—the guys who feel they have been gentlemanly, supportive, considerate. All of a sudden the message they are getting is one of distrust, as they're portrayed as abusers, ne'er-do-wells, drug abusers and cheats. And after struggling to survive the street, college and/or military service and the day-to-day strife of the work world, they are being sent messages that say women's struggles make theirs pale by comparison. Not only that—they are the ones responsible for it!

Liberation. Independence. They're words that imply hard-won, new-found freedom. Freedom from the shackles of the past. That should include the freedom to look at relationships in a new light. Taking one or two bad experiences into each relationship thereafter is not being liberated. It is being shackled, weighed down, by your past. Understanding that the changes that took place for women also changed the perspective of many men is important. It means that realignments in relationships are necessary.

I once had the experience of working with a group of five women. All of them had previously worked together and had been friends for some time. Their businesslike demeanor made me want to straighten my tie, let alone my files and desk. We would have group meetings prior to every division meeting. They would stress how we would go in as a group, pose a common front. But once inside the meeting, something interesting happened. They broke ranks, and each tried to impress the boss. How? By fluttering eyelashes, flashing toothy smiles and laughing at all his dumb jokes.

It caused one of my male coworkers to remark, "You know who the new woman is? She's the old woman, only she can't cook"—a sexist response evoked by a group of women who lapsed into a stereotypical role.

As bleak as some of this many seem, things are actually getting better. Change did move in very swiftly, and we are all, men and women alike, getting used to it. Certainly most of us over 30 grew up in an America where girls played nurse and boys played soldier. So it will take a while. But regardless of the changes, and the time it takes, there will always be a misread signal somewhere.

And it will *always* be on a cold night.

You Men Want It Both Ways!
Betty Winston Baye

I thought the 1980's would be different, especially after the revolutionary sixties, when it was common to hear some Black men hollering about how Black women should walk ten paces behind their "kings" and have babies for the revolution. I thought that in the eighties, Black men and women had declared a truce in the war between the sexes and that we had reached, or were striving to reach, a level where we could enjoy each other's company as equals.

Betty Winston Baye, "You Men Want It Both Ways," *Essence,* July 1985. Reprinted by permission of the author.

I know, now, however, that I hoped for much too much. Though I don't presume to paint all Black men with one broad brush stroke, it seems to me that there are men—too many—who, for reasons that only they and God understand, find it necessary to lie and pretend that they just love independent women. That's what they say at first, but as their relationships develop, it becomes painfully obvious that what they really want are women who work to help bring home the bacon but also cook, clean, and take care of them and their babies on demand. These new men want women who are articulate and forceful when they're taking care of business—but who, behind closed doors, become simpering sycophants who heed their every wish.

I am an independent woman, and I'll tell anybody that what my mother and many of the women of her generation did to keep home and family together I won't do, not for love or money. Whenever I meet a man who says he's interested in me, I tell him up front that I don't do no windows. I don't love housework. I don't love to cook, and I certainly don't reach a climax thinking about having to clean up behind a bunch of kids and some mother's son. If a man wants somebody to make him home bread and fresh collard greens every night, then I'm definitely not the girl of his dreams.

Now, I realize that I'm not every man's cup of tea. But take it or leave it, that's where I'm coming from. I'll gladly work every day to help bring home the money so that my man and I can pool our resources to go out to dinner every once in a while, take a few trips during the year and to pay somebody willing (or needing) to cook, clean and do laundry.

Surprisingly, my attitudes don't turn too many men off—in fact, brothers seem turned on by my honesty and independence. My ex-husband is one case in point. At the dawn of our relationship, he swore to me that I was just what the doctor ordered. Said he'd never met a woman like me—intelligent, witty, educated, self-sufficient and not all that hard on the eyes. He went on about how he was just so thrilled that I had "chosen" him.

At first, everything was wonderful. But soon after I acquired a sweet contract to write my first book, the shit was on. It occurred to me that my beloved husband was just a bit jealous of my success. Before I knew it, I realized that he got some kind of perverse pleasure out of trying to insult me and make me look small in the eyes of my friends and professional colleagues. I remember how one time, for no special reason, he got up and announced in front of my childhood friend, her husband and their children that I was "a stupid bitch." Now, he had already published a novel, and to me he was a fine writer who could handle the English language as smoothly as butter sliding down a hot roll. But my book, and the money I got, just seemed to set him off. Not surprisingly, the marriage was finished before the book hit the shelves.

Had what happened in my marriage been an isolated case, I might have concluded that it was just "my problem"—something we women tend to do a lot. But it wasn't isolated. All around me, women friends of mine were and still are bailing out of relationships with men who say one thing, then do another.

A friend of mine got married a few years ago to a man she'd been dating for more than a year. This was a marriage made in heaven, or so she and we thought.

Both she and her husband were talented go-getters who seemed to want the same things out of life. When they first met, she says, he told her he didn't dig her just for her body but also for her sharp mind. Before long, however, it became clear that the only thing he wanted to do with her mind was to cause her to lose it. She says he wanted her to be dynamic by day and servile by night. Finally, after much verbal and physical abuse, she split. Thankfully, her memorable excursion into his insanity didn't last for long. Now she's recovering quite nicely.

Strong, dynamic, intelligent, independent women are what men of the eighties say they want. They claim they want their women to go that extra mile, but what they really mean is that we should work twice as hard but not forget our responsibilities at home. When a woman spends time with *their* children, cleans the house or cooks for *their* family, it often goes unnoticed. No matter how tired she is after a demanding day at work, the expectation is that these are *her* responsibilities. But when a man spends time with *their* children, cooks food for *their* family, or cleans *their* house once a month, he acts like he deserves an Academy Award.

Money is another area that has the brothers confused. For example, there are the men who say that if we women want to be truly liberated we should be willing, on occasion, to pick up the tab for dinner or for a night on the town. The fact that many of these same men often get their jaws wired when women, in the presence of a waiter or others at the table, reach for their wallet and pull out the cash or credit card says they're not ready for liberation. They don't mind a woman paying but would much prefer that they slip them the money under the table, the way women used to do.

And there are also the double-talking men who claim they can handle a woman who makes more money than they do. At first, everything is all right, but in order to assuage their egos, some men start thinking that "just because" they are men, they must exert control over their women's money and become personal financial managers of sorts. She's smart enough to make the money, he knows, but he believes she doesn't have enough sense to know how to spend it, invest it or manage it. "Are you sure you can afford this?" is a common question, but one rarely asked out of concern for a woman's finances. He knows she can afford it; he'd prefer to think she can't.

Many of the same men rattle on about how if we women want equality, we should buy gifts for them, as they allegedly have always done for us. Gift giving is nice, but for women; it can be a double-edged sword. One well-known singer tells the story of how she bought gifts for her man, which he gratefully accepted. But she says that after a time, the man got real nasty and told her that he couldn't be bought—he wasn't for sale.

And, of course, there are the men who seem to think that success drops out of the sky—that it doesn't require hard work and long hours. I've seen men hotly pursue women who they know are busy and then get bent out of shape if the sister pulls out her datebook to see when she's free. These women say they are tired of feeling guilty and trying to explain to some yo-yo that they can't just saunter off to dinner on the spur of the moment when they've got a report to finish or a meeting to attend.

Brothers are all for liberation when it works to their advantage. Yet, what we have found out is that when men don't want a serious commitment, they encourage us to be independent—to be open-minded enough to accept the terms of an "open relationship." But try that same rap on them, and we're in for trouble. Try saying, "Okay, baby, I don't want a commitment either"; or better yet, beat them to the punch. All of a sudden they've decided that they're in love and want to settle down. They get jealous and accuse us of "using" them.

And what about men who claim they want total honesty with their women? For many men, total honesty means that they want the freedom to talk openly about their prior involvements, including relating to their women intimate details about how many other women they've slept with or how many have aborted their babies. In return, a man like this often demands that his woman tell her business to keep things in balance. Unfortunately, what many sisters have found—often after they are laid out on a stretcher or when they've had their past sexual exploits thrown in their faces in the heat of an argument—is that many men can't handle total honesty, especially if it's sexual honesty. Many men still seem to buy into the Madonna/whore syndrome. They still believe that their peccadilloes are understandable because everyone knows that "boys will be boys." Women, however, especially *their* women, are supposed to be innocents who somehow, perhaps through osmosis, instinctively know how to turn them on in bed.

There are dozens of other ways that men send out mixed signals to the women in their lives and show, through their words and deeds, that they really want it both ways. They want us to drive the car—but from the backseat. Mostly what they want is for things to be the way they used to be. That, however, is a pipe dream. Black women, like their counterparts of other races, are liberating their minds and their bodies from the shackles of the past. Increasingly, women are refusing to waste their lives trying to decode men's mixed messages and buying into some man's macho fantasies. Instead, many women who are or want to be high achievers are accepting the fact that the price of success may be temporary loneliness. And even that loneliness is relative, since many of us have learned that having a man isn't all there is to life.

Professions for Women

Virginia Woolf

When your secretary invited me to come here, she told me that your Society is concerned with the employment of women and she suggested that I might tell you something about my own professional experiences. It is true I am a woman; it is true I am employed; but what professional experiences have I had? It is difficult to say. My profession is literature; and in that profession there are fewer experiences for women than in any other, with the exception of the stage—fewer, I mean, that are peculiar to woman. For the road was cut many years ago—by Fanny Burney, by Aphra Behn, by Harriet Martineau, by Jane Austen, by George Eliot—many famous women, and many more unknown and forgotten, have been before me, making the path smooth, and regulating my steps. Thus, when I came to write, there were very few material obstacles in my way. Writing was a reputable and harmless occupation. The family peace was not broken by the scratching of a pen. No demand was made upon the family purse. For ten and sixpence one can buy paper enough to write all the plays of Shakespeare—if one has a mind that way. Pianos and models, Paris, Vienna and Berlin, masters and mistresses, are not needed by a writer. The cheapness of writing paper is, of course, the reason why women have succeeded as writers before they have succeeded in the other professions.

But to tell you my story—it is a simple one. You have only got to figure for yourselves a girl in a bedroom with a pen in her hand. She had only to move that pen from left to right—from ten o'clock to one. Then it occurred to her to do what is simple and cheap enough for all—to slip a few of those pages into an envelope, fix a penny stamp in the corner, and drop the envelope into the red box at the corner. It was thus that I became a journalist; and my effort was rewarded on the first day of the following month—a very glorious day it was for me—by a letter from an editor containing a cheque for one pound ten shillings and sixpence. But to show you how little I deserve to be called a professional woman, how little I know of the struggles and difficulties of such lives, I have to admit that instead of spending that sum upon bread and butter, rent, shoes and stockings, or butcher's bills, I went out and bought a cat—a beautiful cat, a Persian cat, which very soon involved me in bitter disputes with my neighbours.

What could be easier than to write articles and to buy Persian cats with the profits? But wait a moment. Articles have to be about something. Mine, I seem to remember, was about a novel by a famous man. And while I was writing this review, I discovered that if I were going to review books I should need to do battle with a certain phantom. And the phantom was a woman, and when I came to know her better I called her after the heroine of a famous poem, The Angel of the House. It was she who used to come between me and my paper when I was writing reviews. It was she who bothered me and wasted my time and so tormented me that at last I killed her. You who come of a younger and happier generation may not have heard of her—you may not know what I mean by the Angel of the House. I will describe her as shortly as I can. She was intensely sympathetic. She was immensely charming. She was utterly unselfish. She excelled in the difficult arts of family life. She sacrificed herself daily. If there was chicken, she took the leg; if there was a draught she sat in it—in short she was so constituted that she never had a mind or a wish of her own, but preferred to sympathize always with the minds and wishes of others. Above all—I need not say it—she was pure. Her purity was supposed to be her chief beauty—her blushes, her great grace. In those days—the last of Queen

Victoria—every house had its Angel. And when I came to write I encountered her with the very first words. The shadow of her wings fell on my page; I heard the rustling of her skirts in the room. Directly, that is to say, I took my pen in hand to review that novel by a famous man, she slipped behind me and whispered: "My dear, you are a young woman. You are writing about a book that has been written by a man. Be sympathetic; be tender; flatter; deceive, use all the arts and wiles of our sex. Never let anybody guess that you have a mind of your own. Above all, be pure." And she made as if to guide my pen. I now record the one act for which I take some credit to myself, though the credit rightly belongs to some excellent ancestors of mine who left me a certain sum of money—shall we say five hundred pounds a year?—so that it was not necessary for me to depend solely on charm for my living. I turned upon her and caught her by the throat. I did my best to kill her. My excuse, if I were to be had up in a court of law, would be that I acted in self-defense. Had I not killed her she would have killed me. She would have plucked the heart out of my writing. For, as I found, directly I put pen to paper, you cannot review even a novel without having a mind of your own, without expressing what you think to be the truth about human relations, morality, sex. And all these questions, according to the Angel in the House, cannot be dealt with freely and openly by women; they must charm, they must conciliate, they must—to put in bluntly—tell lies if they are to succeed. Thus, whenever I felt the shadow of her wing or the radiance of her halo upon my page, I took up the inkpot and flung it at her. She died hard. Her fictitious nature was of great assistance to her. It is far harder to kill a phantom than a reality. She was always creeping back when I thought I had dispatched her. Though I flatter myself that I killed her in the end, the struggle was severe; it took much time that had better have been spent upon learning Greek grammar; or in roaming the world in search of adventures. But it was a real experience; it was an experience that was bound to befall all women writers at that time. Killing the Angel in the House was part of the occupation of a woman writer.

But to continue my story. The Angel was dead; what then remained? You may say that what remained was a simple and common object—a young woman in a bedroom with a inkpot. In other words, now that she had rid herself of falsehood, that young woman had only to be herself. Ah, but what is "herself"? I mean, what is a woman? I assure you, I do not know. I do not believe that you know. I do not believe that anybody can know until she has expressed herself in all the arts and professions open to human skill. That indeed is one of the reasons why I have come here—out of respect for you, who are in process of showing us by your experiments what a woman is, who are in process of providing us, by your failures and successes, with that extremely important piece of information.

But to continue my story of my professional experiences. I made one pound ten and six by my first review; and I bought a Persian cat with the proceeds. Then I grew ambitious. A Persian cat is all very well, I said; but a Persian cat is not enough. I must have a motor car. And it was thus that I became a novelist—for it is a very strange thing that people will give you a motor car if you will tell them a story. It is a still stranger thing that there is nothing so delightful in the world as telling stories. It is far pleasanter than writing reviews of famous novels. And yet, if I am to obey your secretary and tell you my professional experiences as a novelist, I must tell you about a very strange experience that befell me as a novelist. And to understand it you must try first to imagine a novelist's state of mind. I hope I am not giving away professional secrets if I say that a novelist's chief desire is to be as unconscious as possible. He has to induce in himself a state of perpetual lethargy. He wants life to proceed with the utmost quiet and regularity. He wants to see the same things day after day, month after month, while he is writing, so that nothing may break the illusion in which he is living—so that nothing may disturb or disquiet the mysterious nosings about, feelings round, darts, dashes and sudden discoveries of that very shy and illusive spirit, the imagination. I suspect that this state is the same both for men and women. Be that as it may, I want you to imagine me writing a novel in a state of trance. I want you to figure to yourselves a girl sitting with a pen in your hand, which for minutes, and indeed for hours, she never dips into the inkpot. The image that comes to my mind when I think of this girl is the image of a fisherman lying sunk in dreams on the verge of a deep lake with a rod held out over the water. She was letting her imagination sweep unchecked round every rock and cranny of the world that lies submerged in the depths of our unconscious being. Now came the experience, the experience that I believe to be far commoner with women writers than with men. The line raced through the girl's fingers. Her imagination had rushed away. It had sought the pools, the depths, the dark places where the largest fish slumber. And then there was a smash. There was an explosion. There was foam and confusion. The imagination had dashed itself against something hard. The girl was roused from her dream. She was indeed in a state of the most acute and difficult distress. To speak without figure she had thought of something, something about the body, about the passions which it was unfitting for her as a woman to say. Men, her reason told her, would be shocked. The consciousness of what men will say of a woman who speaks the truth about her passions had roused her from her artist's state of unconsciousness. She could write no more. The trance is over. Her imagination could work no longer. This I believe to be a very common experience with women writers—they are impeded by the extreme conventionality of the other sex. For though men sensibly allow themselves great freedom in these respects, I doubt they realize or can control the extreme severity with which they condemn such freedom in women.

These then were two very genuine experiences of my own. These were two of the adventures of my professional life. The first—killing the Angel in the House—I think is solved. She died. But the second, telling the truth about my own experiences as a body, I do not think I solved. I doubt that any woman has solved it yet. The obstacles against her are still immensely powerful—and yet they are very difficult to define. Outwardly, what is simpler than to write books? Outwardly, what obstacles are there for a woman rather than for a man? Inwardly, I think, the case is very different; she has still many ghosts to fight, many prejudices to overcome. Indeed it will be a long time still, I think, before a woman can sit down to write a book without finding a phantom to be slain, a rock to be dashed against. And if this is so in literature, the freest of all professions for women, how is it in the new professions which you are now for the first time entering?

Those are the questions that I should like, had I time, to ask you. And indeed, if I have laid stress upon these professional experiences of mine, it is because I believe that they are, though in different forms, yours also. Even when the path is nominally open—when there is nothing to prevent a woman from being a doctor, a lawyer, a civil servant—there are many phantoms and obstacles, as I believe, looming in her way. To discuss and define them is I think of great value and importance; for thus only can the labor be shared, the difficulties be solved. But besides this, it is necessary also to discuss the ends and the aims for which we are fighting, for which we are doing battle with these formidable obstacles. Those aims cannot be taken for granted; they must be perpetually questioned and examined. The whole position, as I see it—here in this hall surrounded by women practicing for the first time in history I know not how many different professions—is one of extraordinary interest and importance. You have won rooms of your own in the house hitherto exclusively owned by men. You are able, though not without great labor and effort, to pay the rent. You are earning your five hundred pounds a year. But this freedom is only a beginning; the room is your own, but it is still bare. It has to be furnished; it has to be decorated; it has to be shared. How are you going to furnish it, how are you going to decorate it? With whom are you going to share it, and upon what terms? These, I think, are questions of the utmost importance and interest. For the first time in history you are able to ask them; for the first time you are able to decide for yourselves what the answers should be. Willingly would I stay and discuss those questions and answers—but not tonight. My time is up; and I must cease.

Ms. Givings

Hilary Cosell

I never forget the commercial.

A montage of fashionable women flashed by in cityscape after cityscape. Woman after woman, each looking more attractive, more important, more in control than her predecessor. Smart tailored suits, attaché cases, shapely pumps, heels clicking on the pavement, legs striding down streets, up stairs, into skyscrapers to rest behind big desks. Makeup perfect, every hair in place in sleek chignons or other graceful, classic hair styles. All projecting an image that said: confident, purposeful, serious. I am a woman who matters. I make a difference.

I think the ad was for a bank and it ran in the early sixties. Needless to say, it made a lasting impression on me. Somehow it fitted right in with the message my collection of Nancy Drews and biographies of Susan B. Anthony, Amelia Earhart, Margaret Bourke-White, and Babe Zaharias sent me. Do something. Be somebody. Grow up to be a woman who counts.

Memory plays tricks, of course, but I think it was the first ad I ever saw in which women weren't portrayed as housewives shilling for cleanser, mothers waxing rhapsodic over detergents or, as little sex kittens, offering themselves as a bonus if you bought their product. Though the women in my ad were obviously models, and there was heavy emphasis on their looks, there was still something different about it. They were businesswomen. Professionals. Successful.

The implications were clear, impressive, and outside the norm of my upper middle class Westchester County world, where mommies didn't work because no mommies "had" to work. So I kept the memory of that ad stored someplace inside me, buried it for future use. A secret, silent motivator. Through my flower-child Fillmore East days, my antiwar years, my style that consisted of two pairs of jeans, a few T-shirts, waist-length hair and no makeup, I never forgot. One day I'll shed this skin and become that. Caterpillar into a butterfly—and I wasn't referring to my looks.

I found a partner to guide me through the tug-of-war taking place inside me during high school, something to remind me that popularity and partying were great, but so was early acceptance by an Ivy League school. I found the women's movement. It reinforced and amplified everything I thought myself, and more.

The days of finding personal reward in being the woman behind the successful man were over. Finished. The days of defining one's worth by the presence of a man, or lack or worth by the absence of one, were over. A woman's place was anywhere she chose to make that place, and if men refused to graciously concede the rightness of our position, we'd take to the streets and the courts to make sure the days of discrimination and second-class citizenry were finished too. In the hearts and minds, as well as the laws, of men. And women.

We had to do it right, though. All the way down the line. Adhere to a position in every part of life. We wouldn't succeed by displaying any traditional kinds of female behavior. No, those had to go, too. What was femininity, anyway, but a male creation? First they shackled our bodies with their silly, restrictive definitions of what was fashion, and what was beauty, and what was the proper height, weight, leg length, breast size, hair color, and eye color. Then they shackled our minds, taught us that ambition, aggression, brains, talent, drive, ruthlessness, independence were all their birthrights. Women who displayed these traits were unfeminine, unattractive, unworthy. The proper province for whatever aggression and drive and competition women had was to compete for male attention and male approval. To win a man and then keep him. By softness, passivity, dependence, nurturing, peacemaking. Control and power by indirect manipulation, all designed to feed the male ego, the male sense of his due, the male definition of his world and everyone else's place in it.

The movement laid it all out for me to see, and when they finished, womankind looked like some washed-up old whore all decked out for one final trick on her bier before retiring to meet her maker. Male, of course. I was aghast. Outraged. So full of righteous anger and indignation I didn't know which way was up or down. Or whom I was more angry with—men for thousands of years of mistreating women, or women for allowing themselves to be willing partners in their own destruction.

And nothing condensed the horror of it all better than the thought that I could wind up condemned to a lifetime of servitude in a kitchen and a nursery. Marriage was a prison, and suburbia death, and children a lifetime of slavery. To end up the dependent and drudge of some man who, if statistics can be trusted, would leave me and our kids six or ten or even twenty years after the ceremony to struggle along on insufficient alimony and child-support payments, most likely in suburbia, was a fate too terrible to contemplate.

No sir, not me. I got the message and the truth set me free. I will be successful. Earn lots of money, be a professional. Ah! I uttered the word in tones usually reserved for brief mentions of the Father, Son, and Holy Ghost. Or a major financial group. Not a career girl, someone filing her nails at her desk, earning a pittance and marking time between college and a husband. Not a working woman, either, doing unskilled, unglamorous work in the pink-collar ghetto.

No, I got the message right, figured out what was being said amid the shouting, finger-pointing, and epithet-hurling. Women are entitled to success. To a real piece of the action. To the American dream. Upscale and upmarket. Upwardly mobile. Today a Jones, tomorrow a Rockefeller, and everyone will be trying to keep up with you. To the job and the money that will buy a house and two cars, a condo and a boat, the TV, the VCR, the Atari, stocks and bonds, tax shelters, whatever is your pleasure and whatever makes you happy.

It sounds pretty good. It makes sense. Why shouldn't women have a chance at these things? Why should they belong almost exclusively to the white male establishment? Besides, if one becomes successful, one is supposed to reap all sorts of extra rewards besides material goods. Happiness and fulfillment. Respect and recognition. Sometimes even fame. Success will make you more popular, more desirable. An object of other people's envy. At the top of everyone's guest list. In demand. And naturally, more desirable than ever before to the opposite sex. Even though one is no longer supposed to care anything at all about whether they find you desirable or not.

And of course success meant other things, too. It meant freedom from economic and emotional dependence on men. It meant you were a special person, a brave and strong pioneer out there fighting a good fight. Hacking your way through the jungle to beat a path for successive generations of women to follow. It made you superior to women without success, several cuts above them. It was proof that you were USDA Prime, while the others were some inferior cut of person. Hiding behind traditional femininity and clutching the very chains that bound them.

But most of all, for anyone of my generation deeply affected by the woman's movement, success would make you active, not passive. You would be in control of your fate and your future, the way men are. You would be safe from victimization. You would be *inviolate.*

Who could turn it down? How seductive. How alluring.

And so I didn't. After studying history and political science for two years at Sarah Lawrence College—and panicking because it was just too liberal arts, and what was I being *prepared* for?—I transferred to New York University to study journalism. To become prepared to be a reporter. I went one step better and got a master's degree in journalism, so that I could perhaps teach if the newspaper I worked for suddenly folded, as they seem wont to do these days. One day you have a by-line, the next day the unemployment line.

That never happened, though. I couldn't get a newspaper job. So many folded that there were seasoned reporters looking for work, people with ten years' experience covering Congress who were willing to spend their days writing obits, if someone would just hire them. So I went into television. It's an expanding market, you see. Also, it pays much, much better.

I began as a production associate for a network news show. I was a "PA" in TV jargon, the lowest of the low, earning a pittance and too often filing my nails, not marking time between Northwestern and marriage, but trying to figure out how to supplant the four people ahead of me who would get promoted to producer first. Not only did I earn a pittance, but there was no overtime, no sixth- or seventh-day pay. But there was lots of overtime and there were lots of sixth and seventh days. On many of those I spent my time logging every word, every gesture, pan, zoom, wipe, and cutaway on Geraldo Rivera videotapes. Or hours on the phone chartering small planes bound for peculiar destinations. Or setting up interviews with people whom I would never meet, for stories I would never help edit, and certainly never come close to producing. In short the job was insufferable but the TV business wasn't. And after all, I was in the "paying your dues" phase of the success mythology.

Almost one year later I got my big break. That's part of the mythology, too. Sooner or later everyone gets the break and I was just lucky. Mine came sooner and I jumped. To another network and another show. At twenty-four I had a new title: network television producer. It seemed to have all paid off: working as a reporter for some Gannett newspapers during college, exchanging de Tocqueville and democracy for Elementary Reporting and the *AP Handbook,* leaving behind the serene academic atmosphere of Sarah Lawrence for the grime and urban blight of NYU. Sure, it was sports, not news or politics, but nothing's ever perfect.

My life changed almost overnight. Not only did my income double, triple and climb even more, but I went from yes-sir-no-sir-anything-you-say-sir to being in charge. Anything you want to do, you just do it, they said, smiling. So I traveled back and forth across the country interviewing athletes, coaches, and team owners. Boxers, promoters, trainers. Athletes on strike, athletes contemplating strikes, athletes who refused to strike. Ones with drug problems, others with alcohol problems. Born-again athletes, retiring athletes, rookies and veterans. I produced a segment called SportsJournal on a show called "SportsWorld." It was the news part of the show, the journalism, the part that showed we cared about more than who won, or lost, or even how they played the game.

I chose the stories. I researched them. I wrote the scripts. Most of the time I did the interviews. The face people saw, the voice they heard, more often than not never did anything. I picked the music, edited the story, and watched it roll from Studio 6A into millions of homes.

And I understood that I had to look my part. Live my part. Dress for success. The jeans and T-shirts moved to the back of the closet to make way for suits. Designer clothes, all cotton, linen, silk and wool, as if I wouldn't be real if the fibers weren't too.

So I traveled every week, and talked to famous people, and walked around looking smug, probably. I've got the world on a string. I've done everything differently from my mother's generation. I've done everything right. I have money, and power, and independence, and a profession, and I am inviolate.

So imagine my shock, my near-trauma, when I realized that I wanted something else. Needed something else. When I realized that I loved my job and I hated it. That it was my whole life. That it was no life at all. That somehow, after years of education and what might be called indoctrination into the virtues of success and the worthlessness of female existence without it, I started to feel empty and isolated and desolate. To feel a need for some kind of personal life that was more than casual, or occasional, unstable and rootless.

There I was, coming home from ten or twelve or sometimes more hours at work, pretty much shot after the day, and I'd do this simply marvelous imitation of all the successful fathers I remembered from childhood. All the men I swore I'd never grow up and marry, let alone be like. (Gloria Steinem once said—cheerfully, I believe—we're becoming the men we were supposed to marry. Great.) The men who would come home from the office, grab a drink or two, collapse on the couch, shovel in a meal and be utterly useless for anything beyond the most mundane and desultory conversation. *Boring.* Burned out. And there I'd be, swilling a vodka on the rocks or two, shoving a Stouffer's into my mouth, and then staggering off to take a bath, watch "Hill Street Blues," and fade away with Ted Koppel. To get up and do it all again.

All the time, of course, in the back of my mind, despite protestations otherwise, was the desire to have something more than my profession. To have a personal life, a future, that somehow included a man and possibly children, although motherhood has never been a big priority of mine. Oh, later on, I'd think, I'll work on it later on, next week after I finish this story, next month when spring training concludes, after the owners' meetings, when the football strike ends, sometime I'll get to it. Just let me get on with this career, it's more important, it's the only vital thing in the world.

But somehow, the life I'd managed to construct for myself—coupled with the prevailing attitudes and popular mythology about success and single professional women—seemed to pretty much preclude the possibility of living much differently from the way I already lived.

First of all, success demands a full-time commitment. Once you become successful, there's no time to relax, or do less than before. Getting in to become successful is only one-third the battle. Staying there takes up most of one's time and energy, and getting even further ahead takes even more.

And then, our culture pretends that creating a social life as an adult in a large metropolitan area—where there is no sense of community and where the old ties of neighborhood, family, and college days have broken down completely—is something people can just go out and do. If they have a mind to. Join a health club! Work on your favorite candidate's political campaign! Take night classes! Talk about feeling foolish. Talk about wearing a neon sign that proclaims: Lonely, need more friends, looking for love. Talk about desperate. And talk about time. Creating a personal life is a task of immense proportion. Like work, it takes time, and it takes energy. How much is there to go around, especially when life is ordered to make success the priority?

And finally, success demands something more from women than it demands from men. And especially from single women, although the demands on married women and working mothers are equally burdensome in different ways. Successful women are asked to continually prove that the company will get a return on its investment. That they will not run off at the first opportunity to wed. Or to have children. That in exchange for the privilege of an employee ID number and a salary that really should be paid to a guy, women will prove that nothing and no one is more important than the job. That life has few, if any other considerations. That this is the normal, reasonable price one pays for the honor of being admitting to the club.

If it were only that straightforward perhaps it would have been easier to swallow. Unfortunately, it isn't. because at the same time, women are also pressured constantly about the status of their personal lives. Don't marry, but why aren't you married? You're twenty-eight? What's wrong with you? Oh, you're married? When are you going to have a baby? Why don't you have a baby? You better not have a baby.

In other words, the messages come thick, fast, and constantly—and conflicting—from women and men alike: when are you going to act like a woman? Why don't you act like a woman? Don't act like a woman, there's no place for it here.

One isn't supposed to pay attention to things like that. One is supposed to be free from considerations for what people think. Peer pressure is an adolescent problem, something to put away with other childish things. One simply carries on, pays no attention, does the job, delivers what has been promised, and what's all the fuss about?

Nothing, really, until one realized that "choosing" success, pursuing it through high school and college and graduate school and on into the business world, is not the simple kind of choice between freedom and bondage people have made it out to be. The battles involved don't cover just things such as comparable pay for comparable work, or a question of learning how to dress, or putting a polite damper on your boss, who's trying to sleep with you.

The price of success is high for everyone, but it is especially high for women, and not just because they fight constant discrimination. For women, the conflicts and the choices involved in dedicating oneself to success are so fundamental, so basic, that sometimes they are unbearable. Conflicts about professional life versus family life, career versus husband and children, and even one's most personal and private perceptions of self and sexual identity.

In order to get ahead, one just dismissed or ignored these conflicts. They were cast aside while we got on with the business of work. Perhaps we refused to acknowledge them in hopes that the problems would just disappear in time. Or because to admit them would give aid and comfort to the enemy: the men and women who insisted that women belonged in the home and nowhere else. That women couldn't handle a professional life, do the work, take the pressure, compete and succeed. That all women ever want—all that ever makes them happy—is a man and a kid and a home to take care of.

So imagine my surprise when I discovered I could no longer dismiss or ignore my own conflicts and questions. When I started to think that if women had erred once before on the side of marriage and motherhood and housewifery, might they be erring again on the side of professionalism, career, and success? That the extreme to which women have gone for past fifteen-plus years may have been as off base as the idea that all women should ever attempt to do is give birth, wax floors, and watch soaps all day?

I did not like asking myself these questions. I do not like being on the "wrong" side of an issue.

But that is where I am. No longer politically correct, or ideologically pure.

At least I am not alone. Like me, other women who have achieved varying degrees of success are also questioning the tenets of their faith. Trying to redefine and reinterpret success in a way that will permit women to incorporate the so-called "feminine" aspects of themselves into a healthier adult life.

Not that we are sure this can be done.

But it behooves us to try.

"I think we are perceiving a real change in attitude," Kate tells me. She is twenty-nine, married, and a writer for a morning television show in New York. Before joining the show a year ago she was a successful freelance writer, work she continues to do. She has also published two books, one nonfiction, one fiction, with a third due soon.

"At first women were forced to go after success on men's terms alone, because they were the only terms available. We had to grab whatever we could and maneuver our way in and prove we could do it, prove that we could handle whatever they chose to throw at us, and we could do it as well as, or better than, any man could.

"Now that women have proven their abilities and done their jobs without falling apart, I think women in their late twenties and thirties are looking around and asking questions all over again, questions about goals and directions and what's really important to them.

"When the women's movement started up, it was led in part by women who were married and had children and they were mostly housewives. Of course there are notable exceptions to that, Gloria Steinem for instance. But the movement really hit home and talked to women who were bored with their lives, or women who lived the dream of marriage and husband and children and found it lacking. Or women who were forced by divorce to go back to work and who discovered that they weren't qualified to do anything, they didn't have experience, and what work they could get didn't pay anything at all. Those women were caught in a terrible bind, and they were very, very angry. Remember how angry they were?

"And so the whole tone of what followed was colored by their particular experiences and prejudices, and much of it was very negative. It was; don't get caught like I did. Don't be a bored, frumpy housewife chasing kids and driving car pools and waiting hand and foot on a husband. It stinks. Women can do better than that and they should do better than that, and the thing to do is to work. Otherwise you might end up on welfare, trying to make ends meet with food stamps, saddled with custody of the kids while your ex-husband joins Club Med and parties all weekend.

"Now, who could argue with the idea that women should work and earn a lot of money and be able to take care of themselves and their children? No one, really, because it's very reasonable, it's smart thinking and common sense.

"At the same time, because they didn't want to offend housewives and alienate such a large bloc of women, there was lots of talk about choices. The movement was going to free everyone to make choices. If you wanted to work, that was okay, if you preferred to stay at home, that's okay, too, just as long as you're not being forced to stay home by your husband or by a society that won't let you go to law school or medical school. The idea was, do whatever suits you best. We were even going to make it possible to trade places and change roles with men.

"And there was lots of talk, too, about how women should never set out to become like men, because their lives were just as rigid and sex-stereotyped as women's lives were. They were victims too. So we were all going to go off and join the labor force and really humanize it. Then everyone would be better off, men and women alike.

"By the mid-seventies, though, practically all pretense about choices and 'do what pleases you the most' was gone. People still said it occasionally, but they didn't mean it. Instead, everything was success, and success meant, climb the corporate ladder and get as close to the top as you possibly can. Push everything out of your life that might deter you, because most of those things don't matter very much anyway.

"You know, it's very easy for women who have been married and who have had children to lecture younger women who haven't, and tell them that marriage and motherhood are not what they are cracked up to be, and to say, don't be like me, profit from my bad example, go off and do something important, something that counts. And let's face it, some of their examples were pretty bad, and I certainly wouldn't have wanted to grow up to be them.

"So I listened and I followed their advice and I called myself a feminist, and I still do. But I think that for most women a time comes when all this success and career obsession starts to become awfully hollow. I started to want marriage, and I started to think about children, and I was terrified to admit it. Partly because I was afraid my desires would be held over my head as proof that women shouldn't be allowed to work in the first place. But I got scared also because I realized that those women of twenty years ago were no longer talking to me, or about me, in the way I once believed they were. I got scared because I realized that they were so busy trying to get in and get their names on the door, that they never bothered to try to build a model for success that takes the fact that we are female into account. Instead, they built one that *denied* it. There's no provision anywhere that really allows us to integrate a significant working life with a significant personal life. We're faced with lousy choices all the time, which isn't comforting when you realize that you might be talking about something as fundamental as having a child, and that's a function which is the single most important thing that separates a woman's professional needs from a man's.

"I used to listen to critics of feminism say how women didn't know how to act like women anymore. I would think, great, because acting like a woman meant giggling and flirting and batting your eyelashes and deferring to men no matter what. Who wants to act like that?

"But I've thought about that quite a bit lately, and I wonder if those people meant something entirely different, something more basic, a kind of warning, almost. If we weren't smarter or more careful, we might make it very hard on ourselves in a different kind of way. Hard to get married and to have children after so many years of placing so much worth on work as the only way to become a worthwhile person. Hard to be appreciated, respected, really, unless you work at least forty hours a week, and bring home lots of money, as well as do everything else a woman is supposed to do. Now the title of your job affects, or reflects, really, the status of the man you're dating or the man you're married to, the same way a clean house and a good dinner was the measure of a woman's worth, and the man's status, years ago. In other words, we may have trapped ourselves into a new identity that has as many, if not more problems built into it than the traditional female role we all disliked so much.

"Now the measure of worth and the definition of a successful woman seems to be 'a person who works full time at a profession, earns good money, attends to her marriage, runs a home or pays someone else to do it for her, has kids but pays someone else to look after them, too.' I've started to think that it's a crazy definition, and I find myself questioning it all the time.

"What I'd really like to know is, what ever happened to all that talk about freedom and choice? All the conversation about choosing a life that suits you personally—not one that suits other women, or your boss, or the men you date, or the man you marry—seems to have just disappeared. What ever happened to those broader definitions of success we all used to talk about?"

There is something I forgot to mention about Kate. She has a particular interest in redefining herself, and success. She is three months' pregnant with her first child.

8 Revising Academic Argument Essays

WHAT IS REVISION?

Many students think that revision means correcting the spelling, punctuation, grammar, and typographical errors in a draft, and that type of activity—editing and proofreading—is certainly important as the final stage of writing a paper. But true revision of early drafts means what the term "re-vision" implies—seeing the writing in a new way and rethinking its every aspect. In revising, therefore, writers rethink *global* essay elements such as overall thesis, quality of research, organization of main ideas, attention to audience concerns, and so on.

When writing teachers refer to "editing," they often mean a conscious process of rereading a text with an eye to possible improvements in paragraphs, sentences, or even word choices. In editing, the purpose is to rethink both *what* we are saying (in local contexts) and *how* we are saying it. When we are wearing our editor's hat (metaphorically speaking), we consider such items as paragraph divisions, sentence styles and grammar, and word-level issues such as specific word (or multi-word expression) choices for intended meanings or tones. And when we wear a proofreader's hat, we are looking for accuracy and conventionality; that is, we are looking to make our writing more *conventionally correct* by closely examining our spelling, punctuation, usage, grammar, and even typography (eliminating those nasty "typos").

Whether we are revising, editing, or proofreading at a given time, we are trying to improve our writing—through additions, deletions, and modifications—for an audience and a purpose. All elements of writing typically operate recursively, meaning that revision, editing, and proofreading occasionally may occur in that exact order, but we normally revise, edit and proofread, revise some more, and so forth—passing through many cycles on our way toward a "final" draft.

Questions for Revisions

To help you make sound revision decisions when rethinking *global* improvements in your argumentative writing, we recommend that you first allow a day or two to pass (more, if time allows) from the time you completed your first draft to the time you're ready to begin revising. Doing so will help you to read your own work more objectively. Then, when you reread your draft, you might consider the following general questions:

1. Does your draft **focus** on an appropriate issue for the assignment and its scope, or have you taken on an issue too broad to discuss with specificity or too narrow to allow you to generate sufficient information? Make sure that your focus is concise enough that you are offering readers specific support instead of generalizations.
2. Is the paper written with a particular **audience** in mind? Have the prior knowledge and possible concerns of that audience been taken into con-

sideration? Have you answered any questions that readers might have about the issue at hand?

3. Have the **context,** background, and direction of the paper been adequately described or summarized early enough in the essay so that even a reader who knows nothing about your assignment will be able to understand your essay's **purpose?** Does the draft fulfill its purpose?

4. Are there **thesis problems?** Is the thesis of your essay a statement of *your own* individual perspective? Remember that the thesis statement of an argumentative essay should reflect the writer's position on a particular debatable issue. Does the paper support all the claims that are asserted in the thesis? Does the paper answer your research question(s)? Make sure that the paper fulfills all promises the thesis makes to your readers.

5. Are **reasons** given for your position? Do the reasons directly refer to the thesis? Are those reasons supported with ample, specific **evidence** and concrete **examples?**

6. Is there an acknowledgment of **alternative views or counterarguments?** If not, the reader may get the feeling that you either haven't thought of other viewpoints or are unable to deal with them. Furthermore, make sure that the paper does not merely acknowledge these concerns but also refutes, concedes, or compromises with them in a **response** or **rebuttal.**

7. Is there a need for additional **facts or information?** Papers weak in **content** lack credibility with readers. Thus, make certain that you have developed and supported your main points with sufficient, reliable and credible research. Additionally, for assigned, multiple source and researched essays, make certain that you are **synthesizing** your sources with each other and with your own ideas—showing composite views where appropriate and possible, rather than single perspectives.

8. Are your ideas presented in a logical, organized manner? Does the **organization** help readers follow the development of the thesis throughout the paper? If not, consider ways in which the paper might work better if you rearranged paragraph or idea order. Also, do you use **transitions** and **metadiscourse** to help readers follow your reasoning from point to point?

9. Is there a **personal voice?** Writing becomes interesting when the reader can sense a committed human personality behind the prose. Do the style and the examples reflect a real person writing? Is the **tone** appropriate to your audience and purpose?

Getting Help with Revision

Many students have a great fear of showing their early drafts to anyone; often they fear that the other person might think that the writing is poor or that the writer is not very intelligent. Yet sharing an early draft with another reader can be extremely helpful, as you talk through your writing project, learn more about how you are presenting your ideas on paper, and decide how to revise to better convey those ideas to your readers. In addition to encouraging conferences with your instructor, many colleges and universities provide a Writers Lab, a support environment where you can take your paper and discuss writing options and strategies—including ideas for revision—with a consultant or tutor. Alternatively, you might have a friend read your draft. Often you may find it difficult to assess the quality of your own writing; you are so close to a paper that you cannot see its loose ends or gaps in development. You probably still see yourself as the *writer* and not as a *reader*. Persons less familiar with the writing may see it differently and be able to communicate to you where (and how) your draft creates problems for them.

Before she revised her paper, our model student Elisa (from the early chapters of this book) took her first draft and the revision questions to her college Writers Lab. There, she and a writing consultant looked over the revision questions and talked about how to revise her draft (which appears on pages 272–273 of this chapter). They decided that the thesis statement did not really reflect what Elisa proposed to say because it gave the impression that the entire paper would be concerned with how the screening committee would violate the rights specified in the U.S. Constitution. Elisa wanted her paper to address several issues beyond that idea. In particular, she wanted to stress the idea that young people cannot become thinking adults if someone does their thinking for them. Elisa and the writing consultant also agreed that her thesis did not reflect her individual perspective because it seemed to be concerned only with the Constitution. They also noted that in her paper's introduction Elisa had not adequately prepared the reader for what the paper was about. In reading her first paragraph, someone not familiar with the situation would be likely to say, "What screening committee?"

In response to the question about personal voice, Elisa and the writing consultant agreed that she had not incorporated any of the material from her prewriting questions and decided that if she did so, her draft might feel more "personal." Elisa thought that she might use some of this prewriting material as examples. In showing her paper to the writing consultant, Elisa also noted that in some places her tone seemed somewhat strident and intractable.

An important question, which the writing consultant asked Elisa, regarded the question of audience (question 2 from the list earlier in this chapter). "For whom are you writing this paper?" the consultant asked. At first Elisa was tempted to answer flippantly that, of course, she was writing her paper to fulfill the requirements of a writing class. But then she considered the question more seriously and realized that her audience would most likely be parents in the community who would be voting on whether to establish a screening committee. These parents might be like Latrice, who had written (Chapter 3) that she didn't send her son to school "to pick up whatever turns him on." To address an audience of concerned adults, then, Elisa decided she might address parents' potential fears about the effects of unrestricted reading.

Furthermore, the writing consultant pointed out that Elisa had not dealt at all with alternative viewpoints (the Brownmiller perspective, for example) or even discussed reasons why anyone would feel the need for a screening committee. After her discussion with the writing consultant, Elisa also decided that she would review the research on her issue to see if there were any relevant sources she had overlooked. Finally, she and the consultant agreed that more recent perspectives concerning the relationship of pornography to violence against women would be useful to have.

Revising, then, means making substantial changes, not just correcting surface errors. Sometimes you can reread a draft and decide right away, on your own, how to make substantial improvements. Frequently, though, you will get more useful revision suggestions or feedback if you read it aloud to someone else or let someone else read it. Exchanging drafts with a classmate or roommate—or working with a consultant in a Writing Center as Elisa did—might give you some additional or more specific ideas for revision. Fortunately, Elisa was able to receive a great deal of feedback, both from her classmates and from the writing consultant she saw. As a result of that feedback, and after much rethinking and rewriting, Elisa decided to revise her paper as follows:

1. Introduce a personal voice right from the beginning.
2. Introduce the situation so the reader understands it. (Set the context.)
3. Develop ideas in addition to those related to the Constitution.
4. Consider the audience.
5. Address the opposing viewpoint and argue against it.
6. Find more recent perspectives on the relationship of pornography to violence against women.

To illustrate these revision decisions, here is a copy of Elisa's first draft, with a few notes and marks to help remind her what she wanted to change:

The First Amendment to the United States Bill of Rights states that "Congress shall make no law respecting or abridging the freedom of speech." That amendment, which is so important to the concept of democracy, has come to mean that citizens of the United States should not be restricted about what they read. <u>Therefore, I am against the screening committee because it would be in violation of the United States Constitution.</u>

> *Not a very exiciting beginning. There is no sense of a real person speaking. Although it establishes the background for the topic, it does not provide enough context for the question of the screening committee. The reader will not know what screening committee is being discussed. Thesis sentence*

First of all, how many books are we talking about anyway? In my high school library,<u> I have never seen a book that could even remotely be considered "unsuitable" in any</u> way at all. Furthermore, Mrs. Gwendolyn Phillips, the librarian in the local high school, states that books are usually ordered by the state, by specific teachers, or librarians and that they act as a sort of screening committee anyway. If we think that another screening committee is necessary, doesn't that say something about our faith in our local school board, our librarians, and our teachers? After all, their main job is to examine the books for the library. Why would we think that we would need an additional committee?

> *Tone is too strident.*
>
> *Does this matter?*
>
> *This paragraph doesn't make a clear point.*
>
> *The question is not answered.*

Another point to consider is <u>whether books really can influence human behavior,</u> since there is a lot of doubt about whether or not this is really true. Ruth McGaffey

> *This is an important point. Develop this in terms of violence and promiscuity.*

points out that no <u>link has been established "between pornography and</u> violent crimes against women" (34) and that messages cannot "magically make people do things they wouldn't otherwise do" (34). If books cannot change behavior, then there seems to be no point to worrying about "explicit sex" and "gratuitous violence" in the school library.

Need more recent information about this.

Moreover, a screening committee to decide on books for the school library is a step in the direction of <u>censorship.</u> We think we live in a freedom-loving society. Yet, according to <u>Frank Trippett in "The Growing Battle of the Books,"</u> "cencorship has been on the rise in the United States for the past ten years. Every region of the country and every state has felt the flaring of the censorial spirit" (39). Because human beings tend to be suspicious of anything new or different from what they believe, people are all too ready to try to censor anything they perceive as threatening.

Important point—links screening committee with censorship

Quotation helps show that we are always in danger of having excessive censorship imposed on us.

History has shown us that past attempts to censor books have resulted in the banning of some fine works of literature such as <u>Catcher in the Rye, A Farewell to Arms,</u> and <u>The Fixer.</u> We may be surprised that these fine works were judged as "unsuitable," but those who favor the censoring of books often have <u>weird ideas</u> about what is appropriate. Unfortunately, these are just the sort of people who would be in favor of a screening committee.

Underline titles

Vague term that needs definition

Young people are exposed to all sorts of influences. Television, rock videos, and movies all contain material that could possibly be judged "unsuitable." To worry about books in the school library seems <u>silly.</u>

This needs to be linked to the main thesis.

Vague, unsophisticated term

<u>In order for young people to become thinking, questioning adults who can function in a free society, they must be able to deal with a variety of ideas, even those with which they might disagree or find "unsuitable."</u> Our country was founded on the principle of freedom of expression. The proposed screening committee for the high school library would not be consistent with the principles of a democratic society.

This idea is not part of the thesis. Maybe it should be further developed.

Following the Writing Center appointment, Elisa went to the library and found these more recent sources:

Cowan, Gloria. "Feminist Attitudes Toward Pornography Control." <u>Psychology of Women Quarterly</u> 16 (1992): 165-177.
Nichols, Mark. "Viewers and Victims." <u>Macleans</u> 11 Oct 1993: 60-61.
Segal Lynne. "Pornography and Violence: What the 'Experts' Really Say." <u>Feminist Review</u> 36 (Autumn 1990): 29-35.

From these articles, Elisa learned that although some research studies show a relationship between viewing pornography and the desire by some men to commit sex crimes, the research findings were not related to possible pornography found in books. She also learned that there was still a considerable division among feminists on whether banning pornography would be worth the loss in freedom of speech. Gloria Cowan's essay, for example, pointed out a belief held by some feminists, "From a free speech perspective, the consequences of censorship are more serious than the effects of pornography, inviting troubling alliances with reactionary and repressive movements" (166). In addition, according to Cowan, feminists do not believe that "banning pornography would eliminate violence against women" (166). Elisa decided that she would incorporate these ideas into the next draft of her essay.

After thinking about the changes she wanted to make and redrafting portions of the paper several more times, Elisa rewrote as follows:

SAMPLE RESEARCHED PAPER (MLA STYLE)

Elisa Jones
English 102-6
Professor Smith
May 1994

To Screen or Not to Screen

When I was about 14 years old, I was looking for a dictionary in my brother's bookcase, when I came upon a well-thumbed novel, The Catcher in the Rye. I was already familiar with the title, because one of my brother's friends had mentioned it. But since I had not read it myself, I opened it and began reading it. That afternoon, when I discovered The Catcher in the Rye, was one of the most wonderful reading experiences of my life, and I always remember it when I think about the issue of censoring books for young people.

Writer establishes personal concern with topic. Incident draws reader into the essay.

Writer uses personal voice.

Introduction of main theme

Recently, a group of concerned parents has proposed the idea of a committee to screen recent acquisitions to the local high school library. These parents claim that several recently acquired books contain explicit sex and gratuitous violence and that these books are unsuitable for their children to read. My feeling, though, is that although this proposal may be motivated by genuine parental concern, there is little evidence to suggest that unrestricted reading of books in a library is a direct cause of violent or promiscuous behavior. More importantly, such a screening committee would be a dangerous step in the direction of censorship and would also generate a restrictive educational climate, which is unsuitable for preparing students to function in a democratic society. Finally, it would deprive students of the pleasures of discovering books for themselves.

Context of screening committee set to orient reader. Background is important here.

Thesis statement. These will be developed in the essay.

The First Amendment to the United States Bill of Rights states that "Congress shall make no law respecting an establishment of religion or prohibiting the free exercise thereof, or abridging the freedom of speech." That amend-

This paragraph establishes that students should be treated as adults and should have the freedom to choose their own books.

ment, fundamental to the concept of a free society, has come to mean that citizens of the United States have the liberty of reading anything they choose. <u>High school students are only a few years away from assuming full rights as citizens, with all of the responsibilities that citizenship brings.</u> Very soon after high school graduation, these students will be eligible to vote and to serve in the military, and many of them will have full-time jobs. <u>By censoring what students are able to read, therefore, the proposed screening committee would deprive the local high school students of their rights as citizens.</u>

Establishes that high school students will soon be citizens.

This point establishes that the screening committee would deprive students of their rights.

This paragraph anticipates opposition.

Some may argue, of course, that screening a few books in a local high school library is a very small violation of First Amendment rights. Yet even a small violation such as this can be regarded as a step in the direction of censorship, and any form of censorship jeopardizes free thought. We think we live in a liberal age, in which freedom is taken for granted. Yet, according to Frank Trippett in "The Growing Battle of the Books," "censorship has been on the rise in the United States for the past ten years. Every region of the country and every state has felt the flaring of the censorial spirit" (39). Because human beings tend to be suspicious of anything new or different from what they believe, people are all too ready to censor anything they perceive as threatening. Surely, this is not an example that should be set in high school.

Quotation incorporated into text.

In-text citation-page number.

One form of censorship can very easily lead to another, perhaps more dangerous, form because of the suspiciousness of human nature. History has shown us that past attempts to censor books have resulted in the banning of some famous and highly acclaimed works of literature, <u>Catcher in the Rye</u>, <u>A Farewell to Arms</u>, and <u>The Fixer</u>, just to name a few examples. We may be suprised that these fine works were judged as "unsuitable," but each age has its own particular notions of propriety and suitability. Those who advocate censoring books are usually those who have very fixed ideas about what is appropriate; often it is only a very small group that feels strongly enough to argue for censorship, and it is this minority that attempts to impose its own views on the majority. Minority rule is also in direct opposition to the concept of democracy.

Supporting point establishes that one form of censorship can lead to another.

Indicates that censorship can become extreme.

To some extent, high school is the place where students receive their preparation for becoming citizens, since, for many, this is their last opportunity for formal education. Being a citizen in a democracy means being able to make decisions, to decide for oneself between right and wrong. As Ruth McGaffey points out, "a self-governing people must be able to discuss all ideas regardless of how repulsive they might be" (52). "Instead of worrying about all the dangerous ideas and pictures and films in the world, we should be worrying about developing minds that are

This paragraph establishes that high school is a training ground for citizenship.

In-text quotation.

Page # cited in text.

Key idea: censoring books prevents development of inquiring minds.

comfortable with uncertainty and complexity, not obedient minds" (52). The idea of a screening committee is in direct opposition to the idea of <u>developing minds</u> because it implies that students are incapable of dealing with ideas that might make them uncomfortable. This is not an environment that is likely to prepare its citizens for responsible participation in society.

Moreover, it is highly unlikely that high school students are exposed to much "gratuitous violence" and "explicit sex" in the school library. Mrs. Gwendolyn Phillips, school librarian, states that books are usually ordered by the state, by specific teachers, or librarians, and that the selection process is very much like a screening anyway. We have delegated responsibility for our children to school boards, teachers, and school librarians because their education and experience have qualified them for our trust. This is not a trust we can assume that a self-selected group of parents can handle as well.

This paraphrase of interview establishes that books are already screened sufficiently.

Of course, those in favor of the screening committee may point to the increasing violence in our society, particularly that against women, which, some say, can be triggered by pornographic material. Susan Brownmiller points out that "pornography is the undiluted essence of anti-female propoganda," (7) and she suggests that pornographic material could well be "a causative factor in crimes of sexual violence" (7). However, in that same article, Brownmiller also states that the President's Commission on Obscenity and Pornography "maintained that it was not possible at this time to <u>scientifically prove or disprove such a connection.</u>" (7) This position is supported by a Danish study (<u>New York Times</u>, Nov. 9, 1970), which "finds that sex crimes have sharply declined in Denmark in the three years since censorship laws have been eased there" (Kauffmann 136). More recent studies as well suggest that there is no clear connection between reading pornographic material in books and violent acts against women. In fact, although a few research studies show a relationship between viewing pornopraphy and the desire by some men to commit sex crimes, there is still considerable division among feminists about whether banning pornography would be worth the loss in freedom of speech. Gloria Cowan's essay, "Feminist Attitudes Toward Pornography Control," for example, points out that some feminists feel that "from a free speech perspective, the consequences of censorship are more serious than the effects of pornography, inviting troubling alliances with reactionary and repressive movements" (166). In addition, these feminists do not believe that "banning pornography would eliminate violence against women" (166).

This paragraph anticipates argument that pornography leads to violence against women.

In-text quotations.

Establishes that it is difficult to establish a connection between books and crimes against women.

Citation of more recent studies showing that no absolute links between pornography and violence have been established.

One feminist position is not clear whether censorship is the answer to pornography.

Given that there is no proof that reading about sex and violence directly leads to the commission of sexually re-

Conclusion.

lated violent crimes or to promiscuous behavior, it would seem unwise for the high school library to jeopardize the First Amendment rights of its students by the formation of a screening committee. My "discovery" of <u>The Catcher in the Rye</u> when I was 14 years old is just one example of the pleasure I now associate with books. Moreover, I am very glad that my own reading was not restricted in high school, since I now feel capable of dealing with a variety of ideas, even those with which I might disagree or find "unsuitable." As a college student who will soon be considered a legal adult, I feel strongly that the proposed screening committee for the high school library would not <u>be beneficial either for students or for the quality of society.</u>

The conclusion returns to thesis and opening anecdote.

Personal voice reestablished.

Reiteration of thesis.

Works Cited

Placed on separate page.

Brownmiller, Susan. "Pornography Hurts Women." <u>Against Our Will</u>. New York: Simon and Schuster, 1975.

Sources arranged alphabetically. Book

Cowan, Gloria. "Feminist Attitudes Toward Pornography Control." <u>Psychology of Women Quarterly</u> 16 (1992): 165–177.

Journal

Kauffman, Stanley. "Pornography and Censorship." The <u>Public Interest</u> 22 (Winter 1971): 112–14.

Journal

McGaffey, Ruth. "Porn Doesn't Cause Violence But a Fear of New Ideas Does." <u>Milwaukee Journal</u> 9 (Sept. 1986): 78–79.

Journal

Nichols, Mark. "Viewers and Victims." <u>Macleans</u> 106.41 (Oct 1993): 60–61.

Journal

Phillips, Gwendolyn. Personal interview. 14 Apr. 1993.

Interview

Segal, Lynne. "Pornography and Violence: What the "Experts" Really Say." <u>Feminist Review</u> 36 (Autumn 1990): 29–35.

Journal

Trippett, Frank. "The Growing Battle of the Books." <u>Time</u> 19 Jan. 1981: 60–62.

Periodical

➤ **Exercise in Analyzing Revisions:** Working in small groups, compare Elisa's first draft with her final draft. Which features of the final draft do you feel are improvements over the first draft? Are there any aspects of the final draft that you feel need additional revision? If so, explain.

➤ **Assignment on Getting Help and Revising:** Using the "Questions for Revision" and/or commentary from your instructor, meet with a Writers Lab tutor, classmate, friend, or family member outside of class and

> discuss possible improvements in your essay. Jot down on your draft any suggestions the two of you generate during your meeting. Next, revise your draft with your revision tasks in mind.

REVISION SUGGESTIONS FOR SPECIFIC ACADEMIC ESSAY TYPES

Just as Elisa's essay improved significantly through revision, you too can strengthen your writing by incorporating revision as a major part of your writing process. Thus, the rest of the chapter is focused upon providing you with specific tips for revising your own essays.

Keeping the Assignment in Mind as You Revise

Although revision processes for different types of academic essays may have many features in common, it's not hard to see that the emphases of different assignments will suggest some relatively situation-specific revision strategies. Thus, the first step to finding clues for necessary revision strategies is to reread your assignment carefully, noting any specific goals of the assignment that must be fulfilled, focus and audience specifications, and any other guidelines that your instructor has offered. In addition to the guidelines provided in the assignment itself, the table below provides a list of areas that might need further attention during revision, depending upon the assignment type. The revision areas are listed in the left (first) column and three types of academic argument essays—a critique, an assigned-sources essay, and a researched essay—appear across the top. Please note which essays are most likely to require revision in which areas. Although this listing is not exhaustive, it may provide you a handy reference tool.

Table 2: Revision Tasks Specific to Assignment Type

	Critique	Assigned-Sources Essay	Researched Essay
Introduction & Conclusion	✓	✓	✓
Focus	✓	✓	✓
Thesis	✓	✓	✓
Summarizing, quoting, and paraphrasing source information	✓	✓	✓
Organization	✓	✓	✓

Table 2: *Continued*

	Critique	Assigned-Sources Essay	Researched Essay
Specific evidence and examples	✓	✓	✓
Transitions & Metadiscourse	✓	✓	✓
Synthesis		✓	✓
Counterarguments and rebuttals	✓	✓	✓
Research			✓
Using ample, credible and reliable source support	✓	✓	✓

➤ **Assignment on Revising Your Critique:** Please read through your essay once as a reader (not as the writer), then ask yourself the following questions about each portion of your essay. Jot down your answers to the questions, paying close attention to those areas needing revision. Revise accordingly.

1. **Introduction:** Is it engaging? Does it introduce the subject of the source you are critiquing? Does it introduce the source and the author(s)? Does it introduce the main point or argument made by the author(s)?

2. **Thesis:** Are your overall evaluation/assessment of the source and the criteria used in your evaluation clear to readers by the end of the introductory or summary portion of your essay?

3. **Summary:** Are the main points of the source clearly presented in your critique? Is there enough summary information provided for readers to get a basic overview of the source's content? Does the critique provide too much summary information? If so, cut out any extraneous material.

4. **Criteria/Analysis Paragraphs:** Do you develop at least three criteria/arguments to support your overall evaluation of the article? Is the criterion that each argument is based upon clearly stated in the topic sentence(s) of each argument paragraph? Does each argument paragraph stay focused on supporting the criterion set up in the topic sentence(s)? Are there at least two pieces of specific evidence (examples) used from the source to support each criterion/argument? Are the argument paragraphs wrapped up well?

5. **Conclusion:** Do you wrap up your overall evaluation and main points well? Do you provide your readers with a recommendation concerning the source's reliability or usefulness on a given topic or issue? Do you bring up any new or irrelevant information? If so, cut out any information that does not help sum up your evaluation, response, or recommendation.

6. **Organization:** Is your essay organized well? Are your argument paragraphs organized in a logical manner?

➤ **Assignment on Revising Your Assigned-Source or Researched Essay:** Read through your essay once as a reader (not as the writer), then ask yourself the "Questions for Revision" listed earlier in this chapter. Jot down any revision strategies you generate right on your draft. Next, revise your draft with your revision tasks in mind.

Improving Titles

Although some see a title to a text as a mere formality, there is more to titling a text than simply tagging on a word or phrase at the top of your essay before handing it in to your instructor. Instead, the title should serve as an attention-grabber by hinting at the controversy at hand, the focus of your argument, or something else that pertains to your text and intrigues readers. For example, read the following title:

Obesity

While this title certainly indicates to readers that the writer will be focusing on the subject of obesity, it neither intrigues readers nor hints at the writer's focus. The following title is more effective:

The Risks of Obesity: What Can We Do to Avoid Them?

This latter title not only does a better job identifying the author's focus but also poses a question that many readers may find intriguing.

➤ **Exercise in Improving Titles:** For the following general subject areas, brainstorm focused and potentially intriguing titles in small groups. Be prepared to share your group's ideas with the class.

1. Stalking
2. The Internet
3. Child Abuse
4. Proficiency tests
5. Multicultural Education

➤ **Assignment on Improving Your Essay Title:** Analyzing the title for the essay you are currently working on, try to determine whether it effectively invites readers to read on and forecasts the specific focus of your essay. If not, brainstorm a list of five additional titles to share with a peer, your instructor, or a tutor. Discuss which new title idea works best.

Improving Introductions

Effective introductions have a "hook" that makes the reader want to read the rest of the essay. This hook could be an engaging anecdote, scenario, question, a surprising example or statistic, or memorable quote—anything that has the ability to draw in readers. Take for instance the hook that Molly uses at the beginning of her essay, "Creating a Smoke-Free Environment" (her essay can be found in its entirety at the end of this chapter):

> Have you ever sat down in a restaurant to enjoy a meal, only to be annoyed with burning eyes and a disgusting stench? How about experiencing the discomfort of trying to eat a meal that tastes like smoke? I'm sure that this scenario is very familiar to anyone who has ever eaten out.

As you can see, Molly's strategy at the outset of her essay is to get readers to recall their experiences at smoke-filled restaurants so that she can forge a bond between writer and reader—an empathy with her claim that a change in policy is needed for restaurants that still allow smoking.

After you *hook* your readers, you will be expected to provide them with a general overview of the issue and the controversy surrounding it, so that they are knowledgeable on the debate before you assert your opinion. Doing so will also make you more credible to readers because it will show them that you examined all sides of the debate before coming to your own conclusions. Thus, after Molly employed her aforementioned hook, she followed it up with a brief summary of the controversy:

> The disturbing effect that smoke has on nonsmokers as they try to eat is sometimes so unbearable that they would rather stay home and eat at their own convenience. Whether or not to ban smoking in restaurants has been an ongoing debate in society. As more and more people realize how danger-

ous and harmful smoking is, they begin to question why it is necessary for people to smoke in social settings—such as restaurants. On the other hand, some people argue that any public facility should give a smoker the freedom to smoke if he/she wishes.

> ➤ **Assignment on Improving Your Introduction:** Reread your introduction and determine whether or not you effectively hook your audience and then provide them a concise, effective overview of the controversy. If you have trouble deciding upon introduction strategies, feel free to discuss possible revision strategies with a peer or writing tutor. Revise the introductory portion of your essay accordingly.

For more advice on writing introductions, refer to Chapter 6, "Writing an Introduction," pages 204–205.

Strengthening Your Thesis

For the academic "argument" essays you write, remember that your thesis (or central argument of your essay) must be debatable—that is, it must establish an arguable position on an issue—and should typically forecast the reasoning you will use to support your overarching claim. The thesis of Molly's "Creating a Smoke-Free Environment" essay does just that:

> I agree with the side of the issue that believes smoking should be prohibited in all restaurants. The reasons supporting my opinion are that smoking affects nonsmokers because of secondhand smoke; some people are actually allergic to smoke; studies have shown that banning smoking would not deter customers; and it is extremely discomforting to eat while others are smoking. I feel that these four points, together, form a strong argument in favor of smoke-free restaurants.

Notice that Molly's thesis makes clear both her position on the controversial issue of smoking in public places, specifically restaurants, and her reasoning for feeling the way she does.

There are no steadfast rules that dictate where you should place your thesis—it can appear as your opening sentence, at the end of your introduction, in the middle of your essay, or as your conclusion. Nevertheless, most writers choose to assert their thesis early in the essay, to let readers know their position and use it as a point of reference for the supporting arguments that follow. In Molly's case, she chose to place her thesis after her overview of the debate, at the end of her introduction. Although in most researched essays the thesis is stated relatively early, the exact location you choose for your thesis depends upon the effect you want to have on your readers and the argumentative style you feel most comfortable and confident employing. For more information on structuring academic arguments, see Chapter 5.

> ➤ **Assignment on Strengthening Your Thesis:** Without prior discussion about the content of your essay, ask peers or a Writers Lab tutor to carefully read your draft. Pay close attention to what they identify as your thesis and its position within the essay. If they can easily summarize your central argument and supporting reasoning, your thesis is most likely clear and focused enough for your readers. If they cannot summarize your central argument and supporting reasoning, you should go back to your draft and look for ways to make them more evident for readers. Next, ask your peers or tutor to comment upon the effectiveness of the positioning of what they identify as your thesis. They may be able to give you suggestions about optimum thesis positioning to assist and persuade readers.

Improving Synthesis

Please bear in mind that synthesis is more than simply including two or more different sources of support for each supporting argument. Most importantly, the purpose of synthesis is to illustrate a reasonable degree of consensus in support of each argument in your essay, by making connections between your own points and evidence provided by credible sources. In making these connections, you will be expected to interpret each piece of source support you use to back your claims and to discuss how the research agrees, disagrees, clarifies, provides examples for, and/or illustrates a cause and effect relationship between your points and the points brought up by your other sources. For example, in the following claim asserted by Molly in her essay "Creating a Smoke-Free Environment," she successfully synthesizes her second supporting argument for her thesis, that smoking in restaurants should be prohibited because some diners may have smoke allergies:

> Not only is smoke harmful to nonsmokers because of the pollutants, but also it is dangerous because some people are allergic to it. I feel that these particular individuals should not have to feel miserable because of people puffing smoke into the air. Philip Wexler, the author of "Passive Smoking" from the *Natural Library of Medicine*, asserts that there are many people who are allergic to smoke and don't even realize it. Wexler **gives a few symptoms** of being allergic to smoke such as eyes watering and itching, coughing, and sneezing almost uncontrollably whenever smoke is in the air (3). I know that if I were allergic to smoke, it would be very disrupting if I was eating and had to wipe my eyes and blow my nose every time my body sensed smoke. The author of "Controversy on Passive Smoking," Frank Dobson, also **agrees** that the banning of smoking sections in restaurants would benefit those customers who sneeze, cough, and tear up because they are allergic to smoke. Dobson maintains, "The discomfort that people who are allergic to smoke endure is sometimes unbearable. To think that this could be prevented if smokers would be courteous enough to smoke outside really disgusts me"(2). Interestingly, a restaurant owner whom I interviewed, Ms. Klingersmith, is allergic to smoke. When I asked her what

motivated her to ban smoking in her restaurant, she replied that she herself is allergic to smoke, so she decided to prohibit smoking. **More specifically**, Klingersmith said, "I've been allergic to smoke ever since I was a little girl, so naturally I wouldn't want my customers (who may be allergic) to have to tolerate the discomfort of being around smoke." After discussing this issue with someone who actually suffers a smoke allergy, I could easily understand how frustrating it must be to not be able to eat in a restaurant without feeling lousy because someone is smoking at the next table over.

Notice that Molly's synthesized use of Wexler for examples, Dobson for agreement, and Klingersmith for clarification and example is clearly signaled by her verb and transition choices. The following table of verb and transition choices may be helpful to you as a guide when you are revising to improve synthesis:

Table 3: Verbs and Transitions That Can Help Strengthen Synthesis

Agreement	Clarification	Example	Cause & Effect	Disagreement
Agrees	Clarifies	Portrays	Causes	Contradicts
Allows	Elucidates	Illustrates	Effects	Condemns
Affirms	Illustrates	Represents	Induces	Disagrees
Approves	Interprets	Depicts	Produces	Differs
Accommodates	Specifies	Paints a picture	Provokes	Dissents
Confirms	Simplifies	Provides a case	Creates	Disputes
Concurs	Explicates	Cites a	Brings about	Denies
Concedes	Shows	model/lesson	Makes (this)	Debates
Consents	Expounds upon	Notes a pattern	happen	Questions
Complies	Makes clear	Explains by	Gives rise to	Opposes
Grants	Further	example	Because of	Protests
In accordance	explains	For example	(this)	Refuses
with	In other words	For instance	Since	Conflicts with
In agreement	That is (to say)	Such as	Due to (the fact	In disagreement
with	In fact	Namely	that)	with
Similarly	As a matter	Specifically	In view of (the	Alternatively
Likewise	of fact	Especially	fact that)	On the other
In the same	More	Particularly	For the (simple)	hand
way	importantly	For one thing	reason that	However
In a like	After all	To illustrate	Therefore	In contrast
manner	Besides this		Consequently	Conversely
By the same	Not only (this)		Thus/Hence	While
token	but also (this)		For this reason	Whereas
Equally	Speaking about		As a result of	Rather
	(this)		(this)	Instead
	Considering		Because of	But
	(this)		(this)	
	To clarify			

> ➤ **Assignment on Improving Your Synthesis in Your Essay:** Reread each of your supporting arguments in isolation, paying close attention to apparent and not so apparent relationships between your source information and your own ideas. Those arguments that are not well synthesized will need to be reworked. Try revising them for better verb and transitions choices to strategically relate your citations to one another and to your argument.

Identifying Source Information and Authoritativeness

Identifying Sources

When introducing the authors of an outside source for the first time, remember to provide readers with their entire names and titles of their work. Also include any information that you may have on their credentials. Once you've given readers these specifics, your later references to the same sources need only refer to the authors by their last names (unless, that is, there are two or more authors with the same last name—then full names are necessary to differentiate between the two). To illustrate, when Molly first brings up her interviewee within her research findings, she makes certain that both the person's name and her credentials are provided:

> While conducting an interview with Cathy Klingersmith, **the owner of a smoke-free restaurant in Hiram,** I asked why she decided to ban smoking in her restaurant. Klingersmith responded by saying, "Smoking is definitely a health hazard to both smokers and nonsmokers. I chose to prohibit this act because I don't think that nonsmokers should have to breathe in hazardous pollutants while they are eating."

While Molly quoted her interviewee's exact words, please note that even if you paraphrase another writer's ideas in your own words, you still must cite your source to give proper credit to the person with those ideas (refer to your style manual or handbook for proper citation format). Even if you don't copy the author's idea word for word, you must still give proper credit to the originator of that idea.

Identifying Authorities

As discussed, you should note the credentials of the authors you cite to lend your arguments more credibility. Additionally, being able to identify and use the most authoritative and reliable sources on your issue will further enhance your credibility, and thus your persuasiveness, with your reader. As an example, readers would be more likely to believe evidence on the negative effects of fertility treatments that appeared in the *Journal of the American Medical Association* than evidence from *Mademoiselle* magazine. To ensure that readers are convinced by her statistics on secondhand smoke, Molly conveys the authoritativeness of one of her sources in the following excerpt:

> Information concerning secondhand smoke is also provided by the Consumers Union of the United States. The Consumer Union of the United States is an organization that did research to determine whether or not secondhand smoke is a threat to nonsmokers. *Consumer Reports* reprinted statistics from the Consumers Union of the United States, which confirms, "People breathing secondhand smoke are eight to 150 percent more likely to get lung cancer sometime later" (28).

Notice that Molly is relying on a study conducted by the Consumers Union of the United States and points out that the evidence came from statistics compiled by that organization, rather than by the source in which it was published (*Consumer Reports*). Similarly, when citing evidence you glean from a source, you should identify the borrowed ideas as belonging to the author or the authority that the author is citing rather than to the source. Note, too, that you only need to establish the authority of a source the first time that you cite it in your essay. You may reasonably assume, in short to moderate-length academic essays, that your readers will remember a source's authoritativeness in subsequent references.

For more tips on identifying source information, refer to Chapter 7.

➣ **Assignment on Identifying Source Information and Authoritativeness:** Reread your essay, paying close attention to the source information you have cited. Then, identify any sources that are not clearly attributed to a particular author. Additionally, replace non-authoritative source support with source support from more credible sources on the issue.

Qualifying Assertions

Qualifiers are words or phrases that help you indicate when, why, and how your claims are valid, logical, and reliable. Most of the time, claims without qualifiers are what we might call "sweeping generalizations," because few claims are entirely true or always right. It's important to note, too, that readers are *most likely* not going to be convinced by your claims if they are based upon generalizations. Some example qualifiers are as follows: *often, generally, probably, possibly, many times, almost always,* etc. Qualifying verb choices such as the verbs *may, might, can,* and *could* can also help you avoid overgeneralizations. An example of an overgeneralization follows:

> Because teenagers are sexually active, which leads to unwanted pregnancies, birth control devices need to be made available in public junior and senior high schools.

A qualified version of this assertion is as follows:

> Because **many** teenagers become sexually active **before they graduate high school,** which **could** lead to unwanted pregnancies, birth control devices should be made available in public junior and senior high schools.

Qualifiers, such as *most* and *could* in the above example, guide readers to the understanding that your claim is conditional rather than absolute. Thus, you're allowing for exceptions in your reasoning. However, keep in mind that using qualifiers does not guarantee that your argument is logically reasoned. Too many qualifications can sometimes signal to your readers that you doubt the substance of your own claims. If you find yourself in this predicament, you need to decide if indeed you have discovered more reasons to doubt your initial claims than to support them. If you have, you can still persuade your readers by acknowledging that your initial hypothesis was found to be untrue after further research and that you therefore have revised your thesis to take into account your discovery. For example, one student writer initially jumped to the hasty conclusion that the water supply for the city in which she lived was contaminated due to the foul taste and odor of the water. After researching the issue further, she found the following:

> Misconceptions and rumors about the quality of the water, information about contaminants taken out of context, and a lack of knowledge about how water treatment plants are monitored by the EPA have caused **many**—including myself—to believe that the drinking water is contaminated. However, after further researching the debate and interviewing personnel at the water treatment plant and the Ohio EPA, I have found that, **unless there is a publicized warning,** residents should feel confident that the water is safe to drink.

After considering these tips on asserting qualified claims, carefully assess the strength and validity of your claims in order to decide where and which qualifiers are needed.

➢ **Exercise in Qualifying Generalizations:** Please qualify the following overgeneralized claims to create claims more likely to be acceptable to college-educated readers:

1. Politicians can't be trusted—they're nothing but lying, cheating money-mongers.
2. Kids today want everything just handed to them, and they have no respect for authority.
3. All teachers deserve to be paid more money.
4. There's a problem with how the police use unnecessary force these days—just look at the Rodney King and Amadou Diallo cases.
5. Homeless people can't get off the streets because they are uneducated and lazy.

> ➤ **Assignment on Qualifying Generalizations:** Reread your essay, looking for overgeneralized claims like those listed in the above activity. Qualify any that you find, using some of the word choice suggestions offered in this section to create claims more likely to be accepted by college-educated readers.

Improving Organization

Organizing to Create Emphasis

Readers often pay more attention to the parts of an essay near the beginning and near the end. Readers who skim for the main idea of a text look to these areas for the most important points. Accordingly, writers often place their strongest, most persuasive arguments either first or last. Those writers who organize their most persuasive point first, after their introduction, believe that doing so captures readers' attention immediately, leaving them more open to accepting the persuasive claims that follow. Those who save their strongest point for last may believe that readers are more likely to be influenced after being exposed to the entire line of reasoning. However, other writers choose to organize their second strongest argument first and most persuasive last, with the least convincing argument(s) sandwiched in the middle, because they fear that organizing their weakest argument first would not capture the readers' attention enough to prompt them to read on. Thus, in placing their second-best argument first, the writers who choose this organization strategy hope their readers will be persuaded enough to read on until they get to the last and most influential argument. Whichever organizational strategy you choose for your essays, it's important for you to make informed choices regarding the arrangement of your main points.

It's also important to note that the length and complexity of each supporting argument tends to indicate to readers the weight of its importance within your overall argument. Most of the time, those points that are more developed and supported by credible, synthesized research will be more convincing for readers—so you should also keep the length and complexity of each point in mind when deciding on the best order for both the purpose of your essay and maximum persuasion. Readers will not tend to consider your major points "major" if you develop them with just a sentence or two, and they easily can be misled by "minor" points to which you allot page after page of detail.

Using Transitions

Transitions can walk your readers through each point in your essay smoothly. They help your readers see how the ideas you are presenting connect to and relate with one another. Do you have transitions between paragraphs? You should. Do you also have transitions within paragraphs, helping readers to see and follow the paragraph's organization, and between individual ideas and their supporting arguments? Also, remember that you must always transition into, or frame, your source materials. See the transition section of Chapter 7 for more details.

> ➤ **Assignment on Improving Your Organization:**
>
> **1.** Reread your rough draft, paying close attention to the length and complexity of each of your supporting arguments and the order in which you present them. Keeping in mind your reasons for the organization strategy outlined above, decide whether your supporting arguments are in the best order for your intended effect on your readers. Make any changes you feel necessary.
> **2.** Double-check your transitions between your supporting arguments and the evidence backing each. Make sure that you have included transitions that help your readers move from one argument to the next and see the relationships between your ideas and source support. Add transitions where necessary and change those that are ineffective.

Effectively Dealing with Counterarguments

Are you aware of concerns some readers may have about your argument as a whole or about some of the main points or reasons supporting your argument? If not, you need to become aware because readers expect you to acknowledge alternative perspectives and to deal with at least some of the concerns they may have.

In order to best address such concerns, you should explain how each disagrees with your thesis or one of your supporting arguments. One logical place to address a counterargument is either before or after the point or reason that it contradicts. If it is a counterargument against your thesis, you might address it right after the introduction or just before your conclusion. Alternatively, counterarguments sometimes can be presented in a paragraph or two, usually near the beginning or end of the paper. (Please bear in mind that you should not leave a counterargument "hanging" or unanswered—even if you must concede its truth—and that counterarguments too near the end of an essay might leave lingering doubts in the mind of the reader.)

As previously mentioned, academic argument calls for the writer to make a response that **refutes** (argues against), **concedes** that an opposing point is valid (but explains that your argument is still the most reasonable), or suggests a **compromise** for each counterargument. This response is often called a **rebuttal**, from the terms of formal debate. Furthermore, in order for the handling of your opposing arguments to be successful, you will need to make it clear to your readers that the counterarguments are not *your* ideas; your ideas are in the response, or rebuttal, to the counterargument. To illustrate, Molly makes appropriate word choices, which have been highlighted, to assure that readers are able to differentiate between counterarguments and her rebuttal:

> One more argument **against prohibiting smoking** in restaurants is that, "Some people will walk out instead of putting their cigarette out" (Sciacca and Eckrem 178). **Although** this may happen infrequently, many studies, such as the one by Biener and Siegel, have shown that many restaurants which do not permit smoking have not lost customers. Those who believe that most smok-

ers would rather avoid the restaurant than go in and eat (without smoking) are simply assuming this. Indeed, the majority of smokers will still eat at the restaurant and wait until after the meal to go outside to light their cigarette.

Some of the word choices that can help identify the opposing arguments and rebuttals are transition choices. The chart below provides suggestions for some of these.

**Table 4: Transitions That Can Help Differentiate Opposing
Arguments from Rebuttals**

Into Counterargument	Into Rebuttal
Alternatively	Still
On the other hand	Yet
However	Nevertheless
In contrast	Nonetheless
Conversely	Despite (this)
While	In spite of (this)
Whereas	Regardless (of this)
Rather	Granted (this)
Instead	However
But	Admittedly
	Though
	Although
	Even so
	Even though

For more advice on effectively handling counterarguments, refer to the counterargument section of Chapter 5.

➤ **Assignment on Effectively Handling Counterarguments:**

1. Reread your rough draft, looking for places where you acknowledge opposing arguments to your thesis and/or supporting arguments. If you do not acknowledge any potential counterarguments, think of some that you might include in your next draft. If you have trouble brainstorming possible counterarguments, ask a peer, your instructor, or a Writers Lab tutor for advice.
2. If you have acknowledged opposing arguments, double-check that you have clearly indicated to readers that the counterarguments being expressed would be the view of another party, not yourself, so that you don't seem to contradict your own thesis. Additionally, make certain that you transition into your response

> to counterarguments, clearly signaling to readers that you are moving from your acknowledgement of opposing arguments into your refutation, concession, or compromise.
>
> 3. Double-check the organization of your counterarguments and rebuttals. Ensure that they are organized effectively. Make any location changes as necessary.

Strengthening Supporting Arguments

Asserting Clear Topic Sentences

Topic sentences are typically the opening sentences to the body paragraphs of your essay. Clear topic sentences are essential to your audience because they inform your readers as to the focus of the rest of the paragraph. Thus, when you define the main idea early in each paragraph, your readers can follow your line of reasoning with ease—not to mention that an early topic sentence can provide you with a handy point of reference for maintaining focus in your paragraph as you write. To better understand this strategy, consider how Molly uses topic sentences to make the four main supporting arguments in her essay "Creating a Smoke-Free Environment" stand out. Excerpts from her paper follow:

> The awareness of how harmful secondhand smoke is to nonsmokers is one reason why I feel smoking should be prohibited in restaurants. In my opinion, people who choose not to smoke should not have to suffer the consequences of smoking because of other people's bad habit. [Argument 1]

> Not only is smoke harmful to nonsmokers because of the pollutants, it is also dangerous because some people are allergic to it. I feel that these particular individuals should not have to feel miserable because of people puffing smoke into the air. [Argument 2]

> The third point that I have against smoking sections in restaurants may be a little surprising. After doing a little research, I have discovered that if smoking were banned from restaurants, it would not keep the majority of customers from eating in these restaurants. [Argument 3]

> Going along with my opening question, it is evident that smoke is extremely disturbing while one is trying to eat. This is my final argument supporting prohibiting smoking in restaurants: It is disgusting to eat in the haze of a smoky room. [Argument 4]

While topic sentences certainly do not need to be as structured as Molly's, it is important that you make your main ideas clear to your readers, because you will be hard-pressed to convince them via the cumulative power of "main" reasons that they do not recognize as such. It is better to be painfully clear to your readers than to have them wondering what exactly you are trying to prove. Thus, we suggest that you first make certain that your topic sentences are explicit; then you may want to go back during the editing stage and polish your style.

➤ **Exercise in Generating Effective Topic Sentences:** For the following topics, working in small groups, determine your stand on an associated issue and brainstorm 3-4 supporting arguments for your stance. Next, generate a clear topic sentence for each supporting argument.

1. Stalking
2. The Internet
3. Child Abuse
4. Proficiency tests
5. Multicultural Education

➤ **Assignment on Topic Sentences and Focus:** Reread your rough draft, paying close attention to your topic sentences. If you do not make the focus of each paragraph clear early on in the paragraph, revise so that it is. Next, read the rest of each paragraph in light of your topic sentence(s). Do you stay focused on the point your topic sentence sets up for the rest of the paragraph? Remember to only include information in each paragraph that directly correlates with your topic sentence(s).

Using Details and Examples

No matter how thoroughly you have researched your topic, how carefully you have worked out your reasoning, and how credibly you have created your "writing self," your reader will be bored and unconvinced if you do not write in a lively style which entails concrete nouns, active verbs, and descriptive details. Specific examples are also useful, as are anecdotes and short narratives, if appropriate. A researched paper about the necessity for antidiscrimination policies that provide women with equal opportunity can be enhanced by a specific reference to a particular woman applying for a particular position. Similarly, if you write a paper about the necessity of restricting medical research done on animals, you would be wise to include descriptions of how certain animals are being mistreated. Likewise, a paper in favor of increased use of information technologies in the classroom might refer to specific examples of information technologies and explain how each is important to specific jobs or professions that students might desire. Examples and details will bring your writing to life and make it accessible to your reader, even when you are writing about a complex issue.

Recognizing an obligation to her readers, Molly chose to include examples and details in her essay "Creating a Smoke-Free Environment." In the following excerpt from her essay, she uses a specific person's experience to back her second supporting argument that secondhand smoke is "dangerous because some people are allergic to it":

Interestingly, the restaurant owner whom I interviewed, Ms. Klingersmith, is allergic to smoke. When I asked her what motivated her to ban smoking in her restaurant, she replied that since she herself is allergic to smoke, she decided to prohibit smoking. More specifically, Klingersmith said, "I've been allergic to smoke ever since I was a little girl, so naturally I wouldn't want my customers (who may be allergic) to have to tolerate the discomfort of being around smoke."

Molly's inclusion of Klingersmith's experience with an allergy to smoke—and her decision to ban smoking in her own restaurant—helps readers to become more personally involved in the debate because they are able to connect a specific name and situation to a problem associated with secondhand smoke. Thus, you too should consider making your points more concrete through the use of specific details.

> ➤ **Exercise in Using Details and Examples:** Read a newspaper for several days and find three controversial issues worth debating. Try to form a statement or a position about each issue. Bring your three issues and three statements into class. Working in small groups during class, share your issues and tentative position statements; then collaboratively write out for each a brief list of details or examples that might be used to develop the position statement into a researched argumentative essay.

> ➤ **Assignment on Using Details and Examples:** Reread your rough draft, focusing on the evidence you provide to support your thesis and supporting arguments. Are you providing readers with specific details and examples throughout? If not, look back though your source information and search for possible specifics that you might include. If none are available in your current sources, you will need to look for additional sources that provide such specifics and/or consider using your own anecdotes and scenarios.

Improving Conclusions

Effective conclusions refocus readers' attention on the issue addressed in the introduction and remind them of why you want them to consider your point of view. Remember, too, that your conclusion is the last chance you have to make an impression on your readers, so you should make it a good one. Tagging on an underdeveloped conclusion is the most common mistake many student-writers make. By the time they get to the end of a draft, they often are either tired of writing or assume that readers should know what they mean and are convinced to accept the writer's point of view. However, you should be wary of falling into this mind set. Remember the four strategies offered in Chapter 6 for effectively wrapping up your essay:

1. Return to something in the introduction.
2. Postulate the implications of your position.
3. Illustrate your position with an anecdote.
4. Summarize your stance and/or reasoning.

For specifics on these strategies and examples of each, refer to Chapter 6.

For example, examine the conclusion that Molly crafted in her essay "Creating a Smoke-Free Environment":

> I feel very strongly that all restaurants should be smoke-free. No diner should have to endure the disturbing effects of smoke or simply try to eat with smoke lingering in the air, especially if they suffer an allergy to smoke. I also believe that secondhand smoke is very harmful to customers' health and therefore should be prohibited in dining establishments as often as possible. Why not prevent the illnesses resulting from secondhand smoke by banning smoking in restaurants? Lastly, if smoking in restaurants is banned, I have discovered that that it would not deter customers who smoke from eating at these places. Because of these compelling reasons, all restaurant owners should make the right decision to prohibit their customers from smoking. I think that nonsmokers have every right to breathe smoke-free air, so smoking should not be permitted in places where nonsmokers are, such as restaurants. I feel that my argument should be seriously considered because the health of many people is at stake. We should do everything possible to eliminate this health hazard. By creating smoke-free restaurants, we can help to solve this problem and create an appealing dining atmosphere for everyone.

Here, Molly employed one of the most common conclusion strategies, the summary. While it may not be as creative as some of the other strategies, it effectively restates her position and the reasoning supporting her thesis. We suggest that you try a variety of closing techniques when crafting your conclusions, to find the ones you're most comfortable with and that mesh with your style of writing. Also feel free to combine approaches. For more advice on writing conclusions, refer to Chapter 6, "Writing the Conclusion," on pages 205–207.

> ➤ **Exercise in Writing Conclusions:** In small groups, skim over Molly's final draft (found at the end of this chapter) and then rewrite three different conclusions, using the other three closing strategies offered above and in Chapter 6. Finally, write one last conclusion that combines at least two of the approaches.

> ➤ **Assignment on Writing Your Conclusion:** Skim back over your rough draft and then write three different conclusions, using one or more of the strategies offered above. Next, share your possible conclusions in small groups and have your peers vote on which conclusion they believe is the most effective.

SAMPLE REVISION PROCESS: THE RESEARCHED ESSAY

The following, final section of this chapter illustrates two steps in Molly Brooks' revision process of her essay "Creating a Smoke-Free Environment" (written in 2000 for an English 112 course at Bowling Green State University). When reading the two drafts of her essay, pay close attention to the improvements made in revision.

Rough Draft

Creating a Smoke-Free Environment

Have you ever sat down in a restaurant to enjoy a meal, only to be annoyed with burning eyes and a disgusting stench? I'm sure that this scenario is very familiar to anyone who has ever eaten out. Whether or not to ban smoking in restaurants has been an ongoing debate in society. As more and more people realize how dangerous and harmful smoking is, they begin to question why it is necessary for people to smoke in social settings—such as restaurants. I agree with these individuals, by saying that I believe smoking should be prohibited in all restaurants. The reasons supporting my opinion are that smoking affects nonsmokers because of secondhand smoke; some people are actually allergic to smoke; studies have shown that banning smoking would not deter customers; and it is extremely disturbing to eat while others are smoking. I feel that these four points come together to form a strong argument in favor of a smoke-free environment.

The awareness of how harmful secondhand smoke is to nonsmokers is one reason why I feel smoking should be prohibited in restaurants. In my opinion, people who choose not to smoke should not have to suffer the consequences of smoking because of other people's bad habit. Published in the *American Journal of Health*, Lois Biener and Michael Siegel wrote an article that talks about the bans on smoking in restaurants. One piece of information that is included in the article is the fact that secondhand smoke causes lung cancer, asthma, bronchitis, heart disease, and many other illnesses. Why should "innocent" nonsmokers have to deal with these illnesses? While conducting an interview with Cathy Klingersmith, the owner of a smoke-free restaurant in Hiram, I asked why she decided to ban smoking in her restaurant. Cathy responded by saying, "Smoking is definitely a health hazard to both smokers and nonsmokers. I chose to prohibit this act because I don't think that nonsmokers should have to breathe in hazardous pollutants while they are eating." Mrs. Klingersmith agrees with me by saying that secondhand smoke causes unfair illnesses to people whom choose not to smoke. Also providing information concerning secondhand smoke is the *Consumers Union of the United States*. The *Consumer Reports* reprinted statistics from the *Consumers Union of the United States* such as, "People breathing secondhand smoke are eight to 150 percent more likely to get lung cancer sometime later." They also inform people that then times the number of lung cancer deaths are because of secondhand smoke. Annually, this statistic is comparable to those deaths resulting from motor-vehicle accidents. To me, this is almost unbelievable—mainly because the deaths caused by secondhand smoke are so preventable.

Not only is smoke harmful to nonsmokers because of the pollutants, it is also dangerous because some people are allergic to it. I feel that these particular individuals should not have to feel miserable because of people puffing smoke into the air. Philip Wexler, the author of "Passive Smoking" from the *Natural Library of Medicine*, asserts that there are many people who are allergic to smoke and don't even realize it. Wexler gives a few symptoms of being allergic to smoke such as eyes watering and itching, coughing, and sneezing almost uncontrollably whenever smoke is in the air. I know that if I were allergic to smoke, it would be very disrupting if I was eating and had to wipe my eyes and blow my nose every time my body sensed smoke. The author of "Controversy on Passive Smoking," Frank Dobson, also agrees that the banning of smoking sections in restaurants would benefit those customers who sneeze, cough, and tear up because they are allergic to smoke. Dobson maintains, "The discomfort that people who are allergic to smoke endure is sometimes unbearable. To think that this could be prevented if smokers would be courteous enough to smoke outside really disgusts me." Interestingly, the lady who I interviewed is allergic to smoke. When I asked her what motivated her to ban smoking in her restaurant, she replied that she herself is allergic to smoke and so she decided to prohibit smoking. More specifically, Klingersmith said, "I've been allergic to smoke ever since I was a little girl, so naturally I wouldn't want my customers (who may be allergic) to have to tolerate the discomfort of being around smoke." Hearing it from someone who actually has to put up with being allergic to smoke, it is easy to see how frustrating it must be to not be able to eat in a restaurant without feeling lousy because someone is smoking at the next table over.

The third point that I have against smoking sections in restaurants may be a little surprising. After doing a little research, I have discovered that if smoking were banned from restaurants, it would not keep the majority of customers from eating in these restaurants. One might think that prohibiting people from smoking would cause them to stay away from that particular restaurant, but studies show that this is not true. John Sciacca and Marty Eckrem wrote an article in the *Journal of Community Health*, which supported this fact. They conducted a study that asked a number of restaurant owners to ban smoking in their businesses. Every owner predicted that they would lose business, but after actually banning smoking in their restaurants, they found this to be untrue. It turns out that they didn't lose any customers at all. I asked Cathy Klingersmith if she has noticed a decrease in customers and she replied, "Absolutely not." That statement tells me that people who do smoke understand that many others do not enjoy eating in a cloud of smoke. A statistic that proves this is that forty percent of adults report having avoided places that were too smoky. In contrast, fewer than nine percent have reported avoiding places because they were smoke-free (Biener & Siegel). With all of the information that I have encountered, I have come to the conclusion that if a restaurant banned smoking, they would not suffer any loss of business. This is definitely a strong point for banning smoking in restaurants.

Going along with my opening question, it is evident that smoke is extremely disturbing while one is trying to eat. This is my final argument supporting prohibiting smoking in restaurants: It is disgusting to eat in the haze of a smoky room. My interviewee informed me that "I personally dislike going to dinner with friends who smoke because the smell and overall presence of the smoke is very disturbing" (Klingersmith). This is sometimes the sole reason why restaurant owners prohibit smoking in their restaurants; it is simply distracting. Just the thought of tasting the bitterness of smoke lingering in the air should be enough to ban smoking in all restaurants (Sciacca & Eckrem). Again, it is very confusing to me why some restaurant owners don't realize that many people (both smokers and nonsmokers) don't appreciate eating in a room full of smoke. Nothing is more unattractive than walking into a restaurant to eat and seeing a layer of smoke just lingering in the air (Biener & Siegel). Perhaps restaurant owners, who don't currently prohibit smoking, should think about the customers who are turned away because of this unattractive sight. As a customer, I would definitely be turned away from a restaurant that appeared cloudy because of smoke. I feel that the fact that smoke really is disturbing to those trying to eat should be a valid reason to prohibit smoking in restaurants.

Just as there are people who agree with me concerning this issue, there are also those who disagree. One point against banning smoking in restaurants is addressed by Jason Harris, who typed an email to the Rhode Island House of Representatives. In this email, Harris asserted, "Any restaurant owner should not be able to interfere with the personal or corporate freedoms of any individual." The freedom that he is referring to is being able to smoke in a public facility. I refute Harris' argument by saying that if someone doesn't step in and ban smoking in restaurants, many nonsmokers will suffer from secondhand smoke-related illnesses. I think that this is worth the personal freedom of smoking in a restaurant being violated. One more argument against prohibiting smoking in restaurants is that, "Some people will walk out instead of putting their cigarette out" (Sciacca & Eckrem). I have already refuted this argument in the third supporting paragraph. Many studies that have been performed have shown that many restaurants which do not permit smoking have not lost customers. Those who believe that most smokers would rather avoid the restaurant than go in and eat (without smoking) are simply assuming this. Indeed, the majority of smokers will still eat at the restaurant and wait until after the meal to go outside to light their cigarette.

After recognizing a few counter-arguments, I am still very strong regarding my opinion that all restaurants should be smoke-free. I don't feel that anyone should have to endure the disturbing effects of smoke if they are allergic, or simply trying to eat with it lingering in the air. I also believe that secondhand smoke is very harmful to customers, and therefore should be prevented as often as possible. Why not prevent the illnesses resulting from secondhand smoke by banning smoking in restaurants? Lastly, if smoking in restaurants is banned, I have discovered that that it would not deter those customers who smoke from eating at these places. Because of these four reasons, why can't all restaurant owners decide to prohibit smoking? I think that nonsmokers have every right to breathe smoke-free air and so smoking should not be permitted in places where nonsmokers are, such as restaurants. I feel that my argument should be seriously considered because the health of many people is at stake. We should do everything possible to eliminate these health hazards. By creating smoke-free restaurants, we can help to solve this problem.

Final Draft

Creating a Smoke-Free Environment

Have you ever sat down in a restaurant to enjoy a meal, only to be annoyed with burning eyes and a disgusting stench? How about experiencing the discomfort of trying to eat a meal that tastes like smoke? I'm sure that this scenario is very familiar to anyone who has ever eaten out. The disturbing effect that smoke has on nonsmokers as they try to eat is sometimes so unbearable that they would rather stay home and eat at their own convenience. Whether or not to ban smoking in restaurants has been an ongoing debate in society. As more and more people realize how dangerous and harmful smoking is, they begin to question why it is necessary for people to smoke in social settings—such as restaurants. On the other hand, some people argue that any public facility should give a smoker the freedom to smoke if he/she wishes. Do these people know of the health effects and discomfort that smoking can cause to those nonsmokers who don't appreciate eating with smoke in the air? I agree with the side of the issue that believes smoking should be prohibited in all restaurants. The reasons supporting my opinion are that smoking affects nonsmokers because of secondhand smoke; some people are actually allergic to smoke; studies have shown that banning smoking would not deter customers; and it is extremely discomforting to eat while others are smoking. I feel that these four points, together, form a strong argument in favor of smoke-free restaurants.

The awareness of how harmful secondhand smoke is to nonsmokers is one reason why I feel smoking should be prohibited in restaurants. In my opinion, people who choose not to smoke should not have to suffer the consequences of smoking because of other people's bad habit. Published in the *American Journal of Health*, Lois Biener and Michael Siegel wrote an article that talks about the bans on smoking in restaurants. One piece of information that is included in the article is the fact that secondhand smoke causes lung cancer, asthma, bronchitis, heart disease, and many other illnesses (2). Why should "innocent" nonsmokers have to deal with these illnesses? While conducting an interview with Cathy Klingersmith, the owner of a smoke-free restaurant in Hiram, I asked why she decided to ban smoking in her restaurant. Klingersmith responded by saying, "Smoking is definitely a health hazard to both smokers and nonsmokers. I chose to prohibit this act because I don't think that nonsmokers should have to breathe in hazardous pollutants while they are eating." Klingersmith agreed with me by saying that secondhand smoke often creates poor health to nonsmokers who don't deserve to be sick because they weren't doing harm to themselves. Information concerning secondhand smoke is also provided by the Consumers Union of the United States. The Consumers Union of the United States is an organization that did research to determine whether or not secondhand smoke is a threat to nonsmokers. *Consumer Reports* reprinted statistics from the Consumers Union of the United States, which confirmed, "People breathing secondhand smoke are eight to 150 percent more likely to get lung cancer sometime later" (28). They also inform people that those who are exposed to secondhand smoke have ten times the risk of developing lung cancer. Annually, this statistic is comparable to those deaths resulting from motor-vehicle accidents. To me, this is almost unbelievable—mainly because the deaths caused by secondhand smoke are so preventable. Because secondhand smoke is such a threat to nonsmokers, I feel that smoking should be banned in restaurants.

Not only is smoke harmful to nonsmokers because of the pollutants, but also it is dangerous because some people are allergic to it. I feel that these particular individuals should not have to feel miserable because of people puffing smoke into the air. Philip Wexler, the author of "Passive Smoking" from the *Natural Library of Medicine*, asserts that there are many people who are allergic to smoke and don't even realize it. Wexler gives a few symptoms of being allergic to smoke such as eyes watering and itching, coughing, and sneezing almost uncontrollably whenever smoke is in the air (3). I know that if I were allergic to smoke, it would be very disrupting if I was eating and had to wipe my eyes and blow my nose every time my body sensed smoke. The author of "Controversy on Passive Smoking," Frank Dobson, also agrees that the banning of smoking sections in restaurants would benefit those customers who sneeze, cough, and tear up because they are allergic to smoke. Dobson maintains, "The discomfort that people who are allergic to smoke endure is sometimes unbearable. To think that this could be prevented simply if smokers would be courteous enough to smoke outside really disgusts me"(2). Interestingly, a restaurant owner whom I interviewed, Ms. Klingersmith, is allergic to smoke. When I asked her what motivated her to ban smoking in her restaurant, she replied that since she herself is allergic to smoke, she decided to prohibit smoking. More specifically, Klingersmith said, "I've been allergic to smoke ever since I was a little girl, so naturally I wouldn't want my customers (who may be allergic) to have to tolerate the discomfort of being around smoke." After discussing this issue with someone who actually suffers a smoke allergy, I could easily understand how frustrating it must be to not be able to eat in a restaurant without feeling lousy because someone is smoking at the next table over.

The third point that I have against smoking sections in restaurants may be a little surprising. After doing a little research, I have discovered that if smoking were banned from restaurants, it would not keep the majority of customers from eating in these restaurants. One might think that prohibiting people from smoking would cause smokers to stay away from that particular restaurant, but studies show that this is not true. John Sciacca and Marty Eckrem wrote an article for the *Journal of Community Health*, which supported this fact. They conducted a study that asked a number of restaurant owners to ban smoking in their businesses. Every owner predicted that they would lose business, but after actually banning smoking in their restaurants, they found this to be untrue. It turns out that they didn't lose any customers at all (176-177). I asked Klingersmith if she has noticed a decrease in customers and she replied, "Absolutely not." That statement tells me that people who do smoke understand that many others do not enjoy eating in a cloud of smoke. A study performed by Biener and Siegel found that forty percent of adults report having avoided places that were too smoky. In contrast, fewer than nine percent have reported avoiding places because they were smoke-free (3). With all of the information that I have encountered concerning the increase/decrease of business because of the prohibition of smoking, I have come to the conclusion that if a restaurant banned smoking, they would not suffer any loss of business. This is definitely a strong point for banning smoking in restaurants.

My next argument against smoking in restaurants is that smoke is extremely disturbing while one is trying to eat. This is my final argument supporting prohibiting smoking in restaurants: it is disgusting to eat in the haze of a smoky room. My interviewee informed me, "I personally dislike going to dinner with friends who smoke because the smell and overall presence of the smoke is very disturbing" (Klingersmith). This is sometimes the sole reason why restaurant owners prohibit smoking in their restaurants; it is simply distracting. Sciacca and Eckrem add, "Just the thought of tasting the bitterness of smoke lingering in the air should be enough to ban smoking in all restaurants" (180). Again, it is very confusing to me why some restaurant owners don't realize that many people (both smokers and nonsmokers) don't appreciate eating in a room full of smoke. Biener and Siegel agree by saying, "Nothing is more unappetizing than walking into a restaurant to eat and seeing a layer of smoke just lingering in the air" (4). Perhaps restaurant owners, who don't currently prohibit smoking, should think about the customers who are turned away because of this unappealing sight. As a customer, I would definitely leave a restaurant that appeared cloudy because of smoke. I feel that the fact that smoke really is disturbing to those trying to eat should be a valid reason to prohibit smoking in restaurants.

Just as there are people who agree with me concerning this issue, there are also those who disagree. One point against banning smoking in restaurants is addressed by Jason Harris, who typed an email to the Rhode Island House of Representatives. In this email, Harris asserted, "Any restaurant owner should not be able to interfere with the personal or corporate freedoms of any individual." The freedom that he is referring to is being able to smoke in a public facility. However, if someone doesn't step in and ban smoking in restaurants, many nonsmokers will suffer from secondhand smoke-related illnesses. I think that this is worth sacrificing the personal freedom of smoking in restaurants. We need to think about whose rights are more important: the rights of someone who is suffering from the actions of smokers or the rights of another who thinks he/she should be able to smoke in restaurants "just because"? One more argument against prohibiting smoking in restaurants is that "Some people will walk out instead of putting their cigarette out" (Sciacca and Eckrem 178). Although this may happen infrequently, many studies, such as the one by Biener and Siegel, have shown that many restaurants that do not permit smoking have not lost customers. Those who believe that most smokers would rather avoid the restaurant than go in and eat (without smoking) are simply assuming this. Indeed, the majority of smokers would still eat at the restaurant and wait until after the meal to go outside and light their cigarette.

I feel very strongly that all restaurants should be smoke-free. No diner should have to endure the disturbing effects of smoke or simply try to eat with smoke lingering in the air, especially if they suffer an allergy to smoke. I also believe that secondhand smoke is very harmful to customers' health and therefore should be prohibited in dining establishments as often as possible. Why not prevent the illnesses resulting from secondhand smoke by banning smoking in restaurants? Lastly, if smoking in restaurants is banned, I have discovered that it would not deter customers who smoke from eating at these places. Because of these compelling reasons, all restaurant owners should make the right decision to prohibit their customers from smoking. I think that nonsmokers have every right to breathe smoke-free air, so smoking should not be permitted in places where nonsmokers are, such as restaurants. I feel that my argument should be seriously considered because the health of many people is at stake. We should do everything possible to eliminate this health hazard. By creating smoke-free restaurants, we can help to solve this problem and create an appealing dining atmosphere for everyone.

Works Cited

Biener, Lois, and Michael Siegel. "Behavior Intentions of the Public After Bans on Smoking in Restaurants and Bars." American Journal of Public Health (1997): 1-4. (http://www.quest.umi.com/pqlink?Ve..00gc3UUW3U2%2fTTGT91YaHimWaG1I2g--).

Dobson, Frank. "Controversy on Passive Smoking Measures." BBC News Online: Health 10 Dec.1998. 29 Feb.2000 (http://www.news.bbc.co.uk/low/english/health/newsid_232000/232364.stim).

Harris, Jason. "Banning Smoking in Restaurants is Wrong!" Email to the Rhode Island House of Representatives. 12 Aug. 1998.

Klingersmith, Cathy. Personal Interview. 19 Mar. 2000.

"Secondhand Smoke: Is it a Hazard?" Consumer Reports Jan 1995. 1 Mar. 2000 (http://researcher.sirs.com).

Sciacca, John, and Marty Eckrem. "Effects of a City Ordinance Regulating Smoking in Restaurants and Retail Stores." Journal of Community Health June 1993: 175-182.

Wexler, Philip. "Passive Smoking." National Library of Medicine 1981: 1-6.

➤ **Exercise in Analyzing Revisions:** In small groups, compare Molly's first draft to her final draft. Which features of the final draft do you feel are improvements over the first draft? Are there any aspects of the final draft that need additional revision? If you believe so, please explain.

Appendix: Working Together

BEGINNING TO COLLABORATE

Most likely, you have had the experience of working together with other people on some project. Perhaps you have worked with a group of friends to plan a party or special celebration. In high school, you may have played a team sport, worked to produce a play, or collaborated with others to publish a newspaper or a yearbook. In previous classes, you may have worked in groups as well. For example, you may have worked in groups in your high school English class to respond to one another's ideas or papers. You may have worked in groups in a science class to perform an experiment or develop projects for a science fair. In any of these situations, you were working in a collaborative group, that is, in a group of people working together to achieve a common goal.

By now you have undoubtedly realized that group work can be an important part of a writing class; however, a writing or English course is not the only class where collaboration may be involved. Many careers and professions routinely entail collaborative work, and an important aspect of college training is learning to work in groups. As a consequence, students in a marketing class may be required to work in teams to research and promote a new product. Likewise, students in a chemistry class may be put into permanent groups for weekly lab work.

You can see, then, that learning to work in groups is an important part of your education. The ability to collaborate successfully with others may also be a requirement in your future career. In addition, group work is a *central* means by which you will learn to be a better writer. For these reasons, we are devoting this chapter to helping you learn more about what collaborative groups are, how they may be used in writing classes, and what responsibilities group work entails.

Reasons for Working in Groups

From this brief overview, you can see that in college you may be working in groups but perhaps you do not understand why. One reason teachers require students to work in small groups is to provide them with greater opportunities to express or clarify their opinions on a wide variety of subjects. In a traditional classroom setting, when a discussion takes place among the members of a whole class, only one person at a time can speak; thus perhaps only 20 percent of the students are able to contribute to a "class discussion." However, when a large class is divided into small collaborative groups, numerous people may express opinions at the same time and, in doing so, learn to address one another, rather than their instructor. Small groups thus offer some students better opportunities to express their opinions, ask questions of others, and talk through their ideas. Talking about ideas and opinions—rather than just thinking about them—is important, because vocalization helps to clarify thinking and provides speakers with a chance to hear how other people respond to their ideas. It also encourages

"Working Together by Alice Calderonello, Donna Nelson-Beene and Sue Carter Simmons, reprinted by permission from *Perspectives on Academic Writing*, 1997, Allyn & Bacon.

students to develop and defend their own points of view, instead of always looking to the teacher for the "right answer."

Small groups are also ideal for ensuring that each student in a class receives individual attention and response. In traditional classrooms, teachers attempt to provide individual attention to each student but are often unable to do so. In classrooms composed of small groups, each group member can be assisted by his or her peers during the class period.

Another reason why small groups are used in many classes is that they are an ideal way to provide students with assistance through all the phases of writing a paper, from invention to final editing. Within collaborative writing groups, ideas for papers can be discussed and developed. Writing groups can also help group members determine various methods for selecting and structuring their ideas and for revising and editing their papers. Group collaborators help one another with all stages of writing.

As mentioned earlier, however, besides the benefits provided to writers, working with a small group can be excellent practice for careers after college. Many professions—including medicine, law, business, science, and technology—rely heavily on consultation and collaboration as the most effective way to operate. Industries, for example, often depend on the effective collaboration of people with a variety of specializations. To produce a product such as a backpack may require the combined efforts of designers, textiles experts, metalworkers, patent attorneys, marketing experts, and publicists.

Types of Collaboration

There are a variety of collaborative activities in which a group can engage. Within a university or college setting, of course, the way in which groups are constituted and how they function can vary across disciplines. Still, people who have studied collaborative groups have identified some common group activities. These are knowledge making, investigating/researching, workshopping, and coauthoring.

- **Knowledge Making.** *Knowledge making* is any activity in which the group's primary purpose is to share knowledge about the subject at hand or to create a new and more complete pool of knowledge. Knowledge making may involve generating ideas, searching memories, or enlarging and expanding points of view. Knowledge making is especially productive in small groups, as the different members are put in dialogue with one another, which leads to broader perspectives or a fuller synthesis of the subjects under discussion. If you watched a group of people involved in knowledge making, they would be talking to one another, with some moments of silence for thinking. You might observe some writing, if, for example, group members were charged with preparing a report for their class or with brainstorming a list to be used in a later activity. Under these and other circumstances, then, group members might occasionally jot down notes; however, in the act of knowledge making, for the most part, group members would be engaged in discussion. Knowledge-making activities may end when the group reaches an agreement or consensus about the subject under discussion or produces a synthesis of or conclusion about the members' points of view. Alternatively, knowledge making may result in different conclusions being reached by different group members.

- **Investigating/Researching.** Collaborative groups can enlarge their knowledge by sharing what they know with one another, yet they can also expand their collective pool of knowledge by investigating a subject together. When library or nonlibrary research can be performed by individuals, it is not uncommon for people in a group to pool their individual research. In addition, people conducting nonlibrary research—for example, conducting an opinion survey—may codesign materials and collect data together. With the sciences and social sciences, research is routinely performed by teams which may (or may not) be led by a "primary" investigator.

- **Workshopping.** *Workshopping* is the term used to describe the kind of help that group members can provide for one another throughout the writing individual projects. It can occur in professional contexts but most often takes place in a classroom setting. Workshopping allows writers to test their ideals and plans with actual readers, to get immediate feedback on drafts, and to get help with editing. Thus workshopping usually involves examining these statements and plans, drafts, or revisions. The procedures groups use for workshopping vary. People may report orally on their plans or read papers out loud, with listeners offering comments, questions, and suggestions orally. Sometimes copies of papers are distributed so that group members can read them silently, write comments on them, and then discuss them together with other group members. In addition, teachers often give groups a written set of directions to follow in responding to drafts, perhaps the criteria by which papers will be graded or an editing checklist.

- **Coauthoring.** When we use the word *coauthoring,* we are referring to a process in which two or more people produce a single piece of writing by working together at every stage, from generating ideas to drafting to revising and editing. Coauthoring takes many forms. One common variation is for a group to decide together what the overall design for a text will be, to draft sections separately, and then to revise and edit together. Another (less common) variation is for coauthors to draft an entire text together, sitting beside one another at a word processor. Depending on the number of writers working on a project, coauthoring can be a highly structured activity coordinated by a particular individual or it can be loose and unstructured with participants adopting a variety of roles.

Although knowledge making, investigating/researching, workshopping, and coauthoring are common group activities, the form these activities take as well as the extent to which they are acceptable practices may vary. Most instructors do not object when students engage in knowledge making; in fact, many colleges and universities provide students with a variety of opportunities to join discussion groups related to their classes, current topics, courses of study, and the like. However, the appropriateness of other collaborative activities is not so clear-cut.

If, for example, students in a particular class are assigned to write individual term papers, the instructor may or may not find it appropriate for them to engage in group investigating/researching. Likewise, students who decide to coauthor a paper without clearing it with their instructor may encounter difficulty. Even workshopping, in which students gain feedback about their papers from others, may be considered inappropriate by some instructors, who may consider it a form of cheating. It is always prudent, then, to be aware of disciplinary or professional conventions regarding group work, as well as the attitude and expectations of your instructor, if you wish to employ collaborative practices in producing your class assignments.

Being an Effective Group Member

Now that you have been acquainted with several kinds of group activities, it is time to learn more about how to make groups work well together. These are two major areas to consider: the different roles people play in groups and effective guidelines for group work.

Different Group Roles. When people work together in small groups, there are many functions they can serve. As you practice these functions, you will get better at performing each one and at becoming more adaptable. That is, if you learn to play the role of a leader at times and of a questioner or a time-keeper at others, you will contribute to the success of any groups you work in. Within a group, members can assume a variety of roles such as researcher, organizer, note taker, leader, and so forth. However, despite this diversity, several roles are crucial in making groups work effectively. As we have suggested, these roles should be assumed by each member of the group on differing occasions. In this way, the group itself will not become overly dependent on the skills of particular individuals who may be absent from time to time, and each group member will become more adaptable. Because people vary in their ability to play particular roles, if you and your peers are given the opportunity to form your own group, you should try to balance your membership. Consider such matters as gender, ethnicity, course of study, and interpersonal skills as you form your collective.

- **Initiator/Facilitator.** A key group role is that of initiator/facilitator. Whoever assumes this role manages group work, initiates discussion, and raises questions that encourage group memebers to respond to issues in detail. Within a linguistics class discussion, for example, the initiator/facilitator might ask, "What are some specific ways that this conversation illustrates the maxim of relevance?" Frequently, a group initiator/facilitator may draw connections among points raised by individual group members. Doing so is important because it allows group members to enlarge their own perspectives in order to see an issue more globally. Finally, the person who assumes this role should work to draw all members into each discussion. If one or more members aren't speaking, the initiator/facilitator might direct questions to specific individuals: "Bob, can you give us another example that illustrates the maxim of relevance?"

- **"The Boss."** As we were trying to come up with a name for this function, we discarded some of these possibilities: the Taskmaster, the Enforcer, the Disciplinarian, and the Wagon Master. As these rather whimsical titles suggest, the person who assumes the role of "the Boss" must work to keep the group on task. That is, as you know from experience, when people get together, even if they are charged with accomplishing a particular goal, it is human nature to digress or to chat with one another. Most people, including students, have tight schedules and need to make effective use of their time. Some of the specific duties of "the Boss" are clarifying directions, setting and keeping time limits, and cutting off or redirecting digressions and unnecessary socializing. A characteristic remark from the individual who assumes this role might be a direct statement that informs group members of time contraints and sets forth a task: "We only have ten minutes left, so we need to think of a couple of examples that illustrate intangible power."
- **Questioner.** Because people who share similar characteristics such as age, background, and so forth may reach a consensus or adopt a particular point of view without much deliberation, an important group role is that of the questioner. The individual who serves this function must play devil's advocate. It is her or his job, then, to ask questions like, "Why are you making that assumption about the result of our survey?" or "What kind of evidence do you have to support the idea that educational level is an important variable related to quality of life in this community?" While we don't want to suggest that the questioner should be combative, we do want to emphasize that this person should invite and sometimes even challenge a group to examine different perspectives and question interpretations and conclusions that have been arrived at too easily.
- **Note Taker/Summarizer.** The person who assumes the role of note taker/summarizer ordinarily does not do as much talking as other group members. This is because he or she is busy taking detailed notes of the group's discussion. Such notes are valuable resources because they provide continuity and a record of all of the ideas, perspectives, and information that the group discovers. In addition, the notes are often a record to help determine the agenda of future group work and may become the substance of a paper that the group will write. Although we have suggested that the note taker/summarizer does not do a great deal of talking, periodically this individual may wish to summarize the group's accomplishments or decisions that have been reached or that need to be made.

Guidelines for Effective Collaboration. For some students, and perhaps for you, working in groups in a classroom setting may be a new way of learning. Reliance on the teacher rather than on peers—and working alone rather than in groups—have been far more often the norms within classrooms. Therefore, you may feel some initial anxiety or uneasiness about group work. For many students, though, uneasy feelings disappear after the first session or two of group work, when they begin to learn more about working effectively together.

Learning to work effectively within a community of writers is not automatic, so it is not reasonable to expect your collaborative group to work easily together at first. Groups need time to gel, to find their own comfort zone—and doing so takes effort from all members of the group. Group members need to determine what responsibilities are entailed in order for the group to work well together. The following guidelines will help you learn to collaborate effectively; if you and the other members of your group adhere to them, you will start to work together effectively in almost no time at all.

- **Think of yourself as an important member of a team.** Just as members of all sorts of teams (athletic teams, for example) have responsibilities to their teammates, you, too, should feel a sense of responsibility to your writing class team. This means that you should attend all group meetings, be on time, and come fully prepared for the task at hand. At your initial meeting, you and your group members should exchange class and work schedules and phone numbers with one another and agree on a means for each member to get materials to the group in the event of an unforeseen illness or conflict. You and your partners should also decide together what the group should do if individuals need to miss meetings or can't come prepared. Agreeing together in advance on such strategies will help ensure that all members are treated consistently and fairly.
- **Socialize briefly, then get to work.** When your group sits down together, it is only natural to greet one another and start talking about something unrelated to your class—the weather, the upcoming football game, or a recent news story. Not only is such dialogue at the beginning of a group session a normal part of group behavior, it also is essential in helping the group establish its comfort zone and sense of identity. However, the members of your group should share the responsibility for *ending* the opening dialogue fairly quickly in order to move on to the assigned task by saying something like "Okay folks, let's get on to this project." Once your group has become engaged in working, members should not bring up unrelated topics of conversation, such as "Hey, did you get your hair cut?" Should such comments occur, group members need to draw the group's attention back to work, perhaps with comments like "Yes, I did. Now what do you think about my conclusion? Do I need to add more details there?"
- **Practice good communication skills.** During each session it will be important for all members of your group to practice good communication skills such as making eye contact with one another and using group members' names when you are referring directly to them. When you are responding to Marina's paper, for example, you should look at her and say, "Marina, I liked the way you started with a question. That got my interest right away." Your group should also make sure that everyone receives an equal amount of time to speak and that anyone who tends not to speak be encouraged to do so. If, for example, you notice that a group member has not contributed to this discussion, you might ask, "Al, you haven't said anything about this paper yet. What do you think about it?" Your aim should be a conversation among all the members; hence you should avoid conversations with only one person in the group, since this will divide his or her attention (and yours) from what the larger group is discussing.

- **When you disagree, be respectful.** Undoubtedly, there will be times when you will disagree with what a fellow group member is saying. When disagreement occurs, it is important not to interrupt another person, but to listen patiently until it is your turn to speak. When you do speak, you should explain your own point of view or your reaction to what is being said in a paper—wthout directly attacking or "putting down" the group member. For example, if you disagree with the stand someone has taken in a paper criticizing affirmative action programs, that person would probably feel you were launching a personal attack if you said, "That's the most stupid argument I've ever heard—affirmative action discriminates against white people! How can you believe that?" Instead of an emotional response that may put the writer on the defensive, a message that describes what has been said or written and how you feel about it is preferable: "Alisha, I know that you think that affirmative action is discriminatory against white people, but I feel that it's necessary to correct a long history of discrimination in employment that you aren't acknowledging in your paper."

  On some occasions, you and your group members may feel that it's desirable to achieve a consensus or agreement on potentially divisive issues, especially if you want to keep working together on a project or to share one another's writing. Realize, however, that there are differences among people that simply cannot be erased. Consequently, at times it may be more respectful to "agree to disagree" with one another than to push toward compromise or agreement.

- **Offer constructive criticism of the writings.** Many times your group will meet for the purpose of discussing one another's writing. During these sessions, you should note particular strengths in each person's paper and offer praise where praise is due. When you note weaknesses, you should be honest yet tactful in describing the problems and in offering explanations or suggestions. Most especially, it is important to offer specific advice or criticism. Global comments such as "I liked it" or "It doesn't flow" are not clear or helpful. Consider how much more helpful the following comments are:

  > *Daniel, I think your main point, about how the essay we read changed your view of hunting, is really clear. I also like the story you open with because it helped me see why you feel the way you do now. But I had some trouble following parts of your paper. When you moved from the story at the beginning to the rest of the paper, it felt pretty choppy. And later, on page 3, I didn't understand why you included the last paragraph. How does it connect to your main point?*

  In addition to being specific about a paper's specific strengths and weakness, to be a helpful group member, you should offer suggestions to your partners and ask questions that will help them clarify thinking, generate ideas, and focus their texts. If, for example, you are unsatisfied with the conclusion of a group member's paper, you might ask questions that would help the writer to see additional reasons why he or she chose to write on this topic or why other people might be interested in the paper.

- **Be open to suggestions.** When your own writing is being discussed by your group members, you should be open to their responses and not be offended by their constructive criticism. Some writers are uncomfortable about sharing their writing with others because they are afraid that someone else—a teacher or a peer group member—will "rewrite" their paper. If you feel this way, realize that you are the author of your own work and are therefore responsible for deciding whether and how to incorporate the suggestions of your readers. Sometimes writers are reluctant to hear feedback from readers for an additional reason: They do not want to hear that the paper isn't finished yet.

    If you are uncomfortable about sharing your writing with group members for whatever reasons, a good way to handle your feelings may be to take more control of the situation. That is, instead of waiting for group members to identify problems in your paper, you may feel more comfortable sharing your own evaluation of the paper first and then soliciting their opinions as in this example: "When I was writing this paper, I wasn't sure if I was being detailed and specific enough. Do you think I need more examples?" An additional strategy that may help gain more control over the feedback process is to ask questions of your group members. If, for instance, someone suggests using more examples, ask what kinds, and where they should be added.

- **Plan time carefully.** Because time passes quickly when groups are busily working together, it's important to budget time wisely. In order to do this at the beginning to each session, your group should decide what you need to accomplish and how you will spend the time allotted. If, for example, your task is to discuss drafts of essays written by the three people in your group and you have an hour to work, you should devote no more than twenty minutes to discussing each text. An appointed timekeeper should keep an eye on the clock and make sure that everyone's work receives an equal amount of time and attention by keeping the group moving forward with comments such as this: "We could probably say a lot more about Ralph's essay, but now we need to move on to Max's paper."

- **Make plans for your next meeting.** Shortly before the close of each session, your group should make plans for the following session and decide what each group member's responsibilities will be to prepare for it. If your group is researching a topic together for a research paper, you might decide to do the following: "At the next class meeting, we will brainstorm what we know already about our group topic. We will each locate three sources in the library and bring our research notes with us." It may be wise for group members to take notes at this point, in order to remember exactly what the group has decided and what individual members are responsible for next time. That is, everyone should write notes about exactly what reading to complete, what writing to complete, and what notes or books to bring to the next meeting.

Although the guidelines we have outlined can help your group function effectively, sometimes collaborative groups can encounter difficulties. One common problem is unequal participation of group members. To resolve problems related to participation, it is always best to try to discover what is affecting a particular group member's behavior. Underlying causes for unequal participation can be diverse. Sometimes an inordinately heavy work or class schedule can make it difficult for a person to attend meetings; group efforts to accommodate such individuals by changing the times or places for meetings or allowing them to do other work in lieu of attending can be effective in these situations. Other times, group members may not respond during discussions or produce much work for a project because they feel that their ideas are not being valued—either by the group as a whole or by an individual who seems to dominate group activities. In these cases, periodic evaluations—in which group members assess the effectiveness of the group as a whole as well as their own contributions—can be helpful.

Ordinarily, when members evaluate the effectiveness of their group as a whole they consider factors such as the extent to which all members have contributed, whether one or more persons have been dominant, whether members have assumed a variety of roles, and so forth. When members evaluate their own contributions they try to determine in what way they have made contributions (by providing leadership, asking questions, etc.) and in what ways they can improve their participation (by listening more and talking less, by building on what others have said rather than disagreeing, by initiating group action rather than waiting for someone else to act, etc.) Sometimes instructors give their students forms to fill out or a series of questions to answer to assess group performance. Even if your instructor does not provide you with such aids, your group should discuss its performance from time to time. The writing assignment at the end of this chapter will help you with that endeavor.

Another common problem that groups experience is in reaching a consensus. As we have said, making an effort to disagree respectfully as well as listening carefully to others' points of views can help groups reach a consensus or decide on a course of action. However, this may not always be possible. If your group cannot decide how to proceed with a project because of strong, irreconcilable differences, it is probably wise to ask your instructor for assistance. In fact, any serious problems that you and your group members cannot deal with on your own—for example, repeated absences by a member—should be discussed with your instructor.

WORKING IN GROUPS

From reading the first part of this chapter, you should have a general understanding that working in groups can be beneficial for both students and professional writers. However, "working in groups" is a broad phrase that encompasses many possible procedures. In this section, we offer guidelines for some of the more commonly used methods of collaboration; of course, there can be numerous variations on these. As you become more comfortable with the process of collaboration, you and your group members probably will want to devise procedures of your own.

Procedures for Collaborating

Because collaborative activities include knowledge making, researching/investigating, workshopping, and coauthoring, a useful way to discuss procedures is within these contexts. The following sections describe procedures for these four kinds of activities, which you and your group members can try out to see how well they work for you. It is important to remember, though, that the first time your group works with a particular procedure, you may not make as much progress as you would like; collaborating effectively takes *practice*.

Knowledge Making. As the phrase suggests, *knowledge making* means combining or synthesizing ideas or information in an original way, thereby creating knowledge that is new. Knowledge can be "made" by one person working alone, of course, but for our purposes we will discuss only the kind of knowledge making that occurs when group members talk or write with one another. Obviously, it would be impossible to exhaust all of the procedures for knowledge making; therefore, we will offer two examples that are intended to help you think of other possibilities.

To help you fully realize the usefulness of the procedures we are recommending for knowledge making, we want you to think of them in the context of the following assignment: Let's say that each student in your class has been assigned to select an article and to write a critique of it (which includes a summary and an evaluation). Although this assignment conceivably could be completed independently, your instructor has asked you to work in small collaborative groups throughout the process. To prepare for your upcoming collaborative session, your instructor has asked everyone to select two possible articles and prepare brief rationale statements about why they might make good choices for the assignment.

The purpose of your first collaborative session, then, would be to help one another decide which of the two articles would work best for the assignment. As you might imagine, in order to have an effective session, the members of the group would not be able to talk whenever they felt like it; instead, they would need to follow a systematic procedure that allowed time for each person to summarize his or her articles and rationale statements and for the other group members to respond. The following are two alternative procedures that could be used:

Procedure 1 for Knowledge Making

Each person is allotted an equal amount of time (say, five minutes) to summarize one of his or her articles and the accompanying rationale statement. Immediately following each person's summary, the group takes five minutes to discuss the benefits and limitations of using the article for the assignment. Each group member contributes to this discussion. After each person's first article has been dealt with in this manner, the procedure is repeated for the second article. This time around, however, the group makes a recommendation regarding the preferred article—or perhaps, a recommendation that neither article should be used for the assignment.

Procedure 2 for Knowledge Making

Each person is allotted an equal amount of time (say, ten minutes) to summarize both of his or her articles and rationale statements. Immediately following each person's summaries, the group takes ten minutes to discuss the benefits and limitations of using the articles for the assignment and makes a recommendation about the preferred choice. Each group member contributes to this discussion.

Investigating/Researching. The point we want to make in this chapter is that working in collaborative groups can greatly increase the effectiveness of researching and investigating. As you would assume, there are numerous workable procedures for collaborating as a "research team"; the following discussion should help you start thinking of various possibilities.

To provide a concrete basis for understanding the options we discuss, we want you to assume that you are a member of a collaborative group that has decided to investigate the topic "gender and interruption" for an introductory linguistics class; that is, you want to learn who interrupts other people's speech more frequently—men or women? Through your research, your group hopes to learn whether there is a significant difference between the genders regarding interruption, whether men interrupt other men to the same degree as they interrupt women, whether women interrupt other women to the same degree as they interrupt men, and so on. This topic could be researched by a group using a variety of procedures, including the following:

Procedure 1 for Working as a Research Team

Following a group discussion of how to divide up tasks, each member of the group is assigned (or volunteers to do) a specific kind of research. This is, one person investigates library sources; one person observes conversations between men and women and keeps track of the interruptions on a self-designed tally sheet; one person interviews a linguistics professor who has done research on the topic of interruption; and one person designs and distributes a survey to find out people's overall perceptions regarding the topic. Each group member is responsible for designing whatever research tool he or she will use (survey, tally sheet, list of interview questions, etc.). The research tools are critiqued by the group so that individual members can make adjustments, if necessary. When all the information has been accumulated, the group members meet to share and interpret their findings.

Procedure 2 for Working as a Research Team

Before any research is conducted, the group works together to design the tools they will use. They collaborate to design a survey; to prepare a list of interview questions; to decide how and when information from observations will be gathered; and to decide on the kinds of library sources that will be used to investigate the topic. After the tools are established, the responsibilities for conducting the research are divided among the group members. When all information has been accumulated, the group members meet to share and interpret their findings.

Workshopping. Perhaps the most frequently used collaborative activity in college classrooms is workshopping. A broad term, *workshopping* refers to the help that group members can give one another during any part of the writing process. It is likely that you already have engaged in workshopping with classmates in college classes or even in high school. Workshopping is used by students and professionals throughout all disciplines.

Because workshopping is used to assist writers at various stages of the writing process, it is necessary to think about workshopping procedures in terms of writing stages. It is not possible to establish procedures that are appropriate for working with all stages of writing, so we offer the following workshop procedures, which are designed to help groups invent, prewrite, and plan; draft and revise; and edit. As with the other procedures we have discussed, these can be varied as a group gains more experience working together.

The first stage in the writing process is the invention of ideas. Ideas are invented in writers' heads, of course, but the physical act of writing them down (prewriting) in the form of notes, diagrams, or lists enables writers to generate even more information and to see connections among ideas. Through prewriting, writers are able to discover and narrow topics, arrive at potential thesis statements, and determine possible strategies for developing ideas within a paper; although these procedures also occur when the writer actually begins drafting, they are begun to a large degree during prewriting. Prewriting often occurs as a solitary act; however, the quality of the prewriting can be greatly enhanced through the help of group members working together. And in general, the more thorough the prewriting, the more effective the paper will be. The procedures that follow illustrate two ways in which group members can assist with prewriting:

Procedure 1 for Workshopping—Prewriting

The group members meet to discuss the prewriting they have done separately in response to a writing assignment. Each person comes prepared with a substantial amount of prewriting. The first person reads his or her prewriting aloud, with the other group members listening carefully. Then the group members respond with questions and comments about the prewriting to help the writer see where ideas are especially convincing, where there are gaps, where additional support is needed, where thinking is unclear, and so on. During this discussion, the writer takes notes on what the others say. Finally, the group works together to help the writer devise a tentative plan for structuring the paper. In the course of the session, every group member's prewriting is dealt with in the manner just described, with an equal amount of time devoted to each.

Please note that in the procedure just described, group members can come prepared with any kind of prewriting they wish, such as freewriting, brainstorming, listing, and so forth.

Procedure 2 for Workshopping—Prewriting

Group members convene in a manner that gives them all visual access to a chalkboard, an easel with a large sheet of paper attached, or another such tool for note taking. One person serves as the note taker while the group works together to help one member at a time prewrite on his or her topic, using any prewriting technique the member chooses. For each writer, the group together comes up with ideas that are especially convincing and well developed. After a writer has been assisted in prewriting, the group works together to help him or her devise a tentative plan for structuring the paper. Each writer copies the notes that the group generates or keeps the notes that were taken by the designated note taker during the discussion of his or her paper. In the course of the session, every group member's prewriting is dealt with in the manner just described, with an equal amount of time devoted to each.

Now, we will offer sample procedures for assisting one another with revising drafts. Such workshopping activities are probably the most common kind that you will encounter throughout your college courses. In providing assistance with revising, group members not only may help one another construct initial drafts, but they may also actively help one another read drafts with a critical eye and make necessary—and often substantial—changes. During this stage of the writing process, instructors often provide students with questions to use as they consider one another's drafts or students devise their own. Here are some typical examples: "What is the thesis or main point?" "How does the writer support or illustrate the main point (list arguments and examples)?" "In what way can the structure be improved?" "Where can additional examples or explanation be added?" "What is the most effective part of the essay?"

Procedure 3 for Workshopping—Revising

After individual group members each have completed a draft of a paper, they bring enough copies to class so that each person in their group can have one—but they do not distribute them right away. During the actual workshopping, the group works through the following directions:

- One at a time, each member reads his or her paper aloud to the group. Other members listen carefully to each reader, with paper and pens ready to jot down notes. While listening to each paper, members take notes on strengths and weaknesses and note any questions they have, any areas where they have difficulty picturing what the writer is trying to convey, and any places where connections are abrupt.

- Immediately after a paper is read, copies are distributed to each group member. Using their notes, the group members mark their copy of the paper with suggestions for revision, focusing their comments on substantive issues: whether the paper has a clear controlling idea, whether the paper has vivid details, and whether the paper presents a distinctive, critical voice, and so on.

- Afterwards, comments are discussed by all group members—including the writer of the paper. In particular, group members focus on problem areas. During this stage of workshopping, problem areas are explained to each writer as precisely as possible so that the writer can understand why particular passages need to be revised. In addition, group members try to offer at least one or two suggestions for revising for each problem area they have identified. Comments that explain problems and offer suggestions for revision are written on copies of each paper and returned to the writer.

As you will see, the following workshopping activity for revision is similar to the preceding activity. In this activity, however, the members of the group bring enough copies of their drafts to class so that each group member can have one—and they *do* distribute them right away.

Procedure 4 for Workshopping—Revising

After the members of the group each have completed a draft of a paper, they bring enough copies so that each group member can have one. They distribute them right away and begin to work through the following procedures:

- One at a time, each person in the group reads his or her paper aloud, with the others following along on their copies. As group members listen to one another's papers, they observe strengths and weaknesses, as well as note any questions they have, any areas where they have difficulty picturing what the writer is trying to convey, and any places where connections are abrupt.

- Immediately after a paper is read, the writer spends a few minutes discussing his or her intentions in the paper and explaining where he or she believes the writing is strong—and where it needs work. The writer identifies any difficulties the paper is presenting.

- Next, the group discusses the paper in terms of the writer's comments and makes suggestions for revision. Comments focus on substantive issues: whether the paper has a clear controlling idea, whether the paper has vivid details, whether the paper presents a distinctive, critical voice, and so forth.

- As the group members discuss their comments with one another and with the writer, they again keep in mind that the writer will benefit most if the group offers precise explanations about why problems exist. In addition, at least one or two suggestions for revising each problem area are offered. Comments are written on copies of each paper and then returned to the writer.

- The previous procedures are repeated for each writer in the group, ensuring that everyone's paper receives equal time.

The final stage in the writing process—editing—sometimes is overlooked by students who are eager to be finished with writing a paper. However, a paper should never be viewed as a finished product until it has been edited, that is, proofread and polished. Editing includes such concerns as spelling, punctuation, usage, verb tense, sentence construction, and word choice. Although we recommend that students strive to learn to be effective editors of their own writing, we also know that workshopping with a group can be a useful way of ensuring that all errors are corrected—as well as a way of helping one another master editing techniques. The following procedures represent two examples of the numerous possibilities for editing with a group:

Procedure 5 for Workshopping—Editing

Each student comes prepared with enough copies of his or her paper for each member of the group. Copies should be typed or "hard copies" (computer printouts) in order to ensure that group members will have no questions about any writer's intentions because of illegible handwriting. Group members read the first writer's paper carefully, marking the paper whenever they see (or suspect) an editing error. When everyone has completed this, the group discusses the paper, paragraph by paragraph, helping the writer to correct his or her errors. If a group is unsure about whether something in the paper is correct, a handbook or the instructor is consulted. This procedure is repeated for each writer in the group so that everyone's paper receives equal time.

Procedure 6 for Workshopping—Editing

Each student comes prepared with enough copies of his or her paper for each member of the group. Again, copies should be typed or "hard copies" (computer printouts) in order to ensure that messy handwriting will not cause misinterpretations. Instead of trying to work on all concerns of editing at once, the group examines a paper for one concern at a time. That is, the group members read each paper several times. On the first reading of a group member's paper, the group may pay attention only to punctuation concerns. On the second reading, the members may review and discuss the paper for spelling. Subsequent readings may focus on usage, word choice, and so on. After one paper has been edited in this fashion, the procedure is repeated for each writer in the group, ensuring that everyone's paper receives equal time.

As we have said, workshopping is an effective activity during all stages of writing a paper. We hope that your group not only will utilize the procedures we have recommended but that together you will design and use some of your own procedures. In particular, editing procedures can be tailored to address the specific editing needs of members in your group.

Coauthoring. The final collaborative activity that we will discuss is coauthoring, the activity that takes place when one or more writers work together to produce one final product. As we said earlier in this chapter, coauthoring is gaining in popularity, both in classrooms and in professional arenas. As you might expect, coauthoring can be accomplished in many workable ways; the suggestions we provide are intended to help you start thinking of various possibilities.

To provide you with a basis for understanding Procedure 1, which follows, we want you to assume that your Sociology instructor has given your class a semester to construct group projects on a social issue of your choice. To fulfill this assignment, your group has decided to coauthor a booklet on the topic "alcoholism." Procedure 1 illustrates one method that would help your group coauthor this project.

Procedure 1 for Coauthoring

In coauthoring your booklet, your group works through the following procedures:

- The members of your group meet to decide on the aspects of alcoholism that you wish to address in your booklet (examples might include causes of alcoholism, co-dependency, family problems and alcoholism, alcoholism and college students, alcoholism and the law, and treatments for alcoholism). As a group, you plan the overall structure for your booklet and discuss points that should be made in each section. When a tentative plan has been made, responsibilities for writing and researching the various sections are divided among group members. In addition to deciding who will draft the various sections, the group selects individuals who are responsible for writing an introduction, a table of contents, and a conclusion.

- Throughout the term, group members meet periodically to assist one another with the drafting process. Group members provide honest feedback and are serious in their efforts to provide useful assistance.

- When the parts of the project have been drafted, they are compiled into one work. Group members then read through the work as a whole and determine where connections need to be made among the sections. Group members work together to write the necessary connections, to revise any parts that need revision, and to produce a final draft of the booklet that reads smoothly and whose parts are logically connected.

In the coauthoring procedure just described, the parts of the booklet are planned by the entire group but most of the drafting is done by members working independently. However, if your group is asked to coauthor a shorter piece, such as an essay, you may want to use a quite different procedure. In the following procedure for coauthoring an essay, notice that all group members are engaged in every stage of writing the piece.

Procedure 2 for Coauthoring

In coauthoring your essay, the group works through the following procedures:

- Group members meet to decide on a topic and tentative thesis for the essay. Together they do substantial note taking on their topic and determine a possible structure.

- The second time the group meets, they work together to actually begin drafting the essay. The group members may choose to sit before a computer screen with one person entering words or they may choose to sit in a small circle with one person writing by hand. (As you might imagine, this activity works best for groups that are composed of only two or three members.) During this stage of writing, group members cooperate to construct the draft but are sure to voice individual opinions about the best strategies.

- When the group has completed the first draft of the essay, some time is allowed to pass before plans for revision are discussed. Then the group works together to determine whether the thesis is adequately supported, whether the argument ever gets off track, whether all parts of the paper are adequately developed with details and examples, and so on. The group works together to make the necessary revisions.

- As a last step, the group works together to eliminate all editing errors.

To summarize this section, knowledge making, researching/investigating, workshopping, and coauthoring are collaborative activities with which we hope that you will gain practice as you proceed through this textbook—and through college and your career beyond. There are multiple procedures that can be effective for each activity, and the more practiced you become with collaborating, the more readily you will design your own procedures.

BRAINSTORMING

We hope that by this point you are not only beginning to see the value of collaboration for a writer but also to understand that collaboration can play a significant role in every phase of the writing process. As we have said earlier in this chapter, prewriting is one phase of the writing process that often is handled independently, but it can be enhanced through collaboration. As we also explained, prewriting can take many forms.

In this chapter, we will introduce you to one widely used method of prewriting: *brainstorming.* Brainstorming is the process of choosing a general topic and then quickly jotting down, usually in the form of a list, ideas you have that are related to the topic. Your prewriting list should include all ideas that occur to you, regardless of how insignificant or unworkable they might seem; oftentimes, the seemingly insignificant or unworkable ideas will trigger some of the best ideas on your list. The process of writing down your ideas in this fashion helps you to probe your memory, generate ideas, and fully develop your topic. A brainstorming list might look like this one by Yolanda that follows. Yolanda's assignment is to write an essay that explains the significance a particular person has had in her life.

MY NEIGHBOR LIZZIE

eccentric woman
seemed old—about seventy?
never smiled at anyone, seemed unfriendly, made me sort of afraid of her
lived in my apartment complex so I saw her coming and going a lot—drove old
   Chevy
chased cats out of the apartment dumpsters so she could browse
tall person, walked proudly, reminded me of a statue
bathrobe
washer her car every day
   even in winter
   used bucket of water and a mop
I imagined scary things about her (will need to explain)
I was afraid
wore curlers in her hair a lot
wouldn't say hello
picked things out of dumpster and put them in her car—lamps, boxes
what happened that made me decide that she wasn't so weird after all—early
   April morning 5:00 a.m., I had to be up to work on a project
   —sun was coming up, beautiful sky
   —saw Lizzie in middle of field behind complex, sitting there watching the sunrise,
   seemed to be meditating
   —seemed to be praying or meditating or something

—wearing straw hat and billowy red pj's
—Lizzie stayed in field till sun was high, then came in carrying cardboard "prayer rug"
Need a good ending about Lizzie's ability to be peaceful or to use her time wisely, how she didn't seem so scary to me anymore, what I learned from Lizzie

As with all brainstorming lists, Yolanda's is made up of phrases and words that appear in no particular order. However, from creating this list, she came to realize that she wanted to focus her paper on the incident that made her aware that her neighbor had more dimensions than Yolanda had earlier perceived. In addition, the list enabled Yolanda to group related items on her list, exclude items that did not really seem to fit, and decide on a tentative organizational plan for her paper.

As you can see, a writer can easily complete a brainstorming activity alone. However, the following activities should help you to see the benefits of working together during the process of brainstorming and will give you practice with both individual and collaborative brainstorming. Activity 1, which follows, will give your group practice with brainstorming together; Activities 2 and 3 will give your group practice in using your brainstorming to draft a paragraph.

Activity 1

The members of your group should spend five minutes or so independently brainstorming a list of details that could be used to construct a paragraph on the topic "Why Writing Is Important." You should write quickly, without worrying about forming complete sentences or using correct spelling or punctuation. The idea is to get your ideas on paper.

Next, the members of the group should meet to compile a collaborative list of details on the topic "Why Writing Is Important". One person in the group should serve as note taker for the day. In collaborating on such a list, it is helpful if everyone in the group can see what the note taker is writing down. A chalkboard or easel works particularly well for group brainstorming, but if one is not available, a large piece of paper, located where everyone can see it, will suffice.

Everyone in the group should contribute ideas to the list. Many of the ideas, of course, will come from the lists that each of you brainstormed independently. However, the process of creating this new, collaborative list will help group members think of ideas that they had not previously thought of; these new ideas, too, should be included in the list. Remember that no idea is too insignificant to be included in the brainstorming.

Activity 2

When your group has developed a fairly substantial list of details (from completing Activity 1), you should discuss possibilities for writing a collaborative paragraph on the topic "Why Writing Is Important." Your group should examine your brainstorming list to determine categories of information and decide which to include or exclude. You should think about ways that you might introduce the topic and ways that you might conclude the paragraph. Your group should work together to decide on the most effective organizational plan. As the members reach agreement, the note taker should be writing down the tentative plan for the paragraph.

Activity 3

After completing Activities 1 and 2, your group is ready to work together to write a draft of the paragraph. During this process, group members should offer ideas, agree and disagree, and reach a consensus regarding the words that will be used. The note taker should write down the paragraph as the group makes decisions. When the paragraph has been written, the group should discuss any changes members wish to make in content, organization, syntax, style, or mechanics, and then, perhaps, construct a revised version.

WRITING ASSIGNMENT

The following assignment builds on the work you completed in activities 1, 2, and 3. It will also help you assess the effectiveness of your group's collaboration and of your own individual contribution to your group. In working through this assignment, first complete Part A and then do Part B. You may wish to hand these in together or to hand them in one at a time, whichever your instructor requires.

Part A

In order to complete Activities 1, 2, and 3, your group worked together as you brainstormed collaboratively and coauthored a draft of a paragraph. For this part of the assignment, you will write two to three pages that *evaluate* how well your group worked together as you completed the activities.

As you write your evaluation, you should be honest and open, yet tactful. You might explain procedural matters, such as how the note taker was chosen, how the group managed (or failed to manage) to stay on task, or how disagreements were resolved. Be sure that your evaluation includes the strengths you saw emerging as your group worked together, as well as suggestions you can offer for the group to try.

After everyone has completed writing an evaluation, your group should meet to discuss them and to collaborate on setting several "group goals" for your upcoming collaborative sessions.

As a reminder, if your group did encounter some problems in working as a team, you should not feel dismayed or as though you somehow failed. As we stated earlier, it ordinarily takes some time for groups to gel. With practice and commitment, your group will develop stronger collaborative skills.

Part B

Again, reflecting upon Activities 1, 2, and 3, think about yourself as a part of your group. For this part of the assignment, you should write two pages evaluating your own role. You might consider some of the following questions: How comfortable did you feel within the group? How did your comfort level make you react? How much and what kind of support did you provide? Based on your experience, do you have personal goals for upcoming collaborative sessions?

After everyone has completed writing his or her two-page self-evaluation, your group should meet to share members' feelings on this topic.

AUTHOR-TITLE INDEX

SUBJECT INDEX